READI

Brad Inwood presents a ays on the philosophy of Seneca, , and tragedian of the first centur -new pieces, and a helpful introduction t reader, this volume will be an essential guide for anyone seeking to understand Seneca's fertile, wide-ranging thought and its impact on subsequent generations.

In each of these essays Seneca is considered as a philosopher, but with as much account as possible taken of his life, his education, his intellectual and literary background, his career, and his self-presentation as an author. Seneca emerges as a discerning and well-read Stoic, with a strong inclination to think for himself in the context of an intellectual climate teeming with influences from other schools. Seneca's intellectual engagement with Platonism, Aristotelianism, and even with Epicureanism involved a wide range of substantial philosophical interests and concerns. His philosophy was indeed shaped by the fact that he was a Roman, but he was a true philosopher shaped by his culture rather than a Roman writer trying his hand at philosophical themes. The highly rhetorical character of his writing must be accounted for when reading his works, and when one does so the underlying philosophical themes stand out more clearly. While it is hard to generalize about an overall intellectual agenda or systematic philosophical method, key themes and strategies are evident. Inwood shows how Seneca's philosophical ingenium worked itself out in a fundamentally particularistic way as he pursued those aspects of Stoicism that engaged him most forcefully over his career.

Brad Inwood is Canada Research Chair in Ancient Philosophy and Professor of Classics and Philosophy at the University of Toronto.

READING SENECA

STOIC PHILOSOPHY AT ROME

Brad Inwood

CLARENDON PRESS · OXFORD

OXFORD
UNIVERSITY PRESS

Great Clarendon Street, Oxford OX2 6DP

Oxford University Press is a department of the University of Oxford.
It furthers the University's objective of excellence in research, scholarship
and education by publishing worldwide in

Oxford New York

Auckland Cape Town Dar es Salaam Hong Kong Karachi Kuala Lumpur
Madrid Melbourne Mexico City Nairobi New Delhi Shanghai Taipei Toronto

With offices in

Argentina Austria Brazil Chile Czech Republic France Greece
Guatemala Hungary Italy Japan Poland Portugal Singapore
South Korea Switzerland Thailand Turkey Ukraine Vietnam

Oxford is a registered trade mark of Oxford University Press
in the UK and in certain other countries

Published in the United States
by Oxford University Press Inc., New York

© in this volume Brad Inwood 2005

The moral rights of the author have been asserted
Database right Oxford University Press (maker)

First published 2005
First published in paperback 2008

All rights reserved. No part of this publication may be reproduced,
stored in a retrieval system, or transmitted, in any form or by any means,
without the prior permission in writing of Oxford University Press,
or as expressly permitted by law, or under terms agreed with the appropriate
reprographics rights organization. Enquiries concerning reproduction
outside the scope of the above should be sent to the Rights Department,
Oxford University Press, at the address above

You must not circulate this book in any other binding or cover
and you must impose the same condition on any acquirer

British Library Cataloguing in Publication Data

Data available

Library of Congress Cataloging in Publication Data

Data available

Typeset by SPI Publisher Services, Pondicherry, India
Printed in Great Britain
on acid-free paper by
Biddles Ltd., King's Lynn, Norfolk.

ISBN 978–0–19–925089–9 (Hbk.)   978–0–19–925090–5 (Pbk.)

1 3 5 7 9 10 8 6 4 2

For Niko

ACKNOWLEDGEMENTS

I owe to the National Humanities Centre and its wonderful fellowship program the realization that I was engaged on a coordinated and long-term project on Seneca. It was during my fellowship there in 1995–6 that several of the essays included here were conceived and either begun or fully written. Without that year, which I spent 'reading Seneca' in the more mundane sense, most of the essays in this collection would never have been written. Further material support came from the Standard Research Grant program of the Social Sciences and Humanities Research Council of Canada, from the Connaught Foundation at the University of Toronto, and from the Canada Research Chairs program of the Canadian government. Moral support of a less tangible but even more important nature has come from my colleagues and friends in Classics, Philosophy, and Medieval Studies at the University of Toronto and from the students who agreed to share the gamble that there might be merit in exploring the philosophical and literary potential of Seneca's prose corpus. I am also very grateful indeed to Stephen Thompson for his exemplary and sensitive editorial assistance.

My greatest debt, though, is to my wife, Niko Scharer, whose love and support have enabled me to imagine this work, to undertake it, and to bring it to whatever degree of completion it has. It is to her that I dedicate this book, for without her neither it nor very much else would have been possible.

CONTENTS

Provenance of the Essays   x
Abbreviations   xiv

Introduction   1

1. Seneca in his Philosophical Milieu   7
2. Seneca and Psychological Dualism   23
3. Politics and Paradox in Seneca's *De Beneficiis*   65
4. Rules and Reasoning in Stoic Ethics   95
5. The Will in Seneca   132
6. God and Human Knowledge in Seneca's *Natural Questions*   157
7. Moral Judgement in Seneca   201
8. Natural Law in Seneca   224
9. Reason, Rationalization, and Happiness   249
10. Getting to Goodness   271
11. Seneca on Freedom and Autonomy   302
12. Seneca and Self-assertion   322

Bibliography   353
Index of Subjects   363
Index Locorum   370

PROVENANCE OF THE ESSAYS

Ten of these essays are reprinted, sometimes with minor adaptations, with the permission of the original publishers and editors as relevant. The details are given below. All twelve chapters have benefited from the comment of many audiences and readers. The enumeration of individual contributions would be impossible, but at least I can indicate the institutions and sponsors whose generous invitations have allowed me to try out my ideas before constructively critical listeners. More particular debts of gratitude are indicated in the notes to each essay.

1. 'Seneca in his Philosophical Milieu' [*Harvard Studies in Classical Philology*, 97 (1995), 63–76] was presented at *Greece in Rome: A James Loeb Classical Conference*, Harvard University, in October 1994; and to the Department of Classics, University of North Carolina Greensboro, in November 1995. Publication permission: Department of Classics, Harvard University.
2. 'Seneca and Psychological Dualism' [in J. Brunschwig and M. Nussbaum (eds.), *Passions & Perceptions* (Cambridge, 1993), 150–83] was presented to the fifth Symposium Hellenisticum, Château de Syam, France, in August 1989. Publication permission: Cambridge University Press. Translations of passages originally given only in Latin have been added for this reprinting.
3. 'Politics and Paradox in Seneca's *De Beneficiis*' [in A. Laks and M. Schofield (eds.), *Justice and Generosity* (Cambridge, 1995), 241–65] was presented to the sixth Symposium Hellenisticum, Cambridge, England, in August 1992. Publication permission: Cambridge University Press.
4. 'Rules and Reasoning in Stoic Ethics' [in K. Ierodiakonou (ed.), *Topics in Stoic Philosophy* (Oxford, 1999), 95–127] was presented to the Sub-Faculty of Philosophy, Oxford

University, and to the B Club, Cambridge University, in February 1996; at Duke University in April 1996; and to the Departments of Philosophy and Classics, Cornell University in February 1998. Publication permission: Oxford University Press.

5. Ancestors of 'The Will in Seneca the Younger' [*Classical Philology*, 95 (2000), 44–60] were presented to the Ohio State University Philosophy Colloquium in October 1996; to the Department of Philosophy, University of Texas at Austin, in November 1996; to the Departments of Philosophy and Classics, Cornell University in February 1998; to the Department of Classics at McMaster University, Ontario, in March 1998; and to the Boston Area Colloquium in Ancient Philosophy at Boston College in October 1998. Publication permission: University of Chicago Press (with whom the copyright resides © 2000).

6. 'God and Human Knowledge in Seneca's *Natural Questions*' [in D. Frede and A. Laks (eds.), *Traditions of Theology: Studies in Hellenistic Theology, its Background and Aftermath* (Leiden, 2002), 119–57] was first presented to the eighth Symposium Hellenisticum in Lille in August 1998; a shorter version was presented to the Boston Area Colloquium in Ancient Philosophy at Boston College in October 1998. Publication permission: Brill.

7. 'Moral Judgement in Seneca' [in J. Zupko and S. Strange (eds.), *Stoicism: Traditions and Transformations* (Cambridge, 2004), 76–94] was presented to the Department of Classics, University of Toronto, and to the second Loemker conference 'Stoicism: traditions and transformations', Emory University, in March 2000; to a conference on Roman Stoicism (hosted by Northwestern University, University of Illinois at Chicago, University of Chicago) in April 2000; to the Department of Philosophy at the University of Victoria and to the departments of Classics and Philosophy at the University of Calgary in March 2001. Publication permission: Cambridge University Press.

8. Ancestors of 'Natural Law in Seneca the Younger' [in D. Runia, G. Sterling, and H. Najman (eds.), *Law Stamped*

with the Seal of Nature (*Studia Philonica Annual*, vol. 15; Atlanta, 2003), 81–99] were presented to the Boston Area Colloquium in Ancient Philosophy in October 1998; to 'Mortal Boundaries', a conference at UC Berkeley, in November 1998; to the Department of Classics at the University of Cincinnati, in February 1999; as the keynote address to the University of New Brunswick Ancient History Colloquium, in March 1999; to the Departments of Classics and Philosophy at Dartmouth College in May 1999; and to the Department of Classics, University of British Columbia in March 2001. Publication permission: Brown University.

9. 'Reason, Rationalization and Happiness in Seneca' [in Jorge Gracia and Jiyuan Yu (eds.), *Rationality and Happiness from the Ancients to the Medievals* (Rochester, NY, 2003), 91–107] was presented to the third Capen conference at the University at Buffalo (Reason and Happiness: From the Ancients to the Early Medievals) in September 2000; to the Department of Philosophy, University of British Columbia, and to the Departments of Philosophy and History/Classics, University of Alberta in March 2001; as a Symposium paper for the Central Division of the American Philosophical Association, in May 2001; and to the Department of Philosophy, University of Ottawa, in November 2001. Publication permission: the editors.

10. Versions of 'Getting to Goodness' [not previously published] were presented to the annual Princeton Ancient Philosophy Colloquium in December 2000; to the Department of Philosophy at the University of Pittsburgh, in March 2002; to the Departments of Philosophy and Classics at Trent University and to the Department of Philosophy at Queen's University, in October 2003.

11. Earlier versions of 'Seneca on Freedom and Autonomy' [in R. Salles (ed.), *Metaphysics, Soul and Ethics. Themes from the Work of Richard Sorabji* (Oxford, 2005), 489–505] were presented to the Josephus conference, York University, in May 2001, to the Department of Classics at New York University, in November 2002, and to the Departments of Classics and Philosophy at Holy Cross College, Worcester

Mass., in March 2003. Publication permission: Oxford University Press.

12. 'Seneca and Self Assertion' [not previously published] was presented to a conference on Seneca and the Self at the University of Chicago, in April 2003 and to the Seminaire de Philosophie hellénistique et romaine at l'Université de Paris XII, in May 2004.

ABBREVIATIONS

Authors and Works

Aristotle
EE   *Ethica Eudemia*
EN   *Ethica Nicomachea*

Cicero
Fin.   *De Finibus*
ND   *De Natura Deorum*
Off.   *De Officiis*

Diogenes Laertius   DL

Epictetus
Diss.   *Dissertationes*
Ench.   *Enchiridion*

Epicurus
KD   *Kuriai Doxai*

Galen
PHP   *De Placitis Hippocratis et Platonis*

Horace
Serm.   *Sermones*

Plato
Apol.   *Apology*
Def.   *Definitiones*
Ep.   *Epistulae*
Grg.   *Gorgias*
Hipp. Maj.   *Hippias Major*
Phd.   *Phaedo*
Symp.   *Symposium*

Abbreviations

Pliny
HN   *Historia Naturalis*

Plutarch
Comm. Not.   *De Communibus Notitiis contra Stoicos*
De Stoic. Rep. *De Stoicorum Repugnantiis*
Lib. Aegr.   *De Libidine et Aegritudine*

Seneca
Ben.   *De Beneficiis*
Clem.   *De Clementia*
Cons. Polyb.   *Consolatio ad Polybium*
Cons. Helv.   *Consolatio ad Helviam Matrem*
Ep.   *Epistulae Morales*
Prov.   *De Providentia*
NQ   *Naturales Quaestiones*
Tranq.   *De Tranquillitate Animi*

Sextus Empiricus
M   *Adversus Mathematicos*

Stobaeus
Ecl.   *Eclogae*

Xenophon
Apol.   *Apology*
Mem.   *Memorabilia*

Other Abbreviations

AJP   *American Journal of Philology*
ANRW   *Aufstieg und Niedergang der römischen Welt*
BMCR   *Bryn Mawr Classical Review*
CHHP   *Cambridge History of Hellenistic Philosophy*
CQ   *Classical Quarterly*
DK   Diels-Kranz, *Die Fragmente der Vorsokratiker*
Dox. Gr.   *Doxographi Graeci*, Diels
EK   Edelstein and Kidd, *Posidonius*
GRBS   *Greek, Roman and Byzantine Studies*

JPh	*Journal of Philosophy*
K	Kuhn, *Galen: Opera Omnia*
LS	Long and Sedley, *The Hellenistic Philosophers*
NAWG, phil.-hist. Kl.	*Nachrichten-Akademie der Wissenschaft zu Göttingen*, Philologisch-historische Klasse
OCT	Oxford Classical Text
OSAP	*Oxford Studies in Ancient Philosophy*
SVF	von Arnim, *Stoicorum Veterum Fragmenta*
W	Wachsmuth, *Ioannis Stobaei Anthologium*
YCS	*Yale Classical Studies*

Introduction

Lucius Annaeus Seneca, known as Seneca the Younger because of the fame of his father, was a Roman senator, a man of letters, an influential political adviser to the last emperor of the Julio-Claudian dynasty, and a philosopher. His importance in literature, politics, and philosophy makes him an unusually interesting intellectual, but in this book only his work as a philosopher will be addressed. In philosophy Seneca adhered to Stoicism and it is as a Stoic philosopher that he has had the most powerful impact on later centuries. I was at first attracted by the problem of his relationship to earlier Stoic philosophy, but before long I found myself fascinated by his philosophical achievement for its own sake.

The twelve essays collected here represent fifteen years of work on Seneca. The earliest, 'Seneca and Psychological Dualism', was first written in 1989, and the most recent, 'Seneca and Self Assertion', was revised for a seminar at the University of Paris in May 2004. With the exception of 'Rules and Reasoning in Stoic Ethics', all were composed originally for presentation at one conference or another and I have not made a concerted effort to erase the evidence of oral delivery; similarly, I have not updated various references to the currency of various pieces of secondary literature which are embedded in many of the essays.

In each of these essays I approach Seneca from the standpoint of an historian of philosophy and not that of a student of Latin literature or Roman cultural history. In order to do so I have tried to take as much account as possible of the historical facts about Seneca: his life, his education, his intellectual and literary background, his career and self-presentation as an author. Within that framework I have made the charitable assumption that Seneca thought and worked as a philosopher, despite his social standing. But I have tried not to extend this charity beyond the limits of plausibility in the interpretation of Seneca's work. What has emerged from this lengthy exercise in reading Seneca philosophically has surprised me. Once it became clear that I was in fact engaged in a long-term project on Seneca, I naïvely expected that a coherent general picture of Seneca's philosophical methods and commitments would readily emerge, a picture that might serve as the basis for a unified treatment of Seneca as a philosopher.

But such a general picture (if indeed there is one lurking in the rich tapestry of Seneca's prose works) has not yet emerged, at least not clearly enough to sustain generalizations that might rise above the banal. It is clear, of course, that Seneca is a highly intelligent, discerning, and well-read Stoic, though a Stoic with a strong inclination to think for himself in the context of an intellectual climate teeming with influences from other schools. And it is clear too that this inclination was facilitated by the fact that Seneca did not teach or study Stoic philosophy in a professional setting and spent much of his intellectual life interacting with broader influences in the political, cultural, and literary climate of Rome. The evidence of his works also shows, I think, that Seneca's intellectual engagement with Platonism, Aristotelianism, and even with Epicureanism was shaped by a wide range of substantial philosophical interests and concerns, and not by a dubious project of philosophical harmonization, as has often been assumed. There is no doubt that his philosophy was shaped by the fact that he was a Roman, but he was a philosopher shaped by his culture rather than a Roman writer blundering about among philosophical themes, as he has often been portrayed. But these observations are not novel and there would be little of interest in a repeated and systematic illustration of the fact that Seneca is a product of his place and time.

* * *

The philosophical interest of various aspects of Seneca's prose writings, whether identified by focusing on a particular work or on a theme running through a range of works, seems undeniable. Yet it is premature, I think, to generalize about an overall intellectual agenda or general philosophical method; at this point I am inclined to conclude that his philosophical *ingenium* probably worked itself out in a fundamentally particularistic way as he pursued aspects of Stoicism that engaged him most forcefully over the course of a long and active life as a writer. Nevertheless, it may be of some use to reflect for a moment on some of the philosophical issues and themes which connect the twelve essays collected in this volume.

The reader will notice very quickly an emphasis on the conservatism of Seneca's moral psychology. He was once thought of as a revisionist in this area of philosophy, but on more critical scrutiny he turns out to be closer to earlier Stoics than has been thought on issues of the passions, the structure of the soul, the nature of the 'will' and the 'self', and so forth. This is argued in Chapters 2, 5, and 12 (and to some extent also in Chapter 11). At the same time, Stoicism itself emerges as being less sharply distinct from 'Platonism' than used to be thought.

Despite this conservatism, though, Seneca appears as an original and innovative exponent of Stoic doctrine, one whose distinctive contribution seems to be a sensitivity to the value of first-hand experience in ethics and moral psychology. Seneca's attention to the 'ordinary man' rather than to the sage is a product of his epistemic humility: in many areas of philosophy the best evidence just *is* first-hand experience and Seneca turns to this to balance the occasional excesses of earlier theorizing. This does not entail major philosophical change, but it does reflect a new intellectual context for his work and a markedly different sensibility than the one which is often imagined for the leaders of the Stoic school in its Athenian period.

Sensitivity to the fact that human beings operate in sub-optimal epistemological circumstances is also reflected in Seneca's discussions of moral theory. This aspect of Seneca's thought, which no doubt underlies the traditional view that Seneca was locked in the embrace of 'middle Stoicism' and cared primarily to develop a second-best moral standard for non-sages, is prominent in Chapters 3, 4, and 7. (These philosophical concerns with the character of epistemic justification are quite general in Seneca, as is shown by his approach to physics, discussed in Chapter 6.) A closely related facet of Seneca's development of Stoic moral theory is his nuanced (and to my mind still traditional) approach to moral rules and natural 'law', a theme which links Chapters 4 and 8 quite closely. Seneca shows himself to be well attuned to situational variability in moral reasoning (much as Aristotle was); again, this is a theme which connects Chapters 4 and 7. Seneca's concentration on the centrality to human beings of social connectedness (as seen in Chapter 3) is also common ground with Aristotle, among others. But this should not, I think, lead us to conclude that Seneca was particularly drawn towards Aristotelian doctrine (any more than other Stoics were), for in ethics he is often quite sharply critical of the Peripatetics. Like many Stoics, Seneca has a powerful interest in and sympathy for the Platonic branch of the Socratic intellectual family. Chapters 8, 9, 10, and 11 reflect this leaning towards 'Platonism', just as Chapters 4 and 10 attest to his interest in the usefulness in ethics of the idealized sage of earlier Stoicism. These interests cohere with Seneca's awareness of the precarious position of human beings poised between the divine and the animal and with the appeal for him of Socratic and Platonic moral rigorism. They underlie his fascination with the nature of rationality, the one trait that unites human nature with the divine and separates us from irrational beasts.

The Socratic tradition had concentrated from the beginning on the importance of improving one's character in order to make possible the living of a happy life. The sage may have reached that goal, but most human beings need to work quite hard to achieve an even slightly improved state. Chapters 5, 9, and 12 reflect Seneca's concern, both theoretical and practical, with the

Introduction

need for moral self-improvement and I argue in those essays that this intense engagement with the techniques of self-improvement is built on an essentially conservative form of Stoicism; and yet because of Seneca's unique literary and rhetorical approach we find that his works have provoked more innovation in the Western philosophical tradition of moral psychology and ethics than is evident in his own works. Seneca's considerable impact on the later tradition should not, I argue, lead us to read those novelties back into his works; but at the same time it would be sheer stubbornness not to recognize the innovative impact his work has had over the centuries.

* * *

It is my hope that philosophers and historians of philosophy will find in at least some of these essays clear support for the view that Seneca is a serious philosophical presence in the Western tradition, worth the time and energy demanded by the study of a body of writing rendered less accessible by the author's literary genius and bravado, by the foreignness of his genres, and by the relative neglect of his philosophy since the seventeenth century. I hope also that those with a passion for Latin prose literature or a deep engagement with the twists and turns of elite Roman culture in the post-Augustan era will be convinced that the philosophy in Seneca's work is a central preoccupation rather than an elaborate excuse for stylistic and rhetorical fireworks; that a just appreciation of his accomplishments as a prose author demands more than the superficial familiarity with Stoicism and other philosophical schools that can be derived from handbooks and general histories; and that a full understanding of Seneca's literary achievement cannot come without the deep and uncompromising engagement in philosophy which Seneca, in his own day, saw as necessary for anyone with an aspiration to live a fully satisfactory human life.

I have not said a word about Seneca's poetic works, his dramas. In these essays I have focused exclusively on the prose corpus. I do so not because I think the dramas are inferior or uninteresting, nor even because I think that Seneca's philosophical commitments are irrelevant to the dramas. My decision rests partly on a sense of my own limitations and partly on the conviction that any philosophical influence probably runs from the prose works to the plays rather than the other way around. Perhaps if one could achieve a more global philosophical assessment of Seneca than I have done it would be wise to revisit this issue, but until then I think common sense dictates that I avoid explaining the *incertum per incertius*.[1] For the purposes of this collection, Seneca the philosopher writes in prose.

[1] My best guess about the way Seneca's philosophical convictions affect his dramas is still summed up in what I said in my review of Thomas Rosenmeyer's *Senecan Drama and Stoic Cosmology* in *Classical Philology* 86 (1991), 248–52.

I

Seneca in his Philosophical Milieu

The philosophical environment in which Seneca wrote was very different from the one which Cicero knew, and I want to present a somewhat exploratory sketch of that environment, one which will show how distinctive Seneca's philosophical world was. No doubt many of the differences between them were matters of personal temperament and decision,[1] and such factors cannot really be understood in a non-circular way. But many other differences were, I think, the result of social and political evolution at Rome; for during the century separating their careers, Roman society underwent a rapid and indeed revolutionary phase of social change. It would be remarkable if such change did not have some impact on the work of pagan Rome's two greatest philosophical writers.[2]

But we should also recall that there are some more specifically philosophical factors which should be taken into account. For

---

[1] Carlos Lévy's discussion in *Cicero Academicus* (Rome, 1992) is the most recent and thorough study of Cicero's personal philosophical stance.

[2] On this broad topic, see the excellent discussion by Miriam Griffin, 'Philosophy for Statesmen: Cicero and Seneca', in H. W. Schmidt and P. Wülfing (eds.), *Antikes Denken—Moderne Schule* (*Gymnasium*, Beiheft 9; Heidelberg, 1987), 133–50. It will be obvious that I owe a great deal to this paper and, of course, to Griffin's *Seneca: A Philosopher in Politics* (2nd edn., Oxford, 1992), which I follow on matters of Seneca's biography.

example, in Cicero's youth Athens was still the centre of philosophical life in the Mediterranean basin; the traditional schools lived and flourished. By the time the upheavals of the first century were over, not only did Rome rule much more of the Greek east than it had before, but the traditional Athenian schools had been closed,[3] philosophical activity there reduced to a shadow of its former self. Alexandria and Rome had become more significant and the importance to philosophers of private patronage in aristocratic houses now rivalled that of organized school life.[4]

There are also some biographical considerations. At some time between AD 37 and 40 Seneca's father composed the preface to book 2 of his *Controversiae*. His middle and homonymous son was somewhere between 38 and 44 years old. The eldest son Novatus was bent on a political career, which later culminated in the governorship of Achaea. The youngest son Mela had already made clear that he preferred the quiet life of an equestrian—a decision that he, unlike Seneca, was able to stick to. Our Seneca had either just completed or was just preparing for the quaestorship and the political career which would soon be cut short by banishment. Political ambitions had not consumed his earlier years, and probably not just because of ill health. If Miriam Griffin is right (as I think she is),[5] Seneca the Younger had avoided taking a political path for as long as possible largely because of his enthusiasm for the philosophical life. Unlike many young Romans, Seneca seems not to have gone to Greece for study, realizing perhaps that the main centres of philosophical activity were now in Rome and Alexandria; he pursued no political office, as far as we know, until well past the normal age—and this despite the advantages he might have had from favourable connections during the ascendancy of Sejanus,[6] con-

---

[3] John Glucker, *Antiochus and the Late Academy* (Göttingen, 1978); John Lynch, *Aristotle's School: A Study of a Greek Educational Institution* (Berkeley, 1972).

[4] P.-L. Donini, *Le scuole, l'anima, l'impero: la filosofia antica da Antioco a Plotino* (Turin, 1982), Ch. 2.

[5] Griffin, *Seneca*, 45–7.

[6] See Zeph Stewart, 'Sejanus, Gaetulicus, and Seneca', *AJP* 74 (1953), 70–85, esp. 70–3; this period of Seneca's life is discussed further and in more detail by Griffin, *Seneca*, 47–59.

nections which would later, of course, have retarded any political advancement after the fall of Tiberius' chief minister.

There is an irony in the remarks by Seneca the Elder in the preface to book 2 of the *Controversiae*. Papirius Fabianus is a featured declaimer in book 2, yet is introduced here as 'the *philosopher* Fabianus, who as quite a youth was no less famous for his declaiming than he was later for his dialectic' (2 Pref. 1, tr. Winterbottom). Fabianus had turned to philosophy, bringing to it his adolescent fame and skill, nearly half a century earlier, before any of the Annaeus boys was born. He followed the path of Sextius, and had eventually made a quite considerable impact on our Seneca.

How, then, does Seneca the father invoke Fabianus the philosopher when introducing him—looking back at least forty years? Surprisingly, with a special appeal to his youngest son Mela, with whose lack of political ambition Seneca senior has evidently come to terms (2 Pref. 3–4, tr. Winterbottom).

I am the more happy to relate this, my dear son Mela, because I see that your mind, shrinking from political office and averse from all ambition, has only one desire—to have no desires. But *do* study eloquence. You can easily pass from this art to all others; it equips even those whom it does not train for its own ends. There is no reason for you to think plots are being laid for you, as if I were planning that you should be held tight by enthusiasm for a study that goes well. No, *I* am no obstacle to a good mind; go where your inclination takes you, and, content with your father's rank, withdraw a great part of yourself from the reach of fortune.

You had a greater *ingenium* than your brothers, completely capable of grasping all honourable arts. And this is in itself the guarantee of a superior mind, not to be corrupted by its good quality into using it ill. But since your brothers care for ambitious goals and set themselves for the forum and a political career, where even what one hopes for is to be feared, even I, who otherwise am eager for such advancement and encourage and praise such efforts (their dangers don't matter, provided they are honourable), even I keep you in port while your two brothers voyage out.

But the practice of declamation will help you in those pursuits to which you are whole-heartedly devoted, just as they helped Fabianus.

At one time, though he was a pupil of Sextius, nevertheless Fabianus went on declaiming and so enthusiastically that you might have supposed he was preparing for that—not being prepared for something else.

How would our Seneca hear this? He himself had done his best to stay out of politics, 'withdrawing a good part of himself from the reach of fortune'. He had followed the philosophical example of Fabianus, with real interest in his rhetorical technique (as the observations on his style found in Seneca's works indicate[7]). He would eventually emulate his model and apply his own rhetorical and literary talents to philosophy. He, Seneca, was surely aware at some level of what history has since proven, that the real *ingenium* in the family lay in himself, not in his younger brother. And yet his father has gone out of his way to emphasize his personal acceptance of Mela's quietism, to reassure him of the value of being content with the example of his father—and has chosen as a vehicle for doing so one of the philosophers who most influenced Seneca himself.

Was our Seneca pressured into accepting the political path which so soon led to the perils of fortune his father predicted? Is that the point of the reference to 'plots' which might be used to entice Mela out of his quietude and safety? Or had Seneca launched *himself* on his political career, perhaps influenced by the *Civilia* of Fabianus and the example of his older brother? We shall, I think, never know. For despite the abundance of his own writings and the scrutiny of generations of scholars, Seneca's own deepest motivations lie hidden behind a façade constructed, paradoxically, largely of his own philosophical convictions.

Seneca's inner motivations may be unreachable, but the image conjured up by his father's remarks tells us something important about the atmosphere in which he lived and wrote. The philosophical environment in which Seneca worked was in the beginning a home environment, or at least not an institutional one. The Sextians with whom he associated included not just the Egyptian Sotion but also Fabianus, a man familiar to

---

[7] *Ep.* 40.12, 52.11, 58.6, 100.

the family since before Seneca was born. Seneca grew up in an environment where a philosophical life was coming to be taken for granted as a realistic option for young Roman men of wealth and standing. It is not that his was the first generation of committed Roman philosophers working in Latin—for Fabianus himself obviously qualifies for that description (in a way that Cicero[8] and Lucretius, and perhaps even Brutus, do not). Rather, Seneca's generation was the first to grow up with such committed philosophers, working in Latin, available as role models. To choose the philosophical way of life was still a struggle, as Seneca's own life shows—but at least he had Roman role models to guide him. Sextius himself had been offered a senatorial career by Caesar and turned it down.[9] Fabianus had chosen philosophy over declamation. Sextius' son followed in his father's footsteps. Other Romans of that generation, Lucius Crassicius and Cornelius Celsus, also chose the philosophical life.[10] For Seneca philosophy was not something essentially Greek, for which he might, like Cicero or Lucretius, be a missionary among the Romans. It was not something which *had* to be done in Greek if it were to be done seriously and in one's own voice, as it evidently had been for Sextius himself. Seneca (owing perhaps to the access he had to Fabianus through family connections) had the luxury of contemplating, without excessive cultural and linguistic conflict, a role model which was at the same time both philosophical and Roman.

It is important too to remember that Seneca's own example proved not to be a trend-setter. Seneca did not mark any major and enduring change in regard to the language of philosophy. Romans who came later would *choose* to practise philosophy in Greek—not just the emperor Marcus, but more pertinently the

---

[8] One might want to make an exception for *Off.* 3 here, or for the *Laelius* and *Cato*. But even if one does, the general character of Cicero's philosophical writing is still 'missionary' writing and Cicero himself is no role model for the philosophical life.

[9] Seneca, *Ep.* 98.13.

[10] Evidence gathered conveniently by Gregor Maurach, *Geschichte der römischen Philosophie: eine Einführung* (Darmstadt, 1989), 79–81.

Etruscan *eques* Gaius Musonius Rufus, a generation younger than Seneca and widely known in the Neronian and Flavian principates.[11] Musonius was, significantly, an intimate of senatorial families; he followed Rubellius Plautus into exile in AD 62 and along with the Greek philosopher Coeranus urged fortitude in the face of death; and he was close enough to Barea Soranus (not to mention politically secure enough) to prosecute Publius Egnatius Celer.[12] This legal vendetta *may* have been driven by philosophical principles, but it also fits squarely into the traditions of Roman political prosecutions; that the defender was another philosopher who worked at Rome, the Greek Cynic Demetrius,[13] familiar to Seneca, reinforces the picture of a Roman philosopher who, like Seneca himself, also lived a highly political life at the centre of power. Musonius could (perhaps should) have done his philosophical work in Latin, but did not.[14] Seneca's choice to think and write in Latin stands out by contrast. The intellectual climate which led Seneca to write in Latin was, in my view, a very local one, a micro-climate if you will, limited in time to the generation shaped by Sextius' students and quite possibly limited to the social circles in which those students happened to move. If we think, as I do, that Seneca was bound to have been influenced by his father's circle, then the micro-climate becomes even smaller.

Another important aspect of Seneca's philosophical milieu was what I take to be the relatively easy bilingualism of his immediate social environment. I think, of course, not just of Nero's eventual philhellenic zeal, but also and earlier of Claudius' freedman Polybius and the (to me) remarkable fact that he

---

[11] Note too that even Cornutus chose to write his philosophical work in Greek, while his literary work was in Latin—and this despite the influence of Seneca. I wish to thank Margaret Graver for reminding me of Cornutus.

[12] The main facts of Musonius' life are collected by Cora Lutz in 'Musonius Rufus: "The Roman Socrates"', *YCS* 10 (1947) 3–147, esp. 14–18.

[13] Ibid. 14.

[14] There is some controversy over whether he also on occasion taught in Latin: see Lutz, 'Musonius Rufus', 17–18 n. 62. I say that perhaps Musonius *should* have worked in Latin more, thinking of the situation envisaged by Epictetus (1.17.16), where a student finds Chrysippean philosophy pretty tough going and asks that it be explained in Latin.

apparently translated Homer into Latin prose and Vergil into Greek prose.[15] Whether this was a mere *tour de force* or actually served some interested audience is not clear, but on either interpretation we find a striking illustration of the intellectual temper of the society in which Seneca lived; it reminds us too that not only were Roman intellectuals comfortable in Greek, but that Greek intellectuals at Rome could be comfortable in and interested in Latin.[16] The recentness of this change is shown by the fact that Epictetus, survivor of the Neronian court, can envisage explaining Chrysippus in Latin, even while teaching in Greece,[17] while in the age of Augustus and Tiberius philosophers like Arius Didymus and Thrasyllus had shown no sign of philosophical interest in Latin, despite their closeness to the emperors.

I am suggesting, then, that Seneca stands out for his striking choice to do what I would call primary philosophy (rather than exegetical or missionary work) in Latin. He was enabled to do so in part because of his unusual early exposure to a man like Fabianus, but also, perhaps, because there existed a critical mass of philosophically interested people, Greeks as well as Romans, whose minds were open to Latin philosophy, as they had not been in Cicero's day.

What else is salient philosophically in the environment of Seneca's thought, beyond this unique attitude to a Latin philosophical life and the familiar tension surrounding the time-honoured options of *otium* and a career of active public service? Let me address this question under three headings. First, one wants to consider the distinctive pattern of interests detectable in much of the philosophical work of the first century AD. Second, we should survey Seneca's position with respect to the various schools whose work shapes the problems and options open to him. And third, I want to look briefly at Seneca's remarkable tendency to shift his interests to technical topics, which displays a rapid shift of perspective and level of detail,

---

[15] See *Cons. Polyb.* 8.2 and 11.5. The term *resoluisti* (11.5) is the basis for thinking that the translations were into prose.
[16] The example of Cornutus (see above, n. 11) is particularly pertinent to Seneca.
[17] *Diss.* 1.17.16.

and a clear grasp of specialist work, features which reveal in brief flashes the real depth of his thought.

The first topic opens up nicely with a consideration of another of Seneca's major philosophical influences, Attalus the Stoic. Let us note that here too (as with Fabianus) we are dealing with a man who turns up in the pages of Seneca the Elder. In the *Suasoriae* (2.12) we read: 'Attalus the Stoic, who was banished thanks to the machinations of Sejanus, was a man of great eloquence, far the most subtle and at the same time the most articulate of the philosophers seen in your generation', meaning, of course, the *aetas* of his sons. Our Seneca describes in warm terms his formal study in the school of Attalus (*Ep.* 108.3). Attalus, he remembers, used to teach a rather interesting form of self-restrained intellectual *askēsis*. These lessons, Seneca says, he remembers from the time 'when I attended his school and was the first to arrive and last to leave, asking him to take up topics for discussion even during his walks; he was not only available to students, but even went out of his way to meet with them.' Attalus was an early influence, is often described as *Attalus noster*, and is usually mentioned only for his moral wisdom. It is striking, then, to hear in another context of his special interest in what is for a Stoic a branch of physics, divination. In the *Naturales Quaestiones* (2.48.2, 2.50.1) Attalus turns up as having made a serious study of the Etruscan art of divination by sky signs, such as thunder and lightning. This branch of physics is, to be sure, closely linked to theology and to ethics. But the conjunction in one influential teacher of predominantly ethical interests with a subsidiary pursuit of physics fits, as we shall see, a pattern of some consequence for Seneca. It is, in fact, the most widespread pattern of philosophical interests found in his immediate intellectual environment. It certainly characterized Papirius Fabianus;[18] and even Musonius Rufus with his heavy emphasis on ethical and social themes evidently acknowledged the crucial role of physics (see frag. 42).

---

[18] Griffin, *Seneca*, 40–1; *NQ* 3.27.3; Pliny, *HN* 18.276.

Seneca's other early teacher, Sotion (*Ep.* 49.2), was also, it seems, a student of Sextius.[19] Certainly he was a man of marked Pythagorean leanings—which fits at least pragmatically with his Sextian affiliation.[20] The rather surprising appeal of Pythagoreanism is of course anticipated by the influence of such ideas on even such a scholarly and political man as Nigidius Figulus two generations before. The Pythagorean justification for vegetarianism is not strictly ethical, as Sextius' was; Seneca strongly suggests (*Ep.* 108.20–1) that Sotion's own abstention from meat was, like Pythagoras', based on belief in transmigration and other substantive cosmological views. But there was no real conflict between Stoics and Pythagoreans on this point in Seneca's day—similar cosmological motivations lay behind Musonius' vegetarianism (frag. 18A).

There is a constellation of philosophical interests here, centered heavily on ethics but with some room for physics, though with the emphasis varying among different philosophers. We see it in Sextius (Pliny *HN* 18.274), in Papirius Fabianus, in Sotion, Attalus, and in Musonius. Epictetus, the student of Musonius, is a less clear representative of this pattern, since his interest in dialectic seems to be much livelier than that of any of those I have mentioned—but Epictetus' formative and influential years come well after Seneca's (it is easy to forget that Epictetus studied under Musonius, and that Musonius was thirty years Seneca's junior). Even the most cursory reflection on Seneca's work confirms exactly the pattern we are considering. His work is fundamentally and professedly ethical, but physics, especially the broader outlines of teleological cosmology, is crucial to it. He is persistently doubtful about the contributions to be made by dialectic itself. The *Naturales Quaestiones* might perhaps come to us as a surprise in Seneca's œuvre, if not for the more widely spread pattern of such interests among the generation from whose example he had learned the most.

---

[19] See Griffin, *Seneca*, 39–40.

[20] *Ep.* 108.17 f.: Sotion explained the different reasons for which Pythagoras and Sextius were vegetarians, which suggests personal knowledge of Sextius' teaching.

This openness to the contributions to ethics of natural philosophy marks Seneca and other Stoics off from the Cynic revival, which was also under way in his own day. We think, of course, primarily of Demetrius, about whom we know relatively little beyond what we learn from Seneca himself, whose report at the beginning of *De Beneficiis* 7 includes a paraphrase of Demetrius' argument *against* the study of physical problems. The role of a Cynic in shaping Seneca's philosophical environment was probably slight—Demetrius came too late to contribute to his intellectual formation and anyway would serve only to accentuate a trend towards practical ethics already well established among Stoic and Sextian philosophers. But even so it is important to recall not just that a Cynic like Demetrius, lecturing in Greek,[21] should make such a profound impression on Seneca, but that he (like Musonius) was intimate with senatorial families and took part in their legal and political struggles.

The decades between Cicero's formative years and those of Seneca saw other developments which affected Seneca's philosophical environment: the decline of Academic scepticism and revival of dogmatic Platonism; the Andronican 'edition' of Aristotle's works and the consequent Peripatetic revival; the founding or refounding of Pyrrhonian scepticism. The one school with respect to which little seems to have changed was Epicureanism. That Seneca and Cicero have such different attitudes to the school is a simple result of their own philosophical perspectives.

Seneca shows considerable, if intermittent, interest in the views of schools other than his own. His view of Epicureanism is perhaps the most complex—wavering from the frankly pragmatic openness to many aspects of its ethical therapy which Seneca displays in the *Epistulae* to the aggressive denunciation, which at times approaches Ciceronian intensity, of some parts of *De Beneficiis* book 4. About the Peripatetics he can be more straightforward. They turn up as holding the wrong view on the passions (urging moderation rather than elimination)— a matter of crucial importance in the treatise *De Ira* and

---

[21] Margarethe Billerbeck, *Der Kyniker Demetrius* (Leiden, 1978), 19 and n. 39.

elsewhere[22]—and on the role of external goods in a happy life[23] (the Peripatetics conceded rather too much to fortune by Stoic standards), and as the source of 'scientific' theories advanced throughout the *Naturales Quaestiones*. He knows other Peripatetic doctrines too, knows them from books rather than teachers, and thinks his audience will care about them. The same is true for his treatment of Platonism, which was in the early stages of its scholarly revival during the first century AD. We find a remarkably detailed discussion of Platonic ontology in the *Epistulae*—letter 58 shows a strong and independent-minded grasp of metaphysical questions going well beyond the more obvious examples of ethically motivated physical theory which typify the philosophy of his era. The same can be said for the letter on causation (*Ep.* 65) which deals with both Platonic and Aristotelian contributions to the issue and for his engagement with the Academic partitioning of philosophy advanced by Eudorus (*Ep.* 89).

These letters have an importance for our understanding of Seneca's philosophical milieu which far exceeds their small bulk in our surviving collection of his writing. For they show a capacity for and an interest in the kinds of philosophical problems which many philosophers of his own day (and perhaps of Cicero's too) and even Seneca himself at some points would have dismissed as irrelevant to human life. We know, of course, that Seneca tends to drop into technical detail somewhat abruptly, either fascinated by some particular aspect of school doctrine or genuinely engrossed by the problems it posed. And he did not just fall into this in his leisurely later years, for we have a striking and self-conscious example of it as early as book 2 of the *De Ira*.[24] Without these rather episodic outbursts we would have a very different picture of Seneca the philosopher, one much more in tune with the 'popular' philosophizing of his

---

[22] See *De Ira* 1.9.2, 1.14.1, 1.17.1, 3.3.1; also *Ep.* 85.3–4, 116.

[23] *Ben.* 5.13.1–2, and the discussion of the *tria genera bonorum* in *Ep.* 88. *Ep.* 92 also contains a critique of their position, though it is not labelled as Peripatetic; the Peripatetics are obviously the unnamed target of several discussions of the nature of the good.

[24] *De Ira* 2.1–4.

day. I would venture the guess that this facet of his philosophical output tells us something important about his philosophical milieu—that his audience included readers who had considerable philosophical training, perhaps even professional teachers of philosophy who cared to read contributions to their problems written in Latin. It also suggests that Seneca was throughout his life interested in their attention and approval. And despite the tendency of some source critics[25] to assume that Seneca preferred to use a small number of intermediary sources, the evidence also suggests that Seneca read serious philosophical literature in Greek, throughout his life, for its own sake, not just in order to digest it for presentation to his peers. His environment probably required the time-honoured Roman disdain for things Greek (one thinks here of his superciliously xenophobic remarks about Chrysippus in *Ben.* 1.4.1); but that contempt was obviously only skin-deep for Seneca—his philosophical milieu also included at least a few like-minded peers. When we read the rather despairing remarks about the current state of philosophy which conclude the *Naturales Quaestiones*, we are not getting the whole story. Technical philosophy mattered to at least a serious core of Latin readers—to believe otherwise would be to suppose that Seneca, a literary animal if there ever was one, continued for decades to throw his published pearls before swine—and this I regard as nearly unthinkable. The truth of the matter must be that his culture took an interest in serious philosophy to a degree which we would not expect to find if we attended primarily to his early works and to the philosophical output of his contemporaries and predecessors.

Before I conclude, I would like to return to a contrast between Seneca and Cicero, a contrast which turns once again on the issue of language. When Cicero wrote philosophy, he created a basic Latin vocabulary for the expression of Greek philosophical ideas. This vocabulary was foundational for later attempts to write philosophical works in Latin, though it was

---

[25] A clear example of this is François-Regis Chaumartin in *Le De Beneficiis de Sénèque: sa signification philosophique, politique, et sociale* (Paris, 1985).

certainly not final or determinative. When we read Cicero, we can almost always do so against the background of our knowledge of the kind of Greek philosophy and terminology which he faced. As a result of this, and because he wrote for the most part to bring Greek philosophical ideas to his Roman audience, we can usually read through his Latin terminology to see the Greek. We see readily, for example, that *assensus* stands for *sunkatathesis*, that *visum* stands for *phantasia*, that *impetus* stands for *hormē*. We can tell, too, that *officium* represents *kathēkon*, though in a case like this the overtones of the Latin term can come to dominate, even distort the Greek ideas that Cicero is purveying. (It is probably significant that the impact of Latinity on Cicero's translations from the Greek is greatest in the *De Officiis*, where Cicero is most on his own philosophically.) Examples of this type could be multiplied almost without limit, and Cicero frequently tells us what he is up to terminologically.[26] He is systematic enough that we can even distinguish the odd case where he gets the sense of a Greek technical term wrong in Latin.[27]

In Seneca things are different. Despite a smattering of technical terms which he deliberately introduces from Greek—*to on, ousia* in letter 58, *kata sterēsin* and *anhuparxia* in letter 87—we find little. Letter 89 gives us Greek terms for the parts of philosophy, letter 81 invokes the *paradoxa* of the Stoics; the *liberales artes* are correlated with the *enkuklioi* in letter 88. And of course there are Greek words dropped in unselfconsciously, as part of the style of a highly educated Roman. The quotation in Greek from Metrodorus in letter 99 is perhaps an instance of this kind of unconscious pretension. Perhaps the extensive use of scientific terms from Greek in the *Naturales Quaestiones* counts as noteworthy, but I think that we should regard that as a different phenomenon. Beyond that, the few invocations of

---

[26] Often the comment comes from the letters. For one particularly interesting case, see Lévy, *Cicero*, 245–8.

[27] *Fin.* 3, in which Cicero gives us a large number of self-conscious translations as well as a substantial apologia for the practice, also includes (*Fin.* 3.32) a translation for *epigennēmatikon* as 'posterum quodam modo et consequens'. But this confuses a form of conceptual supervenience with temporal and causal relationships.

Greek terms stand out. *aochlēsia* is rendered *quies* in letter 92; more interesting are two passages where the looseness of fit between the Greek term and the obvious translation of it provoke explicit comment. In letter 9 (9.2) Seneca notes that if you just go ahead and translate *apatheia* as *impatientia* you will wind up with ambiguity and perhaps even communicate the opposite idea to what is intended. Once this is noted, Seneca does not waste his time trying to find the best single word for the Greek—he describes and talks about the substantive issue in his own non-technical Latin. In the *De Tranquillitate Animi* (2.3) he tells the reader that he is wrestling with the Greek term *euthumia*, and has chosen *tranquillitas* as the Latin stand-in for Democritus' term. Seneca feels he has to defend this translation for not being isomorphic with the Greek term (it is not composed of a prefix and some term for 'spirit'): 'the very thing at issue should be picked out by some noun, which ought to have the *force* of the Greek term rather than the *form* of it.'

Clearly Seneca is reacting, here and in the case of *impatientia* (which is isomorphic with its Greek target), against a strategy of translating isomorphically and symbolically, a technique which works best if the reader already knows the Greek term in question and ultimately requires as much explanation as would be needed by simply dropping in the Greek word itself. What this shows about Seneca's attitude to writing philosophy in Latin is simple: that he prefers to work his ideas out in Latin, in Latin terms, because that is the language he thinks in. Seneca, much more than Cicero, is thinking creatively and philosophically in Latin. The result of this for us is mixed. On the one hand, we can be much closer to Seneca's own intellectual creativity than we would otherwise be, but on the other, he is less easy than Cicero to coordinate with the Greek background which we sometimes seek when reading Latin philosophy. Seneca is a vexingly slippery 'source' for Hellenistic philosophy; but he is as a result (and as a result of the unique environment in which he worked) a rare example of first-order Latin philosophy.

Let me illustrate this point with an example, as I do so tipping my hat with respect to a recent collection of essays edited by Pierre Grimal on this theme,[28] and especially to Grimal's own contribution on 'Le vocabulaire de l'interiorité dans l'œuvre de Sénèque'. First, and most familiar, think of Seneca's term *voluntas* and the verb *velle* in some of its more self-conscious uses.[29] As is well known, his use of the term is new; the obvious Greek counterpart *boulēsis* simply does not mean the same thing. When Seneca says that our 'will' to do something is the focal point of a moral decision or evaluation, it is virtually impossible to turn this back into Greek without significantly altering what he seems to mean. Perhaps the closest Greek parallel to the meaning and use of the term which we can find is the term *prohairesis* as used by Epictetus. But there is, I am sure, no serious argument to be made that Seneca was reacting to that term—Epictetus simply came too late and there is no clear sign that the distinctive features of his use of the term are rooted in any tradition Seneca could know. There is, I think, a much better argument to be made for the suggestion that Epictetus' departure from earlier Stoic uses of the term *prohairesis* might be influenced by Seneca.[30] Such a discontinuity, both terminological and conceptual, seems to me to be a result of the fact that Seneca took his understanding of philosophical issues out of Greek and into his own language, the fact that Seneca really did think things through, philosophically, in Latin. There has long been a tendency, even while recognizing the originality and distinctiveness of Seneca's thought, to attribute his originality to his Roman culture or to his openness to *Erlebnis* in contrast to school dogma.[31] These are no doubt important factors. What

---

[28] P. Grimal, *La Langue latine, langue de la philosophie: actes du colloque organisé par l'École Française de Rome* (Rome, 1992).

[29] See too A.-J. Voelke, *L'Idée de volonté dans le Stoïcisme* (Paris, 1973), pt. 2, ch. 3.

[30] This was hinted at by Charles Kahn in 'Discovering the Will', in J. M. Dillon and A. A. Long (eds.), *The Question of 'Eclecticism'* (Berkeley 1988), 252–5. John Rist, *Stoic Philosophy* (Cambridge 1969), 230–1, pointedly declines to consider this possibility, attributing the similarities between Seneca and Epictetus to their common position as teachers and spiritual directors. But the very different social and political positions of the two, and the fact that Seneca never formally taught as did Epictetus, make this speculative explanation doubtful at best.

[31] I have in mind M. Pohlenz, 'Philosophie und Erlebnis in Senecas Dialogen', *NAWG* phil.-hist. Kl. 1.4.3 (1941), 55–118. See John Rist's critique in *Stoic Philosophy*, 224–8. My suggestions differ from Rist's position subtly but importantly. He

I suggest is that the key factor is the directness of his philosophical thought in Latin, following the model of his teachers.

Another facet of Seneca's fresh thinking on the philosophy of mind also comes out of reflection on the role of *voluntas*. In addition to adding the notion of 'will' to the Stoic tradition, Seneca also rethought to some important degree the earlier Stoic conception of assent—this rethinking is expressed in the early pages of *De Ira* book 2, in the discussion of 'preliminary passions'. I have aired my thoughts on this elsewhere,[32] and so can only allude to it now. But I should note in passing that in this case the terminology of assent seems stable enough; what changes is the nature of assent itself, and it changes in a way that coheres nicely with the idea of *voluntas* as a basic psychological power which we see elsewhere in Seneca. This confirms, for me at any rate, that the change introduced by Seneca within the Latin terminological framework was motivated primarily by philosophical considerations.

The most important thing about Seneca's philosophical milieu is its combination of frank Romanness and Latinity with its philosophical creativity. With much of his philosophical work, despite its inevitable and somewhat conventional stance of reaction against things Greek *qua* Greek, Seneca has made his own milieu. Failure to see that, and a reluctance to acknowledge that here, if nowhere else in pagan Latin philosophy, the lines of philosophical influence just might run *back* from Latin to Greek, have (I think) blinded many students of ancient philosophy and culture to the depth and complexity of Seneca, who was in his own way as important a contributor to ancient philosophy as he was to Roman politics.[33]

---

is most concerned to deny, against Pohlenz, that there is anything 'particularly Latin...about Seneca's position'; that is true as far as it goes, but I hold that the development and articulation of his Stoic views in the Latin language make a substantial difference to the shape and impact of his theory. Rist's emphasis on the compatibility of Seneca's position with Chrysippus' moral psychology (230) overshadows the importance of Seneca's new and (in my view) influential version of the earlier Stoic position.

[32] 'Seneca and Psychological Dualism', Ch. 2 below.

[33] I leave these speculations about *voluntas* unchanged, although a rather different line of interpretation can be found in Ch. 5 below, 'The Will in Seneca'.

2

Seneca and Psychological Dualism

SENECA AND ORTHODOXY

Seneca's 'philosophy of mind' presents us with many puzzles, but in this it is no more than a faithful mirror of his philosophy as a whole. In this essay I am interested in how his views on the structure and operations of the human soul relate to those of so-called orthodox Stoics, and how one goes about assessing such an issue. That Seneca is not a slavish or unimaginative representative of Chrysippean Stoicism seems clear from the most casual reading of his work and the most cursory glance through the abundant secondary literature. But it is not clear just how his views on the soul differ from those of the early Stoics.

Seneca is sometimes described by the (traditionally pejorative) term 'eclectic'. But as Pierluigi Donini and others have shown,[1] we can no longer take for granted the usefulness of that simple description in the study of later ancient philosophy; indeed, it is not clear that we can readily agree about its meaning. I want at least to set aside the negative associations of the word: even if Seneca is in some sense an 'eclectic' it should not

---

[1] Pierluigi Donini, 'The History of the Concept of Eclecticism', in J. M. Dillon and A. A. Long (eds.), *The Question of 'Eclecticism': Studies in Later Greek Philosophy* (Berkeley, 1988).

be assumed that he is for that reason a derivative, less powerful, or less interesting thinker.[2] Further, I want to argue that in one important area of the philosophy of mind, the theory of the passions, we should not be calling Seneca an eclectic at all. His approach is open, but not eclectic. He is prepared to propose changes in traditional Stoicism, but those changes never threaten the core of Stoic ideas—as a change from psychological monism to dualism (let alone tripartition) would do.[3]

Seneca's orthodoxy is inevitably judged by comparison with the early Stoic scholarchs. What it means to be a Stoic is determined in large measure by a thinker's relation to Chrysippus, Cleanthes, and Zeno; in the normal way of treating the development of Stoic thought, these three philosophers constitute a benchmark to use in measuring the 'Stoicness' of other thinkers. Before proceeding too much further we should pause to reflect on one of Seneca's own statements on the question of school allegiance and orthodoxy.

Hoc Stoicis quoque placere ostendam, non quia mihi legem dixerim nihil contra dictum Zenonis Chrysippive committere, sed quia res ipsa *patitur* me ire in illorum sententiam, quoniam si quis semper unius sequitur, non in curia sed factione est.[4]

---

[2] I follow P. Donini, *Le scuole, l'anima, l'impero: la filosofia antica da Antioco a Plotino* (Turin, 1982), ch. 4, in his general estimation of Seneca's 'eclectic' character: his proneness to adopt and integrate facets of other schools' thought into his own basically Stoic framework is a mark of his ability to appreciate the larger significance of philosophical theories and tailor them to his own insights and needs, a sign, that is, of his freedom from the restrictions of unreflective school loyalty.

[3] The sense I assign to the terms 'psychological monism' and 'dualism' is only that described in B. Inwood, *Ethics and Human Action in Early Stoicism* (Oxford, 1985). See in particular chs. 2 and 5. To quote from p. 28: one must distinguish two questions: 'does the soul in its entirety or just the *hēgemonikon* have a multiplicity of powers? and the more important question, does the mind...have in it a power which can oppose reason and impair its functioning in the control of a man's actions and life? The latter is the key psychological question which bears on Stoic ethics.' And it is the key diagnostic question to ask when assessing a theory for monistic or dualistic character. This central point seems to have been missed by A. M. Ioppolo, 'Il monismo psicologico degli Stoici antichi', *Elenchos*, 8 (1987), 449–66.

[4] *De Otio* 3.1. This text and several others are discussed by J. Rist, 'Seneca and Stoic Orthodoxy', *ANRW* 36.3 (1989), 1993–2012. See esp. 1999–2003 for his discussion of the subjects which I will discuss at length below.

I will show you that the Stoics also hold this view – not because I have bound myself to undertake nothing in opposition to the dictates of Zeno or Chrysippus, but rather just because the facts of the matter *permit* me to support their opinion. For if one always adheres to the opinion of some one person, one is a partisan rather than a senator.

For Seneca, being a Stoic does not mean following an inflexible rule to abide by the views of Zeno and Chrysippus; but it does involve following their doctrine when the facts themselves permit him to do so; the initial expectation is that Stoic views will be accepted, but Seneca assumes no obligation to do so. When, in his own view, their doctrine conflicts with the facts, then the facts prevail. Of course, this leaves out the difficult questions of how Seneca goes about determining what the 'facts' are and how strict a notion of conflict he employs; but I will not try to explore those complexities here.

So how in practice can we assess Seneca's orthodoxy? Let us concede, first of all, that orthodox consistency in early Stoicism is not something to which we have direct access; rather, it is a methodological construct. I do not mean that orthodoxy itself is a myth, nor do I doubt that it remains proper to regard the first three scholarchs as a kind of criterion of what it meant to be a Stoic. After all, even Epictetus used to lecture to his aspiring philosophers on Chrysippus.[5] But the picture which modern scholars have made for themselves of an orthodox Stoicism teaching internally consistent doctrine, grounded on clear general principles—this picture seems to me to be an artefact of our reconstructive methodology.

We generate such a construct by means of tacit assumptions which most scholars make when attempting a reconstruction of early Stoic doctrines: we assume (1) that school doctrine was on most points fairly unified, (2) that the high-level philosophical motivations for these doctrines were fairly consistent, and

[5] I do, however, mean to doubt that agreeing in all significant points with that 'holy trinity' was often regarded as a criterion for considering oneself a Stoic, or being considered a Stoic by others. Seneca bears comparison with the even more difficult case of Marcus Aurelius; see J. Rist, 'Are You a Stoic? The Case of Marcus Aurelius', in B. F. Meyers and E. P. Sanders (eds.), *Self-Definition in the Greco-Roman World*, vol. 3 of *Jewish and Christian Self-Definition* (Philadelphia, 1982).

(3) that each of the early scholarchs held determinate and internally coherent views on most issues, and held them in more or less one form over his entire career.

And yet, these are all questionable assumptions. The chances that any of them was strictly true in the real world are small. We have evidence of divergences among the three scholarchs on important theories in physics, logic, and ethics; but when there is little or no convincing evidence of divergence we tend to postulate doctrinal harmony, taking comfort from the ancient testimony about the internal consistency of the school in its early phase. Moreover, within the work of one of the early scholarchs we assume a fairly high degree of internal cohesion, referring often to *the* Chrysippean theory on this or that topic. But consider the length of Chrysippus' working life, the size of his corpus: compare this to the working life of Plato or Aristotle and to their respective corpora. Do we speak with comfort of *the* Platonic theory of forms? or *the* Aristotelian doctrine of substance? Of course not; or at any rate we should not. Why then do we speak of *the* Chrysippean theory of the *pathē* or of the early Stoic conception of the soul?

On many, if not most, topics we must reconstruct the doctrines from scattered bits of primary and secondary evidence of quite various degrees of reliability. But although most of the applicable parallels militate against a harmony postulate strong enough to support a definite reconstruction, without something of the sort we cannot effectively proceed. And we have good reason for doing so: anything else would make the reconstruction of philosophically interesting theories virtually impossible and reduce the historian of thought to an activity little better than doxography.

The limitations of our reconstructive method matter little for the early Stoa considered on its own, since we can do nothing about the loss of direct evidence from the period. But things are different when we come to an author like Seneca, for whom we have a large part of his total philosophical output. We tend to judge him by comparison with early and orthodox Stoics in two ways: we ask how much he diverges from them, and we ask whether he was as rigorous as they. On both counts a more sober appraisal of our knowledge about the early Stoa will work to Seneca's advantage: it is harder than we like to think to show that a given doctrine diverges from orthodoxy, and it is highly unlikely that Chrysippus was ever as internally consistent as we might wish to present him as being. His doctrine of the passions leaves us with some uncomfortably loose ends to tie up for ourselves. Perhaps things are not all that different with Seneca; perhaps the looseness sometimes detected in his theory was not all that different from what we might find in the work of Chrysippus if we recovered it tomorrow.

What I will be doing in this discussion is to take a very familiar text, *De Ira* 2.1–4, for closer examination and use it to try to show how Seneca's openness operates in one particular case, and how it differs from derivative eclecticism. But before doing so I will need to comment briefly on the recent work of Janine Fillion-Lahille[6] on the *De Ira* (for my approach to Seneca is quite different from hers) and to reflect on three preliminary issues: the significance of literary form, the importance of distinguishing the different kinds of dualism which we may find in a philosophical text, and apparent examples of explicitly dualistic statements.

OLD PROBLEMS AND NEW APPROACHES

My method here represents a long-standing dissatisfaction with the procedures of *Quellenforschung*. In the detailed discussion below I take issue with Holler[7] in particular, since it is his work which most clearly reveals the limitations of that method in advancing our understanding of ancient texts. Moreover, Holler is in a way the classical representative of the view that Seneca was a confused eclectic. In Holler's view Posidonius is most to blame for the dualistic muddle to be found in Seneca's work.

---

[6] J. Fillion-Lahille, *Le De ira de Sénèque et la philosophie stoïcienne des passions* (Paris, 1984).
[7] E. Holler, *Seneca und die Seelenteilungslehre und Affektpsychologie der Mittelstoa* (Kallmünz, 1934).

More recently there has been another and better study of Posidonian and other influences on the *De Ira*, by Janine Fillion-Lahille. For the particular text which interests me (i.e. the early chapters of book 2), she too finds significant Posidonian influence. The foundation of her analysis of the *De Ira* is, without a doubt, traditional *Quellenforschung*. A detailed analysis of Galen's *De Placitis Hippocratis et Platonis* and other sources (such as Cicero's *Tusculan Disputations*) is used to reconstruct in great detail the plan and doctrine of Chrysippus' and Posidonius' books on the passions. The quality of the analysis is higher than is found in Holler's work and the results are presented with a much more realistic caution. As far as the *De Ira* is concerned, her conclusion is that book 1 is basically of Chrysippean inspiration and book 2 of significantly Posidonian inspiration. Her further arguments about influences in the latter part of book 2 and in book 3 are new, but not relevant to my immediate concerns. More interesting is her fundamental reevaluation of the relation between Chrysippean and Posidonian philosophies of mind.

The traditional view, which I still hold despite Fillion-Lahille's argument, is that Posidonius' analysis of mind and the passions is plainly inconsistent with Chrysippus'. By contrast, Fillion-Lahille regards them as being complementary and argues at some length that we should regard Posidonius as being essentially orthodox,[8] blaming Galen for the common misperception of Posidonius as a radical innovator. The overall effect of her study, put bluntly, is that she retains the old-fashioned *Quellenforscher*'s theory of Posidonian influence in book 2 of the *De Ira*, but strips that theory of what is to me one of its most unacceptable corollaries, viz. that Seneca is a muddled eclectic.

If one were concerned to do no more than rehabilitate the philosophical reputation of Seneca, this would be a tempting theory to support. But my concerns about the traditional view are also founded on a deep scepticism about the possibility of

---

[8] Esp. 154 ff. She outlines three key theses which define orthodoxy. But these are insufficient to define orthodoxy; and the evidence cited seems insufficient to support the claims made.

reconstructing Posidonian or other lost views by traditional methods. In that regard, Fillion-Lahille has not advanced much. Her *Quellenforschung* is better, but we are still shuffling back and forth the familiar counters: Cicero, Galen, Arius Didymus, Plutarch, Diogenes Laertius; and we are still resting hypotheses on unanswerable questions such as: is Galen more misleading when giving us evidence about Chrysippus or about Posidonius? (I tend to think he is most misleading about Chrysippus, Fillion-Lahille stresses how misleading his Platonizing version of Posidonius is.)[9]

What I am trying to do in this essay is to break free from such sterile analysis and to ask afresh whether we have adequate grounds for even suspecting 'foreign' influence on the early chapters of *De Ira* 2. Fillion-Lahille's analysis of the Posidonian elements in 2.1-4 (pp. 163 ff.) leaves Seneca committed to a form of dualism incompatible with views of Chrysippus, whereas I do not think that dualism is to be found there any more than it is to be found in Chrysippus himself. Once again the appeal of Posidonius has encouraged a *Quellenforscher* to postulate inconsistency in Seneca's text.

Of course I still rely, for better or worse, on my own understanding of the early Stoic doctrine of the passions. Fillion-Lahille's analysis of it is noticeably different, and different in ways which make it easier for her to argue that Posidonius is not fundamentally at odds with the early Stoics, as Galen claims. For what it is worth, my analysis of the early Stoic theory allows Posidonius to play the role that Galen gives him.[10]

---

[9] I have benefited from reading an unpublished paper on Posidonius' doctrine of the passions by John Cooper, 'Stoic Theories of the Emotions'. He is critical of Galen's portrayal of Posidonius.

[10] Of the texts cited to justify rejecting Galen's view (pp. 123 ff.), only the Plutarchan *Lib. Aegr.* 6 (in fr. 154 EK) is of any weight at all; and even this does not say what Fillion-Lahille hopes it says. It does not say that 'desire, fear, and anger are nothing but judgments'. What it does is to give a description to distinguish purely psychic *pathē* from others: in contrast to mixed and bodily *pathē*, these involve judgments and suppositions. Fillion-Lahille says that this formally contradicts the assembled evidence of Galen (p. 124). Well, it does not. Cooper ('Stoic Theories', n. 15) has a more plausible view of the passage.

In other respects too Fillion-Lahille differs from me on the earlier Stoic theory. In particular (see pp. 128–30), she does not see that the key issue for orthodoxy is not the relation of irrationality in the soul to the passions, but whether or not there is any irrational part. By tackling the theory of passions on its own, outside the context of the entire analysis of mind and action, she enables herself to present Posidonius' addition of irrational powers as a minor complement to Chrysppean theory which helps with the causal explanation of the *pathē*.[11] And perhaps from that narrow point of view it is no more than that. But as Galen saw, such an addition is in fact of much greater philosophical significance.[12]

Perhaps the simplest description of my position on the early chapters of *De Ira* 2 is this. Posidonius is not overtly invoked in the chapters in question. Seneca claims to be following the views of his school, and there is good reason to doubt that Posidonius represents that view. Consequently I limit myself to direct examination of this text in comparison with earlier Stoic doctrine. Fillion-Lahille has no difficulty in holding that Seneca's philosophical stance is significantly different in books 2 and 1, though she tries to play down the difference by bending Chrysippus and Posidonius towards each other (in my view unsuccessfully); I, however, prefer to assume that the two books are in harmony until forced by evidence to postulate internal contradiction. I do not think that book 2, properly interpreted, conflicts with anything in book 1. Let us turn to the other preliminaries.

---

[11] The clearest index of how different our views of Chrysippean monism are comes from the fact that she argues (160 ff.) that it is a mark of compatibility with Chrysippean philosophy of mind that Posidonius locates the irrational powers in the heart, rather than in a Platonically inspired lower part of the body. But the issue is whether the soul contains any irrational powers, not where they are located.

[12] In addition, I would want to disagree with Fillion-Lahille about the importance of assent, the nature of the excess which constitutes a passion, the proper understanding of Posidonius' *pathētikē holkē* (156 ff.), and about the relation between Zeno and Chrysippus. Fillion-Lahille holds that Posidonius revived the dualism of Zeno (see esp. 163) and reasserted it against Chrysippus; since the case for Zeno's 'dualism' is weak (Inwood, *Ethics and Human Action*, 29 ff.), Posidonian dualism, if such it be, would be a more serious departure from orthodoxy, and Seneca's acceptance of it would be a much more serious departure from his normal attitude to the early scholarchs than Fillion-Lahille believes.

THE IMPORTANCE OF LITERARY FORM

With few exceptions we have very little detailed information about the literary form and technique of early Stoic treatises.[13] But that many works of Chrysippus had a literary form is certain;[14] Cleanthes' poetry and Zeno's book titles also point in that direction. We may be confident that the doxographical writers and later authors who discuss the early Stoics have stripped off what they understood to be the irrelevant literary apparatus which might mislead us, and in so doing they may have got things right or wrong. But with Seneca, the problem of controlling the literary apparatus is much more immediate and acute. We possess Seneca's works, and therefore must decide for ourselves how to handle the question of literary form. We cannot forget, as we might be tempted to do when dealing with Chrysippus, that Seneca, like Plato, writes deliberately in a literary genre, or genres, and the apparatus which naturally accompanies such work tends to exert an influence on our interpretation of his philosophical doctrine.

It is not possible to provide a general theory of the interaction between philosophical content and literary form; the observations which follow are best regarded as an exhortation to caution in approaching the text of a literary philosopher: I do not claim that there is a single right way of interpreting metaphors and similes in philosophical texts, merely that a close and sceptical look will never be a waste of time.[15]

---

[13] See L. Stroux, 'Vergleich und Metapher in der Lehre des Zenon von Kition', Diss. (Heidelberg, 1966) and K.-H. Rolke, *Die bildhaften Vergleiche in den Fragmenten der Stoiker von Zenon bis Panaitios* (Hildesheim, 1975).

[14] The extensive amount of quotation from Euripides' *Medea* in his *On Passions* is the clearest sign. In the same work he makes crucial use of an illustrative comparison with a runner (*SVF* iii. 462), and this will be relevant to our appraisal of Seneca.

[15] One might sketch out a typology of the relationships between metaphor and philosophical content. (1) The metaphor may be purely ornamental and evidently so, such that one feels no temptation to impute doctrinal significance to it; (2) at the other extreme, the metaphor may be an essential component of the philosopher's conception—his doctrine may have been developed by thinking through the metaphor itself and so the two are inextricably intertwined (the work of G. Lakoff and

I believe that one reason for imputing to Seneca an 'unorthodox' philosophy of mind flows from his use of images to portray more vividly psychological relationships and actions. Consider the theory of the passions, the central problem area for later Stoic psychology and the one in which suspicions of unorthodoxy and eclecticism are most likely to arise. The 'orthodox' Stoic view is that all passions are causally dependent on rational decisions of the mind, and that a conflict between one's rational decision-making powers and the passions of the soul, of the sort which Plato attributes to Leontius in *Republic* IV, is simply not possible. Yet in many passages Seneca writes as though the passions had a kind of life and force of their own, which enables them to take up a position in opposition to reason; and this has encouraged scholars, most noticeably Holler, to impute an eclectic form of psychological dualism to Seneca. A good example of this can be found in *De Tranquillitate Animi* 2.8, where the absence of inner harmony is described in terms which suggest dualism:

Tunc illos et paenitentia coepti tenet et incipiendi timor subrepitque illa animi iactatio non invenientis exitum, quia nec imperare cupiditatibus suis nec obsequi possunt, et cunctatio vitae parum se explicantis et inter destituta vota torpentis animi situs.

Then they are seized by regret for what they have begun and by fear of the next undertaking. They begin to suffer insidiously from an agitation of the mind, which cannot come to a resolution since they can neither command their desires nor obey them, from hesitation about a life which cannot sort itself out, and from the sluggishness of a mind which sits paralyzed amidst its abandoned hopes.

M. Johnson, *Metaphors We Live By* (Chicago, 1980) is interesting in this connection); (3) the metaphor may be used to enliven or reinforce the impact of a theory without being meant to determine the content of that theory, and in so doing it (i) may or (ii) may not introduce misleading elements or ideas; (4) there may be self-conscious analogies drawn to familiar experiences, analogies whose implications are meant to help determine the sense of a doctrine, and these analogies (i) may be essential to the justification of the theory or (ii) may be purely illustrative. There are surely many other possible categories. The kind of cases I am interested in fall into types (3) and (4); (3.i) is the type most relevant to the parts of Seneca under consideration.

Seneca and Psychological Dualism

Most of the psychic instability here appears to be a matter of temporal vacillation, a perfectly orthodox analysis:[16] at one moment the agent feels or wishes one thing and shortly afterwards something else. But the phrase *quia nec imperare cupiditatibus suis nec obsequi possunt* hardly admits of that interpretation: to speak of giving orders to or obeying the orders of one's desires would suggest the sort of quasi-independence for the desires which orthodox Stoic theory does not permit. Yet from the larger context of this work it is clear that Seneca is not turning to Platonism or to some sort of Posidonian amalgam of Platonic and Stoic psychology. The figure of speech which Seneca uses here would, if pressed for its literal descriptive significance, entail a non-monistic view of the soul. The question interpreters must ask is whether a given passage should be so pressed.

Another text, this one not from Seneca, shows how difficult it is to determine whether to take such language literally. In Stobaeus' report of Arius Didymus' doxography,[17] there occurs a well-known borrowing from Plato's *Phaedrus*. The Stoic idea of excessiveness in the passions (*sphodrotēs*) is illustrated by the Platonic image of a horse which is disobedient to its master; this is supported by a quotation from Euripides which puts cognitive powers (*gnōmē*) into conflict with the nature (*phusis*) of the agent. If one takes seriously the Platonic allusion, then this text reveals an openness to a synthesis of Platonic and Stoic psychologies. If one attends more to the Euripidean quotation, then things are less clear—for to find someone's 'nature' to be in conflict with his powers of rational decision is much less clearly inconsistent with what we understand as Chrysippean psychology. The 'nature' in question could be understood as bodily. As has been recently argued (though perhaps not as sharply as one might wish),[18] there is a kind of dualism in Chrysippean

---

[16] Better seen in *Ep.* 52. Cf. Inwood, *Ethics and Human Action*, 138.

[17] *Ecl.* ii.89.4 ff. See Inwood, *Ethics and Human Action*, 142 and notes.

[18] L. Couloubaritsis, 'La psychologie chez Chrysippe', in H. Flashar and O. Gigon (eds.), *Aspects de la philosophie hellénistique* (Entretiens sur antiquité classique, t. 32; Geneva, 1986). We should also distinguish metaphysical dualism, which deals with the principles underlying Stoic physics, from psychological

Stoicism, a body/soul dualism which is compatible with monism as applied within the soul.[19] If, in the passage of Stobaeus now before us, we focused on the Euripidean text, nothing would determine for us which kind of dualism we should attribute to the author; it is only by giving primacy to the *Phaedrus* allusion that we feel confident in concluding that the psychology is unorthodox.

The delicacy of this interpretation is enhanced by reflection on the evolution of Plato's own psychology. The dualism between reason and desire is, at its first appearance in the *Phaedo*, a body/soul dualism; great weight is placed on the internal unity of the soul. A reader of the *Phaedo* must take the phenomena associated in the *Republic* or *Phaedrus* with a lower, irrational part of the soul as being mere bodily disturbances. If we put ourselves in the position of someone who believes that the differences in psychological doctrine between the *Phaedo* and the later dialogues are superficial, it becomes more difficult to decide whether a Platonically flavoured dualism is or is not compatible with Stoic views. David Sedley's paper 'Chrysippus on Psychophysical Causality' is acutely and correctly sensitive to the relevance of the *Phaedo*, read in the context of the rest of Plato's corpus, to the interpretation of Stoic thought.[20]

---

dualism. Thus the Stoic division between god and matter can be seen as a form of dualism, and so can the distinction between god (or providence) and the cosmos. These metaphysical dualisms appeal to Seneca, and he sometimes finds in them (correctly, I would say) similarities to important Platonic ideas—see esp. *Ep.* 65 and the *NQ*, esp. the proem to book 1. I owe this observation to P. Donini. It may also be true that Seneca, in Stoic fashion, understands the importance of the parallel between the microcosm of man and the macrocosm of nature, according to which the god/cosmos or god/matter contrast is analogous to the mind/body opposition in man. But even so, this sort of dualism is not relevant to my analysis of Seneca's position on psychological dualism, which turns exclusively on the relations within the soul of man.

[19] I cannot discuss fully here the question of how Stoic materialism as applied to the soul is compatible with dualism. Suffice it to say that there is no *a priori* need for the two entities opposed in a dualism to be of different ontological orders—as body and soul are in a Platonic dualism. The corporeal status of soul and its perfect blending with body are compatible, as far as I can see, with an ethically relevant dualism between body and soul.

[20] D. Sedley, 'Chrysippus on Psychophysical Causality', in J. Brunschwig and M. Nussbaum (eds.), *Passions & Perceptions* (Cambridge, 1993), 313-31.

Because it is so easy to blur the issue of Platonic dualism, it becomes more and more difficult to decide whether a given problematic discussion by a Platonically prone Stoic is or is not 'orthodox'. It is at this point that the nature of the text becomes crucial. If we are considering a doxographical report, like that in Arius Didymus,[21] it seems reasonable to press the significance of the allusions and quotations quite hard. It is hard to argue that Arius or his source is using this deliberately borrowed Platonic allusion in a casual or merely literary way and that he does not realize that his readers will assume that he is endorsing a full *Phaedrus*-style dualism. With the Senecan text we have considered above, it is more difficult to be sure, but I suggest that the general nature of the text and immediate context should dispose us to strip off the figures of speech and leave Seneca with a reasonably orthodox if not technically precise theory, at least in this place.

Seneca's own explicit views on the use of figures of speech are also worth considering. In *Epistulae Morales* 59, which is distinguished for its self-conscious attention to the technical accuracy of style, his own and Lucilius', Seneca offers some remarks on metaphor and simile (*translationes, imagines*) in philosophical writing. Despite the accuracy of Lucilius' style, Seneca does find some examples of these figures of speech (59.6): he groups them as 'comparisons' (*parabolae*), and adds:

quas existimo necessarias, non ex eadem causa qua poetis, sed ut imbecillitatis nostrae adminicula sint, ut et dicentem et audientem in rem praesentem adducant.

I think they are necessary, not for the same reason that they are necessary for poets, but as compensations for our weakness, in order to bring both the speaker and the listener into direct contact with the matter at hand.

The effect of a good *imago* or *translatio* is simple, to compensate for our weaknesses as readers and writers and bring us face-to-face with the reality of what we are trying to say. Sextius,

---

[21] For Arius' character see C. H. Kahn, 'Arius as a Doxographer', in W. W. Fortenbaugh (ed.), *On Stoic and Peripatetic Ethics: The Work of Arius Didymus* (New Brunswick, NJ, 1983).

whose influence on Seneca is visible in a number of places, is offered as an example of this kind of philosophical writing; Seneca then translates and paraphrases an extended comparison between a man's relationship to his virtues and a general's relationship to his troops when on the march in hostile territory. The central point of comparison is made explicit (59.7–9):

Quod in exercitibus iis quos imperatores magni ordinant fieri videmus, ut imperium ducis simul omnes copiae sentiant, sic dispositae ut signum ab uno datum peditem simul equitemque percurrat, hoc aliquanto magis necessarium esse nobis ait. Illi enim saepe hostem timuere sine causa, tutissimumque illis iter quod suspectissimum fuit: nihil stultitia pacatum habet; tam superne illi metus est quam infra; utrumque trepidat latus; sequuntur pericula et occurrunt; ad omnia pavet, inparata est et ipsis terretur auxiliis. Sapiens autem, ad omnem incursum munitus, intentus, non si paupertas, non si luctus, non si ignominia, non si dolor impetum faciat, pedem referet: interritus et contra illa ibit et inter illa. Nos multa alligant, multa debilitant. Diu in istis vitiis iacuimus, elui difficile est; non enim inquinati sumus sed infecti.

We see this happening in armies organized by great generals: all the troops become aware of the leader's command simultaneously, since they are marshalled in such a way that the signal given by one man passes simultaneously through infantry and cavalry alike. He [Sextius] says that this is somewhat *more* necessary for us. For they [the army] have often had a groundless fear of the enemy—their safest march turns out to be the one they were most apprehensive about. But stupidity knows no peace. It is afraid of what is above and below; both flanks make it tremble; perils pursue it and meet it head on. It trembles at every occasion and is driven to panic by its own allies. The wise man, though, is fortified against every assault and on his guard. He won't retreat before the attacks of grief, humiliation, or pain; he will confront them and even walk among them fearlessly. Many things tie us down and weaken us; we've wallowed in those vices for a long time and it is hard to cleanse ourselves. We aren't just smeared with them—they are dyed into us.

Another splendid illustrative *imago* is used at letter 72.8, this one being the work of Attalus. The 'fool' is like a hungry dog being tossed tidbits by his master; whatever he gets he swallows whole and then gapes for the next morsel. The point of the parallel is once again made explicit: Fortune is like the master, and fools who devote themselves to anticipation of good things wind up not enjoying them. The use of this *imago* does not commit Attalus to a belief in a personal Fortuna, any more than the image of the general and his troops commits Sextius to a belief that virtue is a distinct component of the mind which issues orders to other parts of one's personality, orders which may travel quickly or slowly.[22] The point of such comparisons is limited and much must be discarded as theoretically unimportant.

The same procedure will be in order when the *imagines* Seneca uses are ones he creates himself. Possibly the best and most important example of this would be at letter 37.4–5, where the highly coloured personification might well be taken as a sign of a dualistic attitude to the relationship between the passions and reason: but the dissection or analysis of the soul undertaken here is much more plausibly regarded as a mark of deliberately vivid presentation.

Humilis res est stultitia, abiecta, sordida, servilis, multis adfectibus et saevissimis subiecta. Hos tam graves dominos, interdum alternis imperantes, interdum pariter, dimittit a te sapientia, quae sola libertas est. Una ad hanc fert via, et quidem recta; non aberrabis; vade certo gradu. Si vis omnia tibi subicere, te subice rationi; multos reges, si ratio te rexerit. Ab illa disces quid et quemadmodum adgredi debeas; non incides rebus. Neminem mihi dabis qui sciat quomodo quod vult coeperit velle: non consilio adductus illo sed impetu inpactus est. Non minus saepe fortuna in nos incurrit quam nos in illam. Turpe est non ire sed ferri, et subito in medio turbine rerum stupentem quaerere, 'huc ego quemadmodum veni?'

Stupidity is a low, base, dirty and slavish thing, subordinate to all kinds of very cruel passions. These masters are very severe, sometimes giving orders by turns, sometimes in concert with each other. Wisdom eliminates them from you and wisdom is the one true freedom. One road leads to freedom, and it is a straight one. You will not go astray; just walk with a steady pace. If you want to subordinate everything to

---

[22] One might compare the externalization of the *pathos* love by Panaetius, as reported by Seneca in *Ep.* 116.5–6.

yourself, subordinate yourself to reason; you will rule many people if reason rules you. From reason you will learn what to undertake and how to do so; you won't just blunder into things. You won't be able to show me anyone who knows how he has come to want what he wants. He has got there not by deliberation but driven by blind impulse. Fortune comes upon us as often as we come upon fortune. It is shameful not to proceed but rather to be swept along then suddenly, in the midst of a vortex of circumstance to be stunned and ask, 'How did I get here?'

EPISTULAE MORALES 92

Let us move on to another traditional reason for a dualistic reading of Seneca. It is usually held that letter 92.1–2 commits Seneca to a Platonic dualism in regard to the soul.[23] And if Seneca is here clearly committed to that position—usually attributed to Posidonian influence—then in other places it becomes quite possible or even likely that he slides into psychological dualism. But if he does not commit himself to such Posidonian or Platonic views here, then it is less reasonable to suspect dualism in other cases. For there is no other text which appears so categorically to commit Seneca to this stance.

But in fact this letter does not commit Seneca to such a position. The dualism is offered only as an agreed basis for discussion, a shared starting point for conversation which Seneca wishes to use in order to show that on this basis too the Stoically appropriate conclusions can be drawn. In other words, it is a merely dialectical or didactic move to agree with the middle Platonic psychology here canvassed.

---

[23] See E. Zeller, *Die Philosophie der Griechen* (5th edn., Leipzig, 1923) 737; Holler, *Seneca*, 11 ff.; M. Pohlenz, *Die Stoa*, 2 vols. (4th edn., Göttingen, 1955), ii. 112; I. Hadot, *Seneca und die griechisch-römische Tradition der Seelenleitung* (Berlin, 1969), 91; A.-J. Voelke, *L'Idée de volonté*, 165; Donini, *Le scuole*, 203. The most detailed discussion is that in Holler, and it depends almost completely on a by now outdated method for reconstructing middle Stoic, esp. Posidonian, doctrine. (One indication of this is the central role he assigns to Seneca's use of Posidonius' definition of anger (e.g. p. 23), which according to our source Lactantius (*De Ira Dei* 17.13 = *De Ira* 1.2) was only one of many cited by Seneca.)

To support this claim, let us look at the letter more closely. Seneca begins (92.1) tentatively enough: 'I think,' he says, 'you and I will agree that external things are acquired for the body, that the body is taken care of for the sake of the soul, and that in the soul there are subservient parts (by which we are moved and nourished) given to us because of the leading part of the soul.' In what follows Seneca slides out of indirect discourse and into direct statement; but it is evident that it is effectively governed by the 'agreement': 'in this leading part there is something irrational and also something rational; the former serves the latter, and this latter is the one thing which is not referred to something else but which refers everything else to itself. For divine reason is in charge of everything and is itself subordinate to nothing, while this reason of ours, which derives from it, is the same.'

There is nothing in the word 'agree' (*convenire*) which commits Seneca to belief in the propositions governed by the agreement. It is quite possible, even likely, that the agreement proposed here (note the use of the future *conveniet*) is merely conventional or dialectical. In a debate we agree to accept certain premises, but it does not follow that we actually commit ourselves to the truth of those propositions. I may well say to my Christian friend, 'OK, we will agree that God sent his Son to save the world from sin, but even so it does not follow that the route to salvation is solely through Christ.' Obviously I am not committed to any Christian beliefs; I am not even expressing sympathy with or openness to such beliefs. Seneca may well be making a dialectical proposal of this type. In 92.2 he goes on: 'if there is agreement between us on this, it follows that we also agree that a happy life depends exclusively on having the reason within us perfected.'

In the paragraphs which follow, the key to human happiness is 'greatness of soul', the ability of man to rise above misfortunes and trials. For Seneca the key to this is the place of human reason in the hierarchy of nature, i.e. at the same level as divine reason. Consequently, it is most important to stress the subordination of other values to those of reason. Hence Seneca returns to the structure of the soul for further dialectical purposes in sections 5–10. When an Epicurean conception of the *telos* is rejected, this rejection is carried out by associating pleasure with the lower parts of the soul and then adding, in section 8, that the previously mentioned irrational part of the soul has the same subdivisions as Plato recognized in book 4 of the *Republic*, the spirited and the appetitive or pleasure-loving part. In rejecting an Epicurean goal, then, Seneca will draw on the conceded Platonic views about the soul: in 9 he claims that the Epicureans have reversed the natural hierarchy of the soul by making pleasure the goal. The shared conclusion of Stoicism and Platonism (that the highest human happiness is to be found in the perfect development of reason, which we share with the gods) is supported more readily on the basis of the conceded Platonic premises than it would be if one worked from the technical standpoint of Stoic psychology.

What we learn from this passage, then, is not that Seneca has come to share Platonic premises in his psychology, but that he is writing in an environment influenced by Platonic ideas and that he finds himself prepared to grant them for the sake of making clear progress on the substantial points of ethics he is most concerned with.[24] And in this letter what is at issue ethically is something on which Seneca and the Platonists agree. His concession of an agreed starting point, then, should be put in perspective: Seneca has not turned dualist in letter 92, he has merely agreed to entertain certain Platonic theses which yield shared conclusions. It is these conclusions he cares about in this letter, and they are just as much a part of orthodox Stoicism as they are of middle Platonism.

So I would claim that we do not find any clear evidence of Platonic dualism in Seneca's own psychological theory, merely an openness to the invocation of it when it suits his purpose. This openness is surely encouraged by the respectability of body–soul dualism in Stoicism and by the ease with which psychological dualism and body–soul dualism can be made to

---

[24] I thank P. Donini for his comments at this point. He directed my attention to the relevance of *Ep.* 58 and 65. The significance of Platonism for Seneca is indicated very clearly in *Ep.* 58.25 ff.

yield the same conclusions (I am thinking of the development from the Platonic views of the *Phaedo* to those of the *Republic*).

The way we interpret other apparently dualistic texts is affected by this reading of letter 92. When Seneca says (*Ep.* 71.27) that the sage himself is composed of two parts, one irrational (and this can be 'bitten,[25] burned and feel pain') and the other rational (and possessed of unshakable opinions), we should not conclude that the dualism invoked here is psychological—the rest of the letter hardly encourages this reading anyway. We should take special note of 71.29, which makes it clear that problematic psychological phenomena, such as the trembling, pain, and pallor of the sage, are mere bodily affects: *hi enim omnes corporis sensus sunt.* We must conclude, then, that the irrational thing which is subject to such sufferings is the body.[26]

We have, then, some clarifications which I hope will be useful in evaluating Seneca. We may distinguish body/soul dualism from psychological dualism; and we may distinguish primarily technical or doxographical contexts from more literary ones. And since there are no texts which clearly commit Seneca to dualism—letter 92 being explained differently—a much more straightforward view of Seneca can be entertained as the initial hypothesis for our consideration of *De Ira*.

THE PSYCHOLOGY OF *DE IRA* 2: *PROPATHEIAI* REVISITED

Holler argued,[27] in keeping with his general account of Senecan psychology, that the doctrine of *De Ira* 2.1–4 owes a very great deal to Posidonius' adaptation of Stoic psychology, and thus

---

[25] See Inwood, *Ethics and Human Action*, 178. Also Rist, 'Seneca and Stoic Orthodoxy', 2001–2.

[26] Pain is not in itself a problematic item here, since it is the term which is standardly used of what is merely bodily, in distinction from the *pathos* pain, which is a mental affect. But the tremors and pallor here, like the non-rational reactions of *De Ira* 2, are harder to dismiss to the level of the merely bodily.

[27] Holler, *Seneca*, 16–24.

that Seneca is committed by this theory to some clearly unorthodox psychological theses.[28] In contrast, the effect of my present approach will be to make the issue of Seneca's alleged eclecticism and dependence on Posidonius secondary, and his use as a source for Posidonian doctrine quite limited. That, however, is a small loss compared with the gain of being allowed to see Seneca's development of earlier Stoic themes in their own right.

In the first four chapters of *De Ira* 2 Seneca examines the genesis of anger, and asks whether it comes about by judgement or by impulse. The causal analysis of anger is of great general significance because anger is a passion. The theory of passions was one of the most vigorously attacked features of early Stoicism, and Posidonius' revised theory shows clear signs of Platonic influence. Moreover, the theory of the passions is a subset of the theory of action;[29] consequently serious revisions to this theory entail a correspondingly significant change in the larger field of the Stoic philosophy of mind. And the theory of anger here has often been suspected of involving such a major revision, indeed of being a sign of eclectic psychological dualism, betraying the direct influence of Posidonius.

---

[28] I do not think that he is right about this, though it does not seem worth the space to present a detailed refutation here. In the discussion below a few particular points can be brought out. But the essential problem with Holler's approach is that he treats Seneca as though he were a doxographical source for middle Stoic ideas, thus subordinating the understanding of Seneca to his plan to find Posidonian fragments in the text of Seneca. Since he antecedently believes Posidonius (and Panaetius too) to be synthesizers of early Stoic and Academic/Peripatetic ideas, he is actively seeking signs of such synthesis in Seneca, since that provides him with 'evidence' for Posidonius' views. The general method he employs for reconstructing middle Stoicism is not well founded. Fillion-Lahille, despite the general superiority of her *Quellenforschung*, succumbs (notably at *Le De ira*, 163 ff.; also 45) to the tendency inherent in the method to find superficial and uncompelling similarities between the well-known author (Seneca) and the hypothetical source (Posidonius) and to use such alleged similarities to support a more sweeping thesis about historical influence. Given the state of our sources, this form of argument cannot be any more convincing than one antecedently wants it to be.

[29] A point which sounds less paradoxical when the Latin *adfectus* is used rather than the Greek *pathos*.

I think that this suspicion is wrong, though it is one I have myself entertained.[30] The development of the Stoic doctrine of the passions which occurs here is a characteristically Senecan development. Without any commitment to theses borrowed from other schools, Seneca modifies in a sensitive and open way the established Stoic doctrine; the result is a theory more closely corresponding to Seneca's own experience and insight but which still entails orthodox conclusions, especially in ethics.

The most important feature of the passions for Seneca and for earlier Stoics as well is that they should be 'rational' in a broad sense: not in the sense that they embody or reflect the correct use of reason in the guidance of human action and reaction, but in the sense that they are products of human reason and so subject to control by that reason. The challenge for the Stoic theory is to account for what seem to be ineliminable affective aspects of human experience;[31] such affective reactions form the focus of Seneca's discussion in the early chapters of book 2, since Seneca wishes to distinguish them from affective reactions, like anger, which are rational in the broad sense, but misguided. The ineliminable reactions are in a sense exempt from moral judgement, since even the sage cannot control them.[32] It is clearly important to understand how such reactions relate to reason, within the context of Stoic moral psychology.

How can affective reactions stand in relation to reason? They can be rational in several senses. (1) They can be the product of assent in a mature rational animal. This reflects the early Stoic theory of action and the passions.[33] (2) In a stronger sense, they

---

[30] B. Inwood, 'A Note on Desire in Stoic Theory', *Dialogue*, 21 (1982), 330, and Inwood, *Ethics and Human Action*, ch. 5, esp. 175-81, my first treatment of *propatheiai* and of *De Ira* 2.1-4; for references to earlier literature, see the discussion there; more recently, note the remarks of Long and Sedley, *The Hellenistic Philosophers*, 2 vols. (Cambridge, 1987), ii.417-18.

[31] See Inwood, *Ethics and Human Action*, 175-81.

[32] See *De Ira* 1.16.7, *Ep.* 57.3-6 and Inwood, *Ethics and Human Action*, 177-8.

[33] I cannot accept the argument of Ioppolo, 'Il monismo psicologico' that Zeno and Cleanthes held a different theory, according to which the impulse (which would include affective reactions) precedes and is confirmed by the assent. Her argument rests on three texts, Cicero *De Fato* 40, Plutarch *Adversus Colotem* 26, and Seneca *Ep.* 113.18. Of these, only the Plutarch text can be said to deal with the pre-Chrysippean Stoa; Cicero's text does not impute Stoic authorship to the doctrine

can be rational in that they are produced by human reason and are correct when judged against the standards of divine reason. Such would be the affective reactions of the sage. (3) They could be rational in the sense that the reaction can be described adequately by the use of intentional language, by spelling out the upshot of the feelings or reactions in *lekta*. In this minimal sense, even the actions and affective reactions of non-rational animals are 'rational', as are the desires and urgings of the epithumetic and thumoeidetic parts of the Platonic soul. (4) They could be rational in the sense that they are the result of conscious deliberation (of an Aristotelian sort) such that the agent can always say that he feels as he does for statable reasons. (5) They could be rational in the sense that good reasons for acting or feeling as one has done can be given after the fact, regardless of whether conscious reasoning of that sort actually caused the action or feeling.

No doubt other senses of rationality could be distinguished, but this provisional list should do for now. For my purposes the central question is whether these ineliminable affective reactions are rational in sense 1 (rational$_1$). Sense 4 is clearly inapplicable; sense 5 is possible, but like sense 2 it is disqualified by the fact that Seneca is concerned with affective reactions which are not ultimately justified, reactions which if confirmed would produce the *pathos* anger.

Sense 3, though, is more important. An affective reaction which is non-rational in this sense would be one which just

---

in question, though it does distinguish it from Chrysippus' views; Seneca makes no mention of early Stoic authorship for the doctrine in question, even though he is careful to distinguish Cleanthes' from Chrysippus' views elsewhere in the same letter (section 23). It is only if the Plutarch text clearly attributes to Zeno (against whom Arcesilaus must be reacting) the theory of impulse before assent that we have any reason to assign the theory to the pre-Chrysippean Stoa. But despite Ioppolo's repeated assertions, this text tells us nothing about the causal or chronological order of impulse and assent; it merely explores the polemical suggestion of Arcesilaus that impulse could occur without assent—a doctrine which Arcesilaus' Stoic opponents naturally reject. It is only Ioppolo's suggestion that the claim that assent is not necessary for impulse to occur entails the claim that assent follows impulse. We should recall that where the problem of ineliminable affective reactions is discussed (as at Gellius, *Noctes Atticae* 19.1), Zeno and Chrysippus are treated together as having the same theory.

cannot be got into words, which even in principle cannot be spelled out in a form appropriate for analysis and approval by reason. Any reaction which is irrational$_3$ is truly irrelevant from a moral point of view, even if such reactions can be made morally relevant by their acceptance. Such acceptance would, I suggest, have to take the form of adding propositional content to the reactions so that they can be approved of and so cause a genuine affective response, one which is rational$_1$. To illustrate: a person may have ice-cold water doused on his back while sunbathing. The shock of such an event inevitably produces an intangible and inexpressible feeling; this feeling is irrational$_3$ and there is nothing anyone can do about it. But if one supposes that the feeling, or some aspects of it, are or become rational$_3$, expressible in *lekta*, then it is possible to scrutinize the reaction and accept or reject it. Whatever reaction is thereby produced is going to be rational$_1$.

In brief, I would hold that strictly orthodox Stoic psychology requires that anything which is rational$_3$ in an adult human is also rational$_1$,—i.e. that people are responsible for all that happens in them which is formulable in *lekta*.

This is, of course, a very strict theory and no ancient evidence unmistakably compels us to attribute it to the early Stoics. But it takes proper account of their determination to advance a theory which justifies strict accountability for all of one's morally relevant actions and reactions. The affective reactions discussed in letter 57.3-6 are plausibly held to be irrational$_3$, and so even the sage is allowed his ineliminable affective reactions. Those discussed by Gellius at *Noctes Atticae* 19.1 are similar; in these texts the emphasis is on the merely physical nature of the preliminary affective reaction:[34] Seneca uses the verb *sentire* and refers to the reaction as a movement; Gellius uses similar language and explicitly denies that any opinion is involved; yet the physical effects on the psychic *pneuma* have the ability to influence the mind; this is what one would expect in a psychophysical theory—Chrysippus even held that a sage could lose his virtue by the effects of alcohol (Diogenes Laertius 7.127).

[34] Cf. *Ep.* 71.29.

The suggestion that irrational$_3$ reactions are converted into rational$_3$ reactions (and thus into rational$_1$ reactions) is derived from the word *prosepidoxazei* in Gellius. His account suggests that the propositional content has to be added to the preliminary and irrational$_3$ experience before acceptance or rejection by reason is possible.[35]

Now, it is clear that one way in which such irrational$_3$ feelings can be caused is by hormetic presentations. That presentations, even rational presentations, should have aspects which are irrational$_3$ seems very plausible—it would be silly to suppose that every aspect of a presentation can be captured in verbal form and that only the verbalizable aspects of such an experience can affect us. The orthodox theory of the passions does not hold that only rational$_1$ events can occur in a rational animal, but merely that all rational$_3$ events are rational$_1$.[36] And it is this orthodox theory which Seneca is working from, extending it and adapting it, though never pushing it over the line into dualism.

[35] Long and Sedley, *Hellenistic Philosophers*, ii.418, suggest that *prosepidoxazei* is equivalent to 'assent'; I think it is more likely to be the necessary preliminary to assent, viz. the addition to an irrational$_3$ experience of explicit propositional content.

[36] M. Frede, 'The Stoic Doctrine of the Affections of the Soul', in M. Schofield and G. Striker (eds.), *The Norms of Nature* (Cambridge and Paris, 1986), claims that each presentation comes with more than propositional content and that in assenting to the presentation one commits oneself to the acceptance of the non-propositional 'way' of receiving the presentation as well. In discussion at Syam, Frede suggested that this broader and looser 'way' of receiving the presentation was an important part of the hormetic presentation and that this hormetic force of the presentation was responsible for the ineliminable reactions Seneca discusses in *De Ira* 2.1–4 under the description of *primus pulsus* etc. But that cannot be quite right, since at 2.3.5 the *prima agitatio animi* is distinguished from the presentation. Moreover, it seems that Seneca thinks of the *primus pulsus* or *prima agitatio* as a kind of *hormē* and not as a component of the presentation. More important for the suggestion I am making here is the apparent fact that every example of the 'way' in which a certain propositional content is thought could also be cashed out in the form of further propositions. This is the crucial fact about the early Stoic philosophy of mind, that everything which one assents to and so is responsible for is something formulable in *lekta*, and that nothing not so formulable is of moral significance. Hence I hold that the early Stoic theory is that assent is properly speaking only given to *axiōmata* (*Ecl.* ii.88) and that references to assent being given to presentations are best understood as loose expressions of the theory (see Inwood, *Ethics and Human Action*, 56–9).

Seneca and Psychological Dualism

In book 1 of the *De Ira* there are several passages of considerable interest as background. Let us look at them to see what philosophical baggage Seneca carries into the passage which concerns us. In 1.3.3–8 an essential Stoic thesis is maintained: the sharp gap between brute beasts and rational animals is made a part of the explanation of human psychology. In understanding anger, Seneca holds that one must remember that only humans can have this passion; any tendency to say that anger might be a useful feeling in small doses, or that it is an ineradicable part of our animal nature and so not subject to strict moral evaluation, should be rejected. What animals have is not anger; anger can only be understood as an expression of reason. This is a crucial theoretical position for Seneca to take, for it ties anger to the activities of reason; just as any phenomenon which occurs in a non-rational animal cannot be anger (on these theoretical grounds), so too any phenomenon which is independent of reason, even in a rational animal, cannot really be anger. When Seneca further specifies criteria for determining what is subject to reason in a person, he will have a basis for distinguishing between anger and pseudo-anger. This he will do in the early chapters of book 2. For now what is most relevant is that the stand he takes here is in every respect an orthodox one.

In chapter 7 Seneca's orthodoxy is equally strong: the comparison between the person falling into a passion, such as anger, and the person losing physical control of his motions because of inertia is drawn directly from Chrysippus.[37] In 1.7.4 this comparison is used just as it was in Chrysippus, and there is no suggestion of dualism:

quarundam rerum initia in nostra potestate sunt, ulteriora nos vi sua rapiunt nec regressum relinquunt. ut in praeceps datis corporibus nullum sui arbitrium est nec resistere morarive deiecta potuerunt, sed consilium omne et paenitentiam inrevocabilis praecipitatio abscidit et non licet eo non pervenire quo non ire licuisset, ita animus, si in iram amorem aliosque se proiecit adfectus, non permittitur reprimere

---

[37] *SVF* iii.462. See Inwood, *Ethics and Human Action*, 155 ff. The term 'inertia' is taken from Galen, *PHP* 4.2.30 (p. 373 K): *rhopē*. See P. H. De Lacy (ed.), *Galen: De Placitis Hippocratis et Platonis*, 3 vols. (*Corpus medicorum Graecorum* V,4,1,2; Berlin, 1978–84), 643 n.

impetum; rapiat illum oportet et ad imum agat pondus suum et vitiorum natura proclivis.

For some things the starting points are in our power but the later developments sweep us away with their violence and do not permit us to turn back. Bodies falling headlong have no control over themselves and once thrown over the edge they cannot stay or delay—rather, the unrecoverable headlong plunge cuts off all opportunity for reconsideration and regret, so that it's no longer possible to avoid ending up where it would have been possible not to go. In just the same way, if the mind once throws itself into anger, love and the other passions it has no further chance to resist the impetus. Its own weight and the 'downhill' nature of the vices must sweep it along and bring it to the very bottom.

But in 1.7.2–3 things may look different:[38] we see here very clear examples of the externalization and objectivization of the *pathē*. But the vivid expression should not lead us to suppose that the reason and the passions are actually distinct; such near-personification need not commit Seneca to any particular doctrinal stance. The external and distinct things which reason opposes are not psychic forces, but, as becomes clear in 1.8.1, the first *inritamentum* and the *semina* of anger—i.e. the presentations which tend to move the mind to anger.[39] These presentations are experienced as *pathos*-producing, and so it is easy to treat them as though they were actual *pathē*, independent psychological states which one might give in to. Note in what follows how Seneca combines a perfectly clear monistic analysis of passion (complete with the voluntary act of reason yielding to the external stimulus) with the apparent reification of the *pathos* as an external thing admitted into the citadel of the soul:

nam si coepit ferre transversos, difficilis ad salutem recursus est, quoniam nihil rationis est ubi semel adfectus inductus est iusque illi aliquod voluntate nostra datum est: faciet de cetero quantum volet, non quantum permiseris.

---

[38] Note especially 1.7.3: *ratio ipsa, cui freni traduntur, tam diu potens est quam diu diducta est ab adfectibus; si miscuit se illis et inquinavit, non potest continere quos summovere potuisset.*

[39] The reactions they do cause, and cannot help but cause, are an important subject of 2.2–4.

Seneca and Psychological Dualism

For if it begins to take us off course, the path back to health is hard, since there is no rationality left once passion has been ushered in and a certain authority has been ceded to it by our own choice. From then on it will do as much as it wants, not as much as you allow to it.

Seneca's view is that our reason yields control and authority to the external enemy when it voluntarily accepts the stimulus to passion. When he says that there is no reason left once passion has been introduced into the mind, he does not mean that one thing is displaced by another: rather, the reason we have is transformed into a corrupt form, which *is* a passion. Our minds are still rational$_1$ minds and still function through reason. What has left us is the correct use of reason (rationality$_2$): passion drives out right reason when our unitary minds cease to use reason properly and when they voluntarily (*voluntate nostra*) give up their authority. Thus 'reason' here means right reason in control, as it often does in Chrysippus too;[40] *pathos* means reason which has turned its back on right reason. But we get the appearance of dualism from the fact that personification and externalization are used. These are effective techniques for vivid presentation, and here we see them unmistakably linked to orthodox monistic psychology.

In the next section (1.8.2) this technique is used even more dramatically to hammer home the moral, which is a simple and orthodox one: one must nip the proneness to a passion in the bud, so that one does not lose control of one's own mental processes:

in primis, inquam, finibus hostis arcendus est; nam cum intravit et portis se intulit, modum a captivis non accipit. neque enim sepositus est animus et extrinsecus speculatur adfectus, ut illos non patiatur ultra quam oportet procedere, sed in adfectum ipse mutatur ideoque non potest utilem illam vim et salutarem proditam iam infirmatamque revocare. non enim, ut dixi, separatas ista sedes suas diductasque habent, sed adfectus et ratio in melius peiusque mutatio animi est.

The enemy must be stopped right at the border, I say. For once it has entered and worked its way within the gates, it doesn't tolerate a limit set by its prisoners. For the mind is not detached and it doesn't gaze

---

[40] Inwood, *Ethics and Human Action*, 156.

upon the passions from the outside so that it can deny them permission to go further than they should; rather, the mind itself is converted into a passion and so cannot get back that healthy and constructive path of life once it has been given up and weakened. For, as I have already said, they don't have two distinct and separate locations; passion and reason just are the transformation of the mind into a better or a worse condition.

Note the effective use of a military metaphor which externalizes and reifies passion as the enemy. But it is also clear just how much of a distortion the metaphor is, and Seneca says as much with his comments on the structure of the soul: what he here explicitly rejects is the kind of Platonizing psychological dualism which one is so often tempted to lay at the door of Seneca the eclectic.[41] Moreover, he goes on to deal with Peripatetic objectors, and it becomes clear in what follows that the externalizing language does more than just make vivid the psychological struggle Seneca is describing. It also gives him a verbal common ground with his opponents and so makes possible the debate. Nevertheless, Seneca is careful to distance himself from the implications of the language.

In the sections which follow (through to the end of 1.11) military metaphors play an important polemical role, as well as providing a unifying literary grace. In 1.9.1 the catapult is used as an illustration of the properly controlled use of the soul's proneness to action (*impetus*): the catapult is effectively used just because the artilleryman in charge of it makes the decision about how much force is to be used in launching the missile.[42] The motive power of the soul which is under rational control is not anger, a passion which is by definition disobedient to reason. In section 4 Seneca alters the military *imago* slightly, concluding that the useful soldier is he who *scit parere consilio; adfectus quidem tam mali ministri quam duces sunt*. By comparing the passion anger to a disobedient soldier Seneca buttresses his

---

[41] For the importance of the theme of psychic transformation, see Inwood, *Ethics and Human Action*, 138.

[42] The parallel to the runner example is quite interesting, though unexploited here. Just as inertia puts the runner's legs outside his control at a certain point, so too the missile is not recoverable once launched, nor is its trajectory alterable.

position against the Peripatetics; but again, doing so entails a certain reification of the passions and also of the motive power of the soul (*impetus*). The best sign that this reification should not be taken to have strict doctrinal implications is perhaps to be found in 1.11.8, where even virtue itself is reified: like the good soldier, *illa certissima est virtus quae se diu multumque circumspexit et rexit et ex lento ac destinato provexit*. The general is portrayed as being distinct from both his good and bad soldiers. We cannot suppose that virtue itself is to be considered as separate from the active reason of the good man;[43] so it would be unreasonable to find dualistic implications in the metaphorical way in which anger is handled.

The general picture which emerges from book 1 is straightforward enough, in my view. The psychological and ethical theses which Seneca wishes to defend seem to be perfectly orthodox and traditional, but the argument against the Peripatetic position, that the passion of anger is good provided that it is moderate, is developed with the aid of an elaborate military comparison which if taken literally would entail some very dualistic-looking views. On balance, though, it seems wrong to attribute to Seneca any proneness to dualism just on the basis of such rhetorically effective devices.[44]

Book 2 begins with a warning: up to this point the discourse has been fairly easy, but more difficult topics must now be dealt with. The first of these, and the only one I want to deal with, is described thus: *quaerimus enim ira utrum iudicio an impetu incipiat, id est utrum sua sponte moveatur an quemadmodum pleraque*

---

[43] In 1.17.2–3 even reason is externalized in this way: *nil aliis instrumentis opus est, satis nos instruxit ratione natura. hoc dedit telum, firmum perpetuum obsequens, nec anceps nec quod in dominum remitti posset. non ad providendum tantum, sed ad res gerendas satis est per se ipsa ratio...quid quod <ad> actiones quoque, in quibus solis opera iracundiae videtur necessaria, multo per se ratio fortior est? nam cum iudicavit aliquid faciendum, in eo perseverat*. Consider too the stance Seneca takes in *Ep*. 113 on the early Stoic thesis that the virtues are animals.

[44] Note too how Galen tries to get dualistic conclusions out of the runner example used by Chrysippus: *PHP* 4.2.28–38 (pp. 372–5 K) also 4.5.12 (394 K) and see De Lacy's commentary on p. 643 of his edition. If even Chrysippus can be smeared with the tar of dualism because of his use of a vivid illustrative image, how much easier is it to treat Seneca this way.

quae intra nos <non>[45] *insciis nobis oriuntur* (2.1.1); and it extends to the end of chapter 4. The question seems a simple one: does anger begin with a judgement (i.e. a rational$_1$ and therefore controllable decision) or with mere impulse (*hormē*, for which Seneca's Latin term is the familiar *impetus*)? What makes the question more difficult is the explication of it introduced by *id est*: I take it that the arrangement of what follows is chiastic, with *sua sponte* fleshing out mere impulse and the rest of the sentence giving further description of mental events which occur by rational decision.

If this is so, then the distinguishing mark of merely impulsive mental events is their causal autonomy; they happen 'of themselves'; and the mark of 'decisions' is the fact that they happen 'in the manner of most mental events which occur *non insciis nobis*', accompanied by 'our' awareness. The 'I' must be reason, which is at the core of personal identity for any Stoic. We do not, then, have a tidily exclusive set of properties to describe the main contrast between impulsive and decided action. The most I would want to conclude from this introductory sentence is this: to preserve consistency with the general thrust of book 1, Seneca should clearly opt for the second choice; the spontaneous and possibly unselfconscious character of impulsive mental events runs counter to the whole Stoic account of anger in book 1.

In 2.1.3 Seneca moves on to a statement of the uncontroversial: the first stimulus of anger is a perception of unfairness, a presentation (*species*) of *iniuria*. Hence the *incipiat* of 2.1.1 is not referring to the first stimulus, but to the first decisive internal component of the complex event known as anger. The contrast of impulsive and decided action is redescribed again: does anger follow immediately on the presentation once it is received, without the consent of the mind (*non accedente animo*), or is it set in motion by the mind's assent, i.e. is it rational$_1$?

---

[45] This supplement, which clearly makes a major difference to the rest of the discussion, seems inevitable in view of the argument in the rest of 2.1–4. But Holler, *Seneca*, 16 n. 40 prefers to delete *sua* and avoid the chiasmus.

Seneca and Psychological Dualism

Seneca follows the Stoic view (*nobis placet*: 2.1.4), that anger does not 'dare' to do anything on its own but needs the approval of the *animus*.[46] The reasons he gives for accepting the orthodox view are interesting—and it is important to see that at this point Seneca is giving reasons for staying with the orthodox view, not simply stating that view. There is, in Seneca's opinion, an impulse which is set going without our *voluntas*, but it is not able to do the kind of processing and quasi-reasoning which is characteristic of a genuine anger-response: for in anger we receive the presentation that we have been treated unfairly and then long for vengeance and then link together the two views: that we ought not to have been harmed and that we ought to fight back. This is a complicated impulse indeed, whereas the other sort, the sort which can occur without our *voluntas*, is simple.[47] The complexity of cognitive structures which the anger-response requires, including understanding, resentment, adverse moral judgement, revenge, simply cannot occur without the assent of the mind to the experiences and thoughts by which it is affected.

The contrast is pursued in the next section (2.2). After clarifying what is at stake in this theoretical debate, namely that if anger can occur without our 'will' it will be immune to rational control (i.e. will be irrational$_1$), Seneca gives a wealth of examples of each kind of mental event. The general principle at issue is clearly stated: *omnes enim motus qui non voluntate nostra*

---

[46] It seems that *illam* must take *ira* as its antecedent, rather than *species*; so once again we may note the reification of a mental state. Contrast the comment of Holler, *Seneca*, 21-2; for him, this treatment of anger is 'eine der wenigen Stellen in de ira, aus denen klar hervorgeht, daß Seneca ein besonderes *thumoeides*...neben der animus...annimmt'. This, he says, is something new: 'halb altstoisch, halb peripatetisch-akademisch'. And he asks, 'Sollte diese Synthese Senecas eigenes Werk sein? Oder ist sie die unbekannte mittelstoische aus dem *Suntagma peri orgēs* des Poseidonios?' Once one acknowledges the importance of Seneca's use of literary techniques, this sort of fancy becomes impossible. Time and again Holler loses his grip on good judgement because of his simplistically doxographical pursuit of Posidonian phantoms.

[47] The simple *impetus* is not impulse proper; note that in 2.3.4 *impetus* without qualification is used of a reaction which is always accompanied by assent. This reflects early Stoic use of the term.

fiunt invicti et inevitabiles sunt.[48] He will allow that there are reactions which are not voluntary, but not that any such reaction could count as genuine anger. To do otherwise would conflict with the stance taken by the early Stoics and reaffirmed in book 1.

These 'inevitable' reactions are interesting. Shivering when splashed with cold water and a creepy feeling when touching certain objects seem to me to be strictly bodily reactions. But the bristling of our hair when frightened by bad news and blushing at improper language—these reactions clearly involve considerable cognitive and social sophistication. Feeling dizzy when looking down from a height seems to fall between the two extremes. A physiological fear reaction to hearing (and understanding) bad news and blushing seem to be rational phenomena; recall Mark Twain's observation that man is the only animal which blushes, or needs to.[49]

Clearly Seneca's criterion for 'rationality'$_1$ in the reaction to potentially passionate stimuli is not that reconstructed for the earlier Stoics, i.e. expressibility in or reliance on *lekta* (rationality$_3$).[50] His own criterion is much narrower and, to our surprise, leaves many clearly cognitive and verbally expressible phenomena on the other side of the line, as irrational or prerational reactions. For Seneca the criterion appears to be susceptibility to change by a conscious rational decision. And one might reasonably conclude that Seneca thinks that the complexity he is describing here gives a better foothold for conscious control than does mere expressibility in *lekta*. And *conscious* control is evidently quite important to Seneca. It follows that 'being in our power' is used in a different sense from what we are used to in earlier Stoic discussions. *Quorum quia nihil in nostra potestate est, nulla quominus fiant ratio persuadet* (2.2.1).

---

[48] This is compatible with the view attributed to Zeno in 1.16.7, that even a sage will have some faint traces of passions—these being inevitable and immune to the perfect rational control of a sage—but no passions.

[49] These examples from *De Ira* 2 are worth comparing to those mentioned at *Ep.* 57.4; even the sage has certain reactions in his soul which are not *pathē*: *non est hoc timor, sed naturalis adfectio inexpugnabilis rationi.* Cf. *De Ira* 1.16.7.

[50] Inwood, *Ethics and Human Action*, 66 ff.

When an early Stoic talks of things being *eph' hēmin* he does not have such a narrow notion in mind.[51]

There is no reason to believe that orthodox Stoics ever propounded the sort of distinction Seneca is outlining here between two kinds of impulse (simple and complex).[52] Of course, they may have done so, or some of them may have at some time; but the relatively tidy reconstruction which makes the most of our scattered sources does not suggest it. Hence my suggestion here is that Seneca himself is offering the distinction in an attempt to justify his retention of the essential element of the early Stoic analysis of anger, i.e. the claim that the passion is rational$_1$.

But does this innovation commit Seneca to any sort of psychological dualism? If we look closely at what Seneca says in these chapters, we do not find him indirectly positing a distinct and non-rational part of the soul. The soul he describes is unitary; the complexity which Seneca introduces centres not on parts or powers, but rather on a *temporally* dynamic process.

---

[51] Ibid. 89–91, app. 4; R. Sorabji, *Necessity, Cause and Blame* (London, 1980), 86, 245, 252.

[52] However, the idea of there being an impulse before assent, the assent being a confirmation for the preliminary impulse, does occur in two places in the Latin tradition: Cicero *De Fato* 40 and *Ep.* 113. In the *De Fato* the theory of an *adpetitus* preceding assent is attributed to anonymous philosophers, neither Stoics nor Antiochean *veteres*, in the context of a polemic about choice and necessity. In *Ep.* 113 Seneca is discussing the Stoic thesis that the virtues are animals, expounding arguments pro and con, but essentially dismissing the idea as ridiculous. In 113.18, part of an argument against the thesis, he presents an analysis of rational action involving impulse preceding assent and confirmed by it—the point being that any rational animal must be capable of this sort of action and that the virtues are not. Earlier in the letter (113.2) Seneca uses the inapplicability of action to the virtues for the same purpose. Here Seneca accepts an analysis of action not attested for the earlier Stoics in order to refute an early Stoic theory—an important indication of his independence of mind. And yet the general result of his theory is still very much in line with Stoic doctrine. When we shift our minds to the *De Ira*, it is clear that the theory of *Ep.* 113.18 is compatible with it, though the *De Ira* text is much less clear-cut and neat. It is hard to tell whether the *De Fato* text presents the same theory, or whether it is meant to present a theory at all. There may be some hint of the origin of Seneca's theory of impulse before assent in Cicero's text, but I doubt it; certainly nothing in Cicero suggests that we tie it to Posidonius or to any form of psychological dualism. For *Adversus Colotem* 1122b–c, see Inwood, *Ethics and Human Action*, 87–8 and above n. 33.

Chrysippus (*SVF* iii.462) described a passion by means of a comparison with the body in motion, so over-committed to its trajectory by its own inertia that it cannot regain self-control and balance; and there are other hints in early Stoicism of what we might call psychological inertia, all readily explicable within the framework of monistic psychology.[53] In book 1 Seneca accepted that comparison and made it his own. In book 2 Seneca goes beyond the Chrysippean theory, but he does so by the enrichment of this essentially Chrysippean insight and by a reasonable reappraisal of the concept of assent. Assent now involves conscious rational control: implicit assent is not good enough for moral improvement—it is probably significant that Seneca shows little interest in the problem of determinism and responsibility which provides the most congenial focus for implicit assent in earlier Stoicism. And the idea of a preliminary, almost mechanical response which is unstoppable and so not subject to the strict moral appraisal which attaches to assented actions grows smoothly out of the idea of psychological inertia already found in early Stoicism.

The criterion which Seneca uses to draw a distinction between a passion and a non-passion is rationality in a new sense, not rationality$_1$, but voluntariness in his own sense. What he asks is: can this mental event be stopped or altered by our rational powers if we consciously suspend the process and apply critical scrutiny to the presentation which sets it in motion? In his view, anything not subject to this procedure is in an importantly different moral category. Thus in 2.2.2 he says that the 'voluntary' vices of the soul are those which can be eliminated by the application of moral precepts. Those which come with the human condition and which no one can avoid are not subject to any conscious control and so are, in the relevant sense, involuntary.[54] Involuntary vices, though they are not discussed here, would seem to be less grave and certainly less amenable to immediate action by the agent. Character flaws

---

[53] See Inwood, *Ethics and Human Action*, 146 ff. on the 'fresh opinion' and the fading of passion with time.

[54] This latter class also afflicts the sage; see *De Ira* 1.16.7, and discussion above.

Seneca and Psychological Dualism

which do not yield to the assertion of will would, on this theory, be exempt from a significant kind of moral blame.

That is why the most important thing to Seneca here is not what I think Chrysippus would have called the mere rationality$_1$ of the presentation and our response to it, but whether it is consciously controllable. Hence the *primus ictus animi*[55] which affects us after we get an *opinionem iniuriae* can be put in the class of involuntary things, even if it is only possible through what I would have to describe as rational mental processes, since they require *lekta*. The linkage between rationality$_3$ and rationality$_1$ is being weakened, but the linkage between rationality$_1$ and morally significant actions is not.[56]

For the psychology of action the most important non-passions in 2.2 are the preliminary passions, the emotional responses which if left unchecked will actually lead to a full-blown passion. But from our point of view the most interesting application of this distinction comes in what follows (2.2.3–6). Here Seneca exempts our emotional responses (for so they must be called) to literary and dramatic experience from voluntariness and so from moral judgement, apparently (and justifiably) on the grounds that the artificiality of the experience causes us to suspend our critical faculties. If we read about moving historical events or see them on the stage, or if the musical accompaniment stirs passions in our souls, or even if a painting with grim subject matter upsets us, still our reactions are not judged in the way that reactions to events in real life are judged. This sort of detachment is, it seems to Seneca, what makes possible that imaginative sympathy with the feelings of portrayed characters which is such an important part of artistic experience (2.2.5). In his view these emotional reactions are no more passions than is the emotion of the actor in expressing himself

---

[55] By this point Seneca is becoming reluctant to describe this non-rational emotional response as an impulse. By 2.3–4 he will have abandoned that description.

[56] Similarly the reactions of the sage described in *De Ira* 1.16.7 seem to involve rational$_3$ mental states but not rational$_1$ assent. This suggests that the doctrine in both books is meant to be the same and that its orthodoxy focuses on the connection between rationality$_1$ and actions or passions, rather than on the connection between rationality$_3$ and rationality$_1$.

or the frisson of fear which a reader feels in reading of the impending Hannibalic attack. From a moral point of view they have more in common with shivers and involuntary blushes.

quae non sunt irae, non magis quam tristitia est quae ad conspectum mimici naufragii contrahit frontem, non magis quam timor qui Hannibale post Cannas moenia circumsidente lectorum percurrit animos, sed omnia ista motus sunt animorum moveri nolentium, nec adfectus sed principia proludentia adfectibus. sic enim militaris viri in media pace iam togati aures tuba suscitat equosque castrenses erigit crepitus armorum. Alexandrum aiunt Xenophanto canente manum ad arma misisse. (2.2.5–6)

These are not cases of anger, any more than it is grief which furrows the brow when one sees an actor shipwrecked on stage, any more than it is fear which courses through the minds of those who read about Hannibal besieging the city walls after Cannae. All those phenomena are movements of minds which do not wish to be moved; they aren't passions but rather starting points which lead up to passions. For it is the same sort of thing when a military man, in civilian clothes during peace time, perks up his ears at the sound of a trumpet; or when army horses get agitated by the rattle of weaponry. It was said that Alexander reached for his weapons when he heard Xenophantus play.

Clearly the theory of aesthetic emotional response which Seneca is invoking here is of considerable interest and might bear comparison with Aristotelian views on tragedy (especially *Poetics* 1455ª30–4) and with Horace's claims in the *Ars Poetica* (101–5). But what is curious and crucial for us is the originality of Seneca's psychological position. He has grouped together a striking range of phenomena under one description: what they all have in common and what justifies grouping them together[57] is that they do not involve what Seneca would consider to be voluntary commitment: they are not the sort of emotional

---

[57] Not all of these should be called preliminary passions, since so many of these responses are not exempted on the grounds that they are too early in their development to merit description as passions; many are privileged by their context and would *never* develop into passions. Some might well be preliminaries to passions, others are merely analogues to them, and others are merely bodily.

Seneca and Psychological Dualism

responses which it is reasonable to expect will be brought before the court of reason for approval or rejection.[58]

The range of these phenomena is remarkable: mere bodily shivers, engaging only the body or the vegetative level of the soul; unavoidable responses to sudden bad news or improper behaviour; vertigo; the emotional response one tends to feel in performing or viewing drama, or in reading history or fiction, or in viewing powerful graphic art, or in our emotional responses to music and sound effects; he is even willing to include the involuntary response to martial stimuli of soldiers, even in peacetime.

These phenomena are all 'involuntary' in a reasonable sense of the word. But it is striking to find a Stoic willing to take them out of the ambit of the passions. At least some of these phenomena express character very clearly; and as expressions of character they are highly relevant to passions and to the moral evaluation of that character. In earlier Stoicism as normally understood we would not find all these reactions grouped with morally irrelevant bodily shivers; there, the criterion of moral relevance lies in the relation of action and thought to character. Moreover, in early Stoicism we find no insistence that the assent given to a stimulus must be voluntary in our and Seneca's sense—that is, a consciously chosen response[59] to a stimulus. For earlier Stoics it is enough if it is a response to a rational$_3$ stimulus in a rational animal.[60]

---

[58] See Holler, *Seneca*, 18–19, for his summary of what these phenomena have in common. He seems to find their grouping less remarkable than I do. What they have in common, according to Holler, is (1) that even the sage is exposed to them, (2) that they are stimulated directly by the *phantasia*, (3) that they are passive not active, and (4) that they are only treatable by habituation and, in short, belong to the irrational part of man. His fourth point is the most problematic. For habituation will have little or no effect on the strictly bodily responses. Moreover, there is no attribution of these phenomena by Seneca to an irrational *part* of man; that is a contribution from Holler's own theory. Nor does Holler distinguish here between the irrational body and the irrational part of the soul, a fuzziness which helps him in his justification of Seneca's grouping of non-rational responses.

[59] Though we start to see this in the phrase *tēs sunkatatheseōs kath' hormēn ousēs*, which occurs in some of our sources for early Stoicism (see Inwood, *Ethics and Human Action*, app. 4).

[60] Inwood, *Ethics and Human Action*, Ch. 3.

In 2.3 the demarcation between passion and action is revisited: the stimuli which do not entail a passion are described as happening *fortuito*, i.e. non-voluntarily. When subject to these, the soul does not act—and that is what is required for a passion to occur. The emotional response which no one can help is a *fortuitus motus*, and simply having that is not very important. What matters morally is yielding to that and confirming it by a voluntary judgement and assent. Again, the examples of involuntary responses are strikingly different from what one would expect of the old Stoa: paleness, tears, sexual arousal, deep sighs, excited gaze (2.3.2), involuntary manifestations of fear or nerves even in a brave soldier, general or accomplished orator (2.3.3). Some of these Seneca is surely right to describe as purely bodily, and so even an early Stoic would be happy dismissing them as non-passionate. But others strike us too much as character-related and cognitively significant to write off as merely bodily. Yet that is just what Seneca does in 2.3.2: *fallitur nec intellegit corporis hos esse pulsus*.[61]

Seneca's position is that anger is different from all of these because it is a deliberate acceptance and confirmation of a starting point which is of this character; it is not just a response (*moveri*) but an excessive one, a runaway response (*excurrere*)—with this Seneca is once again invoking the Chrysippean idea of 'psychological inertia'. That is because anger is a genuine *impetus* (*hormē*) and so is dependent on assent—as the first or primitive emotional/bodily response (now called an *agitatio*, not an impulse) is not. And since it needs assent, it must come under conscious mental control (2.3–4). For the soul would be aware of the sort of activity needed for anger: the sort of quasi-inference we met above. Here Seneca is integrating his new criterion of conscious voluntariness with the earlier Stoic idea of assent. At 2.3.4–5 anger is presented as a response of the reason to the soul's prior response to a stimulus, and that prior response is no more anger than the stimulus itself (*species*) is.[62]

---

[61] Cf. *Ep.* 11.5–7; 71.29.

[62] See above on the idea of an impulse before assent, which is confirmed or rejected by it. While Seneca has no hesitation about calling this preliminary response an *impetus* in *Ep.* 113, in this text he shows a more proper and orthodox

Seneca and Psychological Dualism

ira non moveri tantum debet sed excurrere; est enim impetus; numquam autem impetus sine adsensu mentis est, neque enim fieri potest ut de ultione et poena agatur animo nesciente. putavit se aliquis laesum, voluit ulcisci, dissuadente aliqua causa statim resedit: hanc iram non voco, motum animi rationi parentem: illa est ira quae rationem transiliit, quae secum rapit. ergo prima illa agitatio animi quam species iniuriae incussit non magis ira est quam ipsa iniuriae species; ille sequens impetus, qui speciem iniuriae non tantum accepit sed adprobavit, ira est, concitatio animi ad ultionem voluntate et iudicio pergentis. numquam dubium est quin timor fugam habeat, ira impetum;[63] vide ergo an putes aliquid sine adsensu mentis aut peti posse aut caveri.

Anger needs not just to be moved, but to surge forward, for it is an impulse. But there is never an impulse without a mental assent. Nor can one act for revenge or punishment without the mind being aware of it. Someone came to the view that he had been injured, he wanted to be avenged, but he settled down again promptly when some cause dissuaded him. I don't call this anger, but a movement of the mind which is obeying reason. Anger is what leaps out ahead of reason and takes it along for the ride. So, that initial disturbance of the mind inflicted by the impression of harm is no more anger than is the simple impression of harm. Anger is the subsequent impulse which doesn't just accept that impression but approves of it; it is an agitation of the mind which is pressing on for vengeance on the basis of a desire and a judgement. There is never a doubt that fear involves flight and anger involves attack. So just see whether you think anything could be either pursued or avoided without the assent of the mind.

Anger occurs by assent, by which Seneca means a consciously voluntary concession to a pre-existing emotional or at any rate non-responsible reaction.

In 2.4 Seneca summarizes his causal account of anger, and distinguishes three distinct *motus* or psychological reactions. First is the *primus motus non voluntarius*, the proto-passion which Seneca has been carefully isolating. Second is the conscious judgement that one ought to act, which he calls assent. It

caution: he at first calls this response an impulse, and then withdraws the label in favour of something quite vague. In *De Fato* 40 the impulse before assent is called an *appetitus*.

[63] At this point *impetum* is not a translation *hormē* but means 'attack' (compare *fugam* above); I thank D. Konstan for this observation.

is cast in Stoic form as a hormetic judgement (the *alter motus* mentioned in 2.4.1). The uncontrolled form of this (*tertius motus*) is the passion of anger.

This passage also gives a justification for regarding the *primus motus* as non-rational and involuntary, a justification which can be put into the form of an inference. (1) The first response, Seneca says, cannot be changed by judgement. (2) But what is produced by judgement can be cured by it (2.4.1–2):

tertius motus est iam impotens, qui non si oportet ulcisci vult sed utique, qui rationem evicit. primum illum animi ictum effugere ratione non possumus, sicut ne illa quidem quae diximus accidere corporibus, ne nos oscitatio aliena sollicitet, ne oculi ad intentationem subitam digitorum comprimantur: ista non potest ratio vincere, consuetudo fortasse et adsidua observatio extenuat. alter ille motus, qui iudicio nascitur, iudicio tollitur.

It is the third motion which is uncontrolled. It doesn't want vengeance *if* it is appropriate but unconditionally; it has conquered reason. We cannot escape that first blow in the soul by means of reason, just as we cannot escape the things which, as I said, just happen to our bodies, such as yawning provoked by someone else's yawn or blinking when fingers are jabbed suddenly towards the eyes. Reason cannot conquer these reactions, though perhaps habituation and constant alertness can mitigate them. But the other kind of motion, which is generated by a judgement, can be eliminated by a judgement.

(3) Therefore the first response must be classified as non-rational. And this will hold good just as long as Seneca maintains (1), i.e. that the emotional responses put into the class of *simplex impetus* or *primus motus* are totally immune to change by rational judgement, and so resemble bodily events more closely than they do rational responses. And it seems that Seneca will do that just as long as he maintains that 'will' rather than expressibility in *lekta* is the crucial mark of rationality.

This is the most spare and clear elaboration of the theory Seneca has been discussing. The three *motus* are distinct: the relationship between the first and third cannot entail dualism because reason has nothing at all to do with the first. And while the third does oppose reason (*rationem euicit*), it is itself a product of judgement and the reason it defeats is not the agent's own, but the right reason which is abandoned by anyone who yields to a passion (i.e. it is rational$_1$ but irrational$_2$).

There is novelty in Seneca's theory. But as far as I can see there is nothing which commits him to psychological dualism or which need owe anything to Platonic or Posidonian influence. The goal of the discussion is the maintenance of Stoic theses in ethics, and the changes have considerable independent interest and merit. We might ourselves want to pursue Seneca's obvious interest in widening the class of emotional experience which is exempt from the strictest moral relevance; that is something anyone concerned about the moralistic constraints of earlier Stoicism would want to do. We may also want to consider the merits of his decision to alter the concept of assent; he does so by linking it to his own notion of *voluntas*, which is a fruitful and original contribution to the development of the Stoic tradition.[64]

But this is not the place for a full consideration of Seneca's contributions. What we have to consider in closing is one last doubt: is there not one respect in which we might detect the cloven hoof of eclecticism? If one thing, reason, is in a position to sit in judgement on something else, which has a kind of life of its own in the soul, do we not find ourselves on the doorstep of dualism?

The answer I give is obviously no, and for familiar reasons. The tendency to speak of reason as distinct from what it is judging is part of the literary apparatus Seneca uses throughout: he is reifying the psychological forces which are the building blocks of his theory. He is no more committed to dualism by this device here than he is anywhere else. The temporally dynamic process which Seneca invokes owes much to Chrysippus'

---

[64] See Kahn, 'Discovering the Will', in J. M. Dillon and A. A. Long (eds.), *The Question of 'Eclecticism': Studies in Later Greek Philosophy* (Berkeley, 1988), esp. 251-5 on Epictetus and Seneca. Kahn offers a larger view of the evolution of the notion of 'will' than I could hope to do, and he puts particular stress on the importance of the shift from early to late Stoicism (typified by Epictetus and Seneca). But he does not provide an account of the philosophical motivations Seneca may have had for the shift towards a 'preoccupation with our inner life' (259); this description is, I think, meant to refer to what I see as Seneca's interest in consciously controllable assent and his reduced interest in overall character.

comparison with the runner, which is used effectively in the orthodox theory. When appraising Seneca's orthodoxy, we should pause to reflect that one of the implications of Seneca's runner example—as an illustration—is, as Galen points out with some satisfaction,[65] that there is a difference between the self which tries to check the inertial drift of the bodily movement and the body itself; it suggests a distinction between reason and the rest of the soul; indeed, Galen insists that the example proves that Chrysippus is committed to accepting not just a separate, but even an irrational part of the soul.

One suggestion which I make is that part of Seneca's innovation is rooted in Chrysippean ideas of psychological inertia, ideas which Chrysippus would have wanted to claim were compatible with his fully rationalistic monism. Seneca, I think, develops some of these ideas in his own way, and certainly drops the commitment to a fully rationalistic account of such experiences. But he does not thereby drop his commitment to monism. What follows for Seneca is that his theory is no more dualistic than Chrysippus'.[66] If, as is so often alleged, we are on the doorstep of dualism with Seneca, then we were already there with Chrysippus.

It is quite possible that we should be re-examining the early Stoic theory for its adequacy; it may, as Galen alleged, contain internal inconsistencies which undermine its integrity (though I personally do not think it does). But if it does, then Seneca will naturally reflect that situation; and the resulting theory will then not properly be described as eclectic or Platonizing: we will simply have discovered more about the Platonic roots of Stoic psychology.

[65] See above n. 44.
[66] The same might be said about the use of medical parallels in *De Ira* 3.10; for these are well documented in the early Stoa, and it is hard to see that Seneca's use of them is unorthodox. Holler, *Seneca*, 23–4, however, takes the language of 3.10, with its emphatic use of personification and reification, as being paradigmatically dualistic, so much so that he uses it to cast doubt on the monistic character of 1.8, with its clear enunciation of monism (1.8.3, see above). As usual, the main effect of Holler's technique is twofold: Seneca becomes self-contradictory and his internal contradictions become crucial evidence in the quest for Posidonian doctrine. Seneca's integrity as a philosopher, even as a writer, is readily sacrificed on the altar of *Quellenforschung*.

3

Politics and Paradox in Seneca's *De Beneficiis*

By the standards of any contemporary western political culture, ancient societies, both Greek and Roman, were strikingly hierarchical. Only in the programmatic dreams of the most wild-eyed reformers could we expect to find an ideological commitment to general social equality. Of course, the notion that there should be equality of political rights among those fortunate enough to be classed as full citizens was somewhat commoner. But what we might call the 'real world' of social relations was based on dramatic differences in status, power, and wealth, which few if any could seriously imagine challenging.

From the fourth century BC onwards political and social thinkers were reflectively aware of the important role played in such a society by the doing of 'good deeds', services or gifts to other members of society for which some sort of return, even if only the expression of gratitude, was normally expected.[1] Although the idea is in some form as old as Greek culture itself, it is fitting that we find clearly expressed in a pseudo-Aristotelian letter to Philip of Macedon the notion that such good

---

[1] Classical Athenian society formalized some aspects of this in the institution of *leitourgia*.

deeds and the return for them served to 'hold together' (*sunechein*) society.[2]

Most philosophers have claimed that doing good deeds is godlike. For, simply put, the giving and interchange of favour (*charis*) holds together the lives of men, some giving, some receiving, and some giving back in return. That is why it is noble and just to pity[3] all those who are undeservedly unfortunate, <especially good men>,[4] (pity being a mark of the civilized soul and hard-heartedness a mark of the uncultivated); for it is shameful and wicked to gaze upon virtue suffering misfortune. Hence I also praise my friend Theophrastus who says that favour should be no grounds for regret and brings noble rewards in the form of praise from those who are benefited. That is why sensible men ought to bestow favour on many, reflecting that, apart from the good repute, there will be a service which can be repaid if fortunes should be reversed. And even if all beneficiaries do not repay the favour, at least one of them will. So try to be ready and eager with your benefactions and restrained in your anger; for the former is regal and civilized and the latter is barbaric and hateful...[5]

Centuries later, Seneca, himself no stranger to the world of higher political power, expressed the same basic idea: *de beneficiis dicendum est et ordinanda res quae maxime humanam societatem adligat* (*Ben.* 1.4.2).[6] Seneca had the advantage of a long tradition of philosophical discussion of social relations which frequently included serious discussions of such good deeds, their social function, and the norms which should govern

---

[2] The main idea here is common enough in genuine Aristotelian works. Note the claim in *EN* 8.1 1155^{a}23–4 that friendship holds states together; the close connection Aristotle recognizes between friendship and *euergesia* has already been mentioned above at 1155^{a}7–9.

[3] As Martha Nussbaum has reminded me, the connection of favour and good deeds to pity, and also to anger, is no accident in ancient culture, whether Greek or Roman. This suggests that a consideration of the connections between Seneca's *De Beneficiis* and his *De Ira* and *De Clementia* would be rewarding. I do not undertake that task in this essay.

[4] Accepting Plezia's supplement (M. Plezia (ed.), *Aristotelis Epistularum Fragmenta cum Testamento* (Warsaw, 1961).

[5] Letter 3 in Plezia, *Aristotelis Epistularum Fragmenta*; letter 4 in the Teubner edition, M. Plezia (ed.), *Aristoteles: Privatorum Scriptorum Fragmenta* (Leipzig, 1977).

[6] See also 1.15.2, 4.41.2.

them. Plato's works contain scattered remarks on the topic;[7] Xenophon's Socratic and other works often reflect an enlightened layman's view;[8] the Aristotelian corpus contains extensive discussion of good deeds in a number of contexts, most notably in connection with friendship;[9] the topic features in the Academic and Peripatetic 'divisions'[10] and in the Platonic 'definitions'.[11] Books on good deeds or the related topic of gratitude (*charis*) are reported for Theophrastus,[12] Demetrius of Phaleron,[13] Stilpo,[14] Dionysius,[15] and Epicurus,[16] among others; even the followers of Hegesias[17] and the Annicereioi[18] had views on the topic.

There was, then, good reason for the earlier Stoics to take a strong interest in this aspect of moral and political philosophy, and clear evidence that they did so. Cleanthes wrote a book on gratitude (*Peri charitos*)[19] and Chrysippus also wrote copiously

---

[7] A sampling would include texts as various as the following: *Apol.* 36c, *Crito* 43a, *Meno* 91c, 92d, *Symp.* 184b, *Grg.* 470c, 506c, 511e, 520e, 522b, *Hipp. Maj.* 281c, *Laws* VIII 850b, *Ep.* VII 332a, 351a.

[8] *Mem.* 1.2.7, 2.1.19, 2.1.28, 2.2, 2.3.14, 2.3.17, 2.4.7, 2.6.5–7, 2.6.21, 2.6.25–6, 2.7.9, 2.9.8, 3.5.23, 3.6.3, 3.11.11 ff., 3.12.4, 4.4.17, *Apol.* 1.17, *Cyropaedia* 1.2.7, 1.6.11, 3.1.28–30, 3.1.34, 3.3.4, 4.4.12, 5.3.31–2, 7.5.60, 8.2.2, 8.2.9 ff., 8.7.28, *Hiero* 7.6, 7.9, 8 ff., *Agesilaus* 2.29, 4.2–4, 9.7, 11.3, *Poroi* 3.11, *Hellenica* 6.5.44, *Anabasis* 2.6.17, 7.6.38, 7.7.23.

[9] The Aristotelian corpus contains far too many texts dealing with favours and good deeds to cite here. Note, though, the concentration in *EE* 7, *EN* 8 and especially *EN* 9 passim; Aristotle's theory of *philia* is sufficiently wide to provide a general framework for a theory of social relations, and this makes it the most important theoretical backdrop for Seneca's writing on *beneficia*. The *Politics* and *Rhetoric* are other rich sources of discussion. *Virtues and Vices* 1251^{b}30 also reflects the common-sense view that 'it is also a mark of virtue to give benefit to the worthy'.

[10] For the 'Academic' divisions, see Diogenes Laertius 3.95–6; for the Peripatetic counterpart, see H. Mutschmann (ed.), *Divisiones quae vulgo dicuntur Aristoteleae* (Leipzig, 1906), 22–3.

[11] *Def.* 412e, 413e.

[12] DL 5.48.

[13] DL 5.81.

[14] DL 2.116.

[15] DL 7.167.

[16] DL 10.28. Compare the views reported at 10.77, 10.118, 10.122, *KD* 1.

[17] DL 2.93.

[18] DL 2.96–7.

[19] DL 7.175.

on the topic.[20] Direct evidence is not readily available (aside from the anecdote of *Ben.* 4.39), but it is hard to believe that Zeno said nothing about benefits and gratitude.[21] Hecaton and his teacher Panaetius were much engaged with this sort of question;[22] and we may suspect that Posidonius' *Peri kathēkontos* touched on the same questions, if only in passing. Stoics who wrote after Seneca, such as Epictetus and Marcus, frequently dealt with the themes of service and gratitude.

The Stoics defined the cosmos as a community of rational beings, including both men and gods;[23] in their ethics and in their physics they exploited the parallelism between real human communities and the cosmos. Physics aside, even in the more strictly political ambit of actual human societies, the social virtues were of crucial importance in Stoic thought, being grounded in the fundamental human tendency to social bonding (a form of *oikeiōsis*[24]).

It is, then, only natural that any Stoic with an interest in ethics or political thought should have regarded questions about the role of good deeds in human societies as important. Seneca, who devoted a treatise in seven books to the topic, was not doing anything unusual, and it is only the accident of transmission which makes his lengthy treatise stand out. It is also worth keeping in mind that he was not devoting himself to a topic which is distinctively Stoic. Any philosopher with a serious interest in moral, political, or social philosophy will have had reason to tackle the topic of good deeds. In the *De beneficiis*

---

[20] As the discussion in *Ben.* 1.3–4 makes clear. Compare too Plutarch's comments cited below, which show that benefits were also discussed in his *Peri katorthōmatōn*.

[21] Especially if M. Schofield, *The Stoic Idea of the City* (Cambridge, 1991) is right in holding that Zeno's *Republic* made erotic relations between fellow citizens important in connection with the problem of its unity. Zeno's contemporary Arcesilaus apparently had a great reputation for the dispensing of favours and good deeds (DL 4.37).

[22] For Hecaton, most of the evidence is in Seneca.

[23] Cicero, *ND* 2.154. Chrysippus at *Ecl.* ii. 184 (*SVF* ii.527). For discussion of this notion of the cosmos, see Schofield, *The Stoic Idea*, Ch. 3.

[24] See *Ben.* 4.17 for the claim that generosity is ingrained in human nature. The language in this section is strongly reminiscent of texts on *oikeiōsis*.

Seneca speaks, as he often does, with a Stoic voice about a topic of broad interest.[25]

Roman society, more than some other hierarchically organized ancient cultures, depended on the reciprocal exchange of services and favours among members of the same social class and also between members of different classes.[26] Patronage and *clientela* are institutions vital to anyone aiming to understand Roman history and the functioning of Roman society. Seneca swam in the sea of patron–client relations; he used them to further his career and to define his position in Roman society. He knew the institution of giving *beneficia* and repaying *gratia* as well as anyone living in Rome. Also, he was a philosopher who read widely and thought acutely about a range of problems, a self-defined Stoic with a solid grasp of the school's traditions, but free of unconditional commitment to specific models and masters.

Seneca's *De Beneficiis*, written between AD 56 and 64, most likely while he was in the active service of Nero,[27] is a somewhat neglected work in the corpus of an often undervalued author. There is, however, one important recent treatment of the treatise, by François-Regis Chaumartin;[28] and of course it features in many general accounts of Seneca or Stoic ethics to varying degrees. But it has not been the subject of searching philosophical appraisal (Chaumartin's treatment being more source-

---

[25] The same could be said about his related treatments of clemency and anger in the *De Clementia* and *De Ira*.

[26] On the topic generally, see R. P. Saller, *Personal Patronage under the Early Roman Empire* (Cambridge, 1982). For a brief overview of Roman imperial customs of social exchange (with more bibliography), see P. Garnsey, and R. P. Saller, *The Roman Empire: Economy, Society and Culture* (Berkeley, 1987), ch. 8. Also A. Wallace-Hadrill (ed.), *Patronage in Ancient Society* (London, 1989); a larger view in P. Veyne, *Bread and Circuses*, trans. B. Pearce (London, 1990).

[27] I follow the dating of M. Griffin, *Seneca: A Philosopher in Politics* (2nd edn., Oxford, 1992), 399, except that I do not see why Seneca should be thought more likely to have finished the work before the retirement of 62.

[28] F.-R. Chaumartin, *Le De Beneficiis de Sénèque: sa signification philosophique politique et sociale* (Paris, 1985), a thesis written under Pierre Grimal; I am particularly indebted to Chaumartin's discussions of the social and historical setting and of the possible sources for the treatise. Other useful treatments can be found in P. Grimal, *Sénèque, ou la conscience de l'empire* (Paris, 1979) and 'Nature et limite de l'éclectisme philosophique chez Sénèque', *Les Études Classiques*, 38 (1970) 14–17.

critical and social-historical), and even the sympathetic eye of Pierluigi Donini finds here 'la meno felice e la meno nuova fra le opere dell'ultima stagione senecana'.[29] All too often students of Stoicism find in this treatise (as von Arnim did) valuable 'fragments' to illuminate the earlier history of the school—a fact which shows how genuinely Stoic the voice of Seneca is in this work—but do not attempt a well-rounded philosophical appreciation of a work which perhaps better than any other illustrates Seneca's own philosophical mind at work, in a Stoic framework, on problems which were real and pressing for his own life in his own time and place.

A fresh consideration of Seneca's 'sources' seems otiose. Chaumartin (part one, chs. 1–3) has now subsumed and replaced earlier discussions of the sources, prefacing his own discussion with a useful account of the origins and development of twentieth-century trends in source criticism. He has modified and to some extent strengthened the arguments for Hecaton's *Peri charitos* as the principal and nearly exclusive source, though one used with considerable freedom. Given the assumptions of conventional source criticism, it is hard to imagine improving on this conclusion (except by substituting the attested *Peri kathēkontos* for the hypothetical *Peri charitos*).[30] But the assumptions of conventional source criticism are perilous. The virtually unquestioned foundation of all reasoning on this topic to date has been that Seneca's principal source *must* have been by the author cited most often in the treatise; Hecaton is cited four times. But how do we know that Seneca used *any* source extensively, or that he named the source he did use?[31] The conclusions generated by such assumptions tend to

---

[29] P. Donini, *Le scuole, l'anima, l'impero: la filosofia antica da Antioco a Plotino* (Turin, 1982), 204.

[30] The former was at least six books in length (see Cicero, *Off.* 3.89), more than long enough to contain one or two books on *beneficia* as a source for Seneca.

[31] I leave aside the dubious value of reconstructions of Hecatonian views. Even in the ideal case where we have a certain reconstruction of one of his views and that view appears in Seneca's work, the conclusion that Seneca used Hecaton's work is dubious. Given Seneca's broad familiarity with Stoicism, we would also have to have good reason for believing that the view in question was uniquely his. And from the little we can tell Hecaton was not a strikingly original philosopher.

be either uninformative or unconvincing. We should note just one example. It seems circular to confirm, on the basis of Seneca's handling of Epicurean ideas, that Seneca used a *Peri charitos* by Hecaton, as Chaumartin attempts to do (pp. 80–92). In fact we know nothing independently about Hecaton's treatment of Epicureanism[32] (let alone his discussion of it in that work) and we have extensive evidence of Seneca's engagement (both critical and sympathetic) with Epicureanism in his extant works. This approach to the question of Seneca's sources can only be the product of methodological blinkers.[33]

What then can we do with the treatise? The most important issue to be clear about is the general character of the work. Is the *De Beneficiis* a social-political or an ethical treatise? Should we locate it in a tradition of theorizing about the operation of societies and political cultures, or in a tradition of discussing the virtues of the individual and their contribution to the good life?

In one sense this is a pointless question. For the political and ethical traditions were never neatly separated in the ancient world.[34] The Stoics, like many others, held that an individual human could only flourish in a social, i.e. a political, context.[35] And the divisions of ethical philosophy make it clear that most discussions of social and political relations would have fallen under the heading *Peri kathēkontōn*.[36] But *we* have a reasonably

[32] Despite the assertion of Grimal, 'Nature et limite', 9 and 'L'Épicurisme romain', in *Actes du VIIIe Congrès de l'Association G. Budé* (Paris, 1969), 144–5. Epicureanism is not mentioned in connection with Hecaton's maxims at *Ep.* 5.7, 6.7, or 9.6, and there is no reason to think on the basis of these passages that Hecaton had 'une familiarité certaine avec la parénétique épicurienne' (Grimal, 'Nature et limite', 9). The argument in Grimal, 'L'Épicurisme romain' rests solely on Hecaton's use of utility in his moral reasoning (*Off.* 3.89), and is quite unconvincing.

[33] It is regrettable that we can learn so little about Seneca's sources, for it probably would matter if we could be sure about how Seneca worked. Seneca's own tag, *et quid interest quis dixerit? omnibus dixit* (*Ep.* 14.18), commands the sympathy of those frustrated with naive source criticism, but is ultimately false.

[34] Though, significantly, Cleanthes did distinguish the ethical and the political part of philosophy (DL 7.41).

[35] In the Aristotelian tradition it was even held that politics was the architectonic branch of knowledge which provided the necessary context for ethics.

[36] DL 7.84; Epictetus, *Diss.* 3.2.4. Eudorus' division of ethics subdivides the heading on *kathēkonta* and *katorthōmata* into those which are concerned with the

clear idea of what is meant by political thought and can sensibly ask whether the social writing of Nero's chief political adviser counts as 'political' or 'ethical'. Does Seneca in this work care primarily about individual virtue, or does he care about the functioning of society in a genuinely political sense?

A clearer way of putting this question might be in terms of Malcolm Schofield's recent assessment of the earlier Stoic tradition of political writing. In *The Stoic Idea of the City* he attempts to chart the development of Stoic political thought from Zeno to the age of Cicero. He sees Zeno's *Republic* as being genuinely concerned with political phenomena—how an ideal state would actually be organized and run—though of course in a manner completely dominated by ethical concerns. But over the course of time a 'category shift' occurs, and in Arius Didymus' summary the political character of the theory has been radically denatured. We have ethical writing about political themes. 'The fundamental object of the exercise... is *simply* to demonstrate that proper application of the [political] predicates in question is contingent on either moral goodness or moral badness, as the case may be, and to show the high moral demands imposed on political and judicial behaviour by a proper understanding of law.' The result is, as Schofield says, 'chapters of political philosophy bereft of virtually all interest in specifically political analysis—or, as one might say, depoliticized' (96–7). What developed, according to Schofield, was 'political philosophy in a quite different style, no longer tied to preoccupation with the *polis*, but focused instead on the moral potentialities of man considered as man, not as citizen' (102–3).

This description of two different approaches to political topics in the school suggests a promising way of assessing the *De Beneficiis*. Does Seneca write real social-political philosophy, or does he write in a purely ethical manner on social

---

agent him- or herself (*kath' heauta*) and those which deal with social relations (*Ecl.* ii.44.20 ff.). The topic of gratitude (*peri charitōn*) falls into this social category, and clearly so would the good deeds so closely linked to it. Eudorus' division shows clear signs of Stoic influence, and is in fact very sensible. But there is no way of knowing how influential it may have been.

themes? The question is interesting in large measure because of Seneca's own political position. We might reasonably expect him to write politically, and that his writings on society would reflect his political views; yet, as Griffin has shown, the relevance of his writings to his practical politics is complex and variable.[37]

Space will not permit a full study of the work from this perspective.[38] What I want to do instead is lay the groundwork for a more comprehensive assessment by considering a single theme. I will not look in detail at the social-historical particulars of the text; for my purposes the specific events and political developments are peripheral, since the issues raised by the work are of general and persistent importance for Roman society; philosophical consideration of them did not need to be sparked by concern with particular cases,[39] though of course they are indispensable as examples.

---

[37] Grimal, 'Nature et limite', 15–16, suggests that the work concerns only private good deeds and generosity, and that the reason for Seneca's intense focus on the inner intention of the giver and receiver is the practical impossibility of a serious consideration of the political significance of good deeds. Under an emperor, 'Sénèque ne pouvait donc élaborer la théorie d'une bienfaisance que privée.' He sees in this a reason for the return of Seneca to the earlier and more purely ethical Stoic approach to social phenomena and the abandonment of the Aristotelian and more openly political tradition which came into the school with Panaetius. This is too simple. True, interior intention is strikingly evident in Seneca's treatment (though the social and external function is amply discussed too), but we do not know that it was absent in Hecaton or Panaetius; and we find clear evidence of it in Aristotle. Nor do we know with any confidence that the 'valeur objective' of good deeds was downplayed by Chrysippus and Cleanthes. Further, the suggestion that Seneca had no choice but to focus on private morality will not stand serious scrutiny. There is considerable (though careful) political comment on the principate and its origins throughout the treatise; and the mere existence of the *De Clementia* proves that *engagé* political writing on a moral virtue was not out of the question. If Seneca emphasizes the interior intention of good deeds, it is for philosophical reasons.

[38] There is more than enough material in the treatise which bears on this question. In fact, it is one of the central issues and recurs in a number of different guises. But the complexity of the topic demands a lengthier treatment than can be managed in the present context.

[39] Hence I do not think that we need to regard the discussion of ungrateful freedmen as having been provoked by the debate of AD 56 on the proposal to revoke the freedom of ungrateful *liberti*. For discussion, see Chaumartin, *Le De Beneficiis de Sénèque*, 330–47; Griffin, *Seneca*, Ch. 8.

Nothing is more distinctive of the Stoic approach to ethics than the central role played by the often paradoxical[40] utterances about the sage and the fool. Claims about these two kinds of agent are the ones most likely to fly in the face of common sense and the generally held views of most people. Hence there is a built-in tendency for such aspects of Stoic ethics to conflict with any system, such as Aristotle's, which is built upon the *endoxa*; and in so far as the Stoic system itself laid claim to the views of people in general as part of its foundation[41] the prospect of self-contradiction loomed. In the areas of ethics which concern us, social and political thought, the relevance of general social attitudes is even greater. Hence it is no surprise that Plutarch twice takes aim at an aspect of Stoic theory which also turns up in Seneca's treatise.

In chapter 12 of his *De Stoicorum Repugnantiis* Plutarch sets in opposition the Chrysippean claim that 'nothing is useful to the base, nor does the base man have use for or need anything' with the equally authentic (though less paradoxical) claim (from book 1 of *Peri katorthōmatōn*) that 'usefulness and gratitude extend to the intermediates', i.e. the indifferents, 'none of which is useful, according to the Stoics'. It follows that the base, i.e. non-sages, have nothing to be grateful for, since no real service can be done for them. In *On common conceptions* chapter 21, Plutarch notes that it is contrary to the common conceptions to hold that the base man is not benefited;[42] after

---

[40] Paradoxical only in the sense that the claims made are in conflict with opinions usually held by people in general: *para ta dokounta*. They violate what Seneca calls *consuetudo* at *Ben.* 2.35.2. This need not, and generally does not, involve any logical oddity. Julia Annas brought this out very clearly in discussion at Cambridge by protesting (quite correctly) that the Stoic paradoxes are, from the Stoic point of view, simply true.

[41] See most recently Brunschwig, 'On the Book-title of Chrysippus: "On the fact that the ancients admitted dialectic along with demonstration"', in H. Blumenthal and H. Robinson (eds.), *Aristotle and the Later Tradition* (Oxford Studies in Ancient Philosophy, Supp. vol.; Oxford, 1991), 81–95.

[42] Plutarch is making, in *Comm. Not.* 21, the excessively strong claim that Stoic views contradict the common conceptions; these, as Myles Burnyeat reminds me, are not identical to the consciously held opinions of the common man; in *De Stoic. Rep.* 12 his claim that Chrysippus contradicts himself seems to be made on the basis of a conflict between technical Stoic doctrine and a Stoic stance which is compatible with views consciously held by the common man.

all, many of them get educated and make moral progress, are manumitted and rescued from siege, and are healed when sick or handicapped. The position which his Stoic opponents are driven to by this criticism is stark: 'When they receive this, they are not benefited, nor are they recipients of good deeds, nor do they have benefactors or neglect benefactors.' It follows, according to Plutarch, that the base are not ungrateful; and since the sensible are not ungrateful either, ingratitude turns out to be non-existent. The Stoic response: that gratification extends to the intermediates and so, while benefiting and being benefited are restricted to the wise, the base are affected by gratification. Plutarch's parting comment is this: 'So, do those who are involved in gratification have no share in usefulness? And is there nothing useful or congenial in the realm of gratification? But what else makes a service a matter of gratification but the fact that the provider of the service is in some respect useful to a man in need?'

This polemic rests on an early Stoic position which eventually appeared in the handbooks which lie behind the compilation we attribute to Arius Didymus; at *Ecl.* ii.104.6–9 we read, 'and the base man is ungrateful, not finding it congenial either to return or to offer gratitude, since he does nothing for the common good nor for friendship nor without calculation'. Seneca reflects this debate about the gratitude of the base man in letter 81.8–14[43] (where he explicitly describes his view as a Stoic paradox) and in the *De Beneficiis* 5.12–17 (where the paradoxical nature of the thesis is also noted[44]).

An equally paradoxical issue is flagged and discussed by Seneca in 2.31–5; Seneca begins thus: *hoc ex paradoxis Stoicae sectae minime mirabile, ut mea fert opinio, aut incredibile est eum, qui libenter accipit, beneficium reddidisse* (2.31.1). This paradox seems congruent with the first; what they share is a marked tendency to dissociate the giving and receiving of services and gratitude from the normal and conventionally understood

---

[43] This letter refers back to the treatise (81.3) and deals with a few additional points relevant to the main theme of the treatise, viz. ingratitude. It is reasonable to regard the letter as a kind of appendix to the treatise.
[44] 5.12.1–2.

conceptions of them, conceptions which (1) involve an acceptance of the normal valuation of those things which the Stoics label indifferent and which (2) locate the service and repayment in the 'goods' so exchanged. The first paradox appears to deny (1) and the second seems to deny (2).

The significance of the gap between common sense and these two paradoxes should not be minimized. For Stoic ethics *needs* common sense in order to get off the ground, and in the case of good deeds Seneca relies on ordinary common sense for important general views about the nature of benevolence. His repeated claim that some particular course of action is not a good deed just because it involves a quasi-commercial exchange of services is supported primarily by the instinctive sense we all have about what counts as generosity.

Let us take a closer look at Seneca's handling of the first paradox. In letter 81 Seneca's main theme is ingratitude (as it is in the treatise). Lucilius complains that he has had to deal with an ungrateful man, and Seneca's response is a curious mixture of impatience and support: it is naïve to be surprised or disturbed by the phenomenon of ingratitude, since it is so common, and Lucilius is encouraged not to let such a turn of events discourage good deeds.[45] They are by their nature uncertain, and it is better to suffer ingratitude than not to give. Not giving would mean not exercising one's virtue and would also deprive one of the satisfaction of encountering the grateful recipient (81.1–2).

So much is derived from the treatise. The material which interests us now arises from a new question,[46] in response to the somewhat casuistical question:[47] if a benefactor subsequently

---

[45] Also an application of the theme familiar from the treatise.

[46] For the discussion of 81.3–8 I have benefited greatly from the need to answer the criticisms made by Pierluigi Donini. Our readings of the passage are still very different, though. His suggestion is to identify the strict judge with the sage and the *vir bonus*, and the *remissior iudex* with the non-sage (e.g. Seneca himself). On this reading, the main point I wish to make would still stand: that in the absence of a sage's exact knowledge of moral values in each circumstance a sensible man would do well to be lenient (*remissior*) in assessing the behaviour of others.

[47] It is typical of the discussion in books 5–7 of the treatise; note the adumbration of it at *Ben.* 3.12.4.

Seneca's De Beneficiis 77

harms us, does that make things equal and cancel out our debt?[48] It is also allowed that the subsequent harm far outweighs the earlier benefit. According to Seneca, a strict judge[49] will assess the benefit and harm and say, 'Although the injuries are greater, let us credit to the benefits what survives the injury.' Seneca means that we must continue to count as a benefit anything of the prior good deed whose effects survive the later hostile behaviour.[50]

Moreover,[51] the assessment in such cases must be made in light of such factors as the timing (extra weight is assigned to the earlier deed) and the state of mind of the other agent (if he had been a reluctant donor then the value of the good deed is thereby reduced); unfortunately, his state of mind is a matter of guesswork and so cannot readily be factored into the evaluation.[52] In the case at hand it is supposed that when the ponderable factors are taken fully into account there is, on the strict assessment, a net injury.

What the good man[53] then does, in contrast to the strict judge, is to draw up this balance sheet in such a way as to favour the

---

[48] The accounting language is normal in the treatise; though Seneca also needs to emphasize that ordinary accounting principles do not apply to good deeds.

[49] Seneca describes his assessment as *recta*. Unlike Donini (in correspondence), I do not think this means that the strict judge is sagelike (though *rectus* often signifies such absolute moral correctness, as when *recte factum* is used to render *katorthōma*). The parallel use of *recta sententia* by Seneca at *Ep.* 94.36 does not flag sagelike correctness either; the opinion is correct, to be sure, but not held in the unshakeable manner in which the sage would hold it. Otherwise, it would not need to be reinforced by *admonitio*. So too here. The strict judge gets the right result (not wiping out the benefit) but not necessarily in the way that the infallible sage would.

[50] A possible illustration: my friend lends me the down payment for my house. I live in it for years, happily. Then later he commits adultery with my wife, arguably a harm far outweighing the loan of the money. Yet the use and enjoyment of the house I live in is still with me and would never have been possible without his generosity. Do I owe him continuing gratitude for the loan? Or does that get wiped out by the insult? The stern judge envisaged here will admit that the injury is greater than the benefit, but still recognize the benefit which I continue to enjoy.

[51] I assume that Seneca moves on to a second point with *plus nocuit* at 81.4.

[52] So I take *nunc coniectura tollatur* in 81.6; compare *Ben.* 4.33.1 and 3.7.7, where it is clear that the relevant kind of guesswork is about the state of mind of another agent.

[53] The *vir bonus* here is not, I think, a sage, but rather the reasonable man of good moral intentions; compare the *stultus* who has a *bona voluntas* (81.8). I concede that

other party by cheating himself on the valuations; given the number of imponderables, this seems more reasonable than restricting oneself to the ponderables, as the strict judge does. Seneca, however, would rather go even further and play the role of a 'slack judge' and urge that we remember the good deed and simply forget the injury. Lucilius 'suggests' that it would be consistent with justice to separate our responses to the benefit and the injury; but Seneca sensibly enough rejects that suggestion. Since the same agent is dealing with us in both cases, there must be an integrated response.[54]

Seneca's general principle,[55] then, is to give greater weight to the good deed than to the injury (81.8), apparently on the grounds that not everyone knows how to be grateful. The ordinary man, with the best of intentions, has trouble assessing the right return to make for a good deed (being unclear about the amount owed, the time to pay it, and the place to pay it); only the wise man knows the true value of each thing and how to repay a favour.

this is an odd usage of *vir bonus* for Seneca. But it will be even more odd to have Seneca here saying that the good man actually *distorts* the value judgements (described as 'cheating himself') in order to justify forgiveness of injury, and then to claim, at 81.8, that he (if he is to be identified with the sage) is the only one who really knows the value of things. Moreover, the *vir bonus* of 81.6 must also be distinct from the *rigidus iudex*; the good man's judgement involves a distortion of the correct assessment, whereas that of the *rigidus iudex* does not. The strict judge acknowledges the greater magnitude of the injury, yet denies that the good done is eliminated just because it is outweighed. Here, the good man actually reduces the perceived magnitude of the injury and increases that of the benefit. The *vir bonus* also appears at 81.15; he may be supremely reasonable (*aequissimum*), but is not a sage. On the present view, the sage comes into the discussion as sole possessor of relevant moral certainty first at 81.8.

[54] The sentence *nam cui . . . debetur* in 81.7 is meant to support this. The argument is that in a case where the injury is forgivable anyway, we would naturally respond to it with something more than forgiveness if there had been a prior benefit. This seems unconvincing, but is intended at least to show that there is a natural connection between our varying responses to the same person.

[55] At this point it is not clear how firmly Seneca is maintaining the distinction between the *vir bonus* and the *remissior iudex*. Both of these characters deviate from the proper assessment of the strict judge, though in different ways (the former by cheating himself on the value judgements, the other by simply forgiving the injury); the *vir bonus* and the *remissior iudex* both stand in contrast to the *sapiens* (who actually can get the value judgements right) and to the strict judge.

At this point the nature of the discussion has shifted noticeably. Until now, the letter has dealt with the practicalities of giving and receiving and has offered advice about personal comportment in these social relations: don't let irritation at ingratitude make you ungenerous; do not be a *rigidus iudex*, since you probably do not know enough to act with certainty; take a lenient evaluation of others in difficult cases; make allowances for the ordinary man's limited grasp of the how-to's of moral life. So much is ethically sensitive advice about the real-world practice of social interchange.

But from there we move on to the contrast of fool and sage. Of what relevance is it to the discussion so far? Since Seneca and Lucilius are not sages, the attitude they take cannot be justified directly on those grounds. Yet the sage is part of the solution to the moral problem being explored by Seneca and Lucilius. Awareness of what a sage *would* do in such circumstances and of the limited moral insight of all fools, including oneself, is meant to justify Seneca's preferred stance of moral leniency. The attitude of the *remissior iudex* is justified by the ignorance of the moral agent. It is not so much that we can imitate the sage; but just knowing that he is there and that we are not wise has an important impact on our behaviour in the practical world of real social relations.

In sections 9–14 Seneca defends the Stoics against a version of the critique we saw in Plutarch, though he does so in an indirect way. He begins by praising the moral aptness of the traditional idiom for repaying a favour, *referre gratiam*. Seneca claims that this idiom is apt in that it expresses the voluntary nature of the act in a way that *reddere, reponere,* or *solvere* would not. The language of commercial and monetary obligation is not appropriate to the sphere of good deeds. Summed up: *qui rettulit, ipse se appellavit.* The sage is a man who remains in control of the social relationships he gets into by considering carefully and correctly what he should receive, from whom, why, when, where, and how. (In this, of course, he is much like the Aristotelian *phronimos*, who can make the right judgements in all these respects.)

This is the context for the introduction of the paradox we are considering, that only the wise man knows how to give a benefit or be grateful for it; the basis for it is clearly laid out before it gets introduced. What the sage has that ordinary people lack is the knowledge of the true value of things and the ability to make reliable assessments of a wide variety of relevant particular factors. The point of saying this is to provide a context for the practical advice given to more typical moral agents. But Seneca's response to the criticism of the paradox does not turn on that justification (and reasonably so, for that would beg the question of the good sense of the advice). Instead, he goes on the offensive, taking the view that the Stoic position is not in fact as paradoxical as it might seem to be at first. He points out that Epicurus himself, or at least Metrodorus, holds the same view. Next, he associates the paradox with two others which are allegedly less objectionable. That only the wise man can love or be a friend seems to provide support, since benefits and gratitude are intimately connected with friendship;[56] and the 'fact' that only the wise man is capable of loyalty also lends support, since (Seneca claims) no one who does not know how to be grateful can be said to be loyal. This defence is weak, since one might easily choose to reject the other two paradoxes; but the envisaged opponents will apparently not do so.

Ordinary agents, then, do not have virtues but merely imitations of virtues (*simulacra rerum honestarum et effigies*, a rather Platonic-sounding phrase). The advice to the ordinary man, then, is to repay good deeds as best he can, given the limits of his knowledge; what makes him a *stultus* is his lack of knowledge, not his lack of intention: *scientia illi potius quam voluntas desit: velle non discitur*. This section of the letter concludes with a reminder of the kind of things which the sage can get right: he is the one who will be able to make apt judgements about particular aspects of individual cases.

In sum, then, the consideration of the paradox here tells us a good deal about the relationship between the paradoxical (or technical, purely ethical) and the practical (socio-political) levels of Seneca's ethics. The function of the 'pure' ethics, the

---

[56] The ambiguity of *amicitia* between the personal friendship and the social or political alliance nicely corresponds to the ambiguity of benefits.

ethics of the sage, is to provide a context and motivation for specific aspects of practical advice to the normal moral agent. The characterization of the sage enables Seneca to distinguish intellectual failings from failures of good will and intention, and justifies the recommendation of leniency in dealing with one's fellow men. The sage becomes not a paradox, but a practically relevant and useful component in the advice given about real social relations.

Let us turn to the discussion of the same paradox in *Ben.* 5.12–17, which is considerably closer in form to what we met in Plutarch. Seneca begins with a disingenuous introduction, treating the issue not straightforwardly as a paradox, but rather as an instance of apparently needless technicality. The value of what follows is said to lie only in a form of mental stimulus: *securitatem ac segnitiam ingeniis auferunt, quibus modo campus, in quo vagentur, sternendus est, modo creperi aliquid et confragosi obiciendum, per quod erepant et sollicite vestigium faciant* (5.12.2).

The rest of 5.12 (3–7) is devoted to a rhetorical elaboration of the dilemma designed to show that there is no such thing as ingratitude. Briefly: the wise man is not ungrateful because he always acts rightly and being ungrateful is inconsistent with always acting rightly. The bad man (1) cannot receive a good deed, since (2) a good deed benefits the recipient and (3) nothing can be of benefit to the bad man; and (4) only someone who has received a benefit can owe a return to the giver, and (5) the ungrateful man is he who owes a return and does not pay it; therefore (6) the bad man cannot be ungrateful. The separation of the bad man from all good deeds is claimed as Stoic doctrine by Seneca (5.12.5: *apud nos*) and developed in 5.12.5–7. The central principle here is that only the *honestum* is good; the paradox clearly rests on the central thesis of Stoic value theory, which entails that all conventional goods are not really goods and so must be redescribed as merely preferred.

The defence of the Stoic view begins with a relaxation of the strict theses of Stoic axiology. The advantages which a bad man can receive are preferred indifferents, but in keeping with the more common and widely shared Peripatetic terminology, he refers to them as goods of the body and of fortune, referring to genuine Stoic goods (i.e. virtue and what partakes of virtue) as goods of the *animus* (5.13.1). The Stoics and the Peripatetics agree that bad men can receive bodily and external advantages, but the latter are prepared to refer to such goods as *minuta beneficia*, whereas the Stoics are not. Seneca does, however, argue that if these pseudo-benefits (*beneficiis similia*) are not returned, then the bad man *in ingrati nomen incidet*. This amounts to a rejection of statement (4) above; Seneca is clearly committed to (4a): someone who receives a benefit or a pseudo-benefit owes a return to the giver.

In 5.13.3 this weakening of (4) to (4a) is challenged: *at quomodo ingratum vocas eo non reddito, quod negas esse beneficium*? Seneca replies with a brief illustration of the kind of figurative language he uses, noting that such advantages are not benefits, but *habent tamen beneficii speciem*. To this the objection is made that it only follows that the bad man is quasi-ungrateful, not actually ungrateful. It is surprising and significant that Seneca rejects this point. The reason as given is this (5.13.4): 'That is not true, because both the giver and the receiver call those [advantages] benefits. So, he who reneges on the apparently genuine benefit is ungrateful in the same way as the man who blended a sleeping potion when he thought he was blending a fatal poison is a poisoner.' Apparently it is the belief of the agents which ultimately determines the moral status of the action—a view vigorously upheld by Seneca in the early books of the treatise. And if the bad man thinks of the advantage given as a benefit and does not return it, then he is committed to ungrateful intentions and thoughts. Hence he is ungrateful, despite the fact that he has not really received a benefit for which gratitude is due: believing that he has been benefited is enough to generate the obligation to repay.[57]

---

[57] This is the obvious sense of the last two sentences of 5.13.4 (*falsum est... miscuit*). It is open to question whether Seneca has thought through this principle sufficiently to be able to treat it as a general maxim. Fully generalized, it might lead to conclusions which would discomfit him as a Stoic. (I am grateful to the discussants at Cambridge, especially Victor Caston, for pointing out how ready Seneca can be to overgeneralize.)

This line of thought is continued through 5.14, where Cleanthes' even more extreme position is brought in as support. Cleanthes uses a counterfactual claim to help uncouple the possibility of ingratitude from strict Stoic axiology: 'Though what he [the bad man] received is not a benefit, he is nevertheless ungrateful because he *would not have* returned it even if he had accepted [a benefit].'[58] The basis for the counterfactual claim must lie in the character of the agent, as is confirmed by Seneca's illustration. A man can be a bandit even before he soils his hands with deeds of violence, providing he is armed and has the intention (*voluntas*) to rob and kill. Seneca's contemporaries would count such a man a criminal even if he were deprived of a ready victim, just as they would punish a sacrilegious man even though the gods cannot actually be harmed by him (5.14.1–2).

In 5.14.3 the interlocutor gives the debate a new twist: it ought to be impossible for anyone to be ungrateful to a bad man, since by definition a benefit cannot be received from such a person. The response is similar: the gift given was deemed a benefit and so should be treated as such for the purposes of repayment. If one accepts as good something indifferent, then one should repay in the same kind of 'currency'. If a quasi-good is received, then a quasi-good should be returned. True benefits are purely intelligible intentions and so can be returned in kind regardless of one's material circumstances.

Seneca urges a certain indifference to the technical terminology here; he likens an overscrupulous reliance on strict terminology to the situation with the language used of monetary debt: *aes alienum* is not repaid in copper coin, and a debt is incurred even if the loan was made in gold coin or even in Spartan leather currency. Someone who claimed to be debt-free because he received no copper would be wrong. What

---

[58] It is not clear from Seneca's Latin (*non fuit redditurus etiam si accepisset*) just what sort of counterfactual is involved here. And yet, as Chris Bobonich pointed out in discussion, the way Cleanthes' position is formulated seems to affect its coherence: for if what is envisaged as having been received is a *real* benefit, then the recipient must be a sage and of course he will return it. Interpretation is difficult, since the point is Cleanthes' and the formulation is Seneca's. For Seneca's immediate purposes, the key point is clarified by the following comparison to a bandit.

counts is that the debt be paid off in the same currency as it was incurred in (5.14.4). The discussion is concluded by a blunt admonition to the non-sage: to him it does not matter whether it is right to use the term *beneficium* for non-moral goods. Though such technical precision has its place, the interlocutor seems to be exploiting it only to the disadvantage of others (*in alios quaeritur verum*), contrary to the general spirit of social bonding. The non-sage should settle for the *species veri*,[59] and while still on the road to moral perfection he should cherish and practise what passes for virtue in his time and place (5.14.5).

This passage bridges the gap between the technicalities of Stoic ethics and useful advice to the non-sage. In particular, it is a valuable application of the fundamental idea of Seneca's theory, the crucial role played by the intention of the agent. The non-sage can at least repay in kind and deal socially with his fellow citizens in the terms, inaccurate as they may be, which are current. The correct axiology can be, and perhaps should be, set aside until a higher state of moral education has been reached. If I interpret 5.14.5 correctly, Seneca has a special criticism to make of those who would mix the technical understanding and the ordinary with an anti-social aim; the *voluntas* of the agent is important even in this second-order question of how to deal with the gap between the two realms of discourse.[60]

From 5.15 to 5.17 Seneca deals with the other side of the paradox. The charge is made that just as in one sense on Stoic principles no one is ungrateful, so in another sense everyone is. For all fools are bad, and he who has one vice has them all; but since all of us are fools, we are all ungrateful. One perfectly reasonable response to this would be to distinguish the senses in which non-sages do and do not have all the vices. That course would be in line with Seneca's penchant for reflection on the role of ambiguity in resolving paradoxes; but he specifically notes that he is not going to defend the proposition on the grounds that it is true in the special technical sense of Stoic

---

[59] Compare *simulacra rerum honestarum* at *Ep.* 81.13.

[60] Of course the enlightened moral teacher also mixes them, but does not use them *against* anyone or to escape responsibilities.

ethical dogma (*nec est, quod hanc nostram tantum murmurationem putes pro pessimo pravoque numerantium quidquid citra recti formulam cecidit*, 5.15.2). Instead, Seneca accepts the truth of the charge in the ordinary and socially shared sense of the terms (note *publica querella* at 5.15.2) and employs it to launch a rhetorical attack against human ingratitude which extends to the end of 5.17, a tirade which puts special emphasis on ingratitude in the political sphere: both cases of generals who were ungrateful to their city[61] and also cases where Rome herself was ungrateful to those who had served her well. *Ingrati publice sumus* (5.17.3) is in Seneca's eyes a fair comment on political life and human nature. Seneca chooses to close on the theme of the more general ingratitude of human nature as manifested outside the political sphere (5.17.3–7). Here again the paradox of technical Stoic ethics is successfully turned to effective social comment.

Let us now turn to the paradox which concludes book 2: *qui libenter accipit, beneficium reddidisse* (2.31.1). Here too Seneca begins from an apparently paradoxical and rigorously ethical thesis and concludes with a position which makes a serious contribution to social thought while still maintaining a consistency with the technical Stoic position.

Seneca begins from the point already established, that everything is referred to the mind, i.e. that in ethics it is intentions which determine the moral character of the actions. As with the exercise of any other virtue we find that we can be grateful by means of our will alone. Would this be fair to the donor of a benefit? Yes, for *quotiens, quod proposuit, quisque consequitur, capit operis sui fructum*, and the donor has fully achieved his aim as long as he has benefited and given the appropriate pleasure to the recipient. This he has achieved just as long as his intention becomes known to me and stimulates in me a reciprocal sense of joy.[62] His intention did not include getting

---

[61] Not missing Julius Caesar, implicated in Pompey's ingratitude (5.16.4) and also ungrateful in his own actions (5.16.5).

[62] Joy (*gaudium, chara*) is the proper Stoic response to any manifestation of the good (in this case, virtue as manifested in the attitudes and intentions of another

something back from me, for that would make his action a business transaction and not a *beneficium* (2.31.2–3).

It is consistent with ordinary opinion that a *beneficium* should have this selfless quality and that the clear expectation of return invalidates its character as a favour. Of course, it is also part of the social custom which binds society together that there should be *some* form of return at some point. Seneca can block an important line of objection to the Stoic position: as long as the donor cannot feel that his action was left incomplete, that his purposes and expectations were thwarted, then he has not been treated unfairly; and if he has not been treated unfairly in the social interchange, then no ingratitude has occurred. The man who receives the benefit in the same enlightened state of mind as characterized the donor has indeed returned what he owes. The crucial point here is the donor's state of mind, which sets the standard for the recipient.

Seneca continues with another argument from common opinions about gratitude: it really would be a *pessima optimae rei condicio* if we depended on fortune for our ability to be grateful (2.31.4). The objection is put, though, that actual return of service for service (or at least the attempt to do so as best one can) is a necessary component of gratitude (2.31.5–2.32). Seneca's first response is a direct extension of the point just made, that *malo loco beneficium est, nisi et excussis manibus esse grato licet* (2.31.5). The objector responds with a clever application of the Chrysippean simile used earlier in the book (2.17), which compared the giving and receiving of benefits to playing catch—a game which requires two people, mutual good will, and cooperation in the application of skilled behaviour.[63] The objector points out that no matter how well you catch a ball in the game, you also have to throw it back well if you want to be a good

---

virtuous agent): it is a response elicited by the awareness that there is good in the world, not by any specific awareness of good for myself.

[63] The relevance of this example to the craft analogy is worth noting, especially in view of Striker's use of sports; see G. Striker, 'Antipater, or the Art of Living', in M. Schofield and G. Striker (eds.), *The Norms of Nature* (Cambridge and Paris, 1986), 185–204.

player. Hence, in social interchanges, you have to receive benefits gracefully but also return them with gratitude.

Seneca's response is in two stages. First, he attempts to deny the exact applicability of the simile on the grounds that it deals with corporeally observable objects and that good deeds deal with the mind—an important disanalogy, and one which shows how dualistic a Stoic can sound without necessarily giving up his corporealism. Seneca also rejects the criticism of a ball player who may have failed to return the ball through no fault of his own (2.32.2). The second stage of Seneca's response is provoked by the objector's quite sensible rejoinder: although the skill of the player might not be deficient in such a case, it is evident that the game itself is incomplete, since the game consists in a two-sided throwing back and forth (2.32.3). This objection is very strong, since everything said by Seneca so far only deals with the state of mind of the 'players' in the social game, and the social custom of *beneficia* which binds a society together really does have an important dimension which goes beyond mere intentions. Even if the giver and receiver have wonderfully clear and virtuous intentions, something will be missing from the social bond if there is no return.

Seneca here (2.32.4) bridges the gap between the ethical and the social sides of his theory by giving in to the objector: *nolo diutius hoc refellere*. He can accept (at least for the sake of argument—the force of *existimemus* is hard to assess) that there is something missing in such a case, even when the intentions of both agents are flawless: *sic et in hoc, de quo disputamus, deest aliquid rei datae, cui par alia debetur, non animo, qui animum parem sibi nanctus est et, quantum in illo est, quod voluit effecit.*

In 2.33 Seneca develops this concession to the real world of social exchange and tries to show how it is compatible with the paradoxical view he has been defending. He does this by developing another analogy with a craft, this time sculpture as practised by Phidias. The fruit of his art (*ars*) lies in his own power, and consists of making exactly what he wishes to make; this is a matter dependent on his own state of mind. But the fruit of his artistic activity (*artificium*) lies in the 'profit' gained by practising his craft, either the glory and fame he gains when recognized as a great sculptor, or the more concrete rewards in the form of *gratia* however expressed or in the proceeds from the sale of his work or some other material reward.

Seneca uses this analogy to show that the material return expected in a case of benefiting is not the remaining component of an as yet incomplete social duty, but rather something added on to an already completed *officium*. Hence the first fruit of a benefit lies in the mind of the giver and occurs when he is able to execute the giving as he wishes to do. The second and third fruits are the good repute and material return which may come back to him in return (*quae praestari in vicem possunt*, 2.33.3). Seneca holds, then, that his original position was strictly speaking correct. The *beneficium* itself was a purely mental event involving giver and receiver. The very real and legitimate expectation of return which attaches itself to a benefit is not a component part of that benefit (*extra beneficium est*). The paradox is softened and the social realities of benefit-giving reconciled with the 'purity' of the ethical evaluation of intent by a model adapted from the common Stoic use in ethics of a craft analogy.[64]

Is the objector then back where he started, with grateful repayment not requiring that we do anything (2.34.1)? No, since in the first place the recipient did indeed do something (*primum fecit*): he met good will with good will and did so as an equal, as required by friendship.[65] And the definitive answer is briefly given again: the benefit is repaid in a different way from a loan and is not evaluable on a commercial basis, and this confirms that the socially required repayment, however real and indispensable it might be, is nevertheless distinct from the actual moral exchange. Seneca concludes: *res inter animos geritur*.

This reconciliation of the purely ethical perspective with the realities attendant on the social function of *beneficia* is elaborated on further in 2.34.2–35. In this concluding section Seneca

---

[64] See G. Striker, 'Antipater, or the Art of Living', in M. Schofield and G. Striker (eds.), *The Norms of Nature* (Cambridge and Paris, 1986), 185–204.

[65] This would be a difficult condition to impose on the material return especially if there were, as there often would be, a significant disparity of resources between the friends.

stresses that the view he defends is in fact not contrary to Liberalis' opinion and that he will acknowledge that this is so if he attends to the subtleties of Seneca's presentation: *quod dico, non videbitur durum, quamvis primo contra opinionem tuam pugnet, si te commodaveris mihi et cogitaveris plures esse res quam verba* (2.34.2). Seneca then gives a short disquisition on the ambiguity of words, especially metaphorically generated terms. His first examples are *pes* and *canis*, obvious and familiar cases of metaphorical ambiguity. He extends this explanation to virtue terms like 'courage' and 'parsimony', which are used both for virtuous states of character and non-virtuous states which somewhat resemble them. The things referred to are different in nature but compelled to share a name by the *inopia sermonis*. The clear implication of this passage is that the non-virtuous states designated by virtue terms are so called by a metaphor, because of some similarity to the genuinely virtuous state. Prima-facie virtues are called virtuous, just as preferred indifferents are called good. The similarity of such states to virtue is sufficient for the cultivation of the prima-facie virtue to be a reasonable start for the non-sage.[66]

This is the model for the relationship between the genuine *beneficium*, an action wholly determined by intentions, and the material of interchange, the 'goods' exchanged in such an action; examples are money, a house, political promotion. Such things share the name with the real good deed, but *vis quidem ac potestas longe alia [est]*. It is not explicitly stated in this paragraph that there is a sound reason for the metaphorical transfer of the name from action to thing, but the suggestion is very strong. Whether this is correct as a matter of linguistic fact is doubtful, but the observation effectively bridges the gap between the technically correct and the ordinary (and therefore socially useful) understanding of *beneficium*.

Hence Seneca concludes (2.35.1) that his theory does not in fact contradict any of Liberalis' common-sense beliefs. It is just that there are two levels of activity in any social exchange, the material and the intentional. They are distinct in a number of

[66] Cf. 5.14.5.

ways, most relevantly in that return may be made on one level but not yet on the other: *voluntati voluntate satisfecimus, rei rem debemus.* The paradox is sanitized by restricting its mode of operation to one level only; the connection of the two levels is assured by the non-arbitrary linkage of the names applied. If Seneca allowed that there was no rational or comprehensible relationship between the two senses of the term, then it would be very difficult indeed to explain the ethical relevance of the social practice. As it is, the connection is easy to see. The material exchange of non-moral goods qualifies as a simulacrum (cf. *Ep.* 81.13) of the genuinely virtuous exchange of real spiritual goods; the realities of social life are reflected in the closing sentence of 2.35.1: *itaque, quamvis rettulisse illum gratiam dicamus, qui beneficium libenter accipit, iubemus tamen et simile aliquid ei, quod accepit, reddere.*

The discussion enters its final phase with a pointed comment on the relation of paradoxical theories to the common-sense views which must lie behind any realistic social theory: *a consuetudine quaedam quae dicimus abhorrent, deinde alia via ad consuetudinem redeunt.* The gap between paradox and social reality intended here is indicated by a list of paradoxes. The sage cannot be injured, yet if you punch a sage you have committed an injury. A fool owns nothing, yet you had better not steal from one. All fools are mad, yet not everyone is treated with psychotropic drugs; we even let those lunatics vote and sit on the bench as magistrates. There is a similar gap in play, Seneca says, when we say that if one receives a *beneficium* in the right frame of mind one has repaid it (though some form of material repayment is still expected).

What is the point of such an indirect way of speaking? Many motivations come to my mind, and I would put special emphasis on the protreptic value of such a two-level mode of discourse. While confirming the average *prokoptōn* in his normal allegiance to the stable social conventions of reciprocal *beneficia* (where the goods exchanged are merely preferred things), the paradoxical level points the agent to something higher and better, a sense of good deed which gives 'good' its full technical sense. The agent cannot, of course, act on that level yet, and will not be able to until he is a sage. But it is crucial that he act in the light of an awareness of the existence of that level.

The justification for such language that Seneca himself gives here is also protreptic, but has a more distinctively social justification. The paradoxical claim, he says, is an *exhortatio*, designed to reduce our uneasiness about being enmeshed in the giving and receiving of good deeds.[67] Seneca fears, with good reason I think, that in a hierarchical society with dramatic disparities of wealth and power people will be reluctant to take on the potentially insupportable burden (2.35.3) of such relationships. The feeling that one can never repay what one has been given is an oppressive one, which undermines the social bonds forged by *beneficia*. Knowing how easy it is to repay the aspect of a benefit which really matters is liberating: *vis reddere beneficium? benigne accipe; rettulisti gratiam, non ut solvisse te putes, sed ut securior debeas* (2.35.5) is the conclusion of this book and well summarizes the genuinely social purpose to which Seneca puts his analysis of the traditional paradox. In the course of this discussion of a Stoic paradox Seneca has shown not just that the rigoristic and purely ethical dogma of the school can be reconciled with the realities of social and political life; he has also argued effectively that the metaphysically bound ethics of pure intention can actually strengthen social and political ties in the real world.

The encouragement to accept social indebtedness with an easy mind is the natural complement to the major message of the whole treatise. From the opening lines to the conclusion of book 7 Seneca is persistently concerned with ingratitude and with the discouraging effect it has on the giving of benefits. Seneca's view, of course, is that man's ingratitude should never incite (and cannot justify) the abandonment of giving. That message, the major message of the treatise, is aimed primarily at the givers of benefits and favours, Seneca's social equals—and betters.

---

[67] Compare what Seneca says about the hortatory effect of *hyperbole* at 7.23.

The two sides of this work are the encouragement to give freely despite the likelihood of ungrateful recipients and the reassurance to recipients that one can be indebted with confidence and dignity. The message to his own peers is stronger and clearer than that to the rest of society, but that is not surprising or unreasonable. The crucial point which Seneca sees and elaborates in such a variety of ways throughout the treatise is that social structure, itself an image of the order of the divinely ordained rational cosmos, is founded on the reciprocal bonds between rational animals, who are capable of appreciating and articulating the conventions which bind them to one another. In a work built on casuistical reasoning and rhetorical elaboration, the two most important points linger in the form of images used by Chrysippus and preserved by Seneca:[68] the three Graces dancing happily in a circle with hands joined (*quia ordo beneficii per manus transeuntis nihilo minus ad dantem revertitur*);[69] and the ball players of 2.17.3–4, the success of whose shared enterprise depends completely on a skill exercised co-operatively and considerately. No more apt model could be imagined for the ideal operation of a community of rational social animals.

CONCLUSION

In the *Nicomachean Ethics* Aristotle notices an important difference between friendships based on virtue and those based on utility.[70] In the latter, quarrels about the value of benefits and repayments tend to arise; it is a complex matter to know how to

---

[68] Not necessarily preserved sympathetically. The first of these is sneered at by Seneca, somewhat churlishly in view of his actual agreement with the point at issue. I suspect the dismissal of Chrysippus here, at the beginning of the work, has as much to do with the common Roman contempt for Greeks (which reflects xenophobia as much as anything else) as it does with philosophical judgement. See 1.4.1: *magnum mehercule virum sed tamen Graecum, cuius acumen nimis tenue retunditur et in se saepe replicatur.*

[69] 1.3.4.

[70] *EN* 8.13 1163^{a}9–23.

assess such relative values. In friendships based on virtue, by contrast, complaints do not occur; for the *prohairesis* of the benefactor functions as a measure, and in matters of virtue and character assessment the dominant consideration must be the *prohairesis*. Such a position mirrors Seneca's insistence on the central importance of *voluntas* as the crucial factor in the assessment of benefits and gratitude. In Aristotle's philosophy of social relations, or at least in the crucial part of it which turns up in *EN* 8–9, he must deal with the same polarity which Seneca faces in the *De Beneficiis*. The proper and definitive account of the matter in hand presupposes virtuous agents interacting voluntarily, and in such a case one can safely concentrate on intentions alone. But the real world of social relations is not like that, and a theory of those relations is also needed. Like Aristotle,[71] Seneca wants very much to find a non-arbitrary linkage between those two. He succeeds, to a great degree, in developing such a linkage, and in the discussion here I hope to have outlined one of his methods, the resolution of the tension between the paradoxes of Stoic ethics and the practical realities of giving morally based advice to real and imperfect people functioning in a real and imperfect society. I hope too that this preliminary and tentative discussion sheds a bit of light on the contrast between the lack of practical realism thought to be typical of early Stoic ethics and the alleged realism of middle and later Stoicism. The contrast is not necessarily a chronological one; in a fully preserved treatise like the *De Beneficiis* it is clear that the two aspects of Stoic ethics coexist in a creative and protreptically effective dialectic. The polarization of purely (and paradoxically) ethical theory and practical social reasoning is, in large measure, of our own making, and if we could but read an earlier treatise on benefits and other appropriate actions (perhaps the *Peri charitos* of

---

[71] Aristotle handles the problem in part by means of his typology of friendships; in that typology, the varying kinds of friendships seem to be connected by their relationship to the prototype, the friendship between virtuous people. Pleasure friendships are closer to the ideal than utility friendships. But this is not the place to pursue Aristotle's theory, despite its importance to Seneca's discussion.

Cleanthes)[72] I feel confident that it would be more like the *De Beneficiis* than many of us have so far thought.[73]

---

[72] Which is almost certainly the ultimate source of the discussion of Cleanthes' views at *Ben.* 5.14 discussed above.

[73] I am grateful to a number of people for comments and criticisms. The participants at the symposium were most generous with their time and energy; I particularly recall the energetic suggestions of Julia Annas, Myles Burnyeat, Chris Bobonich, Victor Caston, and Martha Nussbaum. F.-R. Chaumartin, Pierluigi Donini, Miriam Griffin, Carlos Lévy, and John Rist have been generous with their comments and criticisms.

4
Rules and Reasoning in Stoic Ethics

Stoic ethics is often criticized for its impractical rigidity and pointless idealism. Its most prominent feature seems to be its proneness to paradoxical theses, such as claims that all moral errors are equal, that only the wise man is free, and that all human passions should be eliminated rather than moderated. Stoic ethics demands that human beings achieve perfect virtue and act accordingly; the alternative is the complete unhappiness from which all of us suffer. And yet at first sight it appears to offer very little in the way of realistic hope or guidance for people who wish to be happy. It seems to be an abstract and Procrustean dogmatism, which deduces from general principles conclusions which have little bearing on the kind of striving and thinking which normally characterizes ethics. It seems to leave little room for progress in an ethics which (like most others in the ancient world) is centred on the improvement of human character.

My principal debts in the composition of this essay are to Gisela Striker and Phillip Mitsis for the original stimulus to think about these problems and for their patience in discussing them with me. I would also like to thank Michael Frede and Malcolm Schofield for their encouragement and Charles Brittain, Steve Gardiner, and Karen Jones for their helpful criticisms.

Since the mid-1960s more sympathetic and sophisticated accounts of Stoic ethics have, of course, begun to tell a different story. But there is still a gap which remains to be filled. One of the issues on which the Stoics have seemed to be most inflexible and unrealistic has been the role of rules, or laws, in Stoic ethics. In this discussion I want to argue that, when we look more closely at how those notions are used in Stoic ethics, we see that, far from being a source of rigidity, rules and law are more closely connected to a theory of moral reasoning which emphasizes flexibility and situational variability. The particular importance of this theme emerges from a picture of Stoic views on the process of moral reasoning (by which I mean figuring out what to do in circumstances which are non-trivial from the point of view of ethical evaluation) which stands in contrast to the one which would follow from their alleged importance in the development of the idea of 'natural law'.[1] Hence I will also have a few remarks to make about the question of 'natural law' in ancient ethics.

Julia Annas has recently helped to clarify the Stoic position on the nature of moral reasoning and its relationship to such general injunctions.[2] On her view, the Stoics have a coherent and interesting account of the role of various kinds of practical injunctions in moral reasoning, one which can be compared fruitfully with Aristotle's own somewhat provisional account. But more still needs to be done: the relationship of such reasoning to 'law' should be worked out, and a more exact account of how such injunctions are meant to work is, I think, within reach.

One common interpretation of natural law in ancient ethics focuses on the image of law as a set of universal prescriptions and prohibitions, the application of which consists in a quasi-deductive application of such generalizations to particular cases. This notion has been encouraged, of course, by the

[1] See most recently Phillip Mitsis, 'Natural Law and Natural Right in Post-Aristotelian Philosophy: The Stoics and Their Critics', *ANRW* II 36.7 (1994), 4812–50. The author kindly sent me extracts from this discussion before publication, for which (and much stimulating debate over the years) I am most grateful.
[2] J. Annas, *The Morality of Happiness* (Oxford, 1993), 84–108, esp. 95–108.

famous opening words of Chrysippus' *On Law* (preserved by the jurist Marcianus): 'Law is the king of all things, both divine and human; and it must be the guardian, ruler, and leader with regard to what is noble and what is base. Consequently, it is the standard (*kanōn*) of what is just and unjust, and for naturally social animals it commands what is to be done and forbids what is not to be done.'[3] This grandiloquent introduction clearly announces an interest in moral prescription, but does not establish how precise or how binding the prescriptions are meant to be. It is compatible with a deontological system incorporating universal, exceptionless, and substantive moral commands, but also with a somewhat looser and more procedural understanding of moral 'law'. On this latter conception 'law' represents the prescriptive force behind the correct moral choice of an ideal moral reasoner, the sage,[4] whatever the content of that choice might be on a given occasion.[5]

---

[3] *SVF* iii.314. For helpful comment on Marcianus' use of Chrysippus, see P. Vander Waerdt, 'Philosophical Influence on Roman Jurisprudence? The Case of Stoicism and Natural Law', *ANRW* II 36.7 (1994), 4857. See below n. 64.

[4] This is roughly the reading I propose of Plutarch, *De Stoic. Rep.*, Ch. 11 (= *SVF* ii.171, iii.175, 520, 521), which is probably based on Chrysippus' *On Law*, cited in 1037–8. See H. Cherniss's notes ad loc. and esp. *SVF* iii.519. The impulse or decision to act is portrayed as the imperative aspect of a person's reason causing action; the virtuous impulses of the sage are further identified with 'law'.

[5] The former interpretation has in recent years been advocated by G. Striker, 'Origins of the Concept of Natural Law', *Proceedings of the Boston Area Colloquium in Ancient Philosophy*, 2 (1987), 79–94, and in 'Following Nature: A Study in Stoic Ethics', *OSAP* 9 (1991), 1–73. She is followed by Phillip Mitsis, 'Moral Rules and the Aims of Stoic Ethics', *Journal of Philosophy*, 83 (1986), 556–7; in 'Seneca on Reason, Rules and Moral Development', in J. Brunschwig and M. Nussbaum (eds.), *Passions & Perceptions* (Cambridge 1993), 285–312; in 'Natural Law and Natural Right' (with J. DeFilippo) in 'Socrates and Stoic Natural Law', in P. Vander Waerdt (ed.), *The Socratic Movement* (Ithaca, NY, 1994), 252–71. The latter view is one I have argued for in the past: see 'Goal and Target in Stoicism', *Journal of Philosophy*, 83 (1986), 547–56 and my comments on Striker in *Proceedings of the Boston Area Colloquium in Ancient Philosophy*, 2 (1987), 95–101; the view is implicit throughout my *Ethics and Human Action*. Recently Paul Vander Waerdt, 'Zeno's *Republic* and the Origins of Natural Law', in *The Socratic Movement*, 272–308, has given this view strong support. The present account rests on roughly the same picture of Stoic moral theory as Vander Waerdt's, but depends less than his on the difficult problems concerning Zeno's *Republic* and its relationship to Socrates and Plato. I try to show here how later and extant sources, especially Seneca, support the same view of the nature of Stoic moral rules.

I shall argue that the latter understanding of law as a *kanōn* is the correct one.[6] In my view the Stoic model of moral reasoning is not very much like conventional rule-case deduction. Rule-case deduction can take two forms. In the case of positive prescriptions, the agent would be thought of as grasping a general command (e.g. protect the interests of the state), seeing that in some circumstances a particular action (such as enlisting in the armed forces) would count as protecting the interests of the state, and then enlisting as a result of this realization. In the case of a prohibition such as 'do not steal' the situation differs, at least in so far as obeying the prohibition does not in most cases require some definite token action (though an instance of resistance to temptation might in some cases be such a token action). But even in cases of universal prohibitions the agent is thought of as bringing particular situations under a universal injunction and acting accordingly.

Some such picture of rule-following has sometimes been assumed to be the only one possible; indeed, one of the main weaknesses of the competing view of rules and natural law in Stoicism has been the absence of a clear alternative account of the role of rules or other commands in Stoic moral reasoning.[7] In the present discussion I will argue that the Stoics advocated a situationally fluid, heuristic process of choice, framed (but not determined) by a general normative context, and that the connection to 'law' is not to natural law as a system of substantive and universal rules. I will question just how rigid Stoic moral injunctions were, and show that if there is a connection between Stoic moral reasoning and a notion of 'law' (beyond the obvious imperatival aspect of law incorporated into the analysis of action by Chrysippus (see n. 5)), it is to non-deductive modes of legal reasoning, one of which I shall exploit in order to bring out the character of the Stoic theory.

---

[6] A key issue in this debate is whether there are in fact any documented examples of substantive and exceptionless moral principles in our evidence for Stoicism. The credentials for the few candidates which have been proposed turn out to be very weak. See below.

[7] P. Vander Waerdt (ed.), *The Socratic Movement* (Ithaca, NY, 1994) does not fully address this need and my earlier accounts have been too sketchy.

The Stoic view of moral reasoning and the place in it of rules will turn out to have an inexactitude reminiscent of that recognized by Aristotle.[8] Like the Stoics, Aristotle recognizes that there must be a balance between articulate deliberation of some sort and the immediate 'perception' of what is morally relevant in a concrete situation.[9] Aristotle is not, of course, committed to the view that an agent can just intuit the right thing to do; it is always a matter of deliberation, and even where action is too immediate for there to have been time for a conscious deliberation, it is still appropriate to provide a justification for it cast in terms of an imputed deliberation. But such deliberations are not straightforward applications of general rules to particular cases. The Stoics will on my account be committed to a similarly flexible view of moral reasoning.

In the final analysis, however, it is very difficult to give a complete and coherent account of Aristotle's position on the use of rules in moral reasoning; as Annas says, 'Aristotle has in fact not thought through the place of rules in the virtuous person's thought.'[10] Some general moral injunctions or rules are clearly at play in the so-called practical syllogism and in the process of character formation. But Aristotle never clarifies how they are to function in particular acts of choice, nor does he show very much interest in determining the limitations of rule-application, though obviously he recognizes that such limits exist. By

---

[8] Aristotle's views on the inevitable inexactitude of ethics have been explored in a recent book by Georgios Anagnostopoulos, *Aristotle on the Goals and Exactness of Ethics* (Berkeley, 1994). See in particular ch. 10. Anagnostopoulos situates Aristotle in a middle ground between a deductive and universalistic conception of moral reasoning and a particularistic view which borders on an intuitionism of particular cases. See also the wide-ranging discussions, focused on *EN* 6, by David Wiggins 'Deliberation and Practical Reason', in A. O. Rorty (ed.), *Essays on Aristotle's Ethics* (Berkeley, 1980), 221–40, and by Martha Nussbaum, *The Fragility of Goodness* (Cambridge 1986), ch. 10 (cf. her 'The Discernment of Perception: An Aristotelian Conception of Private and Public Rationality', *Proceedings of the Boston Area Colloquium in Ancient Philosophy*, 1 (1985), 151–201). Annas (*The Morality of Happiness*, 87–90) has given a particularly clear account of where Aristotle should be thought to stand on the issue of intuitionism in ethics.

[9] Op. cit. 89 and n. 139 Annas assesses the importance of Aristotle's claim that moral judgement is 'perception'.

[10] Op. cit. 94. Cf. the remarks of Nussbaum, *The Fragility of Goodness*, 299–300.

contrast, the Stoics were more explicitly interested in rule-like moral commands, just as they were interested in the actual procedures of moral choice. We can, therefore, despite the fragmentary state of our sources, hope for a more complete account.

One more similarity should be noted. Just as Aristotle needs to distinguish between the reasoning of a fully virtuous agent and that of someone who is in the process of moral development,[11] the Stoics also have two markedly different kinds of agents to account for. Far more sharply than Aristotle, the Stoics distinguish the wise man, or sage, from the ordinary moral agent (even one who has made considerable progress); the moral capacities of these two kinds of agent are crucially different, and so the Stoics eventually came to use two distinct terms for moral deliberation: 'selection' and 'choice' in the narrow sense (*eklogē, hairesis*).[12] This explicit duality in their formal account of moral deliberation reflects a sort of dualism of moral agents. The gap between the wise and the rest of us looks very sharp indeed.

There is a conventional understanding of this dualism which is quite misleading.[13] It has often been held that the gap between the wise and the non-wise reflects a basic ethical dualism, that the Stoics offered *two* moralities, one for the wise and one for the rest.[14] That this is not so is indicated by the basic Stoic claim

[11] Annas, *The Morality of Happiness*, 89–90.

[12] I have given an account of this difference in ch. 6 of *Ethics and Human Action*, esp. 206–15.

[13] See 'Stoic Ethics I', in K. Algra et al. (eds.), *Cambridge History of Hellenistic Philosophy* (Cambridge, 1999), 675–6; *Ethics and Human Action*, Ch. 6.

[14] This interpretation of the history of Stoicism was advanced forcefully by A. Schmekel, *Die Philosophie der mittleren Stoa* (Berlin, 1892). This interpretation was encouraged, possibly even suggested, by what Seneca says about Panaetius at *Ep.* 116.4–5. But the distinction between the wise man and the fool there is limited to the issue of practical advice about self-control. See my discussion in 'Why do Fools fall in Love?', in R. Sorabji (ed.), *Aristotle and After* (Bulletin of the Institute of Classical Studies, Supp. 68; London, 1997), 55–69. On the influence of this idea, see the summary survey by I. Hadot, *Seneca und die griechisch-römische Tradition der Seelenleitung* (Berlin, 1969), 71–8. Hadot's own view (78) still takes the notion of a middle Stoa (which is not attested by any ancient sources) rather too seriously, though it is a great step forward over most of the tradition.

that the characteristic act of the wise man, a *katorthōma*, is itself a kind of *kathēkon* or appropriate action.[15] Yet there are important differences between wise men and other kinds of moral agents, and the most important of these lies in their different relationship to moral rules or to laws. Whatever the role of rules or other prescriptions in the moral life of ordinary men, it is clear that ideally wise moral agents (however rare they may be) are reported to have a different relation to them.[16] The wise man is said to have a special kind of authority with regard to normally binding moral rules.[17] It is presumably in connection with such special authority that both Zeno and Chrysippus allowed that in some circumstances such taboo activities as cannibalism and incest would be permissible.[18] Wise men and the rest of us seem to have different relationships to moral rules.

The Stoic analysis of moral choice needs to be situated in the framework of two distinctively Stoic theories. First, their articulation of the different kinds of values of things or states of affairs (roughly, the sorts of things which can be the central objects of moral choice) needs to be taken into account; second, the sharp distinction drawn between appropriate actions (*kathēkonta*) and morally right actions (*katorthōmata*) is relevant, as are some distinctions among different kinds of appropriate acts. As far as the theory of value is concerned, a summary account should suffice. For the relevant range, everything can be classified as either good, bad, or indifferent.[19] The only goods are

---

[15] *Ethics and Human Action*, 208 and n. 120; see also Cicero, *Fin.* 3.59 and below, n.53.

[16] The nature of this difference is, however, controversial. See the exchange between myself and Mitsis in *Journal of Philosophy*, 83 (1986), 547–58.

[17] DL 7.121 juxtaposes the acknowledgement that the most sacred taboos can be broken in some circumstances with a key definition of the sage's freedom: it consists in his 'authority to act autonomously' (*exousian autopragias*). In 7.125 it is noted that such complete authority is granted to sages by 'the law'. Similarly at *Ecl.* ii. 102. 8–9 the wise man is said to be law-abiding just because he is the only proper interpreter of the law. Cf. *Ecl.* ii.108.28, where the wise man is said to be king because only kingship entails the highest authority, one not subject to accountability (*anhupeuthunon archēn*).

[18] For the evidence on this, see Vander Waerdt, 'Zeno's *Republic*', 300–1, with notes.

[19] The classification of things into good, bad, and indifferent is important enough that it is used by Stobaeus (or his source) as the opening theme of his Stoic

virtue and what 'participates' in virtue; conversely for bad and vice.[20] Everything else is 'indifferent', though here again a distinction is drawn between things which play a positive role in a normal, healthy life (preferred indifferents) and those which play a negative role (dispreferred indifferents).[21] Health is a typical preferred and illness a typical dispreferred. There are also 'absolute indifferents' which play no role at all—such as whether the number of hairs on one's head is odd or even. This doctrine is the key to understanding the latitude for choice which Stoicism leaves to the rational agent. A startling range of things, indeed virtually everything that human beings normally think about when making morally significant choices, falls into this category. Yet the 'good', virtue and what participates in virtue, is the real determinant of moral success. Preferred things, such as health and wealth, may be natural to us as humans; but they cannot be guaranteed to be the appropriate things to pursue in all circumstances; the recommendation implicit in labelling them 'preferred' can operate only at the level of general types, since in some concrete cases they might in fact be disadvantageous. In contrast, virtue is always and in every case beneficial—just as one might expect on the basis of Socratic theory.[22]

Moral injunctions and recommendations, 'laws' and rules, all typically deal with actions rather than things, and the Stoic classification of morally pertinent actions is closely parallel to their classification of the objects of choice. Appropriate actions

doxography (*Ecl.* ii.57.18–58.4); the tripartition underlies parts of the organization of Cicero's and Diogenes Laertius' presentations of Stoic ethics.

[20] DL 7.94; *Ecl.* ii.57.20–58.4.

[21] See DL 7.102–7 and my discussion in 'Stoic Ethics I', *CHHP*. H. W. Ausland ('On the Moral Origin of the Pyrrhonian Philosophy', *Elenchos*, 10 (1989), 380 ff.) refers to a Stoic view which sorted indifferent things 'in accordance with several degrees of indifference'. The 'several' is puzzling; I do not see much in Stoic sources which makes it natural to speak of 'degrees' of indifference—except, that is, for the contrast between utterly insignificant things and the preferred/dispreferred. His discussion of the orthodox Stoic classification of indifferents at 398–400 seems to me to strain at fine distinctions in order to enhance its parallelism with Pyrrhonian 'theory'.

[22] See the debate between Ariston of Chios and more conventional Stoics as represented in Sextus *M* 11.64–7; cf. my discussion in 'Stoic Ethics I', *CHHP*.

correspond roughly to preferred indifferents and morally correct actions correspond to the good. The former can only be specified in a general way, at the level of types, and the generalizations can be no more than approximate. Hence the most enlightening definition of appropriate action is as 'that which, when done, admits of a reasonable defence';[23] what is required is not a probative or certain justification, nor a justification in terms of moral rightness or virtue. The standard of judgement here is quasi-forensic, as suggested by the use of the technical term *apologia*. By contrast, morally right actions are defined in terms of their relationship to rightness or virtue[24] and so are either concrete tokens (i.e. all pertinent acts performed by a sage) or universal but vacuous generalizations (such as 'prudent walking').[25]

Against the background of such a classification of actions and objects of action, rules and recommendations can be tricky. Types of actions are described as appropriate or non-appropriate; but there is always a further judgement to be made on the level of tokens: each individual action is itself either correct or wrong (*katorthōma, hamartēma*). There can be no universal and substantive rules about choosing or acting—appropriate actions are subject to 'special circumstances',[26] which in the extreme case might even justify cannibalism,[27] and preferred

---

[23] DL 7.107.

[24] See *Ecl.* ii.96.20–2. They are also defined in relation to appropriate actions (they are 'perfect' appropriate actions (*Ecl.* ii. 85.9–20, 2.93.14–16)).

[25] See Annas, *The Morality of Happiness*, 97–8. The connection between preferred indifferents and appropriate actions is very close; generally speaking, an appropriate action is one aimed at gaining a preferred indifferent, just as a morally right action is one aimed at a genuine good as such.

[26] See White, 'Two Notes on Stoic Terminology', *American Journal of Philology*, 99 (1978), 111–19. Acts which are appropriate only in special circumstances must be what Philo has in mind at *SVF* iii.513: *to mē kathēkon estin hote dratai kathēkontōs*.

[27] At DL 7.121 eating human flesh is mentioned as something that the sage will do in special circumstances. DL 7.121 also reports the common view that the sage will participate in political life unless there is some relevant obstacle. For cannibalism and incest (in particular Chrysippus' treatment of Oedipus and Jocasta), see Vander Waerdt 'Zeno's *Republic*', 300–1 and nn. 102–4. What makes DL 7.121 so important for present purposes is the connection it makes between taboo-breaking and the freedom of the wise man. On DL 7.121 and 7.125 (and on other comparable evidence) see n. 18 above.

indifferents are often to be avoided. Only virtue is always beneficial and only an action defined with intrinsic reference to virtue is always appropriate.[28] There is no determinate action type which is in itself right or wrong, except under vacuous descriptions which contain a built-in reference to virtue or vice: 'prudent walking', or more generally 'virtuous

---

[28] *aei kathēkonta* DL 7.109. The only example given is 'living according to virtue'. Mitsis ('Natural Law and Natural Right', 4837) puzzlingly adds 'honouring one's parents, brothers and country, and living in the society of friends' to this category; the same move is made again in DeFilippo and Mitsis, 'Socrates and Stoic Natural Law', 267 n. 23. Mitis appears to follow the *inference* made in Long and Sedley, *The Hellenistic Philosophers*, i. 366, rather than the clear evidence of Diogenes Laertius' text. Mitsis does not quote the primary evidence upon which he relies. (Long and Sedley give no argument on the point.) Vander Waerdt, 'Zeno's *Republic*', 274 n. 10 reports DL 7.108–9 correctly when he says: 'Thus "living according to virtue" is the only example we are offered of an *aei kathēkon*.' Another possible source of support for Mitsis's view, Cicero, *Fin*. 3.32, does not determine the issue. (The contrast is only between acts, such as betraying one's country or attacking one's parents, which are good examples of overt (*in effectu*) bad actions and passions which are not necessarily overt; Cicero is not saying that there is a universal rule not to do those things.) It would, at any rate, be wrong to claim that Stoics believe that we should unconditionally honour our parents and other family members (except in the sense that 'honouring', as a virtue-word, includes the presupposition that the act is done virtuously). See e.g. Epictetus, *Diss*. 3.3.5–10 which shows that any choice between virtue (the good) and one's father would be made in favour of virtue; *Ench*. 30 shows only that in the normal case honouring a parent is incumbent on the agent, not that it is exceptionlessly obligatory (see *Diss*. 2.10.7 for the list of filial duties). Further, in any given case it is open to question what particular action would count as honouring a parent. That there could be debate about this kind of issue is suggested not just by Cicero's representation of such a debate at *Off*. 3.90 and by Epictetus' many allusions to the issue but also by the numerous debates reported by the Elder Seneca in his *Controversiae* which turn on a conflict of obligations between father and son. The Younger Seneca notes (*Ben*. 2.18.1) that one has to *learn* how to handle the *officia* involved in the father–child relationship; *Ben*. 3.31.3 argues that mere parenthood is not enough to establish unconditional obligations; and at *Ben*. 6.4.2 the repudiation of a bad father is clearly contemplated. But the clearest proof that honouring one's parents is only held to be unconditionally obligatory if by it we mean doing what is morally right can be found in Musonius, *Diatribe* 16; in the Socratic spirit of the early Stoics, Musonius argues that refusing to obey a parent is not disobedience if the command is morally wrong and that doing what is morally right is obedience *even if the parent does not instruct the child to do it*. Near the end of *Diatribe* 16 a father forbids his son to study philosophy, but the obligation to study philosophy overrides the short-sighted parental command (cf. Epictetus, *Diss*. 1.26.5–7). Vander Waerdt ('Zeno's *Republic*', 301 n. 105) reports another unconvincing candidate for being an exceptionless moral rule, the injunction against building temples, but rightly rejects it.

action'.[29] Such evaluative descriptions of course pick out correct actions, but not in a way which is directly informative or useful to the agent. Contrast them with types of actions described in a way which is immediately meaningful to an ordinary deliberating agent but which can only be evaluated as being *generally* appropriate.

This shows how much flexibility in choice is recognized in basic Stoic theory. It also underlines certain important similarities with Aristotelian theory, where the concrete particularities of a situation calling for moral choice must be taken into account by the *phronimos*, who alone can be counted on to give a correct assessment of such factors as the 'how', the 'when', 'with respect to whom', and so forth. We began from Julia Annas's lucid discussion of the difficulties long recognized in reconciling Aristotle's incipient interest in moral 'rules' with such situational variability. If the Stoics explicitly recognize a similar need for situational sensitivity and combine this with a developed interest in systematic moral injunctions (whether called 'rules' or 'natural law'), how can they escape dealing with the dilemma which Aristotle only avoided by leaving his theory of rules vague?

Of course, we do have clear evidence that this need for situational sensitivity and variability was recognized by Stoics throughout the school's history. Indeed, Ariston of Chios was, as has long been recognized, so concerned with such variability that he rejected general precept-giving of any substantive sort

---

[29] *Ecl.* ii. 70.11, DL 7.94. The phrases *hosa mē hairei logos* and *hosa hairei logos* at DL 7.108 do not indicate unconditional injunctions to act issued by reason, though as the contrast with *apagoreuei* in 7.109 shows it is imperatival. Long and Sedley (*The Hellenistic Philosophers*) seem to mistranslate the key phrase *hosa mē hairei logos*. They say 'ones which reason does not dictate our doing'; but that produces nonsense when the examples are considered. 'Neglecting parents, not caring about brothers', etc. are not merely things which reason does not require us to do; they are things which reason urges us not to do. One should translate 'things which reason tells us not to do'. (See H. W. Smyth, *Greek Grammar* (Cambridge, Mass., 1956), 2692, for the construction.) The use of *hairei* does not entail an exceptionless prescription; Vander Waerdt translates it 'prevails upon' ('Zeno's *Republic*', 274 n. 9), which seems too weak but at least flags the non-universal nature of the prescription.

altogether,[30] opting for a position which Annas rightly calls 'the only explicitly intuitionist theory in ancient ethics'.[31] Seneca, who is a crucial source for our understanding of Stoic views on moral injunctions, also recognizes the importance of such situational factors. In *Ep.* 71.1 he explicitly claims that 'the majority of deliberation turns on the immediate circumstances' (*magna pars consilii in tempore*), and that the particularities of an action (the 'when' and 'how', as he puts it) cannot be dictated universally. That is why it is so useful to have an adviser right at hand, in the form of a close friend. The lengths to which such flexibility might go are clear from an earlier letter (*Ep.* 22.7–8). Having noted (*Ep.* 22.2) that universal instructions cannot deal satisfactorily with particularities (such as *quando fieri debeat aut quemadmodum*), Seneca goes on to discuss how to help Lucilius to disengage from an excessively busy professional life, and has first offered him an Epicurean perspective.

I think you are now asking for a Stoic view too. Don't let anybody slander them to you for boldness. Their caution exceeds their bravery. Maybe you think that they will say to you: 'It is shameful to yield to a burden; struggle to fulfil a task once you have taken it on. He who avoids effort is not a brave and energetic man unless the difficult experience makes his spirit stronger.' They *will* say this to you—*if* perseverance turns out to be worth the effort and as long as you don't have to do or suffer anything unworthy of a good man; *otherwise* he will not wear himself out with base and despicable effort nor will he stick to the business just for the sake of it. He won't even do what you think he will: endure the turmoil of being involved in political affairs. Rather, when he sees the difficulties in which he is entangled, the uncertainties and the risks, he will withdraw—not run away; but gradually he will fall back to safety.

This acknowledgement of how a positive moral trait such as determination can be situationally inappropriate makes a striking contrast to the common picture of Stoic endurance: on this Stoic view, constant reassessment of the pay-off in any situation

---

[30] See my discussion in 'Stoic Ethics I', *CHHP*; A. M. Ioppolo, *Aristone di Chioe lo stoicismo antico* (Rome, 1980) 152–4, 181–3, and recently Ausland, 'On the Moral Origin', 381 ff.

[31] *The Morality of Happiness*, 102.

is called for. This confirms the view that Stoics are not wedded to a theory of moral recommendations or rules which are substantive, universal, and exceptionless. It follows from all of this that the recommendations about moral choices based on Stoic axiology work as non-universal generalizations.

The debate with Ariston raises some crucial questions about the role of rules and generalizations in ethics. In an important discussion of 'natural law', 'Natural Law and Natural Right',[32] Phillip Mitsis pursues the contrary line of argument, which holds that natural law consisted in a set of invariable rules about good which have a substantive content definite enough to dictate what a moral agent must do in a concrete circumstance. As we have seen, one very serious problem with this position lies in the difficulty one has in finding in our sources any such thing, called a 'law' or even a 'rule', which is more determinate than injunctions to live virtuously, act rightly, and so forth—for this is the level of generality which one sees in Chrysippus' *On Law* and elsewhere.[33] Such advice is sound enough, if you know how to apply it. That it is exceptionlessly right to pursue virtue and choose the good is true enough, and *in some sense* not vacuous; but from the point of view of the choosing agent who is not yet a sage it is hard to see how this would provide any substantive guidance. Another problem might be found in the flexible nature of rule application in the few texts where Stoics or Stoic-influenced writers actually talk about what might pass for 'rules'.

It has long been recognized that the most important discussion of such 'rules' in Stoicism can be found in two letters by Seneca, numbers 94 and 95. At least since Ian Kidd's pathbreaking 'Moral Actions and Rules in Stoicism'[34] it has been normal to read these letters, which constitute an intricate

---

[32] *ANWR* II.36.7, 4812–50. In doing so, he is following a view first developed by Gisela Striker, 'Origins of the Concept of Natural Law'. See above n. 5 for other references. Mitsis is followed by Annas, *The Morality of Happiness*, 107.

[33] Above and n. 28. In fact, in one key passage (DL 7.88) the life according to nature is described as 'doing nothing which the common law *generally* forbids'. This text constrains the grand exordium of Chrysippus' *On Law* at *SVF* iii.314.

[34] In J. M. Rist (ed.), *The Stoics* (Berkeley, 1978), 247–58.

examination of the place in ethical theory and practice of *praecepta* (or moral instructions) and *decreta* (or moral principles), as being about 'rules'; Kidd also established that the relevant context for this discussion was the more general Stoic theory of values and kinds of action. The tradition of interpreting *praecepta* and/or *decreta* as rules has been very hardy, despite the difficulties occasioned by the Stoics' acknowledgement of variability and flexibility in moral action, features which make 'rule' (with its connotations of fixity) subtly inappropriate. The further move, initiated by Striker in 1987, of associating such rules with natural law only exacerbates the problem.

Phillip Mitsis addresses the tension between the fixity suggested by 'rules' and the subtlety of Stoic moral practice in his 'Seneca on Reason, Rules and Moral Development',[35] arguing that *praecepta* and *decreta* should be understood as 'rules', that 'moral judgement and development are structured at every level by rules; and [that] these rules are grasped by reason alone' (291). He then acknowledges the force of several critiques of rule-based ethics (291–3, 295–7) and sets out to show how Seneca's theory of moral decision-making has the resources to survive many such objections. His analysis of letters 94 and 95 is in most respects convincing; but in the end it is not clear that he has justified the traditional identification of *praecepta* and/or *decreta* with rules, in the sense of moral injunctions which are at the same time substantive and exceptionless.[36]

It is important to get straight about this issue, since the 'rules' putatively identified with natural law are of considerable importance in Stoic moral reasoning. If they are exceptionless principles enjoining definite act types, then the use of these rules (whether called *decreta* or *praecepta*) in moral reasoning will be subject to the sorts of criticism levelled at any deductive model of ethical reasoning.[37] What is needed at this point is a

[35] The account in 'Natural Law and Natural Right', 4844–50 is similar.

[36] In 'Natural Law and Natural Right' he attempts to give examples of such injunctions under the guise of *aei kathēkonta*. See esp. 4837–8. But the only substantive obligation of the type which he can cite is in fact based on no direct textual evidence. See above, n. 28.

[37] On the general issue, see the discussion in Mitsis, 'Seneca on Reason, Rules and Moral Development'.

way forward which avoids merely terminological solutions and can give an adequate account of the following: the pervasive generality of moral injunctions; the utility of moral injunctions in guiding choice in concrete situations; the susceptibility of substantive injunctions to exceptions; and the apparent authority of the wise man to decide on permissible exceptions. If we can preserve a connection between such injunctions and a notion of 'law', then that will be a bonus; and it will be a further advantage if the Stoic theory of recommendations and precepts can be cast as dealing with 'rules'.

One account which seems particularly promising in this regard is that given recently by Frederick Schauer in *Playing by the Rules*,[38] following in part the work of Rawls in 1955.[39] One of Schauer's main concerns—and one which goes to the heart of our concern with pragmatic exceptions to rules—is with the obvious fact that rules when applied to situations can conflict with the background justification which grounds the rule. When such a conflict does occur, rule-following reasoners can react in different ways: they can reassess the situation and decide in view of the values and assessments which underlie the background justification, in which case the rule is a dispensable rule of thumb; they can find reasons to relocate the case in hand *outside* the scope of the rule to which it prima facie applies; or they can decide in accordance with the rule (perhaps in a modified form). This last reaction is hard-core rule following, and is characteristic of situations and institutions in which the rule is (in Schauer's terms) 'entrenched', that is, followed even when it conflicts with the substantive justification for the rule's existence.

The relevance of Schauer's work on rules to the Stoic problem is this: he shows how something can be a rule and still be completely defeasible by situational moral reasoning—it is then

---

[38] F. Schauer, *Playing by the Rules: A Philosophical Examination of Rule-Based Decision-Making in Law and in Life* (Oxford, 1991).
[39] J. Rawls, 'Two Concepts of Rules', *Philosophical Review*, 64 (1955), 3–32. There is also an interesting discussion of the flexibility and rigidity of legal and moral obligation in John Finnis, *Natural Law and Natural Rights* (Oxford, 1980), ch. 11, esp. 11.3.

a rule of thumb. Moreover, he provides a convincing discussion of the reasons for which one might want to entrench rules *even when* they are certain to yield sub-optimal results in many cases. Since *praecepta* are important in Stoic moral reasoning, it helps to compare such *praecepta* to Schauer's rules. Like them, *praecepta* are always subject to what he calls situational inadequacy; and nevertheless, as we shall see, there are good reasons to entrench them, reasons which include justifiable doubts about the ability of the typical rational agent to decide correctly in many circumstances, the intractable mass of information relevant to a particular decision, and the inevitably open texture of moral decision contexts.

Schauer's work shows that practical reasoning can employ rules and yet escape most of the common grounds for criticism of rule-based systems, and that deductive rule-case reasoning is not the only way to use rules which preserves their normative force.[40] Hence it helps to create room for a more flexible assessment of the Stoic account of moral reasoning, leaving scope for its compatibility with the autonomy and freedom of the wise man. For the generality and defeasibility of rules on this view is compatible with insisting that they should function as constraining rules or generally stable guidelines for *ordinary* decision-makers and also with allowing an *idealized* moral reasoner to set aside the rule, to de-entrench it and treat it as no more than a dispensable rule of thumb, an aid and guide to moral reasoning but no more. None of the theoretical discussions of rules normally invoked can account for the distinct ways in which rules function for the wise man and the mere progressor; Schauer's can. A further advantage will be that his theory provides a framework which works for a range of texts wider than the two key letters of Seneca, including Cicero's *De Officiis* and other works of Seneca.

---

[40] By contrast, the typical view of moral rules forces us to choose between regarding them as mere rules of thumb without independent normative force and a view which endows them with some ultimate and general normative power independent of particular situations. Nussbaum's posing of the dilemma at *The Fragility of Goodness*, 299–300, is typical; Mitsis and Striker make the same assumption, though not so overtly.

Rules and Reasoning in Stoic Ethics

Confusions about the status of rules in Stoicism dissolve when one resorts to a fully articulated theory of rules like Schauer's. Thinking of Ariston's challenge to mainstream Stoicism (as reported by Sextus in *Adversus Mathematicos* 11.64–7), we can now say that mainstream Stoics did not insist on the universal connections which Ariston demanded and were prepared to talk about natural preferability (preferred status) without insisting that it represent a class every token member of which is worth choosing.[41] Ariston, unlike Chrysippus, does not want any moral agent to be guided by defeasible rules—he will insist on obedience to such invariant rules as 'pursue the good' or on deliberation which is based directly on substantive background justifications. The mainstream Stoic will allow the wise man to reason in that direct way, if he sees fit, but offer to all other moral agents entrenched but modifiable general rules prescribing appropriate actions as a framework for their thinking. This freedom to reason directly in terms of substantive justifications is the basis for what our sources recognize as the sage's authority to act on his own, even in contradiction of the 'rules'.[42]

It is vital to moral reasoning that the agent know which kinds of actions are normally appropriate and why. That is why they are the subject of 'rules' or instructions (*praecepta*). But it is also crucial that the agent be good at spotting relevant exceptional circumstances. What the Stoics need—and I hope to show that they have it in the *formulae* and *regulae* found in Seneca and Cicero—is a set of tools for moral reasoning which link up their general principles with concrete actions and decision contexts.

The distinction between normally and exceptionally appropriate actions operates at the level of types; it is a distinct point about token actions that the concrete particulars of each situation, including the character of the agent and the place of the action in his life as a whole, determine the final moral evaluation of that particular action. And even when the particulars of the agent's character and situation determine that a given action was wrong, the action may well turn out to have been appropriate; as

---

[41] See 'Stoic Ethics I', *CHHP*.   [42] See nn. 13, 24 above and esp. DL 7.121.

long as the action, when done, admitted of a reasonable defence or justification, then it was appropriate. The dialectical/rhetorical notion of the 'reasonable' and the forensic notion of a 'defence' help to characterize Stoic moral reasoning (which centres on determining what action is appropriate in a given context) in a way that mediates between the need for situational sensitivity and the demand for stable general principles.

For an illustration of how this connection between contingent moral reasoning and more permanent values might work, we might look to Seneca's *De Beneficiis*. That treatise is intensely concerned with the practicalities of ethical reasoning. But what most clearly makes the connection we need now is found in 4.9–11. In 4.9.3 Seneca says: 'We pursue what is morally fine (*honestum, kalon*) only for its own sake; nevertheless, even if there is nothing else worth pursuing, we still investigate what we should do, and when, and in what manner.[43] For it [the morally fine] comes to exist through these factors (*per haec enim constat*).'[44] In what follows, Seneca stresses that the point of moral goodness is to be found in the rationality of the *procedures* of choice.[45]

Returning a deposit is something desirable in itself. Nevertheless, I will not always return one, nor will I do so at any old place or time. Sometimes it makes no difference whether I deny the deposit or return it openly. I shall consider the interests of him to whom I am to return it and I will refuse to return something which would harm him. I shall do the same thing with a benefit. I shall consider when I give, to whom, in what manner, why. For nothing should be done without rational reflection (*sine ratione*); for only what is given on the basis of rational reflection is a benefit, since rational reflection is the invariable companion of moral fineness.[46]

[43] Note the similarities to Aristotle's approach, which reflects the looseness required by any realistic account of moral reasoning. Cf. *Ep.* 95.43.
[44] Cf. the similar account in *Ep.* 81.
[45] Cf. *Ep.* 84.11 on the role of *ratio* and *adsidua intentio* in each moral decision.
[46] *Ben.* 4.10.1–2. Compare *Ben.* 3.14, which emphasizes that the injunction to 'give back what you owe' is not in moral matters subject to legal enforcement because it is merely formal. No law, he says, can regulate the return of morally significant favours; one has to rely on the good faith of other people. Part of the reason lies in the difficulty of assessing the value of things and so estimating what one really does owe.

This, I think, is a clear example of Stoic moral reasoning at work (on a notably traditional problem): situationally sensitive thinking within the framework of a general rule which is defeasible but at least partly entrenched. In this case, only a very sophisticated moral reasoner should make the judgements anticipated by Seneca—a moral klutz or a man with limited self-knowledge will clearly do less harm by following the rule than by thinking for himself. This illustrates one of Schauer's justifications for entrenching defeasible rules.[47]

There is another Stoic doctrine which can be illuminated by this approach:[48] suicide is permissible in early Stoicism, but only when a clear and correct judgement can be made about one's situation in life. No one but a wise person can do so; so only a wise person ought to commit suicide. The paradox that only a man endowed with perfect happiness should kill himself did not escape their critics, but the view makes sense: there is a general rule against suicide, based on our natural preference for life, but it is a defeasible rule of thumb. Still, only a truly wise man can be relied on to make the decision well. So the rest of us normally follow the rule, the more urgently in the case of a decision which cannot be reconsidered should new information come to light or additional reflection indicate a different choice.[49]

In both of these cases, deciding whether to repay a debt or whether to commit suicide, there is a general injunction in play; there is also a host of particular factors which must be taken into account. It might in principle be possible to analyse the Stoic understanding of such situations in terms of a large number of exceptionless general rules, perhaps hierarchically arranged, so

---

[47] Compare Finnis, *Natural Law and Natural Rights*, 308–10, on promising.
[48] See *SVF* iii, ch. 11.
[49] Of course, in Seneca this attitude to suicide changed considerably, in effect by allowing a wider range of moral agents to reason not in terms of the rule but fallibly, in terms of the substantive justifications for the rule. See *Ep.* 70.11: 'So, when external violence brings imminent death, you cannot make any universal pronouncement about whether to pursue it or to wait for it; there are many considerations which might draw in either direction.' Clearly Seneca thinks that the ordinary, non-wise moral agent is supposed to be making these difficult evaluations, whereas an earlier Stoic would have restricted such choices to the wise man.

that (as Striker[50] and Mitsis might wish) even the sage's decision could be seen as the result of entrenched rule-following of a particularly complex sort; the same situations could be understood as the outcome of making intelligent situational exceptions to general rules. Allowing, for the sake of argument, that either model could provide an adequate rational reconstruction of the phenomena, I would claim that the latter model fits better with the evidence we have about Stoic procedures of moral reasoning, none of which seems to invoke the intersection of various rules or hierarchical structures of rules (these being the principal alternative strategies for reconciling universal rules with situational variability).

It is regrettable that, despite our wealth of information about the general doctrines of Stoic ethics, we do not possess a single treatise dealing specifically with how to make moral choices: the early works *On Appropriate Actions* are all lost.[51] As we have seen, Seneca's *De Beneficiis* and *Epistulae* are of some help. We can also look to Cicero's *De Officiis*, an idiosyncratic work (based in part on Panaetius' *On Appropriate Actions*), but one which Cicero himself says is most closely concerned with precepts applicable to the *vita communis*.[52] The basic plan of the book turns on the practical moral reasoning of ordinary agents, and Cicero reports on the general kinds of questions which engage them. In *Off.* 1.9 he writes (trans. Atkins):[53]

[50] For Striker's commitment to the use of higher-order rules, see the reprinting of 'The Origins of the Concept of Natural Law', repr. in *Essays on Hellenistic Epistemology and Ethics* (Cambridge, 1996), 219–20 n. 8. For a more subtle view of the issue, see Schauer, *Playing by the Rules*, 45 n.7: 'Thus, the difference between a rule with exceptions and simply a narrower rule is semantic and not structural, and there is no difference that matters between modifying a rule and adding an exception. The difference that *does* matter is the difference between a modification (or an exception) that applies only in future cases and one that is applied to the very case that prompted it.'

[51] We know of works on this theme by Zeno, Cleanthes (but, significantly, not Ariston or Herillus), Sphaerus, Chrysippus (at least seven books (*SVF* iii.688)), Hecaton (a student of Panaetius), and Posidonius.

[52] *Off.* 1.7. Note that Cicero goes out of his way to assert that such precept-based *officia* are in fact pertinent to the goal of life, but that this fact is less obvious. It is not completely clear to me what is meant by *vita communis* here, but *communis* probably has the same sense that it has at *Fin.* 3.59 (see above n. 15).

[53] M. T. Griffin and E. M. Atkins (eds. and trs.), *Cicero: On Duties* (Cambridge, 1991).

There are in consequence, as it seems to Panaetius, three questions to deliberate when deciding upon a plan of action. In the first place, men may be uncertain whether the thing that falls under consideration is an honourable or a dishonourable thing to do; often, when they ponder this, their spirits are pulled between opposing opinions. Secondly, they investigate or debate whether or not the course they are considering is conducive to the advantageousness and pleasantness of life, to opportunities and resources for doing things, to wealth and to power, all of which enable them to benefit themselves and those dear to them. All such deliberation falls under reasoning about what is beneficial. The third type of uncertainty arises when something apparently beneficial appears to conflict with what is honourable: benefit seems to snatch you to its side and honourableness in its turn to call you back; consequently the spirit is pulled this way and that in its deliberation, and it arouses in its reflection a care that is double-edged.

Cicero goes on to complain about topics omitted by Panaetius. Two of these are trivial. But more important is Cicero's complaint that Panaetius omitted any treatment of how to resolve apparent conflicts between the morally right and the advantageous. This is the topic which Cicero himself develops in book 3—which may be why he goes to the trouble to highlight Panaetius' omission. We will return to Cicero's own contribution shortly.

We are also fortunate to have two letters of Seneca which provide valuable insight into earlier Stoic approaches to moral reasoning. I do not mean to neglect the equally important letter 71, but the pertinence of the debate with Ariston makes letters 94 and 95 more interesting for present purposes.[54] They, of course, present a controversy in the early Stoa about the role of practical advice-giving (parainetic philosophy), between Ariston and more mainstream Stoics, represented by Cleanthes.[55]

---

[54] See also *Ep.* 109.14 ff. on the practical deliberations of the wise man.
[55] It is difficult to tell how much of the critique attributed to Ariston and how much of the defence associated with Cleanthes stems directly from those philosophers. As David Sedley pointed out in conversation, it is *Seneca* who constructed this debate out of materials provided by the tradition of the school's history. (The same point should be made with regard to Cicero's presentation of the debate between Antipater and Diogenes in *Off.* 3 below.) But, however much Seneca may have elaborated Ariston's position, the case attributed to him is still in broad

The debate turns on a simple but crucial point, whether or not this branch of philosophy (identifiable with the *topos* on encouragements and discouragements)[56] was or was not useful. A closely connected question arises from Seneca's defence of the utility of parainetic, whether or not it is sufficient for moral progress (treated in letter 95). Seneca's position on this too is typical of mainstream Stoicism; he holds that general moral theories are necessary, and indeed, as Cleanthes held (94.4), that advice-giving is ineffectual unless it flows from the general theory, which consists in *decreta* and *capita* (*dogmata*). Scattered throughout these letters are many indications of the kind of considerations which played a role in Stoic moral reasoning.[57] We need to dwell on these briefly, in the form of a selective paraphrase with added comments.

The parainetic branch of philosophy consists largely in issuing to individuals instructions or precepts[58] (*praecepta*) appropriate to their role and station in life. 'How to live with one's father', 'how to live with one's wife' are examples of the ground covered by parainetic discourse (94.5; see also 94.14–15); they involve enjoining non-circumstantial *kathēkonta*. Ariston's objections to such precepts focus on the claims that they are redundant (if a person has virtue then such instructions are not needed, and if a person does not, then they are useless (94.11)) and that they are indeterminate (people's circumstances and roles are so varied that *praecepta* must be infeasibly detailed and specific (94.15–16)), and such indeterminacy is in

agreement with the views of Ariston we know from Sextus Empiricus. Ariston in these letters is no more of a historical fiction than most long-dead philosophers become when their views are discussed in later centuries.

[56] DL 7.84. Note that it immediately follows the topic of appropriate actions. It is possible that these topics should be grouped in an unconventional way, with a *peri* introducing each one. Thus we would have a single topic 'on primary virtue and actions' and another 'on encouragements to appropriate actions and discouragements [from the opposite]'.

[57] Much of the detailed discussion by Mitsis in 'Seneca on Reason, Rules and Moral Development' is of considerable interest in the analysis of this material and is in broad outline compatible with my interpretation. Where we disagree is over how best to describe the role of rule-following.

[58] See too *Ben.* 7.1.3–7 for views similar to Ariston's put into the mouth of the Cynic Demetrius.

conflict with the character of philosophy as a general discipline. (With this point we see Ariston in effect offering a defence of what I have stigmatized as vacuity: at least, he thinks, his stripped-down, abstract theory is guaranteed to be true in virtue of its universal character.)

This kind of criticism is what we would expect of Ariston; it is no wonder that he, unlike Zeno, Cleanthes, Chrysippus, and others did *not* devote a treatise to the topic of appropriate actions. His view would seem to be that there is no point in giving general guidelines for ethical decision-making, that one cannot in fact say anything useful about what is generally appropriate. And, if one cannot do that, then the kind of moral guidance which comes via precepts will be just as useless.

Seneca counters that such *praecepta* play a vital role in ethics. Though it is true that our job is to follow nature, and that if we do not acknowledge that fact we will suffer from a form of moral blindness which no *praeceptum* can cure, still, even when the scales fall from our eyes, we do not immediately see what is to be done: nature does not tell us what it is appropriate to do, but *praecepta* are required to point the way (94.18–19). The barrier to doing the right thing is not only our general moral character, he says, 'for it is not only the passions which prevent us from doing praiseworthy actions, but also inexperience in figuring out (*inperitia inveniendi*)[59] what each situation requires' (94.32).[60]

Some *praecepta* are consequently just as useful to the morally earnest person as they are to the bad person who needs to be encouraged to direct his efforts to the good (94.22–4); and even if the bad cannot be saved by *praecepta* alone, it does not follow that *praecepta* are pointless. Moreover, Seneca says, *praecepta* can remind us of moral facts which we once knew but have

---

[59] Cf. *Ben.* 5.25.6 where *bona voluntas* is said to be blocked either by general moral failings (note *deliciae, situs*) or by *officii inscitia*.

[60] Seneca is in fact choosing to place an educative goal ahead of evaluation here; Ariston stands out as unusual and peculiarly 'rigorous' because of his narrower focus on evaluating. He is prone to emphasize that each action and each person is either right or wrong and that there is little more to be said about the matter. Perhaps that is true from the point of view of assessing the success or failure of the agent in attaining the goal of life, but most Stoics did not limit themselves so narrowly to a single perspective.

forgotten (94.21, 25–6); they can make the relevant facts of a particular case perspicuous in a way that the vagueness of a more general principle cannot (94.21). The very generality of the principles can militate against their utility in the practical and specific tasks of the moral life (94.31); both give instructions in their own way, but the specific character of *praecepta* makes the instructions more useful to the moral agent.

Though *praecepta* themselves do not *prove* anything and do not demonstrate the goodness of a particular course of action, they still aid the agent in deciding what to do. The authority of an advisor is of some weight, if the advisor is well chosen (94.27);[61] certain moral principles seem to lie dormant in our minds, but when even an unargued precept is uttered, it can serve to wake up our moral intuition and so get us started on the road to moral improvement (94.28–9, 31).

More interesting for present purposes, the connections between moral principles which we may in fact have might easily escape our notice until a *praeceptum* jars us into making the juxtaposition (94.29–30):

Moreover, some considerations may well be in our minds, but yet not sufficiently accessible; we begin to get at them only when they are spoken aloud. And other things are there, but scattered in widely separated [mental] locations, and the untrained mind cannot bring them together. So we have to bring together and juxtapose such considerations, so that they can have more impact and do more good to our character.

This is a crucial function in the economy of moral reasoning, the synthesis of previously unconnected guidelines in a way which bears on the specific needs of the immediate situation.

---

[61] Significantly for our comparison to the law, Seneca compares the authority of an adviser to that of a jurisconsult, whose considered opinions have weight even if a *ratio* is not given; as a legal adviser might give an opinion before working out the supporting reasoning, so too in moral reasoning. This is one of the more important ways in which case-by-case individual assessments interact with the application of general principles. Clearly it is not a case of deduction from the justifying general principle, nor is the particular judgement the basis for deriving the principle. The distinctively legal style of reasoning is equally applicable in moral deliberation. See Hadot, *Seneca*, 174. Cf. *Ben.* 5.25.5–6 on encouraging one's friends to remind us of our *officium*.

Seneca also notes that *praecepta* play a role in character formation. As in Aristotle, just doing the right thing in itself helps to form a better moral character; and following *praecepta* enables us to do the right thing before our characters become well formed (94.33–4, 42–51). Closely related to this is the favourable impact on our characters of the company of the good men who are our moral advisers (94.40–1),[62] of other sorts of moral suasion (94.39), and of the examples of good and bad lives which are used to inculcate and reinforce *praecepta* (94.59 ff.).

In *Letter* 95 Seneca turns to the fortification of Cleanthes' claim that *praecepta* alone will not *suffice* for moral progress. From the beginning of his discussion (95.4) his argument is based on the fact that right action (*katorthōma*) is needed if the moral life is to attain its goal, and that right actions do require a full grasp of the general moral principles which form the general theory. This leads him to give an explanation of what is meant by 'covering all the aspects' in the contrast between appropriate actions and right actions. 'Unless formed and shaped from the beginning with a complete rationality, a person cannot carry out all the aspects so that he knows "when" and "how much" and "with whom" and "how" and "why" he ought [to do something]. He cannot strive for what is morally fine with his whole heart, let alone steadfastly and gladly, but will look back and hesitate' (95.5). The theory must be fully internalized for this kind of comprehensive and therefore stable morality to be part of one's actions (cf. 95.12).[63] A life lived according to *praecepta* alone will therefore be incomplete, not achieve its goal; it will be pointless to give people *praecepta* unless the obstacles which might bar their good effect are eliminated (95.38). If one acts well without knowing why, the rightness of the act will be unstable; the agent who is to act well consistently must have a standard (*regula*) to apply which will certify the rightness of actions (95.39); interestingly, this

---

[62] Cf. *Ep.* 71.1, 22.1–2 and M. Graver, 'Therapeutic Reading and Seneca's Moral Epistles', Diss. (Brown University, 1996), 60–2, 74.
[63] Compare this to Chrysippus in *SVF* iii.510.

word *regula* is as close as we get to the term 'rule' in Stoic moral reasoning, and here it probably corresponds to the Greek *kanōn*, the word used by Chrysippus to describe 'law' in the exordium to his treatise *On Law*. Yet here, at any rate, the function of a *regula* seems to be epistemological and justificatory, not prescriptive.[64] Genuine stability of moral action can only come if there is a clear way to connect the point of the action to the goal of life, to which all actions are to be referred (95.45); this consists in a set of beliefs, known with certainty, which deals with life as a whole (*persuasio ad totam pertinens vitam* (95.44)). That is what counts as a principle, and no *praeceptum* is enough unless it can make that connection between the particular circumstances and the overall point of life. Hence the first example of such a principle which Seneca offers is a statement of the *telos* or goal of life (95.45–6).[65]

Seneca goes on to give other examples of the kinds of general principles he has in mind. One deals with the gods (95.47–50). A distinct issue follows (*altera quaestio*), our relations with other humans (95.51–3); the crux of the matter is a maxim (*formula*)[66] similar to one which we will meet shortly in Cicero, *De Officiis* 3: it makes no more sense, Seneca says, to harm each other than it does for one body part to attack another. The third example is the set of principles dealing with the value of things—that is, the basic axiology as discussed above (95.54). Fourth is the theory of virtues in their relationship to action (95.55–9), a topic also dealt with in Cicero's *De Officiis*.[67] A careful reading of our evidence from Seneca and the *De Officiis* will confirm that the

---

[64] Cf. *Ep.* 13.7; also *Ben.* 4.12.1, where, according to J. M. Cooper and J. F. Procopé (*Seneca: Moral and Political Essays* (Cambridge 1995), 283) *regula* is the translation for the Greek *kanōn*. They suggest that Seneca is there quoting the opening phrases of Chrysippus' *On Law*. If so, it is particularly important that Seneca here says that a law, qua rule (*regula*), is not something to be chosen for its own sake. I take it that this means that a substantive law can be no more than a rule of thumb in Schauer's sense.

[65] Cf. *Ep.* 71.2.

[66] This is not the only use for the term *formula* in Seneca. In *Ep.* 124.14 he offers a *formula* or practical criterion as an aid to self-assessment rather than moral choice.

[67] These general principles can be helpfully compared to those attributed to the Cynic Demetrius at *Ben.* 7.1 ff. and to those alluded to by Epictetus (e.g. *Diss.* 2.14.9–13).

principles at issue here, the *dogmata*, are by and large general theses in Stoic physics and ethics and not (as Mitsis has suggested)[68] substantive rules.[69] This is evident from what Seneca says about *decreta* in the practical arts (especially the *liberales artes*) at 95.9: most of these arts have *decreta* as well as *praecepta*; in fact Seneca suggests that the difference between different schools of medicine lies primarily in the principles rather than in the actual precepts and procedures which guide practice. These precepts, Seneca implies, may be shared despite the difference in *decreta* which underlie the differences between the schools of Hippocrates, Asclepiades, and Themison.

Consider too Seneca's explanation of what a *decretum* is at 95.10: he says that it translates the Greek *dogmata* and that *placita* and *scita* are other acceptable translations. He specifically notes that you find *decreta* also in geometry and astronomy. (These are noted as theoretical sciences, not practical, but the point of comparison remains: ethical *decreta* are normally theories with ethical import, not rules.)

It is easy to slip into treating *decreta* primarily as rules. For the term 'principles', like the Latin *scita*, can be ambiguous; moreover, the general principles are in fact cited to *justify* injunctions to act. To illustrate this, we can glance back at *Ep.* 95.52–3, which Mitsis paraphrases thus: 'a *decretum* enjoining that we respect other persons as mutually related parts of God

---

[68] 'Moral Rules and the Aims of Stoic Ethics', 557; repeated in 'Seneca on Reason, Rules and Moral Development', 290 n.15. At pp. 299 ff. a more subtle account is given of *decreta*, but the evidence of Cicero and *Ben.* is not taken into account. Hence his difficulties confessed on p. 302. It is clear that the disagreement between Mitsis and myself turns largely on terminological confusion: the rules which I think the sage can break are mere *praecepta* and not injunctions to act morally. The burden of Mitsis's objection to my claims in 'Goal and Target' rests on the belief that I think that such injunctions can be violated. The kind of rule discussed here and exemplified in a *praeceptum*, in the *regula* of Seneca, or the *formula* of Cicero is, however, breakable *salva moralitate*. What I aim to do in this discussion is to show the moral function of rules which do not apply universally and exceptionlessly even for fools, let alone for wise men.

[69] Although 94.31 complicates the issue by claiming that the difference between *decreta* and *praecepta* is merely one of generality. Cf. 95.12 where the difference is compared to that between *elementa* and *membra: haec ex illis dependent, illa et horum causae sunt et omnium.*

and nature'.[70] What Seneca writes is subtly different in emphasis. In explaining why he gives precepts such as that one should avoid shedding human blood, help a shipwrecked person in distress, show the way to a lost person, or share food with a starving person, Seneca says:

Why should I state all the services which should be done and avoided, when I can communicate to him [an interlocutor] briefly this maxim (*formula*) for appropriate human behaviour (*humani offici*[71])? This universe which you see, in which all things human and divine are included, is a unity; we are limbs of a gigantic body. Nature brought us forth as blood-relatives, for she created us from the same elements and in the same element. It is she who gave us reciprocal love and made us social. She established what is fair and just; by her dispensation it is more wretched to harm than to be injured.[72] Let this verse be on your lips and in your heart: 'I am a man, and think no human matter foreign to me.' Let our possessions be for the general good; we were born for it. Our society is just like a stone archway which would fall down unless it exerted reciprocal pressure on itself and is thereby kept up.

Mitsis takes this as a *decretum* in the sense of an injunction to act. But though the actions enjoined by the *praecepta* follow directly from it, there is very little injunction in what Seneca says—it is (as we would expect from Seneca's introduction of *decreta*) an assertion of Stoic physical principles (holism, rational teleology, a part–whole understanding of the cosmos) and of the natural foundation of human sociability. It is not a universal rule or law of nature *enjoining* these behaviours in all particular cases. Rather, the *praecepta* which enjoin more specific type-actions of mutual respect flow from it.

---

[70] 'Seneca on Reason, Rules and Moral Development', 303.

[71] Cf. *Ep.* 103.3. Note too *servilis officii formulam* at *Ben.* 3.21.2. Actions can be appropriate to a person qua human or in virtue of some specific social role. See below on *personae*.

[72] This might be thought to be a good candidate for an exceptionless general principle with content specific enough to be useful as a rule in Mitsis's sense; indeed, he suggested that in conversation. But in fact the notion of harm used here must be the special, transvalued meaning of harm which accompanies the notion that true benefit is the moral good. And so it brings with it the kind of technical and tautological sense that makes the 'rule' useless to anyone but the already wise agent.

Rules and Reasoning in Stoic Ethics

At this point I should add, at least parenthetically, that if one studies Seneca's own usage for 'law of nature', the prescriptive element does not bulk very large. A more thorough study would be necessary, but provisionally I would say that typically *lex naturae* and similar expressions refer to brute facts such as the mortality of human beings and the perishability of the cosmos.[73] In this regard much of what Seneca says about laws of nature bears a closer resemblance to *decreta* without overt prescriptive force than to moral injunctions which give commands to act (as *praecepta* do). Seneca's terminology is, to be sure, somewhat fluid here.[74] But it is typical of Seneca *not* to limit himself by rigid terminological decisions;[75] the contrast between theories and the precepts grounded by them is the crucial point, and Seneca maintains it despite his deliberately nonprofessional style.

In order to round out our picture of moral reasoning, let us return to Cicero, and in particular to his own treatment (which follows Stoic principles) of the topic omitted by Panaetius. In book 3 of *De Officiis* the question is restated in terms which respect the basic framework of Stoic axiology: it is allowed that genuine benefit could never conflict with moral value, since they are in fact identical.[76] But conflict can legitimately occur, in Cicero's view, in cases where there is doubt about the moral quality of the proposed action. 'For often circumstances determine that what is generally considered to be shameful is found

---

[73] See Ch. 8 below. Mortality as the law of nature: *NQ* 6.32.12; *Cons. Helv.* 13.2 Constant material change: *Cons. Helv.* 6.8. Negative inevitabilities of human condition: *Vita Beata* 15.5. Natural inevitability of human sociability (descriptive, not prescriptive): *Ben.* 4.17.3. Natural limits set to pleasure and wealth (Epicurean sense): *Ep.* 4.10, 25.4, 27.9, 45.9, 90.4 (prescriptive as well as descriptive). Large-scale scientific regularities in physics: *NQ* 3.15.3, 3.16.4. Prescriptive uses I have noted include: ideal of kingship (natural king) *Clem.* 1.19.2; natural, rather than political freedom: *NQ* 3 Pref. 16.

[74] Note also that the relevant maxim here is actually termed a *formula*, not a *decretum*. (Similarly in *Ben.* 7.1–2 we see *praecepta*, *lex*, and *regula* used in a very confusing way. It is evident that more serious work needs to be done on such terminology in Latin philosophy.)

[75] See my remarks in 'Seneca in his Philosophical Milieu', Ch. 1 above.

[76] ...*cui quidem ita sunt Stoici adsensi, ut et quidquid honestum esset id utile esse censerent, nec utile quicquam quod non honestum* (*Off.* 3.11).

not to be shameful' (*Off.* 3.18–19: *Saepe enim tempore fit ut quod turpe plerumque haberi soleat inveniatur non esse turpe*). If someone believes that a given action is shameful (morally bad), then a morally earnest agent (whether *prokoptōn* or sage) could not hesitate about choosing, over it, the alternative, no matter how disadvantageous (and vice versa). But, in the real world of moral choice, we spend much of our time trying to decide on the moral character of unclear actions. According to Cicero (and nothing here seems uncharacteristic of the Stoics) the proper place for the debate about the relative merits of the *utile* and *honestum* is this sort of grey area.

From the point of view of moral reasoning, Cicero's recommendations for such ambiguous areas are most instructive (*Off.* 3.19–20). Drawing on the resources of Roman legal reasoning (note that we return to a legal source here, which ought to reassure us about the relevance of an analysis like Schauer's), he looks for a maxim or procedural rule (*formula*) to use in the comparative assessment of possible courses of action; following it would prevent us from straying from appropriateness in our actions. I take it that this means that a reasonable justification of our action once done would be based on the claim that we followed such a *formula*. But for this procedure to provide a reasonable justification for specific actions—which is the standard to be aimed at in choosing the appropriate thing to do, the *officium* in each circumstance—it will itself have to be a generally defensible rule. And Cicero goes on to provide just that, a formula which is, he says, 'most consistent with the line of reasoning and the teaching of the Stoics'. The *formula* he proposes is also, he says, compatible with Academic and Peripatetic ethical practice, in the sense that it would in actual instances of moral reasoning lead to the same outcomes and would also cohere in a pragmatic way with their doctrines.[77] The general

---

[77] Compare Seneca's remarks at *Ep.* 95.9, which suggest that *praecepta* about what to do might be shared by various schools of medicine, while the theoretical principles or *decreta* might serve to distinguish them. So too here; the principles are clearly Stoic in their rigour, which Cicero regards as the distinguishing feature of the school's ethics, but the Academics and Peripatetics share the practical outcome: they too place *honesta* ahead of *utilia*.

principle (and such a principle should remind us of those discussed by Seneca in letters 94–5) is simple, practical, and grounded in the Stoic theory about the nature of man. Cicero's introduction of it should be quoted at length (*Off.* 3.20–2, tr. Atkins):

But I return to my rule of procedure. Now then: for one man to take something from another and to increase his own advantage at the cost of another's disadvantage is more contrary to nature than death, than poverty, than pain and than anything else that may happen to his body or external possessions. In the first place, it destroys the common life and fellowship of men: for if we are so minded that any one man will use theft or violence against another for his own profit, then necessarily the thing that is most of all in accordance with nature will be shattered, that is the fellowship of the human race. Suppose that each limb were disposed to think that it would be able to grow strong by taking over to itself its neighbour's strength; necessarily the whole body would weaken and die. In the same way, if each one of us were to snatch for himself the advantages other men have and take what he could for his own profit, then necessarily fellowship and community among men would be overthrown. It is permitted to us—nature does not oppose it—that each man should prefer to secure for himself rather than for another anything connected with the necessities of life. However, nature does not allow us to increase our means, our resources and our wealth by despoiling others.

In much of the rest of book 3 Cicero devotes himself to the application of this formula to what strike him as problem cases in moral reasoning. It is impossible to follow him through the details of this reasoning, just as it is impossible to survey the entire *De Officiis* for the other examples of the interplay between *praecepta* and *decreta* which it offers;[78] but it is evident

---

[78] The emphasis on *praecepta* begins in *Off.* 1.4–7 and never lets up. The general discussion of how our *kathēkonta* are rooted in the theory of the virtues illustrates, in my view, one way in which *praecepta* and *decreta* interact—for the theoretical account of the virtues which dominates book 1 is part of the *decreta* of Stoic ethics, and the rules for appropriate action which form the focus of the book are *shown* to flow from such principles. They are, in Cicero's words, the *fontes* or *fundamenta officii*. In several places (e.g. 1.30–1) Cicero points out the usefulness to moral reasoning of having the right theoretical principles. In 1.30 Cicero notes how our capacity for self-deception makes a general rule useful—thus paralleling one of

that the particular conclusions which Stoics might come to on each problem can vary considerably in any given particular case. Note the famous case involving the morality of full disclosure in a market economy (3.50–3).

The scenario is as follows. An idealized moral reasoner (a *vir bonus et sapiens*) is sailing to Rhodes from Alexandria with a full cargo of grain; there is a grain shortage in Rhodes. Our sage knows that many other merchants have set sail for Rhodes with grain to sell. Should he mention this in Rhodes, or should he keep silent and sell his cargo for the best price he can get? *Ex hypothesi* the merchant will not keep silent if he judges that to be shameful or wrong; but is it?

Two Stoic philosophers are presented as debating the issue. Diogenes of Babylon and his student Antipater systematically disagree about cases of this type in the following way. They agree that the agent should not do anything shameful; and they agree that man is a fundamentally social creature. But Diogenes holds that disclosure need only be made to the degree that civil law requires it and that treachery (*insidiae*) should be avoided; once those considerations are satisfied, the best price possible may be sought. Antipater's line or reasoning (*ratio*) is opposed to this; the context is clearly dialectical. As so often in such debates, the point thought to be central to his case is made salient by means of a rhetorical question sharpened with an *ad hominem* barb (*Off.* 3.52, tr. Atkins):

What are you saying? You ought to be considering the interests of men and serving human fellowship; you were born under a law, and you have principles of nature which you ought to obey and to follow, to the effect that your benefit is the common benefit, and conversely, the common benefit is yours. Will you conceal from men the advantages and resources that are available to them?

Schauer's justifications for entrenchment. Other particularly interesting passages from books 1 and 2: 1.42, 1.49 on *beneficia*, 1.59–60 with its use of the metaphor of calculation for moral reasoning in which *praecepta* are balanced by an estimation of particular circumstances, 1.148, 2.44–51, 2.54, 2.71 (which makes the relationship between the rule and the moral theory underlying it particularly clear).

In the response suggested for him by Cicero,[79] Diogenes at no point challenges the principle that we have a basic obligation to our fellow men. But he advances a subtle distinction between keeping silent and concealment, maintaining that one is not obliged (on pain of being accused of concealment) to tell someone everything which it might be of use to them to know, spicing the point with an *a fortiori* consideration: there are some truths (such as basic philosophical knowledge about the gods and the goal of life) that are more valuable than cheap grain. There is an implicit challenge to Antipater to produce some non-arbitrary account of which kinds of useful information one is obliged to share and which not—since one cannot be obliged to share all. Antipater is imagined as simply refusing this challenge: 'But no! he will answer, It is necessary, if indeed you remember that men are bound together in fellowship by nature' (*Off.* 3.53, tr. Atkins). Diogenes replies by conceding the principle adduced by Antipater but challenging its scope with a *reductio ad absurdum*: surely it does not mean that there should be no private property and that we should give things away rather than selling them.

Here, two Stoic experts come to opposite conclusions in a concrete case *without at any point* disagreeing about the principles involved, only about the way they bear on the case in hand.[80] The same is true for the other illustration Cicero advances (3.54–5), which deals with the obligations of the vendor

---

[79] For my purposes it makes no difference how historical Cicero's account of the debate is. No doubt there was a core of historical truth, but the elaboration is Cicero's. (The same may well be true for Seneca's account of the debate between Ariston and Cleanthes in *Ep.* 94–5.) See n. 55.

[80] Compare the discussion by Julia Annas, 'Cicero on Stoic Moral Philosophy and Private Property', in M. Griffin and J. Barnes (eds.), *Philosophia Togata* (Oxford 1989), 151–73. I do not agree, though, with her contention that Diogenes and Antipater are really addressing different issues in this debate. What she misses is that Cicero's main interest in the debate is in their common ground: that *despite* their disagreement on the right thing to do, they nevertheless agree on the much more important principle that one should never do what one concedes to be morally wrong. If one wants there to be a single correct Stoic answer to such problem cases, then one must decide either that Diogenes or Antipater is wrong, or that they are not really disagreeing; but if, as I contend, Stoics can legitimately disagree on the application of principles which they share, then such manoeuvres are not needed.

of an unsound house. What better illustration could there be of the fact that Stoic ethics does not dictate determinate actions to moral agents, but rather prescribes methods of procedure within a framework of sound general principles?

Cicero, of course, does settle the debate for himself by using the rule of procedure outlined in 3.20–2 to settle the question about the boundary between concealing and merely remaining silent.[81] What seems to be typical of Stoic practice in this case is the use of general principles in a kind of moral casuistry. The rule of procedure just considered is such a principle, and it (like the *formula* and *regula* found in Seneca) seems to form a bridge between the most abstract principles of Stoic ethics (such as statements of the goal, or the claim that men are naturally social, or the assertion that virtue is sufficient for happiness) or physics and concrete decisions to act. Such debates were clearly far from unusual in Stoic ethics. Hecaton is said to have filled book 6 of his treatise on appropriate actions with cases of the sort discussed by Cicero here (3.88–9), and the debates between Antipater and Diogenes of Babylon on such cases are also of this type. What we can derive from this book for our general consideration of Stoic moral reasoning is twofold: its general structure (problem cases settled in the light of a general principle—seen also in the Seneca) and the character of the *formula* chosen. What we do not get is any sign of rule–case deduction, nor any moral principles which are simultaneously (i) imperatival, (ii) universal, and (iii) substantive. In its place we find a more dialectical and rhetorical style of reasoning, one as characteristic of the deliberative and forensic spheres as it is of the philosophical schools.

The kind of discussion which we see reflected in Cicero's discussion is in important ways typical of Stoic moral reasoning. It deals with indifferents primarily, but always within the context of a general moral theory founded on a definite conception of a virtuous life. Stoic moral reasoning deals with concrete decisions about things which are not in themselves of moral value, but which do matter for a normal and 'natural' human

---

[81] *Off.* 3.57.

life. The issues are genuinely open to debate about what one should do—we are not being asked to decide whether to follow the path of virtue or not. Such decisions are described as 'selections'; and the open-ended nature of 'selection' is to be taken seriously. In no useful sense does Stoic moral theory tell the agent what is to be done in a concrete case.

Rather, it defines the framework and sets the terms within which such a choice is to occur. A successful selection will be one which constitutes an appropriate action, an action which has a reasonable justification, an act for which an adequate, though not certain, defence could be given in some idealized court of 'law', where one need not demonstrate the ultimate moral rightness of the act in order to win one's case. The framework of the moral theory, including the axiology, the general principles, the conception of the *telos* and the virtues, and the naturalistic foundations of the system, will help to determine which selections are reasonably justified—that is, which actions represent the successful functioning of human reason in a concrete situation.

Another important category of factors to consider in selecting the right action and in giving a reasonable justification of one's selection will be the individual identity and character of the agent and the particular relationships in which she finds herself.[82] Stoic ethics lays down general principles which apply to all persons, but it would be a strange agent-centred ethical theory which did not in its theory of moral reasoning provide for the relevance of the particularities of each agent. The *persona* theory first reported for Panaetius (*Off.* 1.107 ff.)[83] is used in exactly this way, but there is no reason to conclude that he is the inventor of the theory.[84] Moreover, the use of a range of different

---

[82] Let me note here that Ilsetraut Hadot (*Seneca*, ch. 2, esp. pp. 27–8, 32–4) seems to underestimate the Stoic interest in individual character and personality. That our essentially human nature should constrain the ideal behaviour for individuals and that individual variation is not a primary *goal* does not entail that a single and essential norm for human behaviour is all that Stoic practical ethics aimed at.

[83] See too C. Gill, 'Personhood and Personality: The Four-*personae* Theory in Cicero, *De Officiis* I', *Oxford Studies in Ancient Philosophy*, 6 (1988), 169–99.

[84] Several considerations ought to incline us to the view that (at least informally) the individual character and situation of the agent were held to be relevant from the

exemplary types of life also confirms the importance of individual factors in the earliest Stoa, as does the very large list of different actions which the sage is allowed to do, if not enjoined to do, under a range of different circumstances. The very theory of actions appropriate in special circumstances points in the same direction. There was never a monolithic ideal of life for the Stoics (in this they no doubt differed from some of the more enthusiastic Cynics); accordingly, the particularities of each agent's character had to have been given considerable weight in selection of the morally correct action. Panaetius' theory of *personae* (reflected later in Epictetus too)[85] was a formalization of earlier modes of moral reasoning, not a new departure.

In its formal and abstract evaluative mode Stoic ethics gives us a language which makes it all too easy to evaluate agents but which provides us with virtually no guidance in moral reasoning. Stoic ethics does, however, contain rich resources for this purpose. First, the basic theory of value sets out a typology of the kinds of objects of practical moral concern—the indifferents—which finds a middle ground between rigid essentialist abstraction and complete situational opportunism. Secondly, the relationship between appropriate actions and morally right actions provides a framework in which reasonable justification (*eulogos apologia*) in a concrete context becomes the proper immediate focus for every moral agent, and this allows the pursuit of abstractly defined moral virtue to fade into the background when one must reason about the selection of what to do; one can focus on the immediate and manageable question of appropriateness because it is a necessary condition for moral rightness and because the very act of rational selection exercises the practical reason, cultivation of which leads towards virtue. Thirdly, Stoic theory justified the common-sense institution of

---

beginnings of the school. Most important is the debate about precepts already considered. Ariston stands out as the voice of protest, and Cleanthes as the defender of the mainstream view. So we must conclude that the use of precepts of the sort outlined in *Ep.* 94 goes back to the earliest days of the school. And those precepts are clearly relevant to and indeed relativized to different social roles. See Gill, 'Personhood and Personality', 175.

[85] 2.10, 4.12.

giving generalized precepts relativized to one's role in life and individual character; such precepts had a clear place in the structure of ethical theory, a place which gave them enough room to function as flexible guidelines for moral reasoning. Fourthly, the use of general rules of thumb as a reference point in moral reasoning enables the moral reasoner to find the balance between abstract theory and the demands of a particular context.

The first two of these tools involve some sort of formal moral theory, an understanding of which had to be presupposed in the agent. But the rest are validations of perfectly ordinary ethical practice, the embodiment of the common sense of the morally serious but imperfect agent of any philosophical persuasion. It would clearly be wrong to claim that anything in Stoic ethics could be separated from the theoretical framework provided by the rest of the system, and the importance of the first two tools should make it clear how essential their general theory is. But the general theory is not, as critics often say, impossibly abstract, nor is the whole business cut off from common sense. When Cicero says that his way of approaching moral reasoning would also work for non-Stoics, he is more or less right. The kind of flexibility we see in his work, and in Panaetius, Seneca, and Epictetus, is not a sign that the Stoics fell away from the pure rigour of some hopelessly abstract moral theory. It is, I think, a central feature of Stoic theory which was present from the very beginning of the school's history.

5

The Will in Seneca

There are few words in the philosophical lexicon so slippery as 'will'. In an attempt to track a history of the idea of will, the most we have going for us is a widely agreed upon lexical correspondence. In modern European languages, so far as I know, we can at least pick out counterparts: will, volonté, volontà, Wille. Push it back a bit further and you arguably add the Latin *voluntas*. But as almost everyone agrees, you cannot push this lexical correspondence back to ancient Greek, where neither *boulēsis* nor *prohairesis*, neither *dianoia* nor any other term quite does the job.[1]

What lies behind these lexical correspondences, though, is considerably less clear. Just what is meant by will and whether

---

I wish to thank the National Humanities Center in North Carolina for support which made work on this topic possible. I have also received a good deal of constructive criticism on early drafts of this essay, most notably from Margaret Graver and Richard Sorabji. I am also grateful to an anonymous referee for *Classical Philology*.

[1] This view is shared by all the authorities on Seneca cited in this essay. Some might argue that *prohairesis* in Epictetus does capture the idea of will. I cannot deal with Epictetus in the course of this essay, though of course his work post-dates Seneca anyway. (Recent work dealing in part with Epictetus and the will includes two excellent discussions: A. Alberti 'Il volontario e la scelta in Aspasio', in A. Alberti and R. W. Sharples (eds.), *Aspasius: The Earliest Extant Commentary on Aristotle's Ethics* (*Peripatoi*, Band 17; Berlin and New York, 1999), 107–41, and S. Bobzien, 'The Inadvertent Conception and Late Birth of the Free-Will Problem', *Phronesis*, 43 (1998), 133–75.)

it exists—or can helpfully be talked about, if one's sympathies run towards instrumentalism in such matters—are all controversial questions. What Anthony Kenny rightly calls 'a view familiar in modern philosophical tradition' holds that

> the will is a phenomenon of introspective consciousness. Volition is a mental event which precedes and causes certain human actions: its presence or absence makes the difference between voluntary actions [*sic*]. The freedom of the will is to be located in the indeterminacy of these internal volitions. The occurrence of volitions, and their freedom from causal control, is a matter of intimate experience.[2]

Kenny rejects this conception of the will, following (as he says) Wittgenstein and Ryle. But he has captured it well. One might bring many different theories of the will to some sort of order by suggesting that they are best understood as various accounts of will in this sense. For the sake of simplicity, I would like to adopt Kenny's description of a traditional sense of the term 'will' as a reference point, adding only one further observation. Although Kenny does not emphasize it (since he dismisses the idea *a fortiori*), it is almost universally assumed by proponents of traditional will that its occurrent volitions are rooted in a faculty of the will, a distinct part of the soul or mind, a set of dispositions devoted particularly to the generation of 'volitions' in the sense just given.

The critique of the traditional sense of will in Anglophone philosophy since the Second World War is so familiar as to need little description. In its place there has grown up a body of theory not designed as a competing account of traditional will, but as a displacement of it, an explicit attempt to account for the 'springs of human action' (to adopt the familiar phrase used by Kenny and advertised in the title of Alfred Mele's recent book)[3] without it. Kenny, in *Aristotle's Theory of the Will*, identifies G. E. M. Anscombe's *Intention*, his own imperatival theory of 'will', and the work of Donald Davidson (at least up to the time of *Essays on Actions and Events*) as central to this project.[4]

---

[2] A. Kenny, *Aristotle's Theory of the Will* (New Haven, 1979), p. vii.

[3] Ibid., p. viii; A. Mele, *Springs of Action* (Oxford, 1992).

[4] Kenny, *Aristotle's Theory*, p. viii; G. E. M. Anscombe, *Intention* (2nd edn., Ithaca, 1969); A. Kenny, *Action, Emotion, and Will* (London, 1963) and *Will*,

He then sets out to track the same style of theory in Aristotle. This project aims to account for the phenomena purportedly accounted for by traditional will and rests on the principle that 'a satisfactory philosophical account of the will must relate human action to ability, desire, and belief'.[5] A related and almost equally influential approach to the problem of the will in this tradition is that of Harry Frankfurt.[6] For Frankfurt, will in its simplest form is our 'effective desire' and is a psychological event which many sub-human animals can share.

In this project, the lexical item 'will' is not supposed to stand for any single mental item. It points instead to a set of *explananda* and it indexes a theory defined in part by the denial that there is any such single mental item as traditional will which coherently accounts for them. The word 'will' as used in this project is an instrumental summary reference to a more complex set of *explanantia*. I will label it 'summary will'. Traditional will and summary will involve very different ontological claims. The corresponding philosophical psychologies cannot be reconciled by terminological stipulations. Since my aim is to consider Seneca the Younger's contribution to the topic of will, it will be important to distinguish clearly between traditional will and summary will. This has yet to be done in considerations of the philosophy of Seneca.

The significance of Seneca for the history of the will has long been appreciated, at least in broad outline. Indeed, since traditional will is generally agreed to be absent in Aristotle,[7] yet is apparently present in Augustine and in medieval philosophy,[8]

Freedom, and Power (Oxford, 1975); D. Davidson, *Essays on Actions and Events* (Oxford, 1980).

[5] Kenny, *Aristotle's Theory*, p. viii.

[6] H. Frankfurt, 'Freedom of the Will and the Concept of a Person', *JPh* 68 (1971), 5–20, reprinted as ch. 2 of *The Importance of What We Care About* (Cambridge, 1988). Frankfurt's approach developed and became more subtle in his later work, and he has decisively influenced several more recent philosophers to work in the same vein (I think in particular of Michael Bratman's recent works *Intention, Plans, and Practical Reason* (Cambridge, MA, 1987) and *Faces of Intention: Selected Essays on Intention and Agency* (Cambridge, 1999)).

[7] See Kenny, *Aristotle's Theory*, p. vii.

[8] The role of Augustine is reasserted by Charles Kahn in 'Discovering the Will', in J. M. Dillon and A. A. Long (eds.), *The Question of 'Eclecticism': Studies in Later Greek Philosophy* (Berkeley, 1988), 237–8, modifying the claims of both Gauthier and Dihle.

and since our lexical correspondence only extends to Latin and not to ancient Greek, interest naturally enough turns to ancient philosophers working in Latin, of whom Seneca is one of the best, best preserved, and most influential.[9]

The importance of *voluntas* in Seneca's work, especially in the *Epistulae Morales* and later treatises such as the *De Beneficiis*, has long been noted. Pohlenz attempted to explain the sharp emergence of *voluntas* as a result of Seneca's Roman experience and language, regarding Augustine's use of the term as the natural culmination of this development.[10] *Voluntas* was Seneca's attempt to render the Greek *dianoia*, Pohlenz thought, and the term shifted markedly in its meaning as a result of the connotations and social practices associated with the term in Seneca's time and place;[11] a voluntarist theory resulted. Rist attempted to mitigate this reading, claiming that 'when Seneca talks about willing and the will, what he is really concerned with is our moral character',[12] and denies a radical discontinuity with earlier Stoic psychology. He urges a view of Senecan *voluntas* which is as innocent of traditional will as was Aristotle's theory or even Chrysippus'.[13]

---

[9] T. H. Irwin has recently advanced a significantly different view of the will in Aristotle in 'Who Discovered the Will?', in J. Tomberlin (ed.), *Ethics* (Philosophical Perspectives, vol. 6; Atascadero, CA, 1992), 453–73. He argues that Aquinas was right to detect a conception of the will in Aristotle's ethics, one that does much of the same work as his own notion of *voluntas* does. But Irwin does not show that Aristotle goes beyond what I have called a summary conception of the will; rather, he argues that the largely intellectualist theory of Aristotle represents *a* theory of the will, but not a voluntarist theory. Perhaps so, though his analysis of *boulēsis* seems open to doubt, and is certainly not one which would naturally occur to anyone not beginning from a reading of Aquinas' discussion of Aristotle. It may be that Aquinas' own explicit theory of the will is intellectualist in character; that goes beyond my competence and present interests. In this essay my concern is only with the development of the distinctively non-intellectualist theory more conventionally associated with the terms *voluntas* and 'will'.

[10] M. Pohlenz, 'Philosophie und Erlebnis in Senecas Dialogen', Anhang, 'Ein römischer Zug in Senecas Denken', in id., *Kleine Schriften*, 2 vols. (Hildesheim, 1965), i.440–6, esp. 446. I take no view on the facts of the matter concerning Augustinian notions of the will, on which there is a large and contentious literature. See most recently J.M. Risth *Augustine* (Cambridge 1994), esp. ch. 5.

[11] Pohlenz, 'Philosophie und Erlebnis in Senecas Dialogen', NAWG, phil.-hist. Kl. 1.4.3 (1941), 55–118; repr. in id., *Kleine Schriften*, 2 vols. (Hildesheim, 1965), i. 445.

[12] J. M. Rist, *Stoic Philosophy* (Cambridge, 1969), 224–8, esp. 227.

[13] The fullest attempt to show that earlier Stoic psychology amounts to a merely summary treatment of the will is in my *Ethics and Human Action*, chs. 2–3.

Yet even Rist concedes that Seneca's use of the term is not fully accounted for in such terms (227), and his reaction against Pohlenz has not been influential. The 'voluntaristic' interpretation of Seneca (which sees in him the roots of traditional will) survives in Ilsetraut Hadot's book *Seneca und die griechisch-Römische Tradition der Seelenleitung*, though her discussion is brief.[14] And this view permeates André-Jean Voelke's *L'Idée de volonté dans le Stoïcisme*,[15] being especially prominent in his chapter on Seneca. Pierre Grimal's treatment of Seneca[16] typically leaves it difficult to tell just what kind of will he attributes to Seneca, though an attentive reading certainly points to the traditional rather than to the summary sense.

In the early 1980s Pierluigi Donini's much closer description of Seneca highlights the role of *voluntas* in the *Epistulae* and the *De Beneficiis*;[17] Donini's frank reference to Seneca's substitution of *voluntas* for Zenonian rationality underpins his bold claim that 'Seneca's notion of *voluntas* is a genuine discovery, one which cannot be contained in any version of Stoic philosophy, and not even, truth to tell, in any version of Platonism'. Shortly thereafter, Albrecht Dihle, searching for the roots of Augustinian (i.e. traditional) will, focuses briefly on Seneca, noting the same tendencies.[18] He summarizes Seneca's position as a 'vague voluntarism'. Pohlenz's hypothesis of Roman cultural influence is developed with special emphasis on the impact of Roman law. Like Pohlenz, Dihle sees Roman culture as pushing Seneca in the direction of voluntarism, against the resistance of the 'intellectualism' of the predominantly Greek philosophical tradition. Kahn's short discussion of Seneca in 'Discovering the Will' aligns itself closely with the voluntaristic and culturally determinist view of Pohlenz, Voelke, and Dihle.[19] Despite the protest against Pohlenz registered by

---

[14] I. Hadot, *Seneca und die griechisch-römische Tradition der Seelenleitung* (Berlin, 1969), 162–3.

[15] A.-J. Voelke, *L'Idée de volonté dans le Stoïcisme* (Paris, 1973).

[16] e.g. in P. Grimal, *Sénèque*.

[17] P. Donini, *Le scuole*, 202–3.

[18] A. Dihle, *The Theory of the Will in Classical Antiquity* (Berkeley, 1982), 134–5, 142; note that the Sather lectures on which this book was based had been delivered in 1974.

[19] Kahn, 'Discovering the Will', 254–5.

The Will in Seneca

Rist,[20] there has been a remarkably homogeneous view of this issue.

It is time to reassess Seneca's contribution to the problem of the will.[21] The urgency of doing so is reinforced by the growing realization that earlier Stoics, especially Chrysippus, should be aligned with Plato and (even more clearly) with Aristotle in holding a merely summary theory of the will. The contrast between traditional will and summary will is much more helpful and revealing than the polarity 'Greek intellectualism vs. Roman voluntarism'. We are looking, then, for clear evidence of traditional will, in contrast to summary will. A review of recent discussions reveals broad agreement about the relevant evidence. The later works of Seneca are the principal focus and provide the key illustrative texts; the 'smoking guns' invoked to establish Seneca's 'new' emphasis on the will, come from the *Epistulae*. There are variations, of course, but as one reads Pohlenz, Hadot, Voelke, Dihle, Kahn, and even Donini a cluster of five proof texts emerges, each of which is invoked by at least two authorities: letters 34.3,[22] 37.5,[23] 71.36,[24] 80.4,[25] and 81.13.[26]

Let us begin with 34.3 and 71.36. In the former Seneca says: 'the *pars magna* of goodness is wanting (*velle*) to become good',

---

[20] Part of the reason why Rist's view has been ignored is that it is too extreme; for it is not the case, as Rist claims, 'that neither Seneca nor Epictetus has made any significant variation on the doctrine of the Old Stoa relating to willing and knowing' (*Stoic Philosophy*, 231–2).

[21] Since my concern is to deal with Seneca's contribution, I pay no attention here to Epictetus, whose work came far too late to influence Seneca. There has, of course, been a tradition of bringing Epictetus' notion of *prohairesis* into discussions of Senecan *voluntas* (see, e.g., Kahn, 'Discovering the Will'; Rist, *Augustine*, esp. 187). But since there is no evidence whatsoever that earlier Stoics, or indeed any philosopher who might have influenced Seneca, anticipated his use of the term, such speculation cannot contribute to an understanding of Seneca's usage.

[22] Pohlenz, 'Philosophie und Erlebnis', 445; Hadot, *Seneca*, 163; Voelke, *L'Idée de volonté*, 170.

[23] Pohlenz, 445; Voelke, 176; Dihle, *Theory of the Will*, 134. See Rist, *Stoic Philosophy*, 225.

[24] Pohlenz, 445; Hadot, 163; Voelke, 170; Dihle, 135. See Rist, *Stoic Philosophy*, 226.

[25] Pohlenz, 445; Voelke, 179; Dihle, 135; Donini, *Le scuole*, 202; Kahn, 'Discovering the Will', 254. See Rist, 224.

[26] Pohlenz, 446; Hadot, 163; Voelke, 175; Donini, 134, 203. See Rist, 225–6.

and in the latter: 'the *pars magna* of moral progress is wanting (*velle*) to make progress'. Here, according to Pohlenz, *voluntas* is made into the decisive factor in moral improvement, and his very wording is echoed closely by Hadot; Voelke takes the same view of the significance of these texts: will is a distinct psychological force, so distinct that it can be recognized as a necessary condition for moral progress (*bonitas* in 34.3, *profectus* in 71.36).[27] These critics see will as a distinct mental event here. But why? Consider 34.2–3 more closely. Seneca is describing with some pride his efforts to improve his friend Lucilius:

Meum opus es. Ego cum vidissem indolem tuam, inieci manum, exhortatus sum, addidi stimulos nec lente ire passus sum sed subinde incitavi; et nunc idem facio, sed iam currentem hortor et invicem hortantem. 'Quid aliud?' inquis, 'adhuc volo.' In hoc plurimum est, non sic quomodo principia totius operis dimidium occupare dicuntur. Ista res animo constat; itaque pars magna bonitatis est velle fieri bonum.

You are my handiwork. When I noticed your potential, I got to work on you, exhorted you, spurred you on, and did not allow you to progress slowly; I drove you constantly. And even now I do the same, but now I am exhorting someone who is already in the race and encouraging me in return. You say, 'what else [would you expect]? I still want it.' Here that is the most important thing, and not just in the proverbial sense that the beginnings are half of the whole. This business turns upon the mind. And so the greater part of goodness is wanting to become good.

Is there a traditional will at work here? Hardly. Seneca merely claims that desire for a given result is crucial, especially when the matter in hand is intrinsically mental. In the much more complex letter (*Ep.* 71), Seneca makes the same point while encouraging Lucilius to persevere with moral progress despite the backsliding which is inevitable whenever one relaxes one's efforts (*Ep.* 71.36):

---

[27] Dihle (*Theory of the Will*, 240, n. 84) correctly sees that 34.3 presumes a traditional psychology and that *voluntas* can sometimes mean nothing more than 'wish' or 'desire', though he wrongly limits that meaning to the tragedies.

Instemus itaque et perseveremus; plus quam profligavimus restat, sed magna pars est profectus velle proficere. Huius rei conscius mihi sum: volo et mente tota volo.

Let us press on and stick to it. There is more ahead of us than we have yet wasted. But a crucial part of making progress is wanting to—and this I am aware of, that I want it and want it with all my mind.

This is one of Dihle's proof texts for 'vague voluntarism'.[28] Here too one might note that the wanting in question is for something mental or psychological. It is second-order wanting, which will be important, but it is not at all clear that we have here a distinct mental act rooted in a special faculty.

Dihle goes further when considering another popular proof text (*Ep.* 37.4–5). He sees Seneca as progressing from 'traditional Stoic intellectualism' to the introduction of 'an independent act of the will rather than reason itself, and he explicitly refuses an explanation of this phenomenon. Seneca did realize that will should be grasped independently of both cognition and irrational impulse' (*Theory of the Will*, 134–5). This closely follows Pohlenz's assessment, and Voelke (*L'Ideé de volonté*, 175–6) seems to take this one step further, regarding the passage as proof that human will can be an irreducible mystery: 'ailleurs il affirme que la conscience ne pénètre jamais jusqu'aux racines du vouloir'. He claims that this passage shows the 'irréductibilité du vouloir au savoir'. What does Seneca say to provoke such an assessment? That if you want to master all, you must submit yourself to reason. Reason will teach you what to undertake and how to go at it and will keep you from just blundering into things (37.5): 'You won't be able to show me anybody who knows how he came to want what he wants; he isn't brought there by planning but driven there by impulses.' (*Neminem mihi dabis qui sciat quomodo quod vult coeperit velle: non consilio adductus illo sed impetu inpactus est.*)

---

[28] Dihle, *Theory of the Will*, 135; see 240 n. 86. Dihle also invokes 80.4 in this sense, for which see below.

The cure for unreflective desires is reason, i.e. thinking and planning.[29] If you look around, you won't find people who know how they have come to have the desires they do. But that situation is a mark of failure. Fools are in a muddle, after all, and Seneca is urging that we take control and develop the self-knowledge we need in order to improve ourselves. There doesn't seem to be any evidence of traditional will here.

What about 80.4? 'And what *do* you need to become good? The desire.' (*Quid tibi opus est ut sis bonus? Velle.*) Seneca is celebrating the benefits of social isolation—everyone who could bother him is off watching the ball game and he is left in peace. The distant noise of the crowd impinges but does not really upset him; for it merely makes him reflect on how much effort is put into physical improvement and how little into psychological betterment. A particular contrast lies in the dependence of the body on other people and external resources: physical training is far from autonomous. But mental training is. Sportsmen need a lot of food, drink, oil, and training. Moral improvement comes without *apparatus* and without *impensa* (*Ep.* 80.4):

Quidquid facere te potest bonum tecum est. Quid tibi opus est ut sis bonus? Velle. Quid autem melius potes velle quam eripere te huic servituti quae omnes premit...?

Whatever you need for becoming good is with you. And what *do* you need to become good? The desire. And what can you more readily desire than to remove yourself from the servitude which oppresses everyone else...?

It is in contrast to the enormous and tyrannical demands of physical training that Seneca says 'all you need is the desire'. It is not plausible to take this as a claim that desire—or will—is totally self-sufficient for moral progress; the point in context is rhetorical. Seneca wants to stress the importance of inner self-sufficiency, and the resolution to improve is the best indication of that. Elsewhere he will emphasize the need for advice, for friends, for philosophical guidance. Here he wants to argue,

---

[29] Rist (*Stoic Philosophy*, 225) is right to reject Pohlenz's reading of this text, but is wrong, I think, in taking it to be strictly in accordance with the orthodox Stoic analysis of action. In particular, it is unlikely that *impetus* here represents *hormē*.

rhetorically to be sure (but this is, after all, the finale to book 9 of the *Epistulae* and Seneca can claim a fitting rhetorical license), that turning inward is freedom, that one's larger social context and one's body are marks of slavery. Notice the trope: 'And what can you more readily desire than to remove yourself from the servitude which oppresses everyone else?' Freedom is the most desirable thing, so this rhetorical question packs great power. But what ties it to its context is the one word, *velle*, which some have wanted to take as evidence of an entirely new theory of the will. It is only by ignoring the context and the nature of Seneca's argument that one can find in this passage clear evidence of a traditional will.[30]

Finally we turn to *Letter* 81, the 'appendix' to Seneca's treatise on favours (*De Beneficiis*). I have recently discussed the argument of this letter,[31] but the essential point of 81.13 needs to be reasserted. The slogan *velle non discitur*, which is so often taken out of context,[32] underlines the importance of know-how in the life of the sage. Only the wise man knows how to be grateful and to repay a favour. A non-sage can only do his best. The difference between the two is the whole point of this passage (which is in the midst of Seneca's explication of the paradox that only the wise man is grateful), so it only makes sense to focus on the point of contrast between the wise man and the fool. One knows how and the other does not, and Seneca

---

[30] Again, Rist (*Stoic Philosophy*, 224) rightly rejects Pohlenz's reading but is insufficiently subtle in his own. That Donini (*Le scuole*, 202), Voelke (*L'Ideé de volonté*, 179), and Dihle (*Theory of the Will*, 135 and n. 86) can see voluntarism, even 'vague voluntarism', here is powerful testimony to a belief in Seneca's commitment to traditional will which is prior to the most cursory reading of the evidence. On the other hand, this usage may fit better into another pattern: sometimes the terms *voluntas* and *velle* can be translated as 'resolve' or 'intend' (though 'desire' may be a more apt sense in these cases). See, e.g., *Ben*. 3.21.2, 3.30.1, 5.4.1, 5.12.7, 5.14.2; *NQ* 2.38.3; *Consolatio ad Marciam* 23.2 (cf. *Ep*. 70.21, 77.6); *Ep*. 95.8, 70.21, 77.6. A string of passages from *De Ira* (1.8.1, 2.1.4, 2.2.1, 2.35) could also in principle be brought under the meaning 'resolve', though it seems that here the real work is being done by the terms 'judgement' and 'decision'. See Ch. 7 'Moral Judgement in Seneca'.

[31] 'Politics and Paradox in Seneca's *De beneficiis*', Ch. 3 above.

[32] Even Rist (*Stoic Philosophy*, 225–6) exploits the passage to make a larger point not warranted by the run of the argument.

goes on to tell Lucilius how the sage does what he does. The shared feature of wise man and fool is their willingness—their *voluntas*—to repay the favour. So Seneca does not want to talk about how to acquire that. When he says *velle non discitur*, he is not claiming that our traditional will is immune to cognitive causation. He is saying no more than that in his contrast between sage and fool (where the fool is *ex hypothesi* a well-intentioned moral agent lacking only that wisdom which sages alone can have) the willingness or desire to repay a favour is not what is at issue. But that is only because Seneca's self-defined interests here are limited, not because he is moving towards a theory of traditional will. In saying that the basic desire to act decently is not learned in the way that moral know-how is learned, Seneca has not moved beyond Aristotle's position. There is nothing here which suggests a distinct faculty or specially reserved set of dispositions whose function it is to generate acts of volition.

So much for the allegedly best evidence for traditional will.[33] As far as these key texts are concerned we have no reason to see anything but summary will in Seneca, and his position is to that extent like Aristotle's or Chrysippus'. But that cannot be the whole story, and it is wrong to claim that there is nothing new or interesting in Seneca's theory of the will. Those who have seen in Seneca's work the beginnings of a traditional will have, I suspect, been encouraged by some genuine features of his work. But in order to see which features of his work might be exploited as evidence of traditional will, we will need to detach ourselves from the lexical framework within which this whole debate has been conducted so far (for *voluntas* seldom means much more than considered desire or willingness). We will have to stop looking for it under the traditional label and cast our net more widely. What we find, I think, is much more interesting. Even though Seneca does not really help to invent the traditional will (for we find nothing inconsistent with summary

---

[33] The *De Beneficiis* has also been seen as a *locus* of the traditional will, but only Donini (*Le scuole*) has attended to the question in any detail. Although the book has a number of distinctive features dealing with Seneca's view of human motivation, the use of *voluntas* in it is clearly compatible with summary will.

will), his work contains features which might well have helped to inspire those who did. But we will not find those key ideas isolated under easily recognizable labels.[34]

Instead, I suggest that we should look for Seneca's indirect and unintended contribution to thinking about traditional will in his reflections on mental causation, self-control, self-awareness, and self-shaping. When Seneca emphasizes our relationship to our own selves, when he focuses on how we treat our own character and temperament as things on which we can reflect and act, on which we can have causal impact, then despite the fact that he is still working within the confines of summary will, he may nevertheless be contributing to the development of a traditional sense of will; certainly he is making it easier for modern critics to interpret him as doing so. It is the second-order quality of our mental lives (i.e. when the mind takes itself as its own object) which plays the most important role in constructing the will,[35] and Seneca, though hardly

---

[34] Not even under the label 'assent', which Voelke (*L'Ideé de volonté*, ch. 3) and Kahn ('Discovering the Will', 245-6) treat as a possible forerunner of the traditional will. But that interest is misplaced, since the earlier Stoic theory is clearly a summary theory of the will. In Seneca, the mental event most clearly associable with will is not assent, and the more carefully one looks at the use Seneca makes of the early Stoic notion of assent, the harder it is to see in it any significant development towards the idea of traditional will. (Assent is, of course, a mental event of considerable importance to Seneca in various contexts, e.g. in *Ep.* 113 and in the early chapters of *De Ira* 2.)

[35] I am aware of the broad similarity between Senecan summary 'will', as I propose to understand it in what follows, and the views about the importance of second-order desires in the work of Frankfurt (see n. 6 above and Ch. 9 below, 'Reason, Rationalization, and Happiness in Seneca'). It would be reckless to overestimate the similarities, but they are nevertheless undeniable. How to account for them? It is tempting to diagnose a simple case of reinvention of the wheel. Frankfurt and Seneca may simply be making comparably acute observations of fundamentally similar moral phenomena. Historical influence can, I think, safely be ruled out. Similarly, the fact that his analysis of the relevant phenomena of mental life is so suggestive of some features of traditional will ought to remind us that, after all, the *explananda* are the same for both summary and traditional will. The philosophical superiority of summary will lies, in my view, in its greater simplicity and economy. The historical superiority of the claim that Seneca does not go beyond summary will lies in the fact that his predecessors in the school and outside it did not, and that there is no evidence at all that Seneca innovated, or even thought of himself as doing so.

unique in his awareness of this aspect of mental life, stands out for the frequency and explicitness of his interest.[36]

Seneca is not, of course, a professional philosopher and teacher, with commitments to the full articulation of theory and to the improvement of other people's souls; this may contribute to his greater concentration on self-improvement and self-shaping,[37] and on the impact one can have on oneself.[38] And the tendency to do so is pervasive; it is found throughout his career, unlike the use of the term *voluntas*. As early as the *Consolatio ad Marciam*, written in the reign of Caligula,[39] Seneca can say (8.3): 'Now you are your own guardian; but there is a big difference between permitting yourself to grieve and ordering yourself to do so.' (*Nunc te ipsa custodis; multum autem interest utrum tibi permittas maerere an imperes*.) In *De Brevitate Vitae* (written between 48 and 55) Seneca shows how wide-ranging this interest is, when he harnesses to the theme of self-reflection and self-assessment the Stoic metaphysical analysis of time (sec. 10). In *De Tranquillitate Animi* we have an illustration of the relationship between self-knowledge and self-management: in section 6 Seneca emphasizes that we need to start from self-inspection (*inspicere...nosmet ipsos*) and self-assessment (*se ipsum aestimare*) before analysing the other relevant aspects of our situation: the tasks we set ourselves and the other people we have to deal with. Self-shaping and the self-conscious management of the relationship between self and others is crucial to achieving tranquillity (see esp. sec. 17).

But the treatise *De Ira* is the most extensive reflection on self-shaping in Seneca's corpus, concentrating, as any treatment of anger would tend to do, on self-control.[40] Throughout the work

---

[36] Important texts on self-shaping: *Ep.* 11, 16, 76.34 (*praemeditatio*), 80, 83, 90.27 (*artifex vitae*), 91.15–6, 98.4.

[37] The craft of self-shaping is still practised among psychologists. For a range of contemporary perspectives and clinical practices, see, e.g., D. M. Wegner and J. W. Pennebaker (eds.), *Handbook of Mental Control* (Englewood Cliffs, NJ, 1993).

[38] When he does think primarily of someone else, as often happens in the *Epistulae* to Lucilius, he will emphasize his causal relationship to him: 'you are my handiwork', as he once said to his friend (*Ep.* 34.2).

[39] For all works I follow Griffin's dating, app. A of *Seneca*.

[40] See especially D. Zillman, 'Mental Control of Angry Aggression', and D. M. Tice and R. F. Baumeister, 'Controlling Anger: Self-Induced Emotional Change',

The Will in Seneca

Seneca shows an acute awareness of the importance of our initial responses to provocation, and of the need to manage them rather than to deny them.[41] This practical goal—the development of an internalized ability to eliminate passions—leads Seneca to take a particular interest in the Stoic theory of *propatheiai* (2.1–4, 1.16.7). And when he turns his attention to remedies, he divides his efforts between character formation (the prevention of irascibility as a character trait) and instruction on how to react under provocation. When discussing character formation Seneca divides his attentions between the shaping of children's characters as they grow up (2.19–21)—actions carried out on others—and advice to adults for shaping themselves.

Seneca's interest in self-shaping continues throughout his career, and there are important reflections on it in his latest works, in the *Naturales Quaestiones* (e.g. 2.59.3, 6.2.1), in the *Epistulae*, and in the socially oriented *De Beneficiis*. For our purposes, we need to concentrate on themes and language which establish the relevance of this to a mental event such as the will. There is a lot to choose from, but in the limited space available I will focus on the following: the language of self-directed commands; explicitly second-order psychological processes; and the role of judgement (*iudicium* and *arbitrium*).

I begin with self-directed commands. Early on Seneca marked the difference between allowing oneself to feel something and ordering oneself to do so; I am thinking of the passage of the *Consolatio ad Marciam* mentioned above. The same ideas are developed many years later in letter 99.15–21: we can either allow tears to fall or (under the influence of socially inculcated conceptions) order them to fall. The naturally occurring tears,

---

chs. 17 and 18 in Wegner and Pennebaker (eds.), *Handbook of Mental Control*. For reflection on the utility in anger-control of the self-conscious manipulation of the description under which one sees things, see J. Kennett and M. Smith, 'Frog and Toad Lose Control', *Analysis*, 56 (1996), 63–73. In the *De Ira* Seneca too shows an interest in this particular technique.

[41] This theme also appears clearly in *Cons. Helv.* 17.1–2, where Seneca concedes (un-Stoically) to his mother that grief is not *in nostra potestate* and argues against mere distraction from grief, on the grounds that admitting its power and defeating it by reason is a more stable resolution.

the ones we can permit but do not order, are said to come *nolentibus nobis* (99.19). This echoes Seneca's view of uncontrollable reactions in the *De Ira* (see <non> *insciis nobis*, 2.1.1; *non voluntate nostra, in nostra potestate*, 2.2.1; *voluntarium... vitium*, 2.2.2; *motus...animorum moveri nolentium*, 2.2.5, etc.) where in-principle controllability (rather than mere causation by one's own desires and beliefs) is taken as a mark of voluntariness.[42] A similar correlation of self-command with self-control and rational reflection is apparent in letter 116.1:

Utrum satius sit modicos habere adfectus an nullos saepe quaesitum est. Nostri illos expellunt, Peripatetici temperant. Ego non video quomodo salubris esse aut utilis possit ulla mediocritas morbi. Noli timere: nihil eorum quae tibi non vis negari eripio. Facilem me indulgentemque praebebo rebus ad quas tendis et quas aut necessarias vitae aut utiles aut iucundas putas: detraham vitium. Nam cum tibi cupere interdixero, velle permittam, ut eadem illa intrepidus facias, ut certiore consilio, ut voluptates ipsas magis sentias: quidni ad te magis perventurae sint si illis imperabis quam si servies?

The question has often been put whether it is better to have moderate passions or none. Our school drives them out, the Peripatetics moderate them. I do not see how any moderately diseased state can be healthy or useful. But never fear: I am not depriving you of anything that you aren't willing to have denied to you. I will show myself to be easy-going and indulgent with regard to the things you pursue and which you think to be necessary to life, or useful, or pleasant. It is the vice which I will remove. For though I forbid you to desire I will permit you to want, so that you can do the same things, but without fear and with a surer counsel, and so that you can better perceive the pleasures themselves. And why shouldn't they make a bigger impact on you if you give them orders rather than taking orders from them?

The language of self-command is used in two different modes. Sometimes Seneca uses explicitly reflexive language (e.g. *De Ira* 2.12.4)[43] where the command is both given and accepted by either the agent or some significant psychological part of the agent; and at other times one part of the soul gives an

---

[42] See 'Seneca and Psychological Dualism', Ch. 2 above.

[43] *De Ira* 2.12.4, 3.13.7, *Ben.* 5.7.5, *Ep.* 26.3, 52.14, 70.25, 78.2, 95.18, 104.3, 117.23.

The Will in Seneca 147

order either to another part or to the agent as a whole (e.g. *De Ira* 2.32).[44] In either mode the effect is the same. Seneca is in most such cases[45] isolating a mental event which has an important, if not decisive, bearing on action and ascriptions of responsibility. This is clear at *De Beneficiis* 5.7.5 where Seneca asks, 'Whom will you admire more than the man who commands himself, who has himself in his own power?' (*Quem magis admiraberis, quam qui imperat sibi, quam qui se habet in potestate?*) It is even clearer in letter 78.2 where Seneca describes his own resolution to live despite suicidal despair at his prolonged ill health:

Saepe impetum cepi adrumpendae vitae: patris me indulgentissimi senectus retinuit. Cogitavi enim non quam fortiter ego mori possem, sed quam ille fortiter desiderare non posset. Itaque imperavi mihi ut viverem; aliquando enim et vivere fortiter facere est.

Often I formed an impulse to kill myself, but the age of my most loving father stopped me. I thought not of how bravely I could die, but of how bravely he would not be able to bear the loss. And so I ordered myself to live, for sometimes it is an act of courage to live, too.

In view of his own despair, this is what most of us would call an 'act of will'. We can see the same connection of self-command with 'will' in a passage of the *De Ira* (2.12.3–4):

'Non potest' inquit 'omnis ex animo ira tolli, nec hoc hominis natura patitur.' Atqui nihil est tam difficile et arduum quod non humana mens vincat et in familiaritatem perducat adsidua meditatio, nullique sunt tam feri et sui iuris adfectus ut non disciplina perdomentur. Quodcumque sibi imperavit animus optinuit: quidam ne umquam riderent consecuti sunt; vino quidam, alii venere, quidam omni umore interdixere corporibus; alius contentus brevi somno vigiliam indefatigabilem extendit; didicerunt tenuissimis et adversis funibus currere et ingentia vixque humanis toleranda viribus onera portare et

---

[44] *De ira* 1.9.2, 2.35.2, 3.23.4, *Tranq.* 2.8, *Cons. Helv.* 18.9, *Ben.* 5.20.7, *Ep.* 18.3, 26.3, 65.1, 66.32, 85.32, 88.29, 90.19, 92.9 and 26, 106.10, 107.6.

[45] In some of the texts it is hard to be certain whether a distinct event is envisaged; in some cases we may be dealing with metaphorical descriptions of internal dispositions of the soul. But many if not most of these texts should, I think, be taken literally, and the others form part of a more general discourse about self-shaping and self-control.

in immensam altitudinem mergi ac sine ulla respirandi vice perpeti maria. Mille sunt alia in quibus pertinacia inpedimentum omne transcendit ostenditque nihil esse difficile cuius sibi ipsa mens patientiam indiceret.

[The Peripatetic] says, 'one cannot remove anger completely from the soul; human nature just doesn't admit of that.' But there is nothing so difficult and demanding that the human mind cannot master it and by constant practice make it habitual; no passions are so fierce and autonomous that they cannot be tamed by training. The soul accomplishes whatever it commands itself to do. Some people have succeeded in never laughing. Some people have completely deprived their bodies of wine, others of sex, others of all forms of liquid. Some other man is content with very little sleep and can stay awake indefinitely without fatigue. Others have learned to run on slender, slanting ropes and to carry huge loads scarcely bearable by human strength, or to dive to incredible depths and endure the sea without pausing for breath. There are a thousand other cases where persistence overcomes every obstacle and demonstrates that nothing is difficult if the mind tells itself to endure it.

What we would without hesitation describe as an act of will, and indeed think of as paradigm instances of will-power, are here portrayed as self-directed commands issued in the pursuit of moral self-control and character improvement. Here we have mental events, acts of 'will', despite the absence of the obvious label which connects readily to modern lexical correspondences. For Seneca, then, it is self-directed acts of command which are acts of 'will'.

In contemporary discussions it is not unusual to look to second-order psychological phenomena in order to isolate what is distinctive about human mental processes as against those shared with animals; the best-known such contemporary treatment is that of Frankfurt and his followers (see nn. 6 and 35 above), and in his seminal discussion, 'Freedom of the Will and the Concept of the Person', he astutely picks out a form of second-orderness as being central to the difference between persons and mere animals. Indeed, one can concede that all relatively complex vertebrates desire and even believe; but only humans, perhaps, can effectively want things and work

The Will in Seneca

at believing things. Second-orderness in this sense is common in Seneca. At the opening of letter 61 he urges:

Desinamus quod voluimus velle. Ego certe id ago < ne > senex eadem velim quae puer volui. In hoc unum eunt dies, in hoc noctes, hoc opus meum est, haec cogitatio, inponere veteribus malis finem.[46]

Let us cease to want what we have been wanting. I certainly work at not wanting the same things as an old man that I wanted as a boy. This is what my days and nights are focused on, this is my labour and my meditation: to put an end to my long-standing mistakes.

Such self-awareness and self-shaping can be used for positive ends (as here) or to deceive others, as in letter 95.2: 'there are many things we want to seem to want, but in fact don't want' (*Multa videri volumus velle sed nolumus*). Making one's own wanting a matter of explicit reflection and even manipulation is a common technique in Seneca. In the preface to *Naturales Quaestiones* 3 (sec. 12) we read: 'What is most important? Being able to bear misfortune with a happy heart, to take whatever happens as though you wanted it to happen—for you would have had to want it if only you had known that everything happens by divine decree' (*Quid est praecipuum? Posse laeto animo adversa tolerare, quidquid acciderit sic ferre quasi volueris tibi accidere. Debuisses enim velle si scisses omnia ex decreto dei fieri*).

This concern with achieving explicit control over one's own desires also manifests itself in his typically Stoic concern with consistency. Always having the same desires becomes a mark of moral progress, even of virtue. This is explicit at letter 20.4–6:

Etiamnunc dicam unde sit ista inconstantia et dissimilitudo rerum consiliorumque: nemo proponit sibi quid velit, nec si proposuit perseverat in eo, sed transilit; nec tantum mutat sed redit et in ea quae deseruit ac damnavit revolvitur. Itaque ut relinquam definitiones sapientiae veteres et totum conplectar humanae vitae modum, hoc possum contentus esse: quid est sapientia? Semper idem velle atque idem nolle. Licet illam exceptiunculam non adicias, ut rectum sit quod velis; non potest enim cuiquam idem semper placere nisi rectum. Nesciunt ergo homines quid velint nisi illo momento quo volunt; in

---

[46] Cf. *Ep.* 27.2.

totum nulli velle aut nolle decretum est; variatur cotidie iudicium et in contrarium vertitur ac plerisque agitur vita per lusum. Preme ergo quod coepisti, et fortasse perduceris aut ad summum aut eo quod summum nondum esse solus intellegas.

And now let me tell you where this inconsistency and the bad fit between actions and plans come from: no one asks himself what he should want, and if he has done so, he does not stick to it but jumps around. He doesn't just change, but also flips back, and returns to what he has repudiated and abandoned. So, to set aside the traditional definitions of wisdom and try to include the entire measure of human life, I can be satisfied with this: what is wisdom? Always to want the same thing and to not want the same thing. You don't even have to add the clause 'providing that what you want is right'. For no one can be always satisfied by the same thing unless it is right. Hence men do not know what they want, except at the very moment when they are doing the wanting. No one has resolved to want or not want for good. Their judgement varies daily and reverses itself; most people live life like a game. So stick to what you started on, and perhaps you will reach the top, or a point which you alone can tell is not the top.

At letter 52.1 this is expressed as 'wanting something once and for all' (*quicquam semel velle*),[47] and in letter 95.58 the connection between 'wanting the same things always' and having 'true desires' (*vera velle*) is again dependent on having a grasp of philosophical *decreta*.[48] The notion of self-conscious control of one's own wants and desires also turns up in letter 37.5, considered above. But what is actually important here is the notion of wanting something *consilio adductus* (upon reflection) rather than *impetu inpactus* (simply driven by psychological causes). What points to the will here is the explicit second-orderness, not the mere word *velle*.[49]

This idea is also apparent in the treatise *De Ira*. At 2.26.4–5 Seneca is arguing against being angry at animals, on the

---

[47] Here, note also the problematization of trying to control our wants.

[48] Consistency with others is as important as consistency with oneself over time: *idem velle atque idem nolle* is a mark of wisdom and true friendship (*Ep.* 109.16); cf. *De Ira* 3.34.2: *quod vinculum amoris esse debebat seditionis atque odi causa est, idem velle*.

[49] The same could be said of *Ep.* 71.36: it is the second-orderness and not the wanting which makes the passage of interest.

grounds that they cannot will (*velle*) to harm us and so do not actually do us any injury (a view about the moral centrality of self-conscious intent which recurs in the *De Beneficiis*): they do us no injury 'because they cannot want to; for it is no injury unless it proceeds from a plan (*nisi a consilio profecta*). Hence they can damage us, as can a piece of iron or a stone, but they certainly cannot do injury to us' (*quia velle non possunt; non est enim iniuria nisi a consilio profecta. Nocere itaque nobis possunt ut ferrum aut lapis, iniuriam quidem facere non possunt*). The key idea is that the kind of desire relevant to a responsible will is one which flows not just from a desiderative state (animals do have those—*consuetudo* and training are mentioned a few lines below), but from a conscious plan: the contrast to habit and training is *iudicium*, a judgement.

From the beginning of conscious reflection on free will and responsibility the idea of a bivalent possibility has been central: the ability to do or not to do something has been taken as a mark of freedom.[50] If that is the mark of morally responsible, free action, then it would not be surprising to see Seneca, in his reflections on what it means to will something, to put a similar condition on wanting. There is a kind of wanting which might turn up in any belief–desire explanation, of course, and that is the commonest use in Seneca. But in many contexts the bivalent possibility is about wanting itself, not overt actions; he emphasizes that the ability to *want or not want* the same thing is what counts. Genuine *velle* entails *posse nolle*. This theme occurs prominently in *De Beneficiis*. Consider 2.18.7–8:

Cum eligendum dico, cui debeas, vim maiorem et metum excipio, quibus adhibitis electio perit. Si liberum est tibi, si arbitrii tui est, utrum velis an non, id apud te ipse perpendes; si necessitas tollit arbitrium, scies te non accipere, sed parere. Nemo in id accipiendo obligatur, quod illi repudiare non licuit; si vis scire, an velim, effice, ut

---

[50] For Aristotle's use of this as a mark of voluntariness, see *EN* 3, 1110ᵃ17–18, *EE* 1225ᵇ8, 1226ᵇ30–2 and R. Sorabji, *Necessity, Cause, and Blame* (London, 1980), 235. Frankfurt's own refinement of the so-called 'alternate possibilities' criterion for moral responsibility is expounded in 'Alternate Possibilities and Moral Responsibility', *JPh* 66 (1969), 829–39; reprinted as ch. 1 of *The Importance of What We Care About*.

possim nolle. 'Vitam tamen tibi dedit.' Non refert, quid sit, quod datur, nisi a volente, nisi volenti datur; si servasti me, non ideo servator es.

When I say that you should choose the person to be indebted to, I exempt, of course *force majeure* and fear: when they are brought to bear there is no choice. If it is open to you, if it is within your ability to decide whether you want to or not, then you will weigh the matter up for yourself. But if compulsion removes the ability to decide, you should realize that you are not receiving a favour but obeying. No one is obligated by receiving something which it was not permitted to reject. If you want to know whether I am willing, make it possible for me to be unwilling! 'But he gave you life!' What is given doesn't matter, unless it was given by a willing donor to a willing recipient. Just because you saved me, it does not follow that you are my saviour.

Of course, this sets Seneca up for a problem when dealing with perfect agents, such as gods or sages. So in a later book (see 6.21–2) Seneca must extricate himself dialectically from potential paradoxes. For present purposes, Seneca's slick argument is less interesting than the terms of debate: he and his interlocutor share the belief that there is a clear moral significance attached to being able to want or not to want—parallel to the issue of being able to do or not to do. Wanting has become a reflective, internalized action.[51]

I have been considering cases where Seneca shows a sharp interest in acts of self-command, and where he is reflecting carefully on our second-order desire, our wanting to want. The final ingredient in Seneca's recipe for traditional will has, like self-command, the character of a mental event. I refer to Seneca's striking use of the language of passing judgement—*arbitrium* and *iudicium* are the key terms.

This use is found prominently in the treatise *De Ira*.[52] Judgement and decision (as I shall translate the *iudicium* and *arbi-*

---

[51] Compare *Ep.* 49.2, 67.2, 95.49, 116.8 for other sharply observed reflections on wanting and ability.

[52] Cf. *Clem.* 2.2.2, where it occurs for the same reasons as in *De Ira*; compare the passage to *De Ira* 2.1.1 where the same contrast of *iudicium* and *impetus* occurs. In the *De vita beata* 5.3 (cf. 6.2, 9.3) *iudicium* is linked to notions of control, not just reason. The *De Beneficiis* presents us with *iudicium* and *arbitrium* in connection with reflective choice; similarly *Ep.* 71.2–3, 87.1.

trium) are part of the language of legal authority. The treatise is addressed, after all, to Seneca's brother the provincial governor, and the ostensible reason for this dedication is that a man in such a position has more reason than most to reflect upon anger and to learn self-control: a great deal of the therapeutic part of the treatise makes better sense when one remembers that it is being addressed to an administrator with virtually unlimited power over non-citizens in his jurisdiction. 2.22–4 is a clear illustration of this. Two contrasting cases are cited to demonstrate the need to pause, in a judicial spirit, for assessment, hearing both sides before coming to a decision on any important matter: the tyrant Hippias who caused his own downfall by hasty reaction to suspicions, and the decision of Julius Caesar to prevent himself from over-reaction by destroying potentially damaging evidence before even reading it.

The general point in this passage[53] is that once one causes oneself to stop to debate the merits of one's reactions to provocation, then any subsequent action taken will be the result of a quasi-judicial decision.[54] Once Seneca reconceptualizes the agent as a judge (*iudex*) the fact that one's mental reactions are self-caused events (like traditional will) becomes clear. As a judge, one must critically assess the fairness of one's own response to events; one's mental life takes on the explicit rationality of the court-room and one's reactions are subject to debate and the expectation of detachment. When in 2.30 Seneca considers situations where the facts are not in question, he urges that we consider a variety of mitigating considerations, especially the intention (*voluntas*) of the agents, before reacting. Like judges, we should strive to consider the broadest possible range of relevant considerations before passing judgement. Note that *voluntas* is not the word for will, but the model of reaction and decision which Seneca invokes here captures a good deal of what traditional will is supposed to involve.

---

[53] The use of the metaphor of judicial processes to capture the phenomena of moral decision-making in this, and many other texts merits a separate study; see Ch. 7 below, 'Moral Judgement in Seneca'.

[54] See also *De Ira* 2.26.6 and 2.28–31.

Political and judicial contexts provide the ideal forum for practising the control of anger and for some of the language in terms of which it can be understood. The interest in this sense of judgement starts in book 1 of *De Ira*, at 1.15.3 where Seneca uses the example of Socrates to urge delay and reflection before punishment. The choice is between hasty, that is, angry, punishment and duly considered quasi-judicial reaction: *cum eo magis ad emendationem poena proficiat, si iudicio + lata + est.*[55] In 1.17.1 Seneca argues against the Peripatetic notion that anger can be used in the war against wickedness because it is unlike other weapons: *bellica instrumenta* can be taken up and put down at the decision of the bearer. The passion anger is not like that. Again, it is the presence of a prior act of considered decision which makes all the difference. The identical idea had been raised earlier at 1.7.4 in connection with the Chrysippean example of the runner.[56]

But it is in the technical early chapters of Book 2 that judgement and decision play their clearest role in adumbrating the scope and role of traditional will. For Seneca sees the task of managing the passions as a matter of imposing on oneself a delay in the reaction which would otherwise occur, a delay which provides the time needed for a considered judgement or decision to be formed. And that involves all of the elements of traditional will: second-orderness; mental events; treating one's own psychological processes as 'other', as something upon which one may act; and the effort required by the task of self-shaping.

At *De Ira* 2.1.1 the question is whether anger is a matter of *iudicium* or *impetus*; the fact that a judgement is required is what brings in *voluntas* and controllability at 2.2.1. Judgement and *voluntas* are yoked again at 2.3.5, and 2.4.2 underlines the role of judgement in distinguishing passions from pre-passionate behaviour. The motion of the mind which is caused by a judgement can also be eliminated by it. This emphasis on control-

---

[55] Cf. *De Ira* 3.12.4–7.
[56] See *SVF* 3.462. The idea that what distinguishes a passionate from a non-passionate response lies in its amenability to decision also turns up at *De Ira* 2.35.2.

lability by an explicit mental act is striking throughout the book, even in passages where *voluntas* is not invoked.[57] In fact, one of the charming conceits of Seneca's strategy in the book is the emphasis he puts on the fact that we can fake anger: in response to Peripatetic suggestions that anger is necessary Seneca several times responds that if ever we do need anger to influence other people then we can pretend.[58]

It is time to conclude this discussion of the various aspects of 'will' in Seneca's works. It is too simple and deeply misleading to invoke various passages of Seneca in which he uses *voluntas* or *velle* to support suggestions that he helped to invent or discover the will as a distinct faculty or set of specialized dispositions. Yet it is equally wrong to retrench around the claim that there is nothing new in Senecan psychology. Conceptual history is a messy business, and all the more so when writers like Seneca (and Plato) who do not use technical terms in a consistent and systematic way play an important role in the process. As I see it, there isn't any new word for will in Seneca, at least not one with a distinctive usage, though *voluntas* may from time to time happen to pick out a phenomenon claimed for itself by traditional will. What matters far more than such lexical considerations is the cluster of key interests which Seneca has, interests which together (but not separately) produce something which covers the phenomena which traditional will is supposed to be uniquely able to accommodate. The interest in second-orderness in the form of talk about self-shaping and self-knowledge; the language of self-command; the focus on self-control, especially in the face of natural human proclivities to precipitate and passionate response; and the singling out of a moment of causally efficacious judgement or decision in the process of reacting to provocative stimuli; these are Seneca's contributions to the development of the will. These

---

[57] The various consequentialist arguments about the utility of anger (e.g. 2.33–6 and 3.14–15) all presuppose that it is controllable. See above Ch. 2, 'Seneca and Psychological Dualism'.

[58] Note 2.17.1; 2.14 reveals the same connection between conscious controllability and feigning.

contributions are fully compatible with the philosophical project centred on notions of 'summary will', and yet evoke phenomena often thought to be explicable only in terms of traditional will. This seems to me to be evidence for a philosophical depth in Seneca's work which continues to demand exploration.

6

God and Human Knowledge in Seneca's *Natural Questions*

In his *Hymn to Zeus*, Cleanthes celebrates the supreme deity, whom the whole cosmos obeys (ll. 7–8), so great is the power of the thunderbolt he wields (9–11). The thunderbolt is the means by which Zeus makes straight the *koinos logos* which penetrates and blends with everything (12–13). As a result, the world is a single coordinated whole (18–21). The moral implications of this order are not neglected (14–17, 22–31). As convention dictates, the hymn ends with a direct prayer for divine assistance (32–39):

But Zeus, giver of all, you of the dark clouds, of the blazing thunderbolt,
save men from their baneful inexperience
and disperse it, Father, far from their souls; grant that they may achieve
the insight relying on which you guide everything with justice,
so that we may requite you with honour for the honour you give us,
praising your works continually, as is fitting

I want to thank Daryn Lehoux for his many helpful suggestions on an early version of this discussion. Margaret Graver was very generous with her help, both substantive and bibliographical, on the earlier and shorter version which I presented to the Boston Area Colloquium in Ancient Philosophy (*Proceedings of the Boston Area Colloquium in Ancient Philosophy*, 15 (1999), 23–43). The participants at the eighth Symposium Hellenisticum in Lille provided both constructive criticism and encouragement. In particular, David Runia, Richard Sorabji, Emidio Spinelli, and Teun Tieleman were generous with written comments.

for one who is mortal; for there is no greater prize, neither for mortals nor for gods, than to praise with justice the common law for ever.

Seneca, of course, knew Cleanthes' work (he alludes to him in the *De Otio* and *De Tranquillitate*, cites him in *De Beneficiis* 5 and 6, and in eight of the *Epistulae Morales*). He even followed the example of Cicero who translated Greek philosophical poetry into Latin verse (*Ep.* 107.10–11), choosing another hymn by Cleanthes to underscore his own argument for the cheerful acceptance of fate.

> Father and master of the lofty heaven, lead
> wherever you wish. I will not hesitate to obey;
> I am ready and eager. And if I am unwilling,
> I shall follow groaning, and be forced to do
> in my wickedness what I could have done as a good man.
> The fates lead the willing, drag the unwilling.

The themes of Cleanthes' hymns lie at the heart of Stoicism and help to flesh out the doctrine of Chrysippus that theology is the culmination of physics.[1] For Stoic physics is by no means the bloodless study of a merely physical (in our sense) world. Like every branch of philosophy, physics is intimately concerned with the place of human beings in the coordinated whole which is run by Zeus. This is familiar enough as a doctrine. But it will be helpful to allude to a summary by Arius Didymus preserved in Eusebius (*SVF* ii.528). This account maintains that the cosmos is not just the *sustēma* of heaven, earth, air, sea, and the natural objects in them; it is also, and more significantly, a 'dwelling place for gods and men', a *sustēma* of gods, men, and the things which exist for their sake. As in a political order, there are leaders and followers: in the cosmos the gods lead and we humans are subordinate, although the *koinōnia* is preserved through the fact that we and the gods have a

---

[1] See *De Stoic. Rep.* 1035a, a direct quotation in which Chrysippus prefers the order logic, ethics, physics, and makes theology the culmination of physics. He shared this view with Cleanthes, if we may infer a judgement on importance from the order of the parts of philosophy listed at DL 7.41. But see also the views of Chrysippus on the order of teaching (DL 7.40): following Zeno he preferred the order logic, physics, ethics.

share in *logos*, which is a law for (or by) nature. The theocentric nature of Stoic physics is further confirmed by the dramatic opening of this extract, which declares that, taken as a whole, together with its parts, the cosmos is properly called god.

Hence when we turn to Seneca's main effort in the area of Stoic physics, the *Naturales Quaestiones*, we really should not be expecting him to be detached from lofty questions of god and man.[2] And indeed he is not. For the *Naturales Quaestiones* is permeated by a vigorous interest in god, man, their relationship to each other, and the way in which the puzzling phenomena of the natural world relate to human life. As one begins grappling with a work which is often dry and impenetrable, it is worth recalling the first thing Cleanthes prayed for at the end of his hymn: 'save men from their baneful inexperience | and disperse it, Father, far from their souls'. *Apeirosunē*, the failure to have and use experience of the natural world,[3] is the evil most to be deprecated. As we shall see, throughout the *Naturales Quaestiones* Seneca works hard to bring together in a single treatment the themes of human and divine relations, the relationship of human beings to the natural world, and human inexperience or ignorance. I shall argue that the cure Seneca proposes for this baneful condition of man is the application of a critically rational approach to the understanding of the cosmos. But what makes the whole exercise a challenge in Seneca's bold—perhaps foolhardy—decision to focus on meteorology,[4] the least promising aspect of natural philosophy.[5] It is impossible to comprehend the effort Seneca poured into this massive work[6] without

[2] For what it is worth, Diogenes Laertius' brief summary of meteorological and astronomical topics at 7.151–5 is sandwiched between his account of *daimones* who watch over human affairs and a treatment of the human soul.

[3] We should recall that Chrysippus defined the *telos* as living in accordance with experience (*empeiria*) of things which happen by nature (DL 7.87, Stobaeus, *Ecl.* ii. 76).

[4] I reject the argument by N. Gross (*Senecas Naturales Quaestiones: Komposition, Naturphilosophische Aussagen und ihre Quellen* (Palingenesia, 27; Stuttgart, 1989)) that the *Naturales Quaestiones* was originally meant by Seneca to be a complete cosmology—a suggestion which requires positing the loss of entire books without a trace.

[5] Contrast the rather easier themes chosen by Cicero in *ND* 2.

[6] His longest unified work surviving, if one recognizes that the *Ep.* are a kind of serial collection. The *De Beneficiis* too was at first a work in four books, with the last three added after the provisional completion of the work (see *Ben.* 5.1.1 and *Ep.* 81.3).

recognizing the nature of his central concerns in the book. The attempt to bring such central issues of Stoicism to his readership by way of such an unpromising vehicle is the mark of a literary genius—or a man who thought himself one. Here, perhaps, is the intellectually proud Seneca whom Tacitus portrays,[7] proposing with an overweening pride to pull off a massive literary and philosophical coup.[8] He will, if he succeeds, put comets, earthquakes, and hailstones to work in justifying the ways of god to man.[9]

Yet Seneca evidently failed in his grand ambition. Consider this representative judgement. In the introduction to his 1974 Munich dissertation, Franz Peter Waiblinger[10] quotes Axelson's 1933 assessment:[11] the *Naturales Quaestiones* is 'das am wenigsten gelesene und geschätzte Werk ihres Autors', the least read and the least appreciated work by Seneca.[12] Despite intermittent attention from a number of hardy and imaginative scholars over the decades (including Gisela Stahl,[13] Gregor

---

[7] *Annals* 13.11; M. Griffin, *Seneca: A Philosopher in Politics* (2nd edn., Oxford, 1992), 7–8, 441–4.

[8] Compare the view in Alfred Gercke, *Seneca-Studien* (*Jahrbücher für classische Philologie*, Supp. 22; Leipzig, 1895), 312, who seems to think that Seneca's response to the appeal of a literary challenge undermines the seriousness of the work.

[9] In approaching this question I am of course presupposing that Seneca was accustomed to detaching the issues of theme and literary form, so that he could consciously choose to package his chosen themes in surprising or paradoxical forms. I believe that his corpus provides abundant evidence for such an hypothesis. Doubters should look again at the metaphor of *De Ira* 2.1.1–2.

[10] Waiblinger, *Senecas Naturales Quaestiones: Griechische Wissenschaft und römische Form* (Zetemata Monographien, Heft 70; Munich, 1977), 1.

[11] B. Axelson, *Senecastudien: Kritische Bemerkungen zu Senecas Naturales Quaestiones* (Lund 1933), 1.

[12] The German-speaking world has done better than we Anglophones, though, with the recent appearance of the bilingual edition of M. F. A. Brok, *L. Annaeus Seneca: Naturwissenschaftliche Untersuchungen* (Darmstadt, 1995). Brok was, unfortunately, unable to take advantage of H. M. Hine's Teubner text (*L. Annaeus Seneca Naturalium Quaestionum Libros* (Stuttgart and Leipzig, 1996)). He is also hampered to some extent by his hasty dismissal of Hine's textual work (p. 3). See also the short section on the *Naturales Quaestiones* in G. Maurach, *Seneca: Leben und Werk* (Darmstadt, 1991).

[13] Stahl, *Aufbau, Darstellungsform und philosophischer Gehalt der* Naturales Quaestiones *des L. Annaeus Seneca*, Diss. (Kiel, 1960), and 'Die *Naturales Quaestiones* Senecas: Ein Beitrag zum Spiritualisierungsprozeß der römischen Stoa', *Hermes*, 92 (1964), 425–54; repr. in G. Maurach (ed.), *Seneca als Philosoph*

Maurach, and Nikolaus Gross[14]) this has remained largely true even now.[15] The recent work by Carmen Codoñer[16] and a series of studies by Harry Hine have to some extent pushed the *Naturales Quaestiones* into clearer view; their work on the text of the *Naturales Quaestiones* and the intractable problem of reconstructing the order of books has perhaps made further progress possible. Indeed, without Hine's new Teubner text[17] and the combined arguments of Hine and Codoñer concerning the book order, it would seem hardly worthwhile to embark on serious thematic study of the *Naturales Quaestiones*.[18] For Hine

(Wege der Forschung, Band 414; Darmstadt, 1975), 264–304; G. Maurach, 'Zur Eigenart und Herkunft von Senecas Methode in den *Naturales Quaestiones*', *Hermes*, 93 (1965), 357–69; repr. in Maurach, *Seneca als Philosoph*, 305–22.

[14] Gross, *Senecas Naturales Quaestiones*, gives the most recent and thorough literature review and an exhaustive treatment of possible sources, structural problems, and thematic analysis. Much of this is inevitably speculative, but his discussion never fails to advance these traditional problems. From the point of view of this essay, though, his analysis is limited by his decision to retain the traditional problematic, which regards the principal thematic issue as the opposition between primarily ethical and primarily scientific aims. I will be arguing that epistemological themes need to be given equal or greater weight.

[15] Throughout this essay I owe a significant debt to the analyses of Stahl, *Aufbau, Darstellungsform* and 'Die *Naturales Quaestiones* Senecas'; Maurach, 'Zur Eigenart und Herkunft'; Waiblinger, *Senecas Naturales Quaestiones*, and Gross, *Senecas Naturales Quaestiones*, as well as the essay by Hans Strohm 'Beiträge zum Verständnis der *Naturales Quaestiones* Senecas', in *Latinität und alte Kirche* (Festschrift Hanslik) (*Wiener Studien*, Beiheft 8; Vienna, Cologne, and Graz, 1977), 309–25. Their interests in this rich work are different both from each other and from my own, and their discussions are still read with profit. None, however, has pursued what I take to be the central role of epistemological concerns in the *NQ*, although Maurach's emphasis on the judicial modes of thinking and argument comes closest (see esp. Maurach, *Seneca als Philosoph*, 316–22). In this essay I hope to complement rather than to displace their work. Brok, *L. Annaeus Seneca*, appears to turn back the clock on the issue of the work's character and purpose, reasserting the unsatisfactory view that it is best understood essentially as a set of *quaestiones* in the tradition of 'scientific' writing on meteorology (pp. 4–5), with the ethical significance to be found in the introductions and excursuses alone.

[16] 'La physique de Sénèque: Ordonnance et structure des 'Naturales Quaestiones', *ANRW* II 36.3 (1989), 1779–1822.

[17] Hine, *Naturalium Quaestionum Libros*. Hine's preface provides a quick and efficient entrée into the voluminous philological literature on the text and book order. His own work on the ordering of books, in my view, renders most of his predecessors' work on the topic obsolete.

[18] Stahl (*Aufbau, Darstellungsform*, and 'Die *Naturales Quaestiones* Senecas') and Waiblinger, *Senecas Naturales Quaestiones*, have both undertaken such studies,

and Codoñer have argued independently on text-critical grounds for the view that the original order was rather: 3, 4a, 4b, 5, 6, 7, 1, 2,[19] and we must assume this order as a basis for exegesis of Seneca's position until new and better arguments come along.[20]

Understandable though it may be, the relative neglect of the *Naturales Quaestiones* is regrettable. For although Seneca's primary interest was certainly ethics and although (as Barnes has recently reiterated)[21] his interest in logic was merely utilitarian, physics is not a marginal or merely subordinate branch of philosophy for Seneca. Not only is a knowledge of physics useful for moral improvement; it is also clearly the superior science in Seneca's eyes (*NQ* 1 Pref.), just as it was for Chrysippus (*De Stoic. Rep.* 1035a–f; see n. 1 above). And for both

---

and both have integrated their interpretative proposals with arguments for the traditional ordering of the books (1–7). Codoñer, 'La physique de Sénèque', and Hine, *Naturalium Quaestionum Libros*, have shown, on largely text-critical grounds, that this cannot have been the original ordering of the books. It is worth noting that the preface of book 1 in the traditional order deals extensively with the themes which I will be arguing are in fact central to the work as a whole. So it would be satisfying if this could be taken as the original introduction to the book as a whole (as it is by Stahl and Waiblinger, followed by Maurach, *Seneca: Leben und Werk*, 146). Gigon ('Senecas *Naturales Quaestiones*', in P. Grimal (ed.), *Sénèque et la Prose Latine* (Entretiens sur l'antiquité Classique t. 36; Geneva, 1991), ch. 8, p. 322) reverts to the hypothesis of A. Rehm, 'Anlage und Buchfolge von Senecas *Naturales Quaestiones*', *Philologus*, 66 (1907), 374–95.

[19] Hine, *Naturalium Quaestionum Libros*, xxiv; Codoñer, 'La physique de Sénèque', 1792.

[20] We are not compelled, however, to assume that the book order is critical to Seneca's argument, since it is possible that the work was organized as a series of essays on related themes and that there was little thematic progression—a pattern visible in the last three books of the *De Beneficiis*. Perhaps the fluid ordering of the *Epistulae* also illustrates the practice. (Brok, *L. Annaeus Seneca*, 4, is firmly committed to this view of the work's ordering and construction.) Gross, *Senecas Naturales Quaestiones*, opts for a book order in the archetype which is incompatible with the findings of Hine and Codoñer, and concludes that not only is our treatise incomplete (that entire books are missing from our tradition) but that Seneca probably did not himself finish the book; this may well be true. I believe, though, that the treatise read in the order indicated does have a discernible thematic progression. After the preface to book 3 (the first book), which adumbrates many of the issues of interest, there is a decline in their apparent centrality followed by a strong crescendo towards the end of the final book (book 2).

[21] J. Barnes, *Logic and the Imperial Stoa* (Leiden, 1997), ch. 2.

philosophers, theology took pride of place within physics. Nor was Seneca's interest in physics restricted to just one period of his life: the *Naturales Quaestiones* is very likely from the latest stage of his career, but the lost work on earthquakes was certainly of early date and our fragments of and allusions to other lost books suggest a fair bit of composition on topics similar to the themes of the *Naturales Quaestiones*: not just earthquakes, but stones, fish, and the geography of India and Egypt.[22]

Of course, herein lies the principal cause of this sad neglect. The physical themes of the *Naturales Quaestiones* are not always the grand cosmological topics which generally excite philosophical interest today[23] (these are seldom principal themes in Seneca's work, except perhaps for the *De Providentia*, to the extent that we regard it as physical not ethical); nor are they the more 'metaphysical' aspects of Stoic physics which we see occasionally in the *Epistulae* (I think of letter 58 on 'being' and letter 65 on causes). The *Naturales Quaestiones* focuses instead on more particular phenomena of the natural world, themes traditionally relegated to 'meteorology'. Book 1 deals with the fiery phenomena of the heavens, book 2 with thunder and lightning, book 3 with water within the earth, book 4(a) with the Nile, book 4(b) with the causes of dew, frost, hail, snow, and clouds, book 5 with the winds, books 6 and 7 with earthquakes and comets respectively. The tradition of advancing speculative explanations for such phenomena goes back to the earliest Presocratic thinkers, was given a characteristically Epicurean treatment in the *Letter to Pythocles*, and had been given further currency by the Peripatetic school in the Hellenistic period. Within Stoicism Posidonius and his students earned the biggest reputation for such work, and a very great deal of the limited work on the

---

[22] On matters of dating, I follow Griffin, *Seneca*. For the lost work on earthquakes, see *NQ* 6.4.2. See Griffin, *Seneca*, 46–7, 175, 399–400; see Brok, *L. Annaeus Seneca*, 1–3.

[23] See the brief discussions by R.B. Todd, 'The Stoics and their Cosmology in the First and Second Centuries A.D.', *ANRW* II.36.3 (1989), 1374–5, and M. Lapidge, 'Stoic Cosmology and Roman Literature, First to Third Centuries A.D.', *ANRW* II.36.3 (1989), 1397–401.

Naturales Quaestiones has focused on situating Seneca with respect to his sources in this tradition.[24]

We should not underestimate the importance of giving rational explanations of such phenomena in the ancient world, both for scientific reasons (reflected in the rich Peripatetic tradition) and for consolatory and ethical reasons (most evidently in the Epicurean traditions).[25] But even in the ancient world (let alone in ours) this is not the kind of topic which consistently excites serious philosophical interest. Here in the *Naturales Quaestiones* more than any place else in the corpus Seneca seems to be caught between the rock of trivial tralatician themes and the hard place of bellelettristic adornment. Add to this dilemma the chaotic state of the books (two of the eight are truncated and until recently there has been no usable consensus on their order), and the neglect ceases to surprise. My goal in this essay is to argue that the *Naturales Quaestiones* contains a good deal more which is of serious philosophical interest, that it contains an important strand of reflection on the relationship between god and man. This important theme is (as is often the case in Seneca) intermittently highlighted against the background of the overtly dominant topic.[26] I will argue, then, that

---

[24] Gross, *Senecas Naturales Quaestiones*, gives the most recent and thorough treatment of the sources for the *NQ*, as well as providing careful analysis of the literary structure of each book. In broad outline his account of the sources is plausible and helpful (he has rejected the 'one-source' models of many of his predecessors and sees how independently, even creatively at times, Seneca uses his sources). See also the remarks by Brok, *L. Annaeus Seneca*, 7. More, I think, could be said about Seneca's reaction to his literary predecessors in Latin, particularly Lucretius and Ovid.

[25] I want to thank Symposium participants at Lille (especially Richard Sorabji) and Margaret Graver (who commented on a shorter version of this essay at the Boston Area Colloquium at Boston College) for emphasizing the centrality of meteorological explanation to the project of rational reassurance in an often threatening world.

[26] This has been recognized to some extent by Stahl (*Aufbau, Darstellungsform,* and 'Die *Naturales Quaestiones* Senecas') but is de-emphasized by Maurach, 'Zur Eigenart und Herkunft' (in Maurach, *Seneca als Philosoph*, 321 n. 62), who holds that since the physics of the *NQ* is subordinate to large-scale cosmology (which he calls 'the physics of the sage') its theological contribution must be limited. I want to argue that it is only the overt theme of the work, meteorological topics, which is to any significant degree subordinate; the latent epistemological theme is, I hope to show, central to the *NQ* and is just as important for Seneca's theological reflections as cosmology would be.

Seneca presents his readers with the fruits of serious thought about the relationship between god and man, and would like to suggest (though proof is not possible) that Seneca's most important concern in the book as a whole is not the overt theme (explanations of traditionally problematic natural phenomena) but the subterranean theme of the relationship between god and man, and most particularly the epistemic limitations of human nature.[27] Seneca's interest in god goes beyond the role of god in Stoic cosmology and extends to more general reflections on the epistemological distance between divine and human nature.[28]

* * *

Space and time do not allow for an exhaustive examination of the *Naturales Quaestiones* from the perspective which I propose. I hope that the selective analysis I offer will persuade;

[27] In what follows I would not want to suggest that Seneca is breaking totally new ground. For as Teun Tieleman and Carlos Lévy remind me, Chrysippus was also very conscious of the need to refrain from hasty judgement when the evidence available on a problem is unsatisfactory. See, e.g., *SVF* ii.763, 885, and his notorious but sensible advice on how to respond to a sorites argument, *SVF* ii.276–7. See also DL 7.46. On Chrysippus' method, see T. Tieleman, *Galen and Chrysippus on the Soul* (Leiden, 1996), pt. 2.

[28] The direct epistemological interests of Seneca in this book have not excited much comment, but I hope to show that they are significant in extent and import. One scholar who does notice them, Pierluigi Donini (in P. Donini and G.-F. Giancotti, *Modelli filosofici e letterari* (Bologna, 1979), pt. 2, Ch. 3), sees the epistemological interests of the *NQ* as evidence of Platonic interests and a general eclecticism. To be sure, parts of the work do rely on a contrast between what can be learned by means of the soul or reason and what can be learned by way of the senses; but this in itself is hardly evidence of Platonism. The contrast between reason and the senses is both old and widespread in ancient philosophy. In this essay I cannot do justice to Donini's bold and intelligent reading of the *NQ* (which I was only able to obtain thanks to the generous efforts of Margaret Graver). Olof Gigon, 'Senecas *Naturales Quaestiones*', remarks on Seneca's interest in the epistemological limitations of human beings and the connection of these limits with the offering of multiple explanations (e.g. 317). Gigon, however, denies that these themes can be of Stoic origin and connects them more with the influence of Cicero's Academic stance (318, 312) and the influence of Peripatetic and Epicurean models (320). Gigon's insistence that Cicero is a central influence on the *NQ* is weakened by the fact that his philosophical works are not mentioned and that he must be postulated as a hidden influence (318, 335). (The one reference at *NQ* 2.56.1 is to his oppressive effect of his reputation for eloquence.) Gross, *Senecas Naturales Quaestiones*, also concludes that Seneca is interested in epistemological questions, but clearly regards this as subordinate to the primarily cosmological and theological aim of the work (330).

a careful re-reading of the treatise as a whole will perhaps reassure the reader that I have not focused unfairly on passages favourable to my suggestions at the expense of potential counterevidence.

Let us begin by considering the preface to book 3 (and to the work as a whole). Seneca emphasizes the magnitude of the task he is undertaking, particularly daunting for someone already advanced in years. The challenge comes both from the global extent of the phenomena to be studied (*mundum circumire*) and from the fact that what is to be pursued are the hidden causes (*causas secretaque*) of nature as a whole. The difficulty is to make knowable to others (*aliis noscenda*) things which are both *sparsa* and *occulta*. The reward, of course, is that such efforts make the mind itself stronger (*crescit animus*). Seneca continues by emphasizing the relative unimportance of the tasks undertaken by historians. Just writing up the deeds of great men is of less importance than the moral instruction one can derive from philosophical reflection on them. It is god, after all, who determines how high or low one's fortunes may be. In 3 Pref. 10 Seneca offers the explanation for our mistaken overestimation of historical greatness: it is because we are 'small' and 'low' (*parvi, humilitate*) that so many things seem great. The implication is that god is the one who sets the standard for what is really great and what is not, that it is only our human limitations of perspective which lead us astray about what is really important in human affairs (*praecipuum*): not the political and military deeds which expand the boundaries of the world, but to have seen the whole of things and conquered one's own failings. These generalizations are punctuated by two claims: that there is nothing mundane which we should yearn for, since whenever we turn away from our dealings with the divine to consider merely human affairs we are blinded and disoriented (rather like those re-entering a Platonic cave);[29] and that our ability to withstand, even accept misfortune, would be greatly enhanced

---

[29] I suspect that the allusion to Platonic themes is intentional on Seneca's part. But in my view this does not mean that Seneca is being strongly influenced by Platonism here.

by knowing that whatever happens does so *ex decreto dei*, that being miserable about mundane events is a kind of disloyalty to god. The piety woven into this blend of physical and ethical reflection is confirmed by 3 Pref. 14, where purity of moral intention is described in terms of the prayers we offer to the gods (*puras ad caelum manus tollere*): moral improvement is something we can aim for not least because it is a game which we can win while no one else loses (*sine adversario optatur*).[30]

At the conclusion of this preface, Seneca underlines the interdependence of achieving an understanding of nature (including our human nature) and moral clarity. In 3 Pref. 18 we learn how the pursuit of natural investigations serves this purpose:

For this purpose it will be beneficial to investigate the nature of things. First, we will escape the tawdry; second, we will withdraw our mind itself (which we need to have in its highest and best condition) from the body; third, our mental sharpness, if exercised on hidden matters, will be no worse in dealing with apparent matters; nothing, however, is more readily apparent than the salutary lessons we learn in our struggle against our vice and madness, things which we condemn but do not abandon.

The purposes envisaged do not include the satisfaction of intrinsic curiosity. Moral improvement would aptly describe the first two reasons, and the third might best be described as epistemic improvement (though the goal of that seems to be moral as well).[31]

God is present throughout the preface, underlying the physical and the ethical themes. And so too are human limitations, the most pressing being the issue of our finite life-span with which Seneca opens the book; but our smallness of vision and inability to see into the heart of nature are also barriers, as are our radical dependency on god for our mundane fortunes and our weakness of resolution in the application of moral precepts. The study of nature is presented as *divinorum conversatio*

---

[30] Compare the theme of a competition in virtue in *Ben.* 1.4, 3.36, 5.2.

[31] 3.1.1 (*quaeramus ergo*) suggests that these are also the reasons for studying more specific phenomena, such as the *terrestres aquae* of book 3.

(abandoning which leads to blindness) and moral weakness is apostasy (*desciscere*). The theological framework articulated here shapes Seneca's reflections on epistemology, on the study of physics, on ethics, and on the relationships among them. None of this is presented aggressively; but it cannot be missed.[32]

The method Seneca displays in book 3 is typical of the treatise as a whole: problems are posed, various proposals for solution are canvassed, the views of earlier philosophers are scrutinized, and Seneca's own thoughtfully articulated arguments are mustered. A frank and open dialectical approach to the problem and previous views is omnipresent and he eschews arguments from Stoic authority. This aspect of Seneca's approach is well emphasized by Maurach in 'Zur Eigenart und Herkunft',[33] but one further feature of Seneca's method is worth a moment's reflection. In much of the *Naturales Quaestiones*, as in book 3, the visible and puzzling phenomena of the world need to be explained in terms of things which we cannot directly observe. Ordinarily Seneca extrapolates in a reasonably empirical manner, holding that the unseen is probably much like what we see, since nature is orderly and uniform. For example, at 3.16, when explaining 'why some springs are full for six hours then dry for six hours', Seneca prefers a general explanation for all such phenomena to a case-by-case approach. Thus he can give a single cause for them all. And the explanation he gives is surprisingly abstract, relying as it does on analogy with other orderly variations in nature (examples are quartan fever, recurrent attacks of gout, menstrual cycles,

---

[32] Seneca's interest in the human focus of natural philosophy comes out in another way which is worth a passing mention. As often in ancient natural philosophy (the *Timaeus* is a clear example), aspects of the natural world are explained by means of a close parallel with human beings. Throughout book 3 Seneca pursues the parallel of man and cosmos with some vigour.

[33] Maurach, 'Zur Eigenart und Herkunft'. His essay brings out very effectively the argumentative character of the work, basing itself on a sample analysis of a part of book 1. A reading of the whole work underscores how consistent and apparent this approach is—indeed, it is hard to fathom the neglect of Seneca's argumentative vigour in earlier scholarship. See most recently Gross, *Senecas Naturales Quaestiones*.

gestational periods, the seasons, equinoxes, and solstices). Why shouldn't other phenomena, such as springs, follow such cycles? It would hardly be surprising given the pervasive orderliness of nature in pursuing its plans. Seneca suggests (3.16.2) that we have no trouble in observing cycles which are short in duration, but that we cannot so easily note the existence of longer cycles, though they are no less definite. With similar confidence Seneca postulates what he takes to be reliable *iura naturae* (3.16.4) under the earth (*crede infra quidquid vides supra*) and goes on to provide examples of subterranean phenomena which are similar to what we see—caves with air, earth, water, and various forms of animal life (3.16.5).

Although this discussion of subterranean waters also forms the point of departure for the next theme (which resumes after the moralizing digression of 3.17–18), the existence of fish in subterranean waters, it is offered in the first instance as proof that natural regularities license us to suppose that things happen in consistent patterns in the unseen world just as they do in the superficial world we see around us. This is offered as the general explanation for the regular pattern of activity in some springs. As feeble as such an explanatory strategy may seem to us, it is an eminently rational approach, and one which will seem more reasonable the longer one reflects on the limited amount of respectable evidence Seneca had at his disposal. Perhaps a permissive attitude towards possible causes, a kind of aetiological '*nihil obstat*' based on analogy (rather like the Epicurean acceptance of multiple explanations in such matters) is not so foolish. Another indication of Seneca's healthy respect for the limitations of human explanation comes with his frank admission at 3.25.11 that 'for some things a cause cannot be given'. The string of such phenomena concludes at 3.26.8 with the frank acceptance that some things are very hard to account for, *utique ubi tempus eius rei de qua quaeritur inobservatum vel incertum est*. Without the appropriate evidence you cannot give a specific cause (*proxima ... et vicina ... causa*) but only a general and rather abstract explanation, based as before on very general patterns of regularity within a certain class of events. Seneca is very aware that it is our limited access to appropriate specific evidence which justifies the kind of abstract and therefore intrinsically less satisfactory explanation which he most often offers. Perhaps this is the best that humans can do, given that direct access to the workings of so much of nature is denied to us. Perhaps this is part of what it means to live 'in accordance with an experience of things which occur by nature'.[34]

Book 3 of the *Naturales Quaestiones* concludes with an extended discussion of the ultimate question concerning *aquae terrestres*, the pre-ordained flood which extinguishes human life on earth at the end of the cycle of change (the counterpart, it seems, of the conflagration). This is obviously not a topic for ordinary empirical investigation and explanation, like the nature and sources of rivers and lakes. But since the occurrence of such a cataclysm is a feature not just of folklore but also of Stoic natural philosophy, it must be explicable in terms of the theory used to account for other watery phenomena and so is included here. Moreover, this theme makes a splendidly apt conclusion to the book, since it provides an obvious moral application (the extinction of humankind in a flood is fitting in view of our moral corruption) and an ideal opportunity for consistent reassertion of the centrality to Stoic physics of the relationship of god (or nature) to man.

In the flood passage as a whole the anthropocentric nature of the deluge is prominent. At the beginning (3.27.1) the sea assaults *us* (*in nos pelagus exsurgat*); the flood has a purpose: *ad exitium humani generis*. The destruction of human settlements is highlighted: villas, flocks and their masters, buildings, cities, walls (3.27.7). It is a *clades gentium* (3.2.27), and after the natural landscape has been described (3.27.8–9) Seneca invokes again the human point of view (*omnia qua prospici potest*) and presents us with the image of the miserable remnants of humanity huddling on the few remaining bits of high ground, puzzled and confused as well as fearful (3.27.11–15). Seneca returns to the human perspective near the end of the narrative

---

[34] DL 7.87, Stobaeus, *Ecl.* ii.76.

(3.29.5–9; 3.30.7–8) underlining the moral purpose of this cleansing destruction.

But the main theme is causal: *how* can the world be overwhelmed by one element? Seneca has to work against the implausibility of such an event, which is inevitably beyond the experience of human observers. In an attempt to make such a unique event plausible he emphasizes, at the beginning and the end of the passage, the unimaginable power of nature: nothing is hard for nature (3.27.2; 3.30.1), and this catastrophe is part of nature's plan from the beginning (3.30.1: *utique <quae> a primo facere constituit; fatalis...dies*, 3.27.1; *in finem sui properat*, 3.27.2; *illa necessitas temporis*, 3.27.3; *mutarique humanum genus placuit*, 3.28.2). Nature brings to bear the full range of watery causes (*omnis ratio consentiat*, 3.27.1; *multas simul fata causas movent*, 3.27.3). The power of nature is overwhelming when applied to the fragile nature of creatures. He reasons analogically again: just as the making of a human being or a city or a forest is a long and slow business but can after all be undone in a flash, so too the earth as a whole is vulnerable to sudden inundation (3.27.2–3).

Seneca considers a range of explanations for the flood, starting with the views of Fabianus (3.27.4). But this explanatory material is set in the context of a moral and theological relationship. Fate's power over man, its ability to command the full resources of the natural world (the tides are described at 3.28.4 as *fati ministerium*), and man's weakness and fragility in the face of divine or natural power (3.27.2–3) form the framework for the detailed explanations Seneca canvasses. But since in the end Seneca's view is that nature or god employs all possible causes in order to bring about the destruction of the human race by flood, the most important feature of the discussion is the polar opposition between divine power and human vulnerability.

And what are the causes? The first theories considered are unsurprising: rain (3.27.4–6) in amounts sufficient to undermine and weaken the foundations of everything (*nihil stabile est*), violent torrents from the hills (3.27.7), rivers rising far above their banks augmented by continued rain and even the rising levels of the sea (3.27.8–10). After a digression on the effects on human life of such causes (3.27.11–15) Seneca returns to his alleged *propositum*, the discussion of causal factors (3.28.1), and begins a debate (*sunt qui existimant; quibusdam placet*) which is typical of the ones he constructs in most of his detailed causal discussions. One party (3.28.1) denies the view Seneca has been developing and claims that excessive rain can endanger the land but not overwhelm it. Others (3.28.2) attribute the flooding to motions of the sea—presumably tidal disasters—holding that none of the causes considered so far can account for destruction on such a scale. Seneca is sympathetic to the combination of both sets of causes, since the lands must be overwhelmed and not just damaged. The effects of rain, streams, and rivers are mere preludes to the marine upheavals which lead to the final and complete inundation. This is reinforced by arguments that tidal floods can readily be understood as able to rise to the height of the land (3.28.3–5) and that observable variation in tidal activity is compatible with the postulate of such an unparalleled (*solutus legibus*, 3.28.7) tidal elevation. Indeed, this tidal hypothesis does violate the 'laws' of observed marine activity. How could this be, Seneca asks? 'By what rational principle (*qua ratione*) can one account for it?'

Just as the conflagration itself violates empirically grounded physical theories, so too does this postulate about marine activity. Seneca's strategy for explanation is based on a theological claim, the view that the *explanandum* is part of a divine plan (*cum deo visum est*) and is a divine decision (*quandoque placuere …placuit*). If that is the case, then, Seneca thinks, one can justify invoking explanations that go so far beyond what anyone has ever seen. Unprecedented rainfall (3.29.5, *plus umoris quam semper fuit*) and unparalleled high tides are complemented by other causes: earthquakes and the movements of the stars (3.29.1). Stellar activity is agreed to be part of the cause of the conflagration, and Seneca regards the inundation as its counterpart so it makes sense to accept such a cause there too. Hence Seneca accepts the validity of these causes and others extrapolated from the explanation of conflagration: it is part of the preordained growth cycle of the world to undergo flood just as it is to undergo fire (3.29.2–3).

All possible causes, then, are accepted as part of the explanation for the flood, which was a result of a decision of nature (3.29.4). The earth itself will contribute to its own demise (3.29.6–7). But the key point here is that the event is part of a law (*lex mundi*, 3.29.3) like that which governs the variation of seasons and the growth and development of living things (3.29.2–3). But this natural law is presented as a decision too (*a primo facere constituit; decretum est*, 3.30.1), as part of a plan formed by nature so that at will she could attack us (3.29.3). Earth's vulnerability to destruction by water is the counterpart of our own bodily weakness (3.30.4) and is the proper reward for our moral failings (when greed prompts us to dig for buried wealth, we find water, the premonition of our punishment, 3.30.3). The world is like our own bodies, kept sound only by constant diligence, and when that is relaxed destruction follows (3.30.5). But the destruction of the earth by water is part of a plan. Nature commands and permits it (3.30.6) and nature will again rein it in (3.30.7) when the time comes.

The opening book of the *Naturales Quaestiones*, then, sets the agenda for the treatise as a whole. Its overt theme is a set of problems and puzzles about a related group of natural phenomena. Seneca grapples with them by means of a carefully considered method,[35] one which rests on theological postulates but also gives considerable weight to a frank recognition of the limitations imposed on us by the fact that we are merely human observers. This recognition grounds both Seneca's readiness to employ controlled extrapolation from the observable to the unobserved and also his aetiological inclusiveness. Seneca wants to allow for all possible causes of the flood because there is no parallel in our experience for such an event being produced by a single cause and because we do not have grounds for ruling out any reasonable cause when the event is (from our limited point of view) unique and unobservable. As we should expect in a Stoic physical treatise, *Naturales Quaestiones* 3 weaves cosmology and theology together with divine purpose

---

[35] As we have seen (3.28), Seneca does not hesitate to create a debate where one is not strictly needed, in order to sharpen his case.

and plan, and there is an ambiguity between law and the decision of nature or god. Seneca does not even try to explain the natural world without intimate and indispensable reference to *our* position in it and god's role in governing it.

In books 4(a) through 5 many of these issues seem to persist, although in a less concentrated form. The truncated book 4(a) does not give us much to compare with book 3. There is certainly a strong moral motivation for the choice of subject matter: at 4a.1.1 Seneca explains to Lucilius that he has chosen to write about the Nile in order to draw his correspondent away from preoccupation with himself and the wonders of his own province. This motivation nicely reflects the lengthy preface on the evils of flattery and one's susceptibility to it (compare 4a Pref. 20: *fugiendum ergo et in se recendendum, immo etiam a se recedendum* and 4a.1.1: *ut totum inde te abducam...in diversum cogitationes tuas abstraham*). The reason for drawing him away from his own province was clearly stated in the preface (4a Pref. 21): *ne forte magnam esse historiis fidem credas et placere tibi incipias quotiens cogitaveris: 'hanc ego habeo sub meo iure provinciam...'*. Pride in his own rule would be as dangerous as the ambitious confusion between *procuratio* and *imperium* (4a Pref. 1); believing historians is equally risky (compare the remarks on what historians celebrate in 3 Pref.). But most of all, there is a kind of flattery to oneself in such pride. Hence the focus on the Nile, an Egyptian theme, while Lucilius is himself in Sicily. The message of this preface is that there is a serious moral drawback in believing what historians have to say about the importance of our affairs. To step back and consider them in the context of nature as a whole, or even in the context of some other part of the natural world, is morally salutary.[36] Natural philosophy, even of the more mundane kind, when practised in a critical spirit, displaces history from its customary role as a source of moral improvement—but it does so because history is limited, even blinded, by its human perspective while natural philosophy goes beyond it.

---

[36] Similarly in book 1 Pref. Seneca reflects on the smallness of human affairs when compared to nature as a whole.

But we do not in fact know how the moral motivation of the book played itself out in what followed, since so much of it is gone. The review of proposed explanations for the flooding of the Nile is lively and critical, and Seneca's intellectual poise is aptly reflected in his criticism of the philosophers in 4a.1. It is noteworthy that Seneca is here rejecting an argument from ignorance: earlier philosophers had thought that since the source was unknown and since the pattern of flooding was similar to the Danube, we should postulate similar causes for the Nile. Now this is a form of inference to which Seneca has no objection—it is not unlike his own method in book 3, where he took it to be acceptable to postulate uniformities in cases where there was no specific discoverable evidence to the contrary. So it is not the form of the explanatory move of which Seneca disapproves. His grounds for dissatisfaction are that by now the source of the Danube has been found in Germany, and without the ignorance and lack of evidence there is no justification for the general licence to invoke unconfirmable analogies; and also that the pattern of flooding is not sufficiently similar to support the inference.

In 4b we lack any hint of the contents of the preface and must plunge into the middle of Seneca's account of hail. Given his methodological self-consciousness so far, it is probably not accidental that he is caught renouncing an overly bold plan: *grandinem hoc modo fieri si tibi adfirmavero quo apud nos glacies fit, gelata nube tota, nimis audacem rem fecero* (4b.3.1). He seems to want to be counted a witness of secondary value, since he concedes that he does not have first-hand evidence (*qui vidisse quidem se negant*). Historians are again offered up as a contrast: *they* will offer one false claim after another and then provide merely token indications of methodological care, when they disclaim *fides* and transfer responsibility to their sources. Seneca is, I think, being ironic when he offers Posidonius as a more trustworthy source on the subject of the formation of hail, since he is willing to *adfirmare* just as though he were a first-hand witness (*tamquam interfuerit*). That Posidonius' confidence is ill-founded is clear. Seneca, then, has positioned himself in contrast to both the historians and the distinguished Stoic

Posidonius as one *auctor*, at least, who can be relied upon, since he does not claim to be authoritative where he cannot be because of his lack of first-hand observation. And of course the topic he is dealing with was not susceptible of first-hand observation by any human. The speculative nature of meteorological investigation seems to have weighed more heavily with Seneca than with other practitioners of the art.

At 4b.3.3 Seneca moves on to a topic about which he feels he can offer a theory, the shape of hail. For although the moment of formation of hail is hidden, analogical reasoning based on first-hand observation is possible: all other cases of moisture forming into droplets show that the condensate is globular. So too, then, for hail. At 4b.3.6 he invites direct comparison with Anaxagoras, claiming that as a philosopher he ought himself to have the same freedom to develop theories as did his famous predecessor. And this freedom to advance theories is further defended on pragmatic grounds at 4b.5.1. Seneca introduces a critique of a Stoic theory. He does not want to advance it (since it is so feeble); but neither does he want to leave it out. He reflects, then, *quid enim mali est aliquid et faciliori iudici scribere?* A strict criterion (*obrussa*) for arguments on such matters would lead to silence. The forensic metaphor continues: *pauca enim admodum sunt sine adversario, cetera, etsi vincunt, litigant.* Hence he feels justified in extending his account with a highly speculative theory. But he has carefully distinguished the risky nature of his own theory; we should recall that he had said at 4b.4.1 that he could justifiably cease his account but wanted to provide a full measure of satisfaction to Lucilius. This unconfirmed theory (4b.5.3) is worth floating for a relaxed and indulgent critic ready to tolerate *molestia* (4b.4.1).

But what it leads to is genuinely strange theorizing. In 4b.6–7 Stoic silliness (*ineptiae*) is pilloried. There are people who think that hail can be predicted and that it is a form of divination which can be the basis for propitiatory sacrifices. Evidently some members of his own school had tried to justify such antiquated and superstitious religious practices, but for Seneca this is nothing but laughable nonsense, the sort of thing which you don't need to be a philosopher to reject out of hand. The inclusion of this nugatory point about hail is puzzling, I think, unless we recognize it as a foil. Seneca is self-consciously presenting himself as a thoughtful and methodologically careful author, unlike so many even of his own school. Of course, this also foreshadows the discussion of Etruscan augury in book 2 and reminds us again that divine–human relations are never far from Seneca's mind in the *Naturales Quaestiones*.

The remaining material in 4b can be handled briefly. Various speculations about whether snow forms high or low in the atmosphere are highlighted by Seneca's reaction to the notion (4b.11) that mountain peaks must be warmer since they are closer to the sun. He rejects this because, he maintains, on the relevant scale such mountains are not in fact 'high'. As he maintained in the discussion of the flood (3.28), on the cosmic scale the minor variations on the earth's surface, such as valleys and mountains, are not of significant size. What seems so impressive from the human perspective is in fact of no cosmic relevance.[37] There is, Seneca seems to think, an arrogance in judging the cosmic relationships relevant to explanations of this sort by merely human standards. Anyone, he says, who believes that lofty mountains get warmer because they are higher might just as well hold that tall people get warmer than short people and that our heads get warmer than our feet (4b.11.4). Such ridicule underlines Seneca's conviction that mistakes of perspective about the scale and relevance of human beings and our concerns lead not just to moral flaws but to bad explanatory science.[38]

Book 5, on winds, lacks a preface to orient the reader. The book opens with a short controversy about the proper definition (*formula*) of 'wind' (5.1) and then plunges immediately into a critical consideration of different theories, beginning with Democritus. Most of this proceeds unremarkably after the pattern set in books 3–4(b).[39] Seneca's own view is that air, like

---

[37] Cf. 1 Pref. 9–11 for this point with an explicit anchoring of it in the contrast of the human and the divine spheres.

[38] The balance of 4b is a moral excursus linked to the use of snow to cool wine.

[39] But 5.4.2–3 contains a not-to-be-missed rejection of the view that winds have their origin in digestive gases produced by the world animal.

other elements, contains a life force within itself and so winds are examples of self-motion (5.5–6). When we turn to more detailed discussion of particular winds (including whirlwinds in 5.13), if there is any particular theme to the critiques offered of various views it would have to be that they all too often involve incomplete generalizations and rest on factual errors. In 5.14 Seneca again (as in book 3) relies heavily on the postulation of features in the unobserved caverns beneath the earth similar to those we can note in our world of observed phenomena. In 5.14.2 he argues for license to make this postulate by saying: *nam ne haec quidem supra terras quia videntur sunt, sed quia sunt videntur; illic quoque nihilo ob id minus sunt quod non videntur flumina*. Hence he can postulate subterranean phenomena to explain the winds which take their origin in the earth. And, he says (5.14.3), *quae si ita sunt, necesse est et illud*. That is, he uses this kind of postulate as a crucial support for further argument. The book is rounded out (after a brief digressive story in 5.15) by a discussion of the classification of winds by direction and location (5.16–17) and concluded (5.18) by an expansive description of the providential nature of winds and our all too human tendency to abuse this divine gift. Seneca insists (5.18.13) that we cannot legitimately complain about the god who made us, if it is we who have spoiled his generous gifts. One of the driest discussions in the entire *Naturales Quaestiones* is brought back to Seneca's general purpose with this conclusion. For it confirms again that the relationship between god and man and the moral standing which men have as a result of how they react to god and/or nature are issues which lie at the heart of the *Naturales Quaestiones*.

The remaining four books represent a crescendo of concentration on these themes.

Book 6 deals with the causes of earthquakes. It approaches the topic with an urgency provoked by the recent occurrence of a major earthquake in Campania, probably in February of AD 62, at a time of year when (as Seneca notes) such disasters were least expected. After surveying the scope of the damage (6.1.1–3) Seneca sets out the motivation for the consideration of earthquakes. It is not just the orderly progression of his work (*propositi operis contextus*, 6.1.3) but also the need to provide consolation and remedy for the fears people understandably feel after such a disaster (6.1.4). He paints a vivid picture of the particular fear inspired in men by earthquakes. The earth is supposed to be the most stable and reliable part of our world. If it crumbles, what can be trusted? Earthquakes leave the victims no place to run, so comprehensive is the disaster (6.1.4–7).

The consolation Seneca offers begins from the fact that *some people* at least think of earthquakes as a particularly horrible way to die (6.1.8). To this the response is simple. Nature is just, and one central feature of its justice is that all forms of death have the same outcome: *cum ad exitum ventum est, omnes in aequo sumus*. Seneca's claim is that the kind of vulnerability which seismophobes feel is quite unreasonable. Such vulnerability is actually universal, part of the bargain we accept when we live on this earth (6.1.9–15). Earthquakes cannot be prevented or predicted; no one promises us stability (6.1.10). So everyone, not just Campanians, lives with the risk. Just as the earth is subject to the same law of vulnerability (*eadem lege*, 6.1.12), so too human beings and our cities are by nature short-lived and perishable servants of fate (6.1.14). If our experience suggests grounds for confidence, that suggestion is deceptive. Although some regions might seem relatively immune from risk (6.1.13), none really is. Yet on the basis of our experience, limited as it is, we humans promise ourselves stability and permanence. Knowing what the rules of the game really are (a knowledge which comes from the study of physics) would humble those who precipitately entrust themselves to confidence, only to fall victims when the unexpected occurs.

But this, as Seneca well knows, is a peculiar comfort. Where (one might wonder) is the remedy in being told that dangers are actually more widespread than we might have thought (6.2.1)?[40] The answer to his own rhetorical question is critical

[40] Of course, the notion that such a reflection is supposed to console a rational person is the core of Stoic (and other) consolatory rhetoric. Seneca is, I suspect, aware that this consideration will provide cold comfort to many. Chrysippus himself was sensitive to the rhetorical and psychological demands of the consolatory process, if I am right in my interpretation of *Tusculan Disputations* 3.74–79 (see Inwood, *Ethics and Human Action in Early Stoicism* (Oxford, 1985), 153–4).

to understanding the *Naturales Quaestiones* as a whole. Seneca recognizes a dual audience: *prudentes* will be freed from fear by the use of reason, and the *imperiti*, those not trained in philosophy, will find comfort in the abandonment of (false) hopes. It is not just that earthquakes can occur anywhere; the prospect of death is omnipresent in the most trivial causes, and the uniformity of the outcome makes the means irrelevant; Seneca concludes with the consoling thought (tinged with his usual irony) that in a way earthquake victims are special favourites of nature: *quid habeo quod querar, si rerum natura me non vult iacere ignobili leto, si mihi inicit sui partem* (6.2.2–9).

But the *prudentes* do not have to settle for this rhetorical consolation. They can grasp the causes of things. In a sentence reminiscent of Epicurean rationalism, aimed at religious sentiments prevalent among his audience,[41] Seneca points out that it is beneficial to be aware that earthquakes and similar phenomena are not caused by individual gods and divine anger (6.3.1): *suas ista causas habent, nec ex imperio saeviunt, sed quibusdam vitiis ut corpora nostra turbantur, et tunc cum facere videntur iniuriam, accipiunt*. It is our ignorance of these natural causes (*nobis ignorantibus verum*), coupled with the rarity of the phenomena, which causes fear (6.3.2). The rarity of the events is important, since (like good naïve empiricists) people are less strongly affected by anything which is a familiar part of their experience.

This is the occasion for one of Seneca's most important methodological reflections. Asking *quare autem quicquam nobis insolitum est* he replies that the error comes from reliance on our eyes rather than our reason: we rely on experience rather than analysis of nature (*nec cogitamus quid illa facere possit sed tantum quid fecerit*). The penalty for this mental laziness is the very irrational fear which Seneca proposes to combat by analysing the causes of earthquakes. Rare events (earthquakes, eclipses, comets) inspire superstitious reactions (*religio*) both public and private, and our astonishment is mixed with fear (*nihil horum sine timore miramur*, 6.3.4).

---

[41] Pliny, *HN* 2.200 reports the widespread view that earthquakes served as warnings of future events.

We need to go beyond naïve reliance on our observational experience if we are to rise above our fear of natural events. Is it not worthwhile to *know* the causes of things, if the reward is freedom from fear? Such an investigation demands complete focus (*toto in hoc intentum animo*); it is not just a sensible course of action for men, but also the most fitting and worthy task (*neque... quicquam... dignius*) for us as rational animals (6.3.4). That is why, Seneca says (*ergo*, 6.4.1), he urges the enquiry on his readers. He begins by describing the phenomena in a way designed to make the enquiry intellectually engaging, one which is worthy of our attention (*dignas res*, 6.4.1). At an imaginary challenge from Lucilius (*quod... erit pretium operae?* 6.4.2) Seneca completes the shift from offering an emotionally utilitarian justification for the enquiry (as he did at the beginning) to the claim that the topic is intrinsically worthwhile: the reward is *quo nullum maius est, nosse naturam. Neque enim quicquam habet in se huius materiae tractatio pulchrius, cum multa habeat futura usui, quam quod hominem magnificentia sui detinet, nec mercede sed miraculo colitur.* We are, as Aristotle knew, creatures who by nature desire to understand things, inspired deeply by a sense of wonder at natural phenomena, and Seneca here acknowledges that as the overriding motivation. To live according to our experience of what happens by nature is our goal not just because it helps to free us from fear, but also because we are naturally contemplative creatures, fellow-citizens of the gods in the cosmic state and born to contemplate as well as to imitate the cosmos, being imperfect parts of the whole.[42]

As a piece of persuasive writing, this introduction is quite successful. Having begun with the charged issue of recent disaster and the natural human panic it inspires, Seneca moves smoothly through a gamut of emotional and intellectual stages (including his disdain for shallow reliance on *mere* experience as opposed to causal analysis) until the deepest motivation is unveiled (one which clearly goes well beyond the motivations adduced in the preface to book 3). Now he can begin (6.5), and

---

[42] Cicero, *ND* 2.37: *ipse autem homo ortus est ad mundum contemplandum et imitandum, nullo modo perfectus sed est quaedam particula perfecti.*

he does so with a critical review of previous and unsatisfactory theories; but although he is frank about the failings of primitive explanations, he confesses a deep respect (reminiscent of Aristotle's) for those who opened up the field of natural enquiry (6.5.1–3). Simply forming the ambition to investigate was the critical achievement; such starting points are naturally crude by the standards of their successors. It is worth noting how Seneca describes their endeavours: they were not content with the *exterior aspectus* of nature, but opened up her hiding places and plunged into the *deorum secreta*. In contrast to the superstitious attention to gods which natural phenomena normally evoke, Seneca equates nature and the gods. These are rational gods whose 'worship' requires that we use the methods of rational investigation to go deep beneath the surface world of our ordinary observational experience.

In his review of theories Seneca begins (6.6–9) with those which rely on water as the explanation. Most such theories, especially Thales', are unsatisfactory, but Seneca is favourably impressed by those which rely on subterranean rivers and lakes (one of several unremarked backward references to earlier books). In the course of developing this view he pauses to justify once again his postulate[43] that there are massive underground bodies of water, and a familiar theme returns. People who deny such waters are naïve empiricists, trusting too much to their eyes and unwilling to project intellectually from the seen world to the hidden world beneath the earth. There follows a series (extending to 6.8.5) of abstract and empirical arguments for at least the possibility of the postulate.

After dealing with water as a cause, Seneca turns to the other two elements which are candidates: fire (6.9–11) and air (6.12 ff.), in each case reviewing earlier theories with a critical sympathy. He takes special interest (6.14) in a theory which exploits the parallel between the earth and the human body.[44] In 6.16.1 he pauses on a distinctively Stoic theory (though he

---

[43] 6.7.5. Hine marks this as the speech of an interlocutor, but I cannot understand why. Gercke in his 1907 Teubner, Oltramare in the Budé, and Corcoran in the Loeb recognize that Seneca is the speaker here.

[44] Cf. book 3 and 5.4.2.

does not describe it as such) which invokes the creative *pneuma* in all things including the apparently inert earth. At 6.16.2 he turns to more powerful arguments in favour of assigning a key causal role to air. He argues first for the existence of a vast quantity of air (6.16.2–4) and for its intrinsically restless and mobile nature (6.16.4–6.17.1). It is only when this natural motility is impeded, Seneca claims, that it shakes and disrupts the earth (6.17.1–6.18.5). This theory is given support (perhaps dubious support) by a further comparison of the earth to the human body (6.18.6–7). Seneca concludes his survey of theories based on air with a scrupulous mention of Metrodorus (6.19).

In 6.20 Seneca digresses to consider two theorists who combine various elemental causes, Democritus and Epicurus. Epicurus' theory of multiple causation is mentioned without disapproval, and it is striking that Seneca's own explicit acceptance of air as the dominant cause is presented as an agreement with Epicurus (6.21.1: *nobis quoque*). Since Seneca frequently entertains a variety of explanations without dogmatic rejection of all but one, this apparently tolerant view of Epicurean multiple causation is striking—another mark, perhaps, of Seneca's methodological independence from his school.[45]

Seneca goes on to discuss the Stoic theories of Posidonius and Asclepiodotus (6.21 ff.) pausing to give strong assent to the collapsing-cavern explanation for many quakes (6.23.1) and to digress briefly on Callisthenes (6.23.2–3). In 6.24.1 he again speaks with surprising forthrightness of his preferred theory, and argues bluntly (note *hoc incredibile est*, 6.24.2) in his own voice about various details of the air theory, invoking yet again the analogy with the human body (6.24.2–3). Seneca is unequivocally in favour of a theory relying on the existence of huge unobserved underground caverns. Hence his earlier remarks about the legitimacy of postulating such unseen phenomena now bear fruit. On his view, the correct explanation of earthquakes does indeed rely on our readiness to put our

---

[45] See too above on his reasons for accepting all possible causes of the cataclysm: if the scale of the event is unique it is reasonable to invoke all possible causes.

minds above our eyes and to abandon naïve empiricism. As he said early in the book, the use of reason and not mere observation is required for a real explanation and consolation.

Seneca closes his general account of earthquakes (6.26) with further methodological reflection. Literary evidence is rejected, even though it might support his own favourite theory. Philosophers[46] are stigmatized (somewhat as historians have been until now) as a *credula natio* for accepting such evidence. The case is closed with terse citation of factual counterexamples (6.26.4), and Seneca turns his attention to a series of things which were allegedly peculiar to the Campanian quake which provoked the entire discussion and other singular features (6.27–31).

At 6.32 Seneca sets aside the causal explanation and turns explicitly to the *confirmatio animorum* which concludes the book, emphasizing that although courage is more in our interest than learning, it cannot be achieved without learning. As at the beginning of book 6 (this whole conclusion is a clear restatement and expansion of the introduction), so too here: it is the *contemplatio naturae* which is made the key to moral virtues. The consolatory discourse which ensues focuses, as did the introduction of the book, on the omnipresence of death and the equality of the outcome. Our happiness and equality with the gods (6.32.5–7) depends on being ready to let go of our life easily. This discourse, surely Seneca's self-conscious reply to Lucretius' own impressive meditation on the fear of death, ranges over a number of familiar consolatory themes and concludes with the reflection that death is inevitable for all creatures, but that the timing of it is none of our concern. In the concluding words of book 6 (the most polished and effective book in the entire *Naturales Quaestiones*) Seneca offers his reply not just to Lucretius but also to Plato:

Death is the law of nature, death is the debt and duty of mortals and the cure for all their misfortunes. Anyone who is afraid wishes for

---

[46] Although all MSS here read *philosophi* many editors have emended to *philologi* and to *historici*. How easy it is to underestimate Seneca's critical detachment, independence, and irony.

death. Lucilius, forget the rest and practise this alone, not to fear the word 'death'. Think on it often and so make it your intimate companion, so that if need be you can go to meet it head on.

Here Seneca fuses his theological, physical, epistemological, and moral concerns more thoroughly than in any earlier book.

The opening of book 7 brings the reader back to the heavens from which he began in book 3. The heavens, that is to say the realm of the divine, stimulate the intellectual excitement of all but the most dull, and especially when something unprecedented or unusual happens. While the philosophically minded find the phenomena of the heavens intellectually and morally uplifting in all circumstances, human nature is such (*ita enim compositi sumus*) that familiar things, even if they are intrinsically impressive, leave us cold, while unusual phenomena, even if they are in themselves unimportant, will be a *spectaculum dulce* (7.1.1): the stars, the sun, and the moon when not in eclipse are normally taken for granted. An unfamiliar event, such as an eclipse, has the power to excite us, even if the reaction is grounded on superstition; the actual causes of an eclipse are important, and well known to the enlightened. But the predictable reaction of human beings (neglect except in the case of novelty) confirms the importance of familiarity (7.1.3–4). People are naturally drawn to amazement at the novel (*adeo naturale est magis nova quam magna mirari*). Seneca sees our natural and healthy empiricism as a mixed blessing; for in the absence of sound explanations of the phenomena it leaves us exposed to fear and superstition. Our reactions to comets illustrate this clearly: for like eclipses they inspire ignorant superstition and insecurity, although a sound understanding of celestial phenomena would liberate us from such panics.[47]

Hence Seneca proposes to approach the understanding of comets from the point of view of their similarity to and difference from better understood phenomena, such as stars and planets (7.2.1–2). Clearly he is aiming to combat irrational reactions to natural phenomena (which by their very nature cannot be proper grounds for such reactions); he is not merely

[47] Cf. *NQ* 6.3.2.

explaining an interesting celestial anomaly because it is an interesting problem. Similarly, Seneca expects that the enquiry in this book will shed light on the question of whether the cosmos is geocentric or not—something worth knowing not just because it is interesting, but because it deals with the relationship of man to god: *digna res contemplatione, ut sciamus in quo rerum statu simus, pigerrimam sortiti an velocissimam sedem, circa nos deus omnia an nos agat* (7.2.3).

With this motivation Seneca tackles the problem of the nature of comets. His aims reveal the interdependence, by now familiar, of epistemological themes and theological issues. And his procedure in the discussion which follows accords with the familiar pattern: critical review and analysis of earlier views tempered with independent argument. Hence Seneca begins with the obvious fact that we need to begin from collections of data accumulated over lengthy periods of time, data which really aren't available to us (7.3). In the absence of this kind of data Seneca must start from a review of the theories of those who appear to be the best sources, Epigenes and Apollonius of Mynda (7.4.1). Epigenes' views, discussed extensively against the background of as much 'evidence' as can be gathered, fare poorly (7.4.10); often the counterargument is simple observation. When Seneca turns to other theories about celestial bodies (7.11–15) he is direct and refreshing in his debunking of half-baked theories.[48] In 7.16 he turns to the discrediting of historians such as Ephorus as sources for observations of the heavens—and it is hard to find fault with his calculated scepticism.

In 7.17 Seneca turns to the other major authority, Apollonius of Mynda, about whom we know, alas, nothing beyond what Seneca tells us. His theory that comets are celestial bodies like planets is rejected briskly, by the simple observation that we can see through comets as we cannot see through any other *stella*, wandering or fixed (7.18.2).[49] Then Stoic theories are outlined

[48] At 7.14.1 Seneca describes the attempt to refute a particularly fanciful theory as a kind of shadow-boxing: *solvere ista quid aliud est quam manum exercere et in ventum iacere bracchia?* He is quite aware of how hard it is to refute theories for which no evidence, for or against, can be found.

[49] But see below for Seneca's own exploitation of this observation. His polemical use of the argument is considerably less nuanced than his own positive use of it.

(7.19–21) and Seneca presents them in sympathetic detail, even using question and answer with an imaginary objector to strengthen the proposal that comets are atmospheric rather than celestial phenomena.

For all that, the standard Stoic view leaves Seneca unconvinced: *ego nostris non adsentior* (7.22.1). In his view comets are among the *aeterna opera naturae*, located beyond the transience of the lower atmosphere. Comets, in Seneca's opinion, are too stable and regular to be grouped with such phenomena (7.22–3). He turns then to further objections to his proposal. In 7.24 it is suggested (by an unnamed critic) that celestial bodies would have to be in the zodiac somehow. The rejoinder appeals to the divine character of the *stellae*: we cannot impose such an arbitrary limit on heavenly bodies. For all we know, some such bodies, all of which we cannot observe up close, might be able to appear from unknown quarters. It is the very limitation of our human ability to gather evidence which makes it irrational for us to impose a limit on entities which are so far beyond human observation (7.24.1), a limit which would have to be arbitrary, given the limitations of our observations. And furthermore, a comet may, for all we know, actually be in the zodiac at some point in its orbit; its orbit may simply be so unusual that our limited observational data have not yet revealed its place in the planetary and stellar system (7.24.2). And can there really be such a small number of planets as five in the vast sweep of our night sky (7.24.3)? Here, Seneca's epistemological modesty has guided him towards an importantly though accidentally correct view.[50]

In 7.25 this uncertainty is compared to our knowledge of the human mind. There are many things, he says, which we know to exist without having to know the details. Since the evidence about comets is thin, we must refrain from forming negative conclusions. We know that we have a mind without being able to agree on all of the details about its nature. So too we should

---

[50] Cf. Favorinus at Aulus Gellius 14.1.11–12 (my thanks to Emidio Spinelli for the comparison).

be able to believe that comets are *stellae* even if we cannot be certain about the details of their nature. As the book began with remarks about how limited our observational data are, so here Seneca emphasizes that our ignorance is commensurate with the limited history of observation (7.25.3–5). Just as several features of planetary orbits were puzzling at first but eventually explained, so too we should expect there to be explanations someday for the puzzling features of the behaviour of comets: our descendants and successors will perhaps answer some of the challenges now posed, so it would be irrational, in the current state of our knowledge of the heavens, to reject a prima facie appealing theory (7.25.6–7).

Seneca is not, of course, claiming that his theories are immune to criticism because cometary science is so young. After all, he had many arguments to make against other theories, and he is therefore obliged in this section of the book to defend his view (which is after all quite modest and sketchy) in ways that are compatible with his own earlier arguments.[51] And he does so, insisting throughout that criticisms of his proposal that comets are stellar be consistent with our general knowledge about heavenly bodies. For example, he rejects the criticism that comets do not have the standard stellar shape (round) not only by arguing that the core of a comet may well be round (7.26.2), but also by rejecting a mechanical requirement of uniformity for all heavenly phenomena (7.27). Nature, he contends, is a powerful force and part of her power lies in her ability to produce exceptional phenomena (7.27.5): as important as consistency among the phenomena is, demands for premature generalizations should be resisted. The less we know, in fact, the more open-minded we should be.

These are only samples of Seneca's style of argument, but I submit that they display both his level-headed empirical respect for evidence and argument and his canny awareness that conclusions can only be as strong and definite as the quality of the

[51] In 7.26.1 Seneca concedes that our ability to see through comets presents a problem for his claim that comets are *stellae*. After all, the point had already been raised at 7.18.2. But consistency is maintained by noting that it is only the tail of the comet that one can see through, not the solid core.

evidence we have to work from. Hence just before the theological peroration of the book, Seneca concludes (7.29.3): *haec sunt quae aut alios movere ad cometas pertinentia aut me: quae an vera sint, di sciunt, quibus veri scientia est. nobis rimari illa et coniectura ire in occulta tantum licet, nec cum fiducia inveniendi nec sine spe.* There is an epistemic humility here of which Xenophanes might be proud.[52]

And such humility is, for Seneca, also an act of piety. In the final section of the book (7.30–2) Seneca brings together themes which have been building slowly. The universe is a divine place, and the heavenly phenomena rank with the divine beings themselves in their claims on our epistemic caution. Aristotle is cited with approval for this notion, and Seneca's concern is to avoid at all costs bold or imprudent claims which run ahead of the evidence and so lead to false claims about the most important matters (7.30.1). Panaetius and the other Stoics are particularly chastised for premature zeal in claiming that comets can be easily explained as atmospheric phenomena. Seneca thinks it critical to allow for how much lies *in occulto* (7.30.2).

The opacity of the works of nature to human eyes (7.30.3: *numquam humanis oculis orientia*) is the theme on which the book closes. Xenophanes again seems to hover in the wings when Seneca says that god has not made everything for us. Our eyes are not the tools to probe the depths of the natural, that is, the divine world. The god who made the world escapes visual inspection and can only be seen by means of *cogitatio*; the supreme spirit (*numen summum*) grants access only to the *animus*. We cannot, he claims, have knowledge of god, the foundation of all things (*quid sit hoc sine quo nihil est scire non possumus*). Why should we be surprised that bits of fire are not exhaustively known when *maxima pars mundi, deus* is himself obscure (7.30.4). Even among the more accessible bodies of knowledge, such as zoology, progress is still being made in his own time. As in the mysteries at Eleusis, so in natural

---

[52] See 21B 18,34 DK. On the possible influence of Xenophanes in later centuries, see Guido Turrini, 'Il frammento 34 di Senofane e la tradizione dossografica', *Prometheus*, 8 (1982), 17–135.

philosophy: something is saved for the final revelation and *rerum natura sacra sua non semel tradit*. We have to expect that there is a great deal for future generations to discover too (7.30.6).

This theological language is not anti-empirical, nor is it anti-rational. Seneca is not saying that there are things which we just cannot understand, that god works in intrinsically mysterious ways. He is making a more modest claim. When the evidence concerning a set of phenomena is weak, the conclusions must be weak. Hence prematurely conclusive theories are bound to lead one astray. The natural world is, he claims, a large and complicated place; there is no good reason to think that it is just laid open for us by the gods. Just the opposite, in fact. A properly pious appreciation of the relationship of human nature to the divine will induce us to be epistemically modest and to anticipate (itself quite a rational view) that progress in the explanation of the natural world will be cumulative and slow. Indeed, Seneca's final assessment (7.31–2) is that, given the state of culture in his own day—a depraved condition in which all ingenuity is squandered on vice and luxury, with nothing left for philosophy (esp. 7.32)—it is not to be expected that great progress will be made in his generation. Even if, he concludes pessimistically, his culture put everything it had into natural philosophy it could hardly expect to get to the bottom of things, which is where truth is to be found (*ad fundum . . . in quo veritas posita est*);[53] but as it is, Roman culture is just idly scratching the surface (*quam nunc in summa terra et levi manu quaerimus*). The impiety which Seneca sees in this situation can readily be inferred. He does not need to spell it out.

In book 7, Seneca denied that comets were an instance of atmospheric fire. Hence the subject matter of book 1, atmospheric fire, follows naturally. Similarly the preface to book 1 comes naturally after the conclusion of book 7. Seneca included in his consideration of comets some thoughtful remarks on the gap between the divine order and human epistemic capabilities and some quite pessimistic comments on the standing of philosophy in his own society. Hence the next book opens with a

---

[53] Cf. Democritus, 68B 117 DK.

preface exploring the value of philosophy and the relationship of man to god.

The preface opens with the claim that the difference between philosophy and the other arts is as great as the difference in value between theology and ethics (*illam partem quae ad homines et hanc quae ad deos pertinet*, where '*hanc*' clearly signals that his current work is theological). In addition to being superior in other ways, theology, as noted in book 7, does not limit itself to the evidence of the eyes (*non... oculis contenta*); not only is it better, but it also eliminates the darkness in which we would otherwise be enmired. As god is superior to man, so physics and theology are superior to ethics (1 Pref. 1–2). The scope of physics is quickly sketched: not just the theory of matter but theology too (1 Pref. 3), where theology includes questions about the nature of god and fate. Seneca avers that his gratitude to nature for the opportunity to study her is so great that it would hardly be worth living otherwise. Not to study nature and god, he thinks, is to reduce oneself to a mere body, a repository for food and drink. Studying the nature of the divine cosmos is, for Seneca, at the heart of what it is to be a human being (*o quam contempta res est homo nisi supra humana surrexerit*). Man is somehow incomplete without the study of physics, which pulls us beyond ourselves and the narrow world open only to the eyes (1 Pref. 4–5).[54]

Seneca then expatiates eloquently on how it is that the study of cosmology carries man beyond his own parochial interests— and parochial they are, since the earth on which we live is so small compared to the size of the universe as a whole (1 Pref. 6–17). In the course of this Seneca confirms the intimate connection between human nature and the study of physics and theology. At 1 Pref. 7 he claims that *tunc consummatum habet plenumque bonum sortis humanae cum calcato omni malo petit altum et in interiorem naturae sinum venit*. In 1 Pref. 12 Seneca asserts the divinity of the mind on the basis of the fact that our mind is nourished by its exposure to the celestial to which it really belongs (*in originem redit*) and is genuinely pleased by

---

[54] On these themes, compare Seneca's remarks at *Ep.* 65.15–22, 90.34, and 117.19.

such studies. The heavens *belong* to the soul (*ut suis interest, scit illa ad se pertinere*). A mind exposed to its true origins comes to despise the earth, which it used to think of as its proper home (1 Pref. 13). The entire quest of the mind, what it seeks while it studies physics, is god:[55]

There it learns at last what it has sought for so long, there it begins to know god. What is god? The mind of the cosmos. What is god? All that you see and all that you do not see. His real greatness, greater than which nothing can be conceived, is only attributed to him if he alone is all things, if he sustains his handiwork from within and from without.

The fact that god is a mind forms a crucial part of the bond between god and man. But the differences between us are just as important. For god is nothing but mind, while in us the mind is merely our better part (1 Pref. 14). And yet, Seneca continues, some people, philosophers as well as laymen, deny the providence and intelligence of god, i.e. nature (1 Pref. 14–15). He concludes with a grandiose rhetorical question about the value of studying theology and physics. Such study, he claims, takes us beyond our own mortal nature and enrols us in a higher class (*in meliorem transcribi sortem*). If you ask, he concludes, what good this will do, he replies: *si nihil aliud, hoc certe: sciam omnia angusta esse mensus deum*. Man is not the measure of all things; god is.

In reviewing the various manifestations of atmospheric fire and light, Seneca begins by raising the question of whether certain unusual phenomena should be viewed as portents—an issue that arose when dealing with comets as well (7.1).[56] Here (1.1.4) such issues are explicitly deferred to a later time (the final book, 2.32 ff.). For there Seneca addresses the major theological issues for a final time. The rest of 1.1 is a critical review of anomalous atmospheric fires and explanations offered for them. 1.2 begins the discussion of haloes and related

---

[55] Note that even here Seneca expresses his sensitivity to epistemological issues, for he neatly divides the realm of enquiry by an epistemic criterion: *quod vides totum et quod non vides*.

[56] And also for earthquakes (6.3.2); Seneca is building towards his final discussion of Etruscan divination in book 2.

phenomena with a similarly undeveloped allusion to their portentous nature. When in 1.3–8 Seneca turns to rainbows (along with mirrors, prisms, and related optical phenomena) he does not invoke issues of prediction and portent, but rather limits himself to a careful and closely argued treatment of the causes, displaying his familiar independence of mind; he trails off in 1.9–11 with a treatment of *virgae* before moving on (1.12–13) to eclipses and a rather heterogeneous collection of optical problems. 1.14–15 return to the kind of unusual atmospheric fires with which comets had been classed and with which Seneca began. But questions of providence and portent, the relationship of man to god, are absent. Instead, Seneca concludes the book (1.16–17) with a moralizing excursus on Hostius Quadra, connected to the rest of the book by the thinnest of threads: his sexual perversion made indispensable use of mirrors. But it would be foolish to grope for a stronger connection to the rest of the book. Here, at least, is a moralizing excursus included for its own sake, and anyone who takes the time to savour it will scarcely question its interest or (admittedly prurient) literary merit.

Book 2 of the *Naturales Quaestiones*, the final book, is also the longest. It begins with an introductory section (2.1–11) which outlines the three relevant[57] parts of physics (*caelestia, sublimia, terrena*) and emphasizes the interdependence of the various components of the system;[58] it focuses extensively on the unity of the world, the nature of the parts within it,[59] and especially on the unique role of air in creating and preserving

---

[57] Relevant not just because these three realms exhaust the range of physics, but also because of the amount of debate about which phenomena are heavenly and which atmospheric (as in the book on comets) and because of the crucial role of terrestrial and subterranean phenomena in so many of his explanations. This tripartition does not represent a basic organizing principle for the entire work.

[58] 2.2 presents a quite technical categorization of the metaphysical underpinnings for the kind of unity which the cosmos has; cf. *Ep.* 102. Seneca's self-consciousness about technicality is reflected clearly in 2.2.4: *vide quomodo auribus tuis parcam.*

[59] Notice the nice distinction between *genera*, which are true parts, and individuals, which are quasi-parts, in 2.4.2. On the Stoic theory of parts generally see J. Barnes, 'Bits and Pieces', in J. Barnes and M. Mignucci, *Matter and Metaphysics* (Naples, 1988), 223–94.

that unity (2.4.1–2), culminating in a minor hymn, one might say, to the power and nature of air.[60] Stoic doctrines about the continuous nature of air and its variability are affirmed. Two epistemological themes emerge in passing: the familiar distinction between things graspable by the senses and those grasped by reason (2.2.3), and the bold claim that the cosmos is epistemically exhaustive: 'the cosmos embraces everything which does or can fall within [the scope of] our knowledge' (2.3.1).[61] There is nothing, then, which a human being can know which is not part of the cosmos—we have, clearly, an important explicit assertion of naturalism; this is welcome, since the repeated emphasis in the *Naturales Quaestiones* on the fact that there are things which the senses cannot grasp or that can only be grasped by reason might lead one to suspect the influence of a quasi-Platonic dualism.[62] But the existence of things graspable only by reason is compatible with Stoic monism, just as much as the distinction in value between earthly and celestial realms (reaffirmed in 2.1.5).

The stated reason for this lengthy account of air is that the phenomena which form the proper topic of the book (lightning, thunderbolts, thunderclaps) occur in the atmosphere, and hence require a general idea of the nature of air in order to control the discussion. And air does play a crucial role in what follows. But so too does the cosmological doctrine that the cosmos is an orderly creation, which emerges from the discussion of unity (see, e.g., 2.13.4: *ordo rerum...ignis in custodia mundi...sortitus oras operis pulcherrrimi*). The importance of air increases in sections 2.15–20, and one of the most important

---

[60] Seneca repeatedly (2.6.2, 2.7.1–2) rejects a corpuscular theory of air in favour of the orthodox continuum theory.

[61] Corcoran's Loeb translation misleads when it says 'the term "universe" includes'. There is no sign in Seneca's Latin that his point is merely semantic. Note too that at 1 Pref. 13 Seneca defined god as *quod vides totum et quod non vides totum*. Since god *is* the cosmos, it follows that what we do or can know (the cosmos) can be divided neatly into the visible and invisible, a conclusion which meshes perfectly with Seneca's other remarks about the relationship between sense-perception and the mind.

[62] As did Donini and Giancotti, *Modelli filosofici*.

ways it bears on explanations rests on the intimate interdependence of air and other elements, especially fire (2.20).

At 2.21.1 Seneca moves on from the straightforward review of earlier theories (including those of Aristotle and a number of Presocratics as well as the Stoics) and strikes out on his own (*dimissis nunc praeceptoribus nostris incipimus per nos moveri*). And this transition is marked as well by a self-conscious transition to grappling with more speculative topics (*a confessis transimus ad dubia*). Sensibly enough, Seneca begins by isolating what is agreed upon (2.21.2–3) and shifting the focus of discussion back to fire from air. For Seneca's own treatment of these phenomena (2.22–6) is indeed characterized by a stronger focus on fire and a de-emphasis of air, at least until he turns his attention back to thunder (2.27–30). Throughout this section he makes use of views advanced by Posidonius and his follower Asclepiodotus.

A remarkably brief expatiation on the wondrous effects of lightning (2.31) forms the transition to Seneca's next major topic. At 2.32 Seneca comes to the question which has been prepared in earlier books and has no doubt been most on his mind throughout the book: the use of lightning and related phenomena to give signs of future events—and not just individual events but entire long series of fated events.[63] Seneca contrasts his own (or perhaps the Roman or the Stoic) approach to that of the Etruscans (*inter nos et Tuscos...interest*). The Etruscans represent a distinctly non-philosophical theological approach to the world. Hence they form the ideal foil (at the climax of his book) for Seneca's own stringently rational yet still theological treatment of the realm of nature. Seneca says of the Etruscans: *omnia ad deum referent* (2.32.2). As we have seen, the same could quite properly be said of Seneca himself. But unlike Seneca they hold, for example, that atmospheric events actually occur *in order to* serve as signs. Seneca's more

---

[63] For pertinent background to Seneca's views here, see the recent discussion of divination by Carlos Lévy, 'De Chrysippe à Posidonius: variations Stoïciennes sur le thème de la divination', in J.-G. Heintz (ed.), *Oracles et Prophéties dans l'Antiquité* (Strasbourg, 1997), 321–43. My thanks to Lévy for a timely offprint. See also Gigon, 'Senecas *Naturales Quaestiones*', 335–9.

restrained theological view (which is more philosophical in so far as it is more responsive to epistemological considerations) is that these phenomena serve as signs because they are part of the divinely structured nexus of cause and effect, not because god takes the time to send specific signs for individual events (2.32.2–4). His objector wonders how any such events can be signs if they are not designed for that purpose (2.32.3); and Seneca replies that this is rather like the situation with bird-omens. Bird signs, like dreams and other forms of augury, are not the particular and individual works of god; but nevertheless they are divine handiwork (*nihilominus divina ope geruntur*, 2.32.4). Simply being part of an orderly and rationally structured sequence of cause and effect is enough to make something a divine sign; by contrast, random events, not guided by a rational order, cannot be useful in divination. But anything for which there is an *ordo* can be the basis for a prediction (2.32.4).

Seneca's characteristic interest in epistemic limitations helps him in what follows. For at 2.32.5 he tackles a question of some import: if anything which is a part of the orderly sequence of cause and effect is potentially significant, why are some things privileged for predictive purposes? What is so special about the eagle, the raven, and a few other birds that they should be predictors of the future? Well, Seneca grants, nothing. The fact that divination uses those birds and not others is a contingency; it is the accident of the availability of observation which limits our science, not the variability among phenomena: *nullum animal est quod non motu et occursu suo praedicat aliquid. Non omnia scilicet [quaedam] notantur.* Predictive signs are relative to the observer (2.32.6), and this applies even to the stellar omens of the Chaldaeans.[64] Just as there are no intrinsically non-predictive animals, so too there are no non-predictive stars. It might seem that the planets are doing all of the causal and so predictive work in the heavens, but this is an illusion grounded in the contingent fact that some stars, like some animals, are easier to observe than others (2.32.7–8).

[64] Cf. 7.4.1 on students of the Chaldaeans.

Thus Seneca launches his rationalistic critique of various aspects of divination and its relationship to religious beliefs (2.33, where the third part directly affects religious practice). In 2.34 he rejects the claim that lightning-based omens override all others. This, he says, cannot be so, since all predictive omens work in the same way, as part of the same system. No truth is truer than any other, and any true prediction has the same weight as any other. There is, Seneca holds, a single system of truth about the world, called fate. It is certainly true that one sort of omen might predict the future better than another, just as one kind of sign might be better than another. But *if* a sign predicts truly, then it cannot be overridden by another. Divination is not a struggle for power among divine forces. It is simply the way we humans attempt to read the fated and rationally regulated future; failures to predict are epistemic failures, not failures of order in the world. Hence in 2.35–6 Seneca quite properly rejects the view that expiatory ceremonies and propitiatory exercises can change the future. Fate, Seneca knows as a good Stoic, is fixed. Attempts to change it might be *aegrae mentis solacia*, but they have no other effect. (And we know from book 6 what Seneca thinks is the proper solace: a rational grasp of the human condition.)[65]

Following this line of thought, Seneca seeks common ground with the more traditionally religious by employing the familiar argument based on *confatalia* (2.37–8):[66] there is a place for expiation and propitiation, but not in such a way that there is real uncertainty about the future. The gods leave some things *suspensa* and so responsive to our prayers (2.37.2); but even so if they are to occur we must pray for them, and those prayers are part of the sequence of cause and effect in the natural world. Hence the diviner does have a function: as a *fati minister* (2.38.4)[67] he is part of the causal chain which leads to my prayers and so to the results determined by fate. There is, on

---

[65] Compare the contrast of *prudentes* and the wise in book 6.
[66] Cf. *SVF* ii.956–8. On this theme, see the recent discussion by Susanne Bobzien in *Determinism and Freedom in Stoic Philosophy* (Oxford 1998), ch. 5. Bobzien has several perceptive things to say about this passage in Seneca.
[67] Cf. 3.28.4 where the tides perform a *fati ministerium*.

Seneca's view as on the orthodox view of his school, no conflict between individual choice (*nostra voluntas*, 2.38.3) and fate.

Having turned his attention to the relationships between the interpreter and the signs as read, in the context of divinely ordered fate, it is natural to continue (2.39 ff.) with a critique of the most authoritative spokesman for the Etruscan science at Rome, Aulus Caecina. (It emerges soon that Caecina is a foil for the Stoic Attalus, Seneca's former teacher, whose views on divination feature prominently in this book.[68]) Whereas Caecina classified lightning signs as being kinds of lightning (in particular: advisory, evaluative, descriptive[69]), Seneca not only takes issue with the details of this classification (2.39.3–4) but also points out that what Caecina was really doing was classifying the kinds of interpretative use and not the kinds of lightning (2.40). Types of lightning should be classified by their behaviour and appearance; but the use made of their significations is relative to the interpreter (cf. 2.32.6). It is a methodological muddle to classify natural phenomena primarily in terms of our use of them.

At this point Seneca turns to further critiques of the Etruscan pseudo-scientific version of divination. Their views about Jupiter's various kinds of lightning are mired in superstition and represent at best a projection onto him of human needs; the ancients, Seneca thinks, did not really believe these myths. The idea of an avenging Jupiter is useful (2.42.3) and the notion that he consults before punishing is a good model for political leaders (2.43). The idea that Jupiter has different kinds of thunderbolt is also symbolically useful (2.44). The Etruscans (and Caecina) are foolish to base their claims on the presumed beliefs of the ancients, whom they clearly underestimated. Jupiter is, as the ancients and Etruscans apparently hold, identified with the one rational fate and providence recognized in Stoic theory (2.45–6). The more challenging issues of theodicy are deferred.[70]

[68] See my brief remarks on Attalus in 'Seneca in his Philosophical Milieu', Ch. 1 above.

[69] *consiliarium, auctoritatis, status.* Corcoran's translations are unsatisfactory.

[70] Contra Oltramare and Corcoran, the reference is not to our *Prov.*, which, following Griffin, *Seneca*, I think was written earlier.

In 2.47–51 Seneca again broaches classificatory issues, finding fault in a detailed way with the Etruscan system and that of Caecina. The Stoic Attalus, often admired by Seneca, had a better system, better (it seems) because it built on the basic insight that the meanings of such signs are relative to the human observer. He goes on to celebrate the power of lightning (2.52–3), capping this section with a restatement of the superiority of philosophy to the Etruscan arts as a way of analysing such matters. And with that he abandons the Etruscans and concludes the book with a consideration of philosophical views: Posidonius, Clidemus, Heraclitus, and his own theories.

Book 2, and the entire *Naturales Quaestiones*, ends like so many of the letters with a consolatory moral application. Lucilius has, in Seneca's conceit (2.59.1),[71] been growing impatient with all of this detail. 'I'd rather lose my fear of thunderbolts than come to understand them, so teach someone else how they occur in nature.' And Seneca, naturally, obliges. The hidden secrets of nature, the pursuit of the divine in the world should yield a salutary moral. So Seneca concludes with a moving rhetorical passage reminding the reader of the message of book 6: that death is universal, natural, and inevitable. Hence there is nothing to fear in lightning. Its strike is fatal, so fear is irrational. If it strikes us, well, death is inevitable and it is not the worst way to die. And if it misses us, then we are fine. The concluding words underscore the astringently rational self-assessment we are used to in Seneca. Fear of lightning is irrational: *nemo umquam timuit fulmen nisi quod effugit* (2.59.13).

* * *

In his old age, Seneca devoted a quite surprising amount of energy to meteorological enquiry. However partial this discussion of the themes of the *Naturales Quaestiones* might be (and it could hardly be anything else), it should by now be evident that the purpose of the work is markedly different from that of other meteorological enquiries. Whether the themes I have chosen to emphasize are central or subordinate, the work offers the reader

---

[71] Waiblinger, *Senecas Naturales Quaestiones*, 71, rather soberly takes this too much at face value.

striking consolation for the fear of death; a sober analysis of the relationship between the cosmic order and human life; challenging epistemological reflections, focusing on the ambivalent nature of human knowledge in a cosmos which is rational but not fully open to our enquiring minds; and a sustained meditation on the relationship of man to a rational god, providential but disinclined to reveal the truth except through his orderly and causally determinate works. These are all well-established Stoic themes, and Seneca has to go out of his way to underline his independence from the theories of his school. This he does with critical (and sometimes waspish) argument and debate.

In the end, we have to ask why he chose to pack all of this into a work on what was evidently the driest and least appealing genre in the philosophical repertoire. None of Seneca's central themes *needed* to be embedded in the framework of a *Naturales Quaestiones*. Most of them, in fact, would be better communicated in works on cosmology, ethics, epistemology, or in letters which are free of most thematic constraints. I conclude by repeating the suggestion I made at the beginning of this essay: Seneca chose to work these ideas out in a meteorological treatise for literary reasons. This, he must have thought, was a challenge worthy of his considerable rhetorical talents. If he could pull this off, he would have an even stronger claim to fame as writer, not just as a philosopher. But such challenges are also risks. The judgement of the centuries has been, regrettably, that Seneca failed. And in literary terms that judgement is perhaps correct.[72] Nevertheless, in the background of this literary challenge Seneca developed independent ideas about physics, theology, and philosophical method of considerable interest and sophistication.

---

[72] Though tastes differ, and some parts of the work, such as book 6, are masterpieces.

7

Moral Judgement in Seneca

We are all familiar with the notion of a moral judgement. In the vocabulary of ethical debate, this term is so common as to be a cliché. While we have different theories about how we make such judgements, it would seem distinctly odd to observe that 'judgement' is a term transferred from another semantic domain and to attempt to sort out its meaning by scrutinizing its source or to impugn the clarity or usefulness of the term on the grounds that it began its conceptual career as a mere metaphor. Whatever origins the term may have had, they now seem irrelevant.

But is this really so? I want to argue that moral judgement has not always been taken as a bland general synonym for moral decisions and that it need not be; to see that we can consider uses of the terminology of moral 'judgement' in which the original semantic sphere for such language (the judicial sphere) is still relevant to understanding how it is used.[1] One such use comes from the Stoic Seneca, and I will argue that he did take the notion of moral judgement as a live metaphor,

---

I am especially grateful to Miriam Griffin for critical comments on an earlier version of this essay.

[1] As Janet Sisson reminds me (in correspondence), the judicial metaphor is also used in relatively straightforward epistemological contexts as well, as by Plato at *Theaetetus* 201. But the issues involved with moral judgement are markedly different, as we shall see.

one which he used to develop his own distinctive Stoic views on moral thinking.

That the particular language we use in talking about moral decision and moral assessment should matter is not surprising. Even for us, this is not the only way to talk about such matters; we also invoke the notions of deducing, calculating, and analysis, for example. Perceptual language is also familiar—we speak of discernment, moral intuition, even perception itself. Such terminology can have an influence on our moral theory, for it may well be more than mere terminology; it may reflect a model or paradigm for moral reasoning. (Of course, the causal relationship may also run the other way; if we are self-consciously critical about our theory we may well make a deliberate choice of terminological model.) If our model for moral decisions is, for example, calculation, we might be drawn unwittingly to certain substantive views in moral theory, such as the notion that there is a single commensurable value at the core of our reasoning. If our model is deduction, we search (perhaps in frustration) for a satisfactorily universal rule under which we might subsume our experience and our deliberations. If we are in the habit of talking about moral discernment or perception, we no doubt tend to seek moral truth in the details. The effect of such models is evident in the ancient tradition too. The so-called 'practical syllogism' of Aristotle is one such model, and so is his use of geometrical analysis in discussions of moral deliberation. At other times he uses the language of perception. Our interpretation of his theory is to some extent guided by our choice of which model to treat as central to his theory.[2]

To speak of moral decision in the language of passing judgement is to adopt one model in place of other possibilities. It is significant for one's moral theory. Yet the term moral judgement seems not to carry this kind of significance any more. I don't know when it ceased to do so, but that would be a question for historians of a later period in the history of philosophy. My

---

[2] In Plato too there are examples of such models. Socrates' account in the *Protagoras* of moral decision as a matter of measurement and calculation is an obvious example of such a philosophical redescription.

attention was drawn to this theme for a simple reason. There is a remarkable absence of this model, based on the activity of legal decision-making, characteristic of a judicial decision-maker, in most ancient texts dealing with moral decisions or moral theory. Not a total absence, of course, just the presence of a quiet whisper to contrast with the noisy omnipresence of this idea in our own discourse.

I only became aware of how scarce this kind of language is in most ancient texts when I began reading Seneca—reading him for his own sake rather than as a source for earlier Stoic ideas. For I was struck by how very frequent the language of judging is in his works. The nouns *iudex* and *iudicium* abound, and not in trivial or trivially metaphorical senses; the verb *iudicare*, which is certainly common in a broadly extended sense in Latin generally, occurs frequently in contexts which invite (or even demand) that we consider the import of the underlying notion of judicial determination. Latin writers do draw on such language more than Greek authors—for the Roman elite seems to have dealt more consistently with judicial experience than their Greek counterparts did, if for no other reason than because every *paterfamilias* held the position of judge and magistrate with regard to his own household.[3] But even the lawyer Cicero does not, in my reading, show such a propensity for thinking and talking about moral assessment and decision in terms of judging and passing judgement.

I doubt that the facts support the extravagant claim that Seneca 'invented' the idea of moral judgement. But his elaboration of the metaphor of judges and judging is pervasive and insistent; its use is both original and illuminating. So I do want to suggest that whatever its *origins*, we find in Seneca an intriguing, influential, and creative exploitation of this notion in the service of his own moral philosophy.[4] In this provisional

---

[3] My thanks to Michael Dewar for this observation.

[4] This nexus of ideas has not been fully explored in Seneca, though I am aware of three helpful discussions. First, Rudolf Düll, 'Seneca Iurisconsultus', *ANRW* II 15 (1976), 365–80; though jejune, it nevertheless confirms the realism and legal accuracy of Seneca's handling of legal concepts. (Indeed, his discussion of the *exceptio* (377–80) would shed useful light on discussions of 'reservation' in Seneca's works,

discussion I can neither explore Seneca's exploitation of this concept thoroughly, nor can I explore the possibility of its influence on later uses of the idea. It will, I hope, suffice if I draw attention to the interest and complexity of his thinking on the topic.

The verb *iudicare* and the noun *iudicium* are common, and while I hope to show that Seneca self-consciously uses them to develop his own original views, it would be difficult to start from those terms. In considering his usage we would certainly find far too much noise and nowhere near enough signal. A more effective entrée into the topic comes from consideration of the agent noun *iudex*. For Seneca says some striking things about judges—moral judges, in particular—and if we can come to an understanding of those oddities we will be well on the way to an understanding of his thoughts on the topic of moral judgement more generally. From the outset I want to make a confession, though. The notion of a moral judge equivocates between two distinguishable ideas: the demands on an actual judge to act by relevant moral standards in carrying out his or her duties as a judge; and the notion that someone making a moral decision or evaluation is to be conceptualized as a judge. My main interest is, of course, in the latter notion. But the

---

though I will not pursue that issue here.) Second, Gregor Maurach makes some tantalizing but underdeveloped suggestions along the lines I pursue here in 'Zur Eigenart and Herkunft' (in Maurach, *Seneca als Philosoph*). The pertinent remarks are on pp. 316 ff. Closer to my argument is Maria Bellincioni's discussion of the judicial metaphor in connection with the theme of clemency: '*Clementia Liberum Arbitrium Habet*', *Paideia*, 39 (1984), 173–83; repr. in M. Bellincioni, *Studi Senecani e Altri Scritti* (Brescia, 1986), 113–25. In this essay, I think, her view of how Seneca uses the metaphor is somewhat one-sided: 'The sense... is, then, always just one: it is an invitation to seek in human relations, such as they are, the sole authentic justice which is born from an attitude of love' (124); compare her remarks about *Ep.* 81 on p. 115, which opposes *clementia* to the rigidity of the *iudex* rather too starkly. I will argue, first, that the judicial metaphor is more of a conceptual tool for thinking through a range of problems; and second, that Seneca makes more positive use of the notion of a moral judge than Bellincioni allows for. Her thesis is (in outline) that *humanitas*, love, and forgiveness stand in opposition to the rigidity of 'judging', whereas I think Seneca leaves considerable room for an idealized form of judging which is practicable only for a sage. I am grateful to Miriam Griffin for pointing out the importance of Bellincioni's work for my discussion. (See too her book *Potere ed etica in Seneca: clementia e voluntas amica* (Brescia 1984).)

morally proper behaviour of a real judge would tend to show many of the same features as the morally proper behaviour of any moral agent acting on the model of a judge; hence I propose to allow these two ideas to blend together for the purposes of this essay.

Several works are of particular importance for Seneca's exploration and exploitation of the idea of a moral judge: *De Clementia*, *De Ira*, and *De Beneficiis* stand out for their close connections, though there does not seem to be a planned co-ordination with regard to the theme.

In *De Clementia* Seneca naturally deals with the proper behaviour of a judge. For much of what the young emperor whom he is advising will have to do will involve acting in his capacity as a judge of other men, indeed a judge from whom appeal is impossible. In 1.5 he argues for the exercise of leniency on the grounds of the extraordinary power of the emperor, but in 1.6 his tack shifts. He asks Nero to consider that his great city would be reduced to a wasteland if its population were thinned out by the judgements of a *severus iudex*, an obvious consideration in favour of not being unduly *severus*. The stern judge is one who never relaxes his judgement in the light of important mitigating factors. I quote from the excellent translation of John Procopé:[5]

Think what an empty waste there would be if nothing were left of it save those whom a stern judge would acquit! How few investigators there are who would not be found guilty under the very law by which they make their investigation! How few accusers are blameless! Is anyone more reluctant, I wonder, to grant pardon than he who has all too often had reason to seek it? We have all done wrong, some seriously, some more trivially, some on purpose, some perhaps under impulse or led astray by the wickedness of others. Some of us were not firm enough in our good intentions, losing our innocence unwillingly, clutching at it as we lost it. Nor have we merely transgressed—to the end of our lives we shall continue to transgress. Suppose, indeed, that someone has so purged his mind as to be beyond further reach of

---

[5] J. M. Cooper and J. F. Procopé (eds. and trs.), *Seneca: Moral and Political Essays* (Cambridge, 1995).

confusion or deception. His innocence has been reached, none the less, through doing wrong.

The stern judge, then, is someone who judges others as harshly as the law permits, despite the fact that such judgement would, if exercised consistently, lead to his own condemnation under the same laws. And even if he is now morally perfect it remains the case that, at some point in his past, a stern judge could have brought his career, if not his life, to an end. A *severus iudex*, then, would be undermining his own credibility as a judge by implicitly relying on a double standard. (More on this below.) He would, then, be weakening his own authority and so compromising his effectiveness as well as behaving unreasonably. Further light on the propriety of passing judgement comes from the closing sections of this fragmentary work, in 2.7. Seneca is discussing the topic of forgiveness:

'But why will he not forgive?' Come now, let us make up our minds as to what pardon is, and we shall realize that a wise man ought not to grant it. Pardon is the remission of deserved punishment. The reason why the wise man ought not to grant this is given at greater length by those whose theme it is. [Here Seneca refers to Stoic philosophers acting in their doctrinally official capacity.] I for my part, as though to summarize a case that is not my own,[6] would say: a person can only be forgiven if he deserves to be punished. But the wise man does nothing that he ought not to do and omits nothing that he ought to do. So he will not excuse a punishment which he ought to exact. But what you want to achieve through pardon [*venia*] can be granted to you in a more honourable way. The wise man will spare men, take thought for them, and reform them—but without forgiving, since to forgive is to confess that one has left undone something which ought to have been done. In one case, he may simply administer a verbal admonition without any punishment, seeing the man to be at an age still capable of correction. In another, where the man is patently labouring under an invidious accusation, he will order him to go scot-free, since he may have been misled or under the influence of alcohol. Enemies he will release unharmed, sometimes even commended, if they had an honourable

---

[6] *tamquam in alieno iudicio dicam*—I think that Procopé's translation is wrong here. I would prefer to translate 'as though I were speaking at someone else's trial'— which he is not really doing, since this issue affects us all.

reason—loyalty, a treaty, their freedom—to drive them to war. All these are works of mercy [*clementia*], not pardon. Mercy has a freedom of decision. It judges not by legal formula, but by what is equitable and good. It can acquit or set the damages as high as it wishes. All these things it does with the idea not of doing something less than what is just but that what it decides should be the justest possible. (tr. Procopé)

The wise man is here envisaged as a judge acting in pursuit of the just outcome in every case. Mercy is a factor internal to the determination of the just decision, whereas pardon is external to that decision. The wise man judges with freedom of decision (*liberum arbitrium*), not constrained by the *formula* which would guide a judge in the court room.[7] This is the latitude which makes it possible for his consideration of relevant factors to be based *ex aequo et bono* rather than on more mechanical considerations. The reformative goal of punishment remains paramount.

Evidently the wise man does not play the role of a *severus iudex* in his dealings with others, whether or not he is an actual judge presiding at a tribunal, and we may infer that the stern judge neglects the broad range of relevant factors because he fails to acknowledge his own human fallibility and its relevance for his own judgements. The wise man of *De Clementia* 2 will have become wise after having erred, and awareness of that personal history will enter into his subsequent judgements. This is in itself an interesting insight into moral judgement, and one which militates vigorously against some models of moral decision-making. One thing of special note, though, is that the insight—which applies to actual judges as much as it does to anyone called upon to condemn or to forgive—is developed and expressed in quite explicitly legal language. For we have not merely the language of the *iudex*, but also other

[7] Bellincioni, *Potere ed etica in Seneca*, 95, comments on the legal metaphor here: '*Liberum arbitrium* is in fact the freedom of judgement of the *arbiter*, who in the Roman legal system is contrasted with the normal *iudex*, who by contrast delivered his verdict for the case in question on the basis of the praetor's *formula* furnished to him on each occasion'. See below on the *arbiter*. Ch. 2 of Bellincioni, *Potere e etica*, 'La clemenza del giudice', is useful background for my treatment of the metaphor. See too Bellincioni '*Clementia*', esp. 120–2.

technical legal terms such as *formula*. In the context of advice to Nero, this is not surprising, but its broader implications are brought out by a consideration of similar ideas in *De Ira*.

For the relevance of such a personal history to the capacity of the sage to act as a moral judge had been of interest to Seneca for some time. In a familiar passage of the treatise *De Ira* (1.16.6–7) the same collocation of ideas occurs. Here Seneca is arguing that the judgement on misdeeds which is required should be carried out in a spirit of quasi-judicial calm and control. Violent emotions are not needed to stimulate the judge to take action. His interlocutor suggests, 'A readiness to anger is needed for punishment.' But Seneca replies (tr. Procopé):

Tell me, does the law seem angry with men whom it has never known, whom it has never seen, whom it hoped would never exist? That is the spirit to be adopted, a spirit not of anger but of resolution. For if anger at bad deeds befits a good man, so too will resentment at the prosperity of bad men. What is more scandalous than the fact that some souls flourish and abuse the kindness of fortune, when no fortune could be bad enough for them? Yet he will view their gains without resentment and their crimes without anger. A good judge (*bonus iudex*) condemns what is damnable; he does not hate it.

'Tell me then. When the wise man has to deal with something of this sort, will his mind not be touched by some unwonted excitement?' It will, I admit it. He will feel a slight, tiny throb. As Zeno says, the soul of the wise man too, even when the wound is healed, shows the scar. He will feel a hint or shadow of them, but will be without the affections themselves.

The good judge envisaged here is a wise man, for only such a person is free of the passions relevant to his situation. And the wise man, in dealing with provocations to anger, will be like that good judge; he will still feel something in his soul, a reminder of the passionate and foolish past which he, like the judge of the treatise *De Clementia*, has had. Like that judge, he will act with an awareness of his former self and its failings. In judging others without anger he will remember his own fallibility.

In fact, this whole section of the treatise *De Ira* (1.14–19) is built on the model of the judge. Consider the description of the *aequus iudex* at 1.14.2–3 (tr. Procopé):

What has he, in truth, to hate about wrong-doers? Error is what has driven them to their sort of misdeeds. But there is no reason for a man of understanding [*prudens*] to hate those who have gone astray. If there were, he would hate himself. He should consider how often he himself has not behaved well, how often his own actions have required forgiveness—his anger will extend to himself. No fair judge [*aequus iudex*] will reach a different verdict on his own case than on another's. No one, I say, will be found who can acquit himself; anyone who declares himself innocent has his eyes on the witness-box, not on his own conscience. How much humaner it is to show a mild, paternal spirit, not harrying those who do wrong but calling them back! Those who stray in the fields, through ignorance of the way, are better brought back to the right path than chased out altogether.

The *prudens* here may or may not be a sage yet; but he is certainly someone in a position of authoritative judgement who acts under two constraints: he must be fair, using the same considerations for his own case and others; and he must act in the light of his own fallibility and proven track record for moral error. Anyone who has ever been in need of forgiveness[8] must extend to the objects of his judgement the kind of well-rounded consideration which makes possible his own forgiveness. He will not act in light of what he can get away with (with an eye to the witness box, believing that no one can *prove* that he has erred) but on the basis of true self-knowledge, in honest realization of his fallible character. As Seneca says in 1.15.3, this judicious attitude is a key to making the educational purpose of punishment succeed. He does not say why this should be so, but it is not hard to see what he has in mind: if the person punished believes that the judge is even-handed and fair-minded, he or she is more likely to avoid the kind of recalcitrance often provoked by the perception of a double standard. In the chapters which follow (1.17–19) reason's judgement is preferred to that of a passion like anger in large measure because the rational

---

[8] *venia*; the term is used differently than in *Clem.* above.

agent has the judicial quality of holding itself to the same standard as others, whereas anger is *in totum inaequalis*, grants itself special standing (*sibi enim indulget*), and impedes any correction of its own judgement (1.17.7).

Seneca returns to this important feature of fair judging in book 2 (2.28). The *aequi iudices* will be those who acknowledge that no one is without *culpa*. What provokes resentment (*indignatio*), he says, is the claim by a judge that he is free of error (*nihil peccavi, nihil feci*), and this resentment at hypocritical double standards makes punishment inefficacious. And in considering the unlikely claim that someone might be free of crime under statute law, Seneca gives yet another reason for preferring a broader standard for judgement than merely legal requirements. The *iuris regula* is narrow, the *officiorum regula* is a wider and more relevant standard (and these *officia* include the requirements for humane and generous treatment of our fellow men). The *innocentiae formula* is a narrow and legalistic requirement for evaluation, Seneca maintains, and we should take into account in our judgements our own moral self-awareness. If we bear in mind that our own behaviour may have been only technically and accidentally proper—though still proper enough to make us unconvictable—then we will be more fair in our judgements of those who actually do wrong (2.28.3-4). Such a broad and inclusive judgement is again recommended at 3.26.3: if we consider the general state of human affairs we will be *aequi iudices*, but we will be unfair (*iniquus*) if we treat some general human failing as specific to the person we are judging.

Seneca is clearly self-conscious in his use of the figure of the judge to sketch a standard of rational fair-mindedness in moral dealings with other people. A central feature of that fair-mindedness lies in knowing oneself, that is, in coming to see that one's own moral behaviour is and has been flawed (although we also have to admit that this is a *relevant* factor in our judgements of others). His systematic use of the model of a trial before a judge extends even to this process of self-knowledge; not only does he contrast working with an eye to the witness box to working with an eye to one's own *conscientia* (above), but even in *De Ira* 3.36, the famous passage recommending Sextius' practice of daily self-examination, the trial model is detectable: each day the mind is to be summoned to give an account of itself; Sextius used to interrogate his own mind—and quite aggressively too. Seneca clearly takes this as a trial: 'your anger will cease or moderate if it knows that each day it must come before a judge' (tr. Procopé). And when he applies this lesson to himself, Seneca again uses trial language: *cotidie apud me causam dico*.

So far we have seen Seneca working with the model of a judge to outline a moral norm, a conception of fair-minded interaction with other people based on certain important general principles. The *aequus iudex* is opposed to the *severus iudex* at least in so far as the latter is a narrow judge of legality, exercising a kind of judgement compatible with a form of moral blindness which undermines his own effectiveness. I want now to shift attention to a later stage in Seneca's career, to the time of the treatise *De Beneficiis* (and one of the *Epistulae Morales* which reflects on the same theme). In *De Beneficiis* Seneca carries forward several of the features of the *iudex* model from these earlier works. Thus in 2.26.2, when discussing the causes of ingratitude, he notes the prevalence of the sort of one-sided and unequal judgement we have noticed already: in the giving and receiving of favours, which is a matter of estimating meritorious service and the value of recompense for it, *nemo non benignus est sui iudex*.[9] We discount the value of what others give us in a way that we do not discount our own services. The *aequus iudex* Seneca has already established would not do that—a *benignus sui iudex* is an *iniquus iudex*. By contrast, in 4.11.5 he points out that even ordinary people can escape this kind of selfish favouritism when conditions are right:

And yet we never give more carefully nor do we ever give our judging faculties a tougher workout than when all considerations of utility are eliminated and only what is honourable stands before our eyes. We are bad judges of our responsibilities (*officiorum mali iudices*) as long as they are distorted by hope, fear, and pleasure (that most sluggish of vices). But when death eliminates all of that and sends an unbribed

---

[9] See below on 3.7.5 on indulgent interpretation.

judge in to deliver sentence, then we seek out the most worthy recipient for our goods; we prepare nothing with greater care than the things which don't matter to us.

In matters of practical reason, we are thought of as judges weighing the merits of various courses of action, our *officia*. Selfish considerations are the bribes which corrupt our moral judgement and the only way an ordinary man can be counted on to set aside such selfishness in his choices is to wait until he is so close to death that he cannot count on benefiting from the choice.[10] At 3.12.2–3 Seneca refers to comparable limitations on the good judgement of a moral judge; the values placed on various kinds of benefits are variable, *prout fuerit iudex aut huc aut illo inclinatus animo*. (Cf. *Ep*. 81.31.)

In a later book of the *De Beneficiis* there is another echo of the *iudex* model developed so far. In 6.6.1–2 Seneca is emphasizing the freedom of judgement of the moral judge. Unlike legally defined offences, favours are bound by no specific laws and the agent plays the role of an *arbiter*, free of the narrow constraints of interpreting specific bits of legislation. In those cases,

nothing is in our own power (*nostrae potestatis*), we must go where we are led. But in the case of favours I have full discretion (*tota potestas mea est*), I am the judge. And so I do not separate or distinguish favours and injuries, but I refer them to the same judge (*ad eundem iudicem mitto*).

The difficult task of weighing benefit and injury must be done in a coordinated way and demands a judge with full power to decide on the relevance of all factors. The *formula* and *leges* which bind an ordinary judge would be unreasonable constraints in such cases; though he refers to himself as an *arbiter* in such cases, it is clear that the *arbiter* is thought of as a judge with particular latitude, but still as a judge.[11]

This contrast between the freedom of the moral judge and the constraints binding the ordinary judge is a disanalogy, and

---

[10] One might compare this to the myth in Plato's *Gorgias*, which tells how the judges of men's lives appointed by Zeus did a poor job as long as they exercised their judgements while still alive.

[11] See Bellincioni, '*Clementia*', 123–4, and below n. 12.

Seneca uses the contrast to give sharper definition to his model of moral judgement. In book 3, sections 6–8, Seneca considers the question of whether it should be possible to bring legal actions for ingratitude.[12] His reply, in brief, is no: this is a job for moral not legal judgement. But in setting out this reply his use of the model of legal judgement gives clearer shape to the concept of moral judgement he has been developing.

It is not the case, Seneca argues, that ingratitude is not a very serious offence; yet the tradition at Rome as almost everywhere else is not to punish it (3.6). One explanation for this is that the assessments involved in such cases are extremely difficult (*cum difficilis esset incertae rei aestimatio*) so that we suspend our own judgements and refer the matter to divine *iudices*. Variable human inclinations cloud human assessments, just as they do the decisions of judges.

In 3.7 he outlines justifications for exempting ingratitude from actual legal judgement and reserving it for moral judgement. The first three do not bear closely on our theme of moral judgement, but at 3.7.5–8 the *iudex* model comes into play again. I translate:

Moreover, all the issues which are the basis for a legal action can be delimited and do not provide unbounded freedom for the judge. That is why a good case is in better shape if it is sent to a judge than to an arbitrator, because the *formula* constrains the judge and imposes fixed limits which he cannot violate; but an arbitrator has the freedom of his own integrity (*libera religio*) and is not restricted by any bounds. He can devalue one factor and play up another, regulating his verdict not by the arguments of law and justice but in accordance with the demands of humanity and pity (*misericordia*). A trial for ingratitude would not bind the judge but would put him in a position of complete freedom of decision (*sed regno liberrimo positura*). For there is no agreement on what a favour is, nor on how great it is. It makes a big difference how indulgently (*benigne*) the judge interprets it. No law shows us what an ungrateful man is: often even the man who returned what he received is ungrateful and the man who did not is grateful. There are some matters on which even an inexperienced judge can give a verdict, as when one must decide that someone did or did not do

---

[12] See Bellincioni, '*Clementia*', 116–18.

something, or when the dispute is eliminated by offering written commitments, or when reason dictates to the parties what is right. But when an assessment of someone's state of mind has to be made, when the only matter at issue is one on which only wisdom can decide, then you cannot pick a judge for these matters from the standard roster—some man whose wealth and equestrian inheritance put him on the list. So it is not the case that this matter is inappropriate for referral to a judge. It is just that no one has been discovered who is a fit judge for this issue. This won't surprise you if you consider the difficulty that anyone would have who is to take action against a man charged in such a matter.

After outlining the range of complicated assessments that would need to be made, Seneca continues:

Who will weigh up these factors? It is a hard verdict, and calls for investigation not into the thing itself but into its significance. For though the things be identical, they have different weight if they are given in different ways. This man gave me a favour, but not willingly; rather he *complained* that he had done so, or looked at me with more arrogance than he used to, or gave so slowly that he would have done me more service if he had said a rapid 'no'. How will a judge go about appraising these things, when one's words or hestitation or expression can destroy the gratitude in a service?

Ordinary human judges would not be capable of the fair-minded and complex assessments which a 'trial' for ingratitude would demand. Yet these are matters which an ideal judge, the sage, could decide on,[13] and although Seneca rather hyperbol-

---

[13] Contrast the view of Bellincioni, who thinks that for Seneca judging *per se* is a bad model for moral behaviour and assessment. At '*Clementia*', 117, a propos of this passage, she overstates the opposition of the *arbiter* to that of the *iudex*, holding that the former is bound by 'nessuno schema giuridico' (whereas there were in fact some procedural guidelines for *arbitri*, though they were, of course, free of the *formula* of a *praetor*). On p. 118 she envisages Seneca propounding as a norm a 'judgement' free of *all* constraints not just of procedure but also of fact. Rather, Seneca merely acknowledges in this text that non-sages cannot be counted on to assess the facts; he is far from urging the positive value of operating without constraint from the facts, guided only by *humanitas* and *misericordia*. Similarly on p. 119 she opposes the constraints of any judicial procedure to an unlimited 'libertà di perdonare', and on pp. 120-1 she opposes the *arbiter* to the *iudex* in a similarly absolute manner. Two texts of which she needed to take more careful account are *Ben.* 3.8.1, cited above: 'it is not the case that this matter is inappropriate for referral to a judge. It is just that

ically contrasts the freedom from constraint of the *arbiter* from the restrictions imposed on a judge (even saying in 3.7.5 that he follows *humanitas* and *misericordia* rather than *lex* or *iustitia*), it emerges from the whole context that the moral judge is expected to weigh facts and assess merit by principles of fairness and justice. The various forms of fallibility which impair the rest of us lead, in such cases, not to more cautious judgements but to none at all. The question of whether a realization of one's personal limitations should induce us non-sages to temper or to avoid passing moral judgements returns in one of Seneca's letters.

Letter 81 introduces one more kind of judge to deal with in outlining Seneca's model of moral judgement. Here he addresses a detailed problem about the assessment of favours. In sections 4–6, Seneca uses the model of judgement to discuss another difficult evaluation (which involves balancing prior good deeds against more recent injuries). But the way he sets out his approach to the decision is important for present purposes. He asks what the verdict of a *rigidus iudex* might be—and it turns out that such a judge would make the difficult assessments which are required to come to a firm assessment of the relative values of benefit and injury, including the detailed assessment of the state of mind of the agents involved. As he says in 81.6: 'a good man (*vir bonus*) makes his calculation in such a way as to limit himself:[14] he adds to the benefit and subtracts from the injury. But that other *remissior iudex*, whom I prefer to be, will order the parties to forget the injury and remember the service.'[15]

---

no one has been discovered who is a fit judge for this issue'; and *Clem.* 2.7.3, cited above, which does not oppose the activity of judging to that of the *arbiter*, but notes that mercy judges with *liberum arbitrium*. Hence the opposition of the *iudex* to the *arbiter* cannot be supported by this passage. It is safer, I think, to take the activity of the *arbiter* as a form of judging (one which has a freedom and sensitivity which the *formula* denies) rather than an activity opposed to the rational activity of judging *per se*.

[14] This is the interpretation of *circumscribere* also arrived at by Bellincioni, 'Clementia', 116. The rejected possibility is that *circumscribere* means 'cheat'.

[15] Compare *rigidus* vs. *remissus* in *Ep.* 1.10.

It is now, I think, clear what is going on in this case.[16] The sage (*vir bonus*) enters into the difficult business of making fine assessments of people's motivations and the values of their actions, while Seneca himself, as an ordinary moral agent, must be a looser sort of judge. He must handle the case in such a way that judgements which he cannot in fact make accurately are not called for. So he does not *reduce* the weighting assigned to the injury, he *eliminates* it, thus simplifying a moral dilemma in a manner with which many who have been faced with the challenge of weighing the imponderable can sympathize. The sage, and he alone, can properly form a *rigida sententia*, a verdict which is both exact and inflexible. It takes enormous self-confidence to formulate such a verdict; no wonder only the sage can do it.

I indulge in a slight digression at this point to bring in an interesting parallel to the sort of self-critical modesty in judgement which Seneca displays here in moral matters. In the *Quaestiones Naturales*—a somewhat neglected work with a strong epistemological subtext not advertised in its title[17]— Seneca shows the same sensitivity. In the fragmentary book 4b Seneca raises a curious Stoic theory about snow (5.1) and at the same time apologizes for introducing a theory which is (shall we say) less than compelling (*infirma* is Seneca's word).

I dare neither to mention nor to omit a consideration adduced by my own school. For what harm is done by occasionally writing for an easygoing judge (*facilior iudex*)? Indeed, if we are going to start testing every argument by the standard of a gold assay, silence will be imposed. There are very few arguments without an opponent; the rest are contested even if they do win.

An easy-going judge is one, I think, who does not impose the highest standards on every theory, simply because he or she is aware that in a field like meteorology the demand for demon-

---

[16] Contrast the discussion by Maria Bellincioni in '*Clementia*', 113–16. She treats the *rigidus iudex* too simplistically when she regards him solely (115) as a foil for what she sees as Seneca's preferred solution based on *humanitas*. See n. 12 above. I also discussed this text in 'Politics and Paradox in Seneca's *De Beneficiis*', Ch. 3 above, written before I was aware of Bellencioni's work.

[17] See 'God and Human Knowledge in Seneca's *Natural Questions*', Ch. 6 above.

strative proof cannot be met. Epistemic humility and pragmatism suggest the wisdom of being a *facilior iudex* where certainty is not attainable. As in the moral sphere, so here, Seneca works out this essentially liberal notion through the metaphor of judging.

If one wants a chilling picture of the results a *rigida sententia* can lead to if it is formed by some lesser man, one need only to turn back to the treatise *De Ira*. In his discussion of the traits of the *aequus iudex* in book 1, Seneca tells the story of one Cn. Piso: 'he was free of many vices, but he was perversely stubborn and mistook *rigor* for *constantia*' (1.18.3). *Constantia*, of course, is a virtue of the sage—Seneca wrote a short treatise on the *constantia* of the sage—and as we see in the anecdote which follows (1.18.3–6, tr. Procopé) *rigor* is the vice which corresponds to it.

I can remember Gnaeus Piso, a man free of many faults, but wrongheaded in taking obduracy (*rigor*) for firmness (*constantia*). In a fit of anger, he had ordered the execution of a soldier who had returned from leave without his companion, on the grounds that if he could not produce him, he must have killed him. The man requested time for an enquiry to be made. His request was refused. Condemned and led outside the rampart, he was already stretching out his neck for execution when suddenly there appeared the very companion who was thought to have been murdered. The centurion in charge of the execution told his subordinate to sheathe his sword, and led the condemned man back to Piso, intending to exonerate Piso of guilt—for fortune had already exonerated the soldier. A huge crowd accompanied the two soldiers locked in each other's embrace amid great rejoicing in the camp. In a fury Piso mounted the tribunal and ordered them both to be executed, the soldier who had not committed murder and the one who had not been murdered. What could be more scandalous? The vindication of the one meant the death of the two. And Piso added a third. He ordered the centurion who had brought the condemned man back to be himself executed. On the self-same spot, three were consigned to execution, all for the innocence of one! How skilful bad temper can be at devising pretexts for rage! 'You,' it says, 'I command to be executed because you have been condemned; you, because you have been the cause of your companion's condemnation; and you, because you have disobeyed orders from your general to kill.' It invented three charges, having discovered grounds for none.[18]

When we consider letter 81 we realize how very risky a *rigida sententia* would be for anyone except a sage. Seneca holds the Stoic view that anyone except a sage is vicious and morally unreliable. So everyone except a sage needs to exercise his role as a moral *iudex* with a self-restraint that the sage would not need. Seneca's respect for the epistemic and moral limitations of ordinary human beings leads him to develop a model of moral judgement worked out in terms drawn from the practices and institutions of *iudices* in Roman society, a model that many of us might still find worth considering. Such judges seek fairness through self-knowledge; they find their way to clemency through reflection on the universality of human failings and the fact that they too share those faults; they work to rehabilitate others more effectively by not placing themselves on a moral pedestal; in unmanageably hard cases they refuse to judge and in others adopt a decision-making strategy designed to obviate the need for exact decisions about the motivations of others which they are in no position to make. The ideal judge and the ordinary judge share one important trait: as moral judges they need to have latitude to consider the widest possible range of relevant factors (though of course they will use this latitude differently). Both kinds of judge make independent decisions guided but not constrained by detailed legislation and the praetor's *formula* for the case.

So far we have, I think, at least prima facie evidence that Seneca was self-consciously and creatively exploiting aspects of the (to him) familiar notion of a *iudex* as a guide to reflection on the kind of rationality appropriate to situations which call for moral decision-making. This is an example of one of the ways Seneca's philosophical creativity emerges in his works. This project can also be observed in his exploitation of the corresponding notion of judgement itself, *iudicium*. I cannot range so widely over the corpus to illustrate this claim, but will simply focus on a small number of especially revealing texts.

[18] Cf. 3.29.2 on *pertinacia*.

I want to recall, first of all, a passage to which I have already alluded. In *De Ira* 3.36 Seneca recommends the practice of daily moral self-examination, and in so doing he presents the review as an internal trial. He brings his awareness of his daily behaviour before an internal judge: *apud me causam dico* he says (3.36.2). There is, in the life of this metaphor, an internal trial at which a verdict can be reached. We might compare here the end of letter 28: 'So, as far as you can, bring charges against yourself, conduct an enquiry against yourself. First, play the role of prosecutor, then of judge and only then, finally, plead for mitigation. Be tough on yourself at last' (*Ep.* 28.10).

This internal judgement is described elsewhere as a *iudicium*. In *De Otio* 1.2–3, for example, Seneca laments the fact that our own *iudicia* are corrupt and fickle (*prava, levia*) and that in our weakness we remain dependent on *aliena iudicia* instead of on our own. There are, in fact, many places where Seneca contrasts this kind of internal judgement (whether of ourselves or of the morally significant factors we face in our life) to that of others, and these passages alone don't suffice to show that the legal model is alive and functioning. After all, *iudicium* is a common enough term in Latin for assessments, beliefs, and decisions of all kinds. Of slightly greater weight, perhaps, is *De Clementia* 2.2.2, where *iudicium* refers to the kind of settled and reflective judgement which confirms tendencies which are otherwise merely matters of *impetus* and *natura* (this is, I suspect, pretty much the sense that *iudicium* has in *De Ira* 2, where it used to demarcate passion from rational action and seems to have close ties (especially in chapters 1–4) to the earlier Stoic notion of assent).[19]

Another aspect of moral *iudicium*, its stability, appears clearly in the treatise *De Vita Beata*. Here Seneca articulates a contrast between judging and merely believing (1.4–5), in

---

[19] Compare *Ben.* 2.14.1: *iudicium interpellat adfectus*. Also *Ep.* 45.3–4 where *iudicium* is contrasted to externally motivated *indulgentia*. Tony Long pointed out that *sunkatathesis* (so important in Stoic analysis of the passions) is originally a legal term for casting a vote at a trial. I have discussed this passage of *De Ira* in 'Seneca and Psychological Dualism', Ch. 2 above.

which 'judging' is clearly an act of fully deliberate and self-conscious moral decision:

> No one goes wrong only for himself, but he is also the cause and agent of someone else's mistake... and as long as each and every person prefers believing to judging he never makes a *judgement* about his life, merely forms *beliefs*, and the mistake passed from hand to hand overturns us and casts us down headlong.[20]

Here 'judgement' in the strong sense is aligned with what is stable, internal, and our own. This is also apparent in section 5: allied with his claim that rationality is the indispensable key to happiness is his summary definition of the happy life: it is a life *in recto certoque iudicio stabilita et immutabilis*. That immobility and consistency yields a *pura mens, soluta omnibus malis*. As he says at 6.2, the happy man is exactly he who is *iudicii rectus*.[21] This remark comes in the midst of his discussion of the role of pleasure in the happy life, a discussion which culminates in section 9.2–3 with an apt statement of the normal Stoic view on pleasure:[22]

> It is not a cause or reward for virtue, but an adjunct [*accessio*] to it. The highest good is in *iudicium* itself and the condition of a mind in the best state, which, when it has filled up its own domain and fenced itself about at its boundaries is then the complete and highest good and wants for nothing further. For there is nothing beyond the whole, any more than there is anything beyond the boundary.

The location of happiness in judgement and the close connection of it to a mental disposition (rather than a transient act of mental decision) suggests that *iudicium* for Seneca plays much the same role that *prohairesis* plays in Epictetus, as a term signifying both a morally significant act of decision-making, a form of assent, and a stable disposition which constitutes the locus of happiness.[23] As in *De Ira* 2.4.2 *iudicium* is connected

---

[20] In 1.5 the term *iudicium* is used generically too—Seneca avoids technical precision and consistency. At *Ben.* 1.10.5 it is *iudicare* which is used for unstable opinion in contrast to *scire*.

[21] Compare *Ep.* 66.32: *sola ratio inmutabilis et iudicii tenax est*.

[22] See DL 7.85–6, where pleasure is an *epigennēma*.

[23] See *Ep.* 108.21: *iudicium quidem tuum sustine*.

closely to the idea of stable and irreversible moral decision. In this sense *iudicium* verges on becoming a faculty—as also at *De Beneficiis* 4.11.5 where we are said to torment our *iudicia* when we work through a tough moral decision. We might say that such decisions are a test of 'character'; for Seneca it is our judicial capacity which is being put to the test.

Throughout the *Epistulae Morales* Seneca uses the language of judgement for moral assessments of many kinds, and a close consideration of how his usage varies and grows would be interesting. But in letter 71 (which deals extensively with moral decisions) Seneca strengthens this connection between a robust notion of judgement and the kind of ideal *prohairesis* which constitutes the stable character state of the sage.

The passage of interest deals with the Stoic paradox that all goods are equal (*Ep*. 71.17 ff.). After some familiar argumentation on the topic, Seneca describes his notion of virtue in lofty terms (18–20). He compares it to the criterion (*regula*, i.e. the *kanōn*) for what is straight (*rectum*) which cannot vary without rendering the notion of straight meaningless. Similarly, virtue is *recta* (indeed, must be if it is to function as a standard of rightness) and so admits of no bending (*flexuram non recipit*). In the corrupt sentence which follows[24] there was clearly some reference to virtue being *rigida* as well—natural enough since it is also said to be unbending, and its unbending straightness could not be preserved if it were not rigid. Virtue, Seneca adds, makes judgements about all things and nothing judges it. Like other standards, virtue is an unqualified instance of the property it measures in others.[25]

This rigidity of virtue, its inflexibility (so termed explicitly at *Ep*. 95.62 also: *inflexibile iudicium*), is tied here to its status as an instrument of judgement. Let us move ahead to section 29,

[24] In Reynolds's edition (OCT) *rigidari quidem amplius quam intendi potest*.

[25] It is the invariability of virtue which forms the basis for the argument in support of the main proposition under discussion, that all goods are equal. Since the other goods are measured by virtue and (as goods) found to measure up to its standard, they must all be equal with regard to the trait measured by that absolute standard (in this case, straightness, *Ep*. 71.20). See also *Ep*. 66.32: *Ratio rationi par est, sicut rectum recto; ... Omnes virtutes rationes sunt; rationes sunt, si rectae sunt; si rectae sunt et pares sunt*.

where Seneca affects to anticipate Lucilius' impatience, as he so often does: *venio nunc illo quo me vocat expectatio tua*. He concedes that the wise man will suffer a variety of physical pains but that these are not bad things unless the sage's mental reaction makes them so. At section 32–3 he summarizes:

> This point can be stated quickly and quite succinctly: virtue is the only good and certainly there is no good without it; virtue itself is situated in the better part of us, the rational part. So what is this virtue? A true and immovable *iudicium*; this is the source of mental impulses, and by this we put to the test every presentation which stimulates impulse. It is appropriate for this *iudicium* to judge that all things touched by virtue are both good and equal to each other.

Here again our judgement is an unchangeable inner disposition, cognitive in its function and determinative in the process of regulating actions. It is, in the relevant sense, our perfected *hēgemonikon*, our *prohairesis*.

I want to conclude by emphasizing just two points. First, it really is remarkable that Seneca uses the language of legal judgement to express this idea. I will concede happily that the noun *iudicium* does not always carry the full weight of a live legal metaphor. But in the context of the brief survey I have offered of Seneca's active and long-term interest in that metaphorical field it seems implausible to suggest that it plays no role here—even if the non-legal idea of *kanōn* is also prominently in play in this letter.

And second, this is a good and effective metaphor with which to work. Consider only the key point of this letter, the notion that the *iudicium* of the sage is unbendable and rigid. Seneca had written elsewhere about rigidity of judgement—we think of the perverse and passionate *iudex* Cn. Piso from the *De Ira*. Yet here judgement in its normative sense is *supposed to be* rigid and unbending. The merely human judge on the bench, like the ordinary man exercising moral judgement, must not be a *severus* or *rigidus iudex*, for reasons we know about from his other discussions of moral judgement: human affairs call for the kind of fine evaluations and judgement calls which lead anyone with a grain of self-knowledge to refrain, to suspend, to wait.

On matters so complex that it is wiser (as Seneca says in *De Beneficiis* 3.6) to refer them to the gods, only the sage, Zeus' intellectual equal, can truly judge. The inflexibility suitable for gods[26] and for the sage would be mad rigidity for us. It is often said that Seneca, like all later Stoics, adopts a double code of ethics, one for the sage and one for miserable mankind. I have argued before that this is not so.[27] What Seneca accomplishes in this bold experiment of thinking by means of a living legal metaphor is to show that despite all of the differences between sage and fool there is still but one norm by which all humans should live. The inescapable fact that we are all moral judges, each according to his or her abilities, unites us in the shared humanity which Seneca urged so ineffectively on Nero in his address *De Clementia*.

[26] I am grateful to Tony Long for directing my attention to what the Stoic Hierocles says about divine judgements in Stobaeus (*Ecl.* i p. 63, 6 W): they are unswerving and implacable in their *krimata*. The virtues on which this rigidity is based are epistemological, of course (*ametaptōsia* and *bebaiotēs*), and shared with the sage.

[27] See 'Rules and Reasoning in Stoic Ethics', Ch. 4 above.

8
Natural Law in Seneca

The theme of natural law has often been controversial in the study of ancient philosophy, in part because its later history is intricately entangled with Christian theology and with seventeenth-century notions of natural law, but also because of an occasional failure to define with sufficient clarity what is meant by the term. It was Plato who first juxtaposed 'law' and 'nature' in the famous speech of Callicles[1] in the *Gorgias*; since then the coupling of terms which had previously and almost inevitably been seen as polar opposites has raised a wide range of problems and puzzles. Many of these involve the fragmentary remains of early Stoicism, and I have made some effort to sort out a few of these issues in a discussion of moral rules and practical reasoning in Stoic thought.[2] Cicero's philosophical works have also provoked interest, especially the *De Re Publica* and the *De Legibus*. But no matter how much sympathy Cicero had for Stoicism and despite his use of characters whose persona is Stoic, he is himself an Academic by inclination as well as by choice, and the synthesizing tendencies of Antiochus of Ascalon left their mark on him. In these two works there is an unmistakable Stoic influence; this extends even to the inclusion of the

---

I am especially grateful to Malcolm Schofield for his detailed written comments on the 1999 version of this chapter.

[1] *Grg.* 483e3, and see Dodds' ad loc.
[2] 'Rules and Reasoning in Stoic Ethics', Ch. 4 above.

famous poem of Chrysippus' *On Law* (*De Legibus* 1.18), though it is highly significant that throughout this work Stoic ideas are attributed not to the school nor even to philosophers, but to 'learned men'. Where Stoics are mentioned, it is in a discussion of the demarcation disputes between various Socratic schools and the importance of focusing on their common ground (*De Legibus* 1.53–6). Overall, the flavour of the books is heavily Platonic and for whatever reason Cicero has chosen to conceal the level of Stoic influence.[3] Hence it is difficult to distinguish with confidence the Ciceronian themes we can claim for the Stoics and those which we cannot.[4]

For now, then, this is as far as I want to go with Cicero's notion of natural law as evidence for Stoic ideas, and so if we want to deepen our understanding of the notion of natural law in ancient Stoicism, another recourse is to turn to Seneca the Younger, the earliest Stoic author from whose pen complete works survive in significant volume.[5] And in Seneca's prose corpus we certainly find an abundant use of the idea of natural law, variously expressed.[6] But perhaps I should say, 'the ideas of natural law', for there is a considerable range of uses of this idea detectable behind Seneca's various wordings, most of

---

[3] See my review of J. Zetzel, *Cicero On the Commonwealth and On the Laws* in *BMCR* (2000).

[4] For a fuller discussion of Cicero's views on natural law, see B. Inwood and F. Miller, 'Law in Roman Philosophy', in F. Miller (ed.), *The Philosophy of Law in Antiquity* (Dordrecht, forthcoming), ch. 6.

[5] It is likely enough that the *Hymn to Zeus* by Cleanthes is a complete work, and it does juxtapose the ideas of nature, *logos*, and universal law in its praise of Zeus; but there is not enough context to determine what he means very exactly. Aratus, the author of the *Phainomena*, was a Stoic, but the amount of usable Stoic doctrine we can detach from the astronomical poem is slight.

[6] Yet he has been oddly neglected in discussions of natural law. Gerard Watson, for example, virtually ignores him ('The Natural Law in Stoicism', in A. A. Long (ed.), *Problems in Stoicism* (London, 1971), ch. 10). Similarly, in the most recent treatment of Seneca's political thought (Miriam Griffin, 'Seneca and Pliny', in C. J. Rowe and M. Schofield (eds.), *The Cambridge History of Greek and Roman Political Thought* (Cambridge, 2000), 532–58) the idea of natural law is not discussed. The themes I deal with in this essay do not, of course, exhaust Seneca's interest in the philosophical applications of the idea of law; he has a particular interest in the conceptual work which can be done with the legal notion of judgement, a theme which I discuss in 'Moral Judgement in Seneca', Ch. 7 above.

which go well beyond Chrysippean usage. And these different applications of the idea of natural law give us an insight into several important aspects of ancient Stoicism in general and, of course, Seneca in particular. In this essay I give a rapid, perhaps even crude, sketch of the range of these senses of natural law and their connections to each other. I then focus on the kind of 'law of nature' which seems most distinctive of Seneca, the law governing human mortality; having done so I want to connect it to a significant Socratic antecedent and to show how careful consideration of this sense of law can help us to resolve a philosophical worry about law-based moral theories, including Stoicism.

'Natural law' and 'law of nature' are now such familiar phrases that their oddity can sometimes escape our notice. Yet when Plato first juxtaposed them the peculiarity of the coupling was the whole point of the exercise. We should keep in mind that 'law' is properly speaking a creation of human social and intellectual activity, so that when we speak of laws of 'nature' we are inevitably transferring some, perhaps not all, of the associations of the term from their proper sphere to a novel environment. Natural law, then, is in its origins a metaphorical concept. We should ask what it is about nature that makes it seem lawlike, and what aspects of law are being projected onto nature when the phrase is used. We will find, as we consider Seneca's conceptions of natural law, that there is some variation in this regard, that natural law in Seneca's works invokes a variety of different associations. And the only way to sort through this variety is to get down to particular applications as directly as possible.

An obvious starting point would be the many cases where Seneca talks about real laws, the ordinances and legal conventions of his own society. In the *De Ira*, for example, Seneca presents the law as a sober and unemotional force, able to punish where need be but without the loss of control and partiality characteristic of an angry man (1.16.5–6). This is an unremarkable connotation for 'law'. Also familiar is the idea that laws are inflexible and often fall short of the subtlety needed to guide moral deliberations and evaluation (an unremarkable point made by both Plato and Aristotle). Hence throughout the *De Beneficiis*, especially in book 3, Seneca argues that the morally significant relationship between willing donor and grateful recipient should not be legislated: too much would be lost. And, again in the *De Ira* (2.28.2), Seneca emphasizes how narrow the focus of the law can be:

Who is there who can claim that he is innocent under all the laws? And suppose that he can: what a narrow form of innocence it is to be 'good' for legal purposes alone! The guidelines for appropriate action extend so much wider than those of the law. Piety, decency, generosity, justice, and honour demand so much, all of which lies beyond the scope of publicly promulgated law (*publicae tabulae*).

In letter 94, on the vexed problem of the utility of moral precepts (*praecepta*), Seneca defends the claim that there is some moral utility in laws, as in precepts (94.37–9), but even in such a context he does not go so far as to claim that laws can capture the content of morality. For it is only if they are framed in such a way as to teach rather than merely command that they can perform a positive function (rather than the merely negative function of dissuading from wrong behaviour by threats). Seneca's final rhetorical flourish (*quid autem? Philosophia non vitae lex est?* 94.39) obviously does not use the term 'law' in its literal sense and so does not actually contribute to Seneca's immediate issue (which concerns whether real laws contribute to moral development).

Nevertheless, the claim that philosophy is a kind of 'law for life' is clearly pertinent to our investigation into natural law, and gives us our first ethically important sense of 'natural law'. For it calls to mind the traditional definition of philosophy as an 'art of life' (*technē tou biou*). Like the skill of a craftsman, law is organized, directive, and (at least as regards the proper function of the art) impersonal. If philosophy is a law for life, it is because it guides us about what to do in an orderly and coherent way. So it is not surprising to find that Seneca very often employs such language in his description of moral principles, though it is just as important to note how general these principles are. For example, in the final book of the *De Beneficiis*

(7.2.2) Seneca is outlining the great invariant moral principles which the *proficientes* must cling to and use as a reference point in all of their practical decisions:[7]

Let him know that nothing is bad except what is shameful and that nothing is good except what is honourable. Let him allot the duties of life by reference to this standard; let him undertake and complete all his duties in accordance with this law,[8] and let him judge to be the most wretched of mortals those who, no matter how great and splendid their wealth may be, are devoted to greed and lust and whose minds lie around in sluggish inactivity.

This is the kind of 'conviction bearing on life as a whole' which Seneca labels a *decretum* (*Ep.* 95.43–4; cf. 95.54 where the values of glory, wealth, etc. are instances of *decreta* which we need in order to interpret *praecepta*). These 'moral laws' determine the basic values of things, and so make up the set of *totius vitae leges* (*Ep.* 95.57)[9] and *vivendi iura* (*Ep.* 119.15). This kind

---

[7] But it is important to remember that such laws are general, and that they do not dictate to the sage what he ought to do in specific cases. Consider *Ben.* 2.18.4 (cf. *De Brevitate Vitae* 15.5): 'Let me remind you repeatedly that I am not talking about sages, who take pleasure in whatever they ought to do and who have control over their own minds and who declare for themselves any law that they want and obey the law they declare.' The self-imposed law of sages will, clearly, be in accord with the law of nature. But they do not experience it as an imposition from outside, dictated by a theory they happen to subscribe to. Rather, the law just is their own decision about what to do in the case at hand—in this passage Seneca is considering choices about who to receive a favour from, an example of the kind of particular moral decision which people must make on a daily basis. But despite the fact that the law is a self-imposed decision, it is no doubt just as deeply rooted in the natural principles which underlie all of the passages we have considered so far. So too in letter 70: 'A wise man, then, lives as long as he ought to, not as long as he can', and the factors which go into deciding how long one ought to live are the kinds of situational particulars with which we are familiar from Aristotle's account of morally sensitive deliberation in the *Nicomachean Ethics*: *videbit ubi victurus sit, cum quibus, quomodo, quid acturus. Cogitat semper qualis vita sit, non quanta sit* (70.4–5). Sometimes circumstances indicate a rapid acquiescence to threatening circumstances (70.5–7), sometimes a delay (70.8–10). There is a particularistic variability in how this kind of situation should be approached. Hence Seneca generalizes: *non possis itaque de re in universum pronuntiare, cum mortem vis externa denuntiat, occupanda sit an expectanda; multa enim sunt quae in utramque partem trahere possunt* (70.11).

[8] *Hac regula vitae opera distribuat; ad hanc legem et agat cuncta et exigat.*

[9] This may be the use of 'law' which we see at *NQ* 3 Pref. 16: *haec res efficit non e iure Quiritum liberum sed e iure naturae.* Cf. *Ep.* 65.20–2 on the freedom which we

of 'law' can be used to guide character development (*ut aliquam legem vitae accipiant qua mores suos exigant*, *Ep*. 108.6). It also serves to set a limit on the role which wealth and pleasure play in our lives, even on Epicurean principles (see *Ep*. 4.10, 25.4, 27.9, where *lex naturae* is used to refer to the limits imposed by nature in Epicurean ethics). In a similar sense Nature is portrayed as our teacher, one whose *leges* we refer to in shaping our lives (*Ep*. 45.9).

In this first application of the idea of law 'laws of nature' are basic principles of Stoic ethics, principles which apply with great uniformity and therefore great generality; they always stand in need of interpretation, and they work, as the passage from the *De Beneficiis* just cited says, as a standard to which we refer when making choices.[10] Such laws are, of course, natural because they are rooted in nature. This is what Seneca says at *Ep*. 90.34:

> You ask what the sage inquired into and what he brought to light? First of all, the truth about nature,[11] which he followed in a manner unlike that of other animals, who use their eyes (which are slow when it comes to the divine). And next, the law of life, which he extended to everything and taught us not just to know the gods but to follow them and to accept the events which occur as commands. He forbade us to obey false opinions and determined the worth of each thing by its true valuation...

Here the content of the 'law of life' is clearly similar basic moral doctrines, but the unmistakable suggestion of the passage is that the investigation of nature which precedes provides a basis for it.

---

have under the law of nature. In both these cases it is our ability to see the minimal value of life and so to part with it readily which constitutes our freedom under natural law. But this assessment of the value of life is precisely one of the basic axiological claims of Stoic ethics. Similarly at *Ep*. 70.14–15: the eternal law makes it easy for us to die, a fact emphasized in its relation to human autonomy at *Ben*. 6.3.1 (*ius mortis*).

[10] Law as a *kanōn* (or standard to refer to) appears in the proem to Chrysippus' *On Law* (*SVF* iii.314).

[11] *verum naturamque*, which I take as a hendiadys.

The foundation of moral principles on an understanding of nature also turns up in another important application. As we saw, in letter 95 Seneca outlines key *decreta* which are used to ground decisions about what to do in life. One of these (95.51–3) asserts the fundamental community of all human beings.[12] It is nature, he says, who has made us all *cognati* and instilled in us a love for our fellow humans. Hence, the basic moral principle which asserts our fundamental social bond to our fellow man is also a law of nature. This particular moral principle is regularly referred to with the language of the law. Let us quickly survey some examples of this usage of the notion of a law founded on nature.

At *De Beneficiis* 3.18.2 the *ius humanum* is an assertion of the common humanity of all, slave and free alike. And in book 7 (7.19.8–9) Seneca invokes the *societas iuris humani* which is broken by the actions of the bloodthirsty tyrant;[13] the same kind of basic bond is referred to as a *lex naturae* at *De Beneficiis* 4.17.3: 'no one has so thoroughly abandoned the law of nature and shed his humanity as to be wicked just for the fun of it' (*animi causa*). In the *De Clementia* the *commune ius animantium* is invoked (1.18.2), presumably an even wider law, while a bit later at 1.19.1–2, Seneca the adviser to young Nero urges that it is a law of nature which dictates that a king should never harm his subjects. (And this is a natural law in a wider sense too, since Seneca supports it by invoking the behaviour of king bees.)[14] More typical is the notion of the *ius generis humani* which Seneca invokes in *Ep.* 48.2–3:

Am I speaking like Epicurus again? Truly, my advantage *is* the same as yours. Otherwise I am not a friend unless whatever is done which matters to you is also mine. Friendship creates between us a shared interest in all things; neither good nor bad fortune applies to us

---

[12] Cf. Cicero, *Off.* 3.20–2.

[13] This is again comparable to the view Cicero takes of Caesar's tyranny in *De Officiis*.

[14] The rhetorical strategy of the *De Clementia* is importantly different from that of other works; hence the invocation of nature here has a generic character not necessarily typical of Stoic doctrine.

separately; we live for the common interest. Nor can anyone live life happily who looks only to himself and turns everything to his own advantage. One ought to live for the other if one wants to live for oneself. This bond, carefully and piously observed, which unites us humans with each other and maintains that there is a common law of humanity, makes a big contribution to that closer bond of friendship I was talking about. For he who shares a great deal with another human being will share everything with his friend.

This law of nature is a law both descriptively and prescriptively; it is the result of nature's arrangements and describes a fact about all human beings, a fact from which general prescriptions for our behaviour follow.

In twentieth-century usage the notion of a natural law most often designates a description of a uniform natural process or the principles which determine it. The underlying notions are fixity and non-arbitrariness, and therefore reliability. Seneca often uses the notion of law in just this way, which gives us our third application of the notion. For example, in the *De Ira* (2.27.2) he is emphasizing the irrationality of projecting onto the gods and the natural world the kind of vengeful mentality humans are capable of.

And so it is madmen and those who are ignorant of the truth who blame the gods for the sea's cruelty, for torrential rains, and for a stubbornly prolonged winter, while all the time none of the things which harm or help us are directed specifically at us. For *we* are not the motivation for the cosmos to bring back summer or winter; they have their own laws, laws by which divine matters are worked out (*divina exercentur*). We think too highly of ourselves if we think that we are worthy objects of such great activities. Therefore none of these things is done to hurt us, rather they are done to help us.

Such 'laws' are echoed in the introductory paragraphs of the *De Providentia*. There, at 1.2, Seneca is stressing that the orderly movements of the world are under divine supervision rather than being matters of mere chance. But his reference is to the normally impersonal divinity of Stoic physics and theology: reason, nature, and god rolled into one. And this is a regular, law-like process: the movements of the heavenly bodies occur *aeternae legis imperio*. Law, not chance, underlies Stoic cosmology. There is a similar use at *Ep.* 65.19 when Seneca asks, 'Shall I not investigate who is the craftsman of this world and by what means (*qua ratione*) such a huge object was brought to regularity and order (*in legem et ordinem venerit*)?' At *Ep.* 117.19 very similar thoughts are expressed:

> Let us investigate the nature of the gods, the nourishment of the heavenly bodies, and these quite complicated orbits of the stars—do our affairs respond to their motions? do the bodies and souls of all things derive their action from them? are even those things which we call fortuitous bound by a fixed law (*certa lege*), with nothing in this world developing in a sudden or disorderly fashion?

In the *Quaestiones Naturales* Seneca inevitably makes frequent reference to such laws: there are beneath the earth *iura naturae* less known to us but no less fixed (3.16.4); various forms of liquid are produced in accordance with a natural law (3.15.3); regular biological phenomena are said to follow a law (3.29.3); nature's laws determine that earthquakes can occur anywhere (6.1.12). Only at the unparalleled moment of cosmic cataclysm are the tides 'released from the laws' which normally govern them (3.29.7). In book 7 laws again are invoked to describe the fixity and predictability of the heavenly bodies. There is a *lex celeritatis* (7.12.4) for stars. Later Seneca observes that people do not notice regular phenomena so much as they do aberrant ones, those which are not *ex consuetudine et lege*; comets provoke wonder because they are not bound by fixed laws (7.25.3). By contrast, any heavenly apparition which is to function as a sign must be *comprehensa legibus mundi* (7.28.2).

Seneca also refers, hypothetically, to special laws of nature which *might* override the regular processes we count on—a curious kind of non-occurrent law which underscores by its absence the normal sort. Thus at *De Otio* 5.5 he wonders whether 'some loftier power could impose a law on individual objects overriding the weight and momentum of their bodies'. If Seneca really does think that this sort of special 'law' can occur in nature, it would point to a greater emphasis in some contexts on the imperatival nature of a law than on its uniformity.[15] But most often Seneca emphasizes the uniformity of natural processes, as at *De Beneficiis* 4.28.3: something put in place for humankind as a whole must inevitably affect even the wicked. Rainfall, for example, is uniform and law-like and good for human beings; *nec poterat lex casuris imbribus dici, ne in malorum improborumque rura defluerent.*

Seneca does not restrict the language of law to individual phenomena which occur in an orderly, predictable, and stable way. In fact, he more often uses the language of law to refer to larger and more comprehensive patterns of events in the cosmos, often making it explicit that this is the same as fate—a generalization of the third sense which might as well be flagged as a fourth distinct sense. This sense is clear in the *De Providentia* (5.6–7):

I am not compelled and I suffer nothing against my will. It is not that I am a slave to god; I give him my assent, all the more so because I know that everything proceeds in accordance with a law which is certain and proclaimed for all eternity (*omnia certa et in aeternum dicta lege decurrere*). The fates lead us and the first hour of our birth determines how much time remains for each person.

This law-like stability and predictability can also be expressed as a feature of the gods' rational determination. In the *Quaestiones Naturales* (1 Pref. 3) Seneca enumerates the important questions one can ask in physics, and these include: 'is god permitted to make decisions even today and to alter in some respect the law of fate?' The answer is given in another work, in the context of his consideration of whether we humans need to feel gratitude to Nature and the gods for the benefits given by providence. (We do owe them gratitude, as it turns out.) At the relevant point he says, 'consider too that external pressures do not compel the gods. Rather, their own will is an eternal law for them' (*Ben.* 6.23.1). In making a law for themselves by their

---

[15] Malcolm Schofield, to whom I am grateful for challenging written comments on an earlier draft of this essay, would put more emphasis on the commanding quality of Seneca's laws and less on their uniformity and predictability. Obviously both aspects will be present in most applications of the idea of law. The reason for my greater interest in the fact that law provides a reliable set of expectations, rather than in its capacity to compel us, will become clear towards the end of the essay.

rational decision the gods provide us humans with the most reliable framework for our own lives, since they cannot deviate from what is already determined to be the best possible arrangement (*nec imbecillitate permanent, sed quia non libet ab optimis aberrare et sic ire decretum est*, 6.23.2). This law-like decree of the gods has built into it a consideration of the best interests of humankind.

The law-like character of fate is also at issue in book 2 of the *Natural Questions*, in the discussion of portents and divination and how they might affect our lives. The Stoics are criticized for making human endeavour useless, since they hold that the fates are unalterable (2.35–8), which they emphasize by the use of the language of law (*ius suum peragunt*, 2.35.2; *nihil voluntati nostrae relictum, et omne ius faciendi <fato> traditum*, 2.38.3). Seneca here defends his own school (*rigidam sectam*, 2.35.1), which he does not always undertake to do, going out of his way to align himself with the difficult views of the school on the matter of human responsibility and choice in the face of fate. (The Stoics regard the expiatory hopes of humankind as the *aegrae mentis solacia*, 2.35.1.) Humans, on the Stoic doctrine, are left with all the choice they need, since (in accordance with the familiar doctrine of *confatalia*) their actions are part of the pattern of fate laid up from all eternity. 'But now I have explained what is at issue, viz. how, if the ordering of fate is certain (*si fati certus est ordo*), the expiations and procedures which deal with portents avert dangers: for they do not conflict with fate but are themselves subsumed in the law of fate (*sed et ipsae in lege fati sunt*, 2.38.3).' Fate, the law of the gods, i.e. nature, is stable and reliable because it is already by definition comprehensive. Neither the gods nor the sage who so emulates the gods should be expected to change (2.36). What matters to us, Seneca thinks, is that we should *know* that the fated sequence of events can be counted on to be consistent and impersonal (*sic ordinem fati rerum aeterna series rotat, cuius haec prima lex est, stare decreto*, 2.35.2). Fate is to this extent like the gods of Epicurus, immune to irrational and emotional influences such as prayer, pity, and favour (*prece, misericordia, gratia*, 2.35.2), but not because the gods neither notice nor care for us; but rather because fate and the Stoic gods are endowed with the detached *apatheia* which is characteristic of normal human laws (see above on *De Ira* 1.16.5–6).[16] One result of this unemotionality is that the events governed by law are predictable by a rational agent.

Of course, it is one thing to know that the events of fate are governed by a law-like rationality and quite another to know the details of what is to come. We turn to letter 101.5:

> Believe me, all things are uncertain even to the blessed. Each person ought to promise himself nothing about the future. Even what he has in hand slips away and chance cuts short the very moment we are bearing down on. To be sure, time does proceed by a fixed law (*rata lege*), but amidst obscurity. However, what is it to me if nature is certain about what I am uncertain about?

Seneca goes on to argue that it is in fact useful to know *that* whatever happens proceeds from a fixed law; and because it is a divine law he elsewhere maintains that this knowledge is a crucial component of piety towards the gods (*Ep.* 76.23: *lege divina qua universa procedunt*). Not to see and accept that such unpleasant eventualities as our own death are governed by this law (stable, predictable, part of a benevolent plan) is ultimate folly (*Ep.* 101.7). Daily uncertainty about such prospects is a source of the wretchedness which comes from *timor... et cupiditas futuri exedens animum* (101.8); the rational solution is to live each day as though it were our last (101.7).

In letter 107 (esp. 107.6–12) the law-like regularity and impartiality of events in the world is again invoked to motivate rational adaptation to the inevitable (note *ius* at 107.6, *legem* at 107.9 and compare *ordine mundi* at 107.12). Reflection on the fact that natural inevitabilities flow from a divine law grounds the ready acceptance of fated events characteristic of a Cato (*magnus animus deo pareat et quidquid lex universi iubet sine cunctatione patiatur*), a great man who faced death with a genuinely Socratic confidence (*Ep.* 71.16). At *Ep.* 76.23–4, though, the implications of knowing that there is a natural law are, if

---

[16] Good human laws are also uniformly applied to all: see *Ep.* 30.11 and below.

anything, more profound. Piety is based on such knowledge, and so is a Catonian tranquillity in the face of events. But Seneca goes on to claim that if the good man knows that things happen 'by the divine law in accordance with which all things occur' then it follows that for him 'the only good will be the honourable, since this is the foundation for obedience to the gods, for not flaring up at sudden events and not lamenting one's fate but rather accepting fate with patience and obeying its dictates'. This is a surprisingly strong claim about the relationship between two senses of the law of nature: fate and the basic Stoic doctrine about the good. But the connection is supplied. For if someone takes anything except the honourable to be good,[17] then he falls prey to *aviditas vitae*, a greedy clinging to life and to the things which adorn life. That kind of lust for instrumental 'goods' is open-ended and unsatisfiable. Hence only someone who recognizes such natural limits can accept that only the honourable is good.

This passage connects the natural law of human mortality (an objective and impersonal part of the grand plan of fate) with two less cosmic laws of nature we have already met—the Epicurean doctrine that there is a natural limit to desires and pleasures (which Epicurus did not describe as a law but Seneca did) and the claim that basic principles of Stoic axiology are laws of nature. In Seneca's mind, then, there is a tight connection between the rational commitment to truth about the world governed by Stoic physical principles (see 76.22) and the Stoic doctrine that virtue is the only genuinely good thing. The connection as asserted here seems to be largely psychological, but it seems clear to me that the psychology of the passage is founded on what he takes to be a conceptual connection between physics and ethics.

Natural laws, for Seneca, include the rational regularities which anyone devoted to a frank assessment of the world unclouded by passionate emotion will come to see. Wisdom, then,

---

[17] *Si ullum aliud est bonum quam honestum*, 76.24; clearly this means, if the agent thinks that anything but the honourable is good. An ethic dative is to be supplied, parallel to *illi* in 76.23.

depends on this kind of acceptance of the facts of nature: 'Meanwhile, as all the Stoics agree, I consent to the nature of things. Wisdom consists in not deviating from it and in being shaped in accordance with nature's law and example' (*De Vita Beata* 3.3). If one wonders why good people have to bear misfortune, we are reminded at *De Providentia* 3.1 that such things are fated facts of life, and that bad things happen to the good by the same law (clearly fate) as governs their very goodness.

As Epicurus focused heavily on the fear of death, so too Seneca concentrates heavily on the inevitability of the transitions and changes dictated by nature. His interest in this feature of the general laws of nature is so strong that it makes sense to mark it as a distinct application of the metaphor. We could label it the *lex mortalitatis*. Such emphasis is naturally prominent in consolatory contexts. In *Consolatio ad Helviam Matrem* 6.8 Seneca refers to the *lex et naturae necessitas* which governs people's comings and goings, and later in the same work (13.2) he explicitly claims that if we regard death not as a penalty but rather as a law of nature we will be able to conquer the fear of death. (As in Epicureanism, the thought that a negative event is being inflicted rather than happening by some impersonal necessity plays a major role in consolation.) In the *Consolatio ad Marciam* Seneca (section 10, esp. 10.3, 10.5) refers to the law governing human life. The *lex nascendi* is that we are mortal and transient beings; being born under the terms and conditions of this law we cannot reasonably complain about it when the inevitable occurs. This consolatory work will be central to the conclusions I want to draw at the end of my essay, so at this point I will pass on to other places where Seneca exploits this particular feature of natural law. In the *Consolatio ad Polybium* the law represents fixed and fair terms, as though in a commercial transaction,[18] not catering privately to individual

---

[18] For the quasi-commercial sense of *lex* as the terms under which life is undertaken, cf. *Ben.* 7.8.3, 7.12.6. If the supplement <*leges*> is right at *Ep.* 48.9 this will be another instance of 'law' indicating the basic ground rules for life as a whole.

preferences but to its own regularities (10.4–5).[19] Death will come—it is the *lex* or *ius mortalitatis* (11.4, 17.2) that it should come to each at its own time.[20] And to grieve irrationally can only be the result of ignorance of this law of nature or impious rebellion against it. At 11.4 Seneca says that he doesn't know which is more foolish, to be ignorant of this law of human mortality or to reject it brazenly. Even Scipio Africanus fell prey to such folly: his *pietas* was *impatiens iuris aequi* (14.4). But all such misfortunes are part of nature's law-governed plan, so that once we have taken on our assignment in this world our job includes bearing all the misfortunes sent our way. At *De Vita Beata* 15.5 this law of nature is compared to the duty of a soldier, and in the *De Ira* (2.28.4) Seneca urges his audience to bear in mind that whatever unpleasantness occurs comes about by the 'law of mortality' not by the malevolence of the gods. Book 6 of the *Quaestiones Naturales* concludes with the ringing declaration that death is the 'law of nature, the duty and obligation of mortals' (6.32.12). The necessity of suffering death is also referred to as a 'law' at *Ep.* 94.7,[21] and at *Ep.* 123.16 death is called 'the just law for human kind' (*mors malum non est: quid <sit> quaeris? Sola ius aequum generis humani*).

In *Ep.* 77.12 Seneca emphasizes again features of the law of mortality into which we are all born: it is fixed and established, necessary, predictable and comprehensible, uniformly applicable to all. Death is a law for humans because it represents the impartial and fair terms under which we all live. Like any just legal regime in the human sphere, nature treats all its subjects alike (*Ep.* 30.11):

---

[19] When Seneca refers to things being mortal *incerta lege* at *Ep.* 63.15 he does not mean that their mortality is at all in doubt; he refers, rather, to the uncertainty we suffer about the exact timing, the fact that we can never know just when someone will die.

[20] Though we may not know when to expect it, see *Ep.* 63.15 (*incerta lege*).

[21] Cf. *Ep.* 91.15–16: the *conditor iuris humani* is presumably the divine force which laid down the rules for human life, rules which include the uniform inevitability of death and our equality in death.

Death brings a fair and inevitable necessity. Who can complain about being in the same condition that everyone is in? For the most important part of fairness is equality. But now it is unnecessary to plead Nature's cause. She didn't want our law to be any different from hers: whatever she put together she dissolves and whatever she dissolves she puts together again.

Again, Nature's law has the same features as a good human law, and it is for that reason that it commands our rational allegiance.

There are, then, five basic uses of the idea of natural or cosmic or divine law in Seneca's work (though the individuation of them is somewhat arbitrary). For the basic principles of Stoic ethics are 'natural' laws for life (1). And the fundamental sociability of human nature is a crucial special case of this (2), one rooted in our biological nature more obviously than are the principles of Stoic axiology. (3) The basic uniform operations of the physical world are also treated as 'laws'; and so too is the entire system of divinely ordained fate (4). But for Seneca, the key sense of natural law emerges as the natural and inevitable fact of human mortality (5), a sense of natural law which draws on all of the other senses of the term.

It has become clear that the various applications of the metaphor of cosmic or natural or divine law in Seneca's work have built in to them (a) the notions of impersonal detachment and uniformity of application which he recognizes in the literal law of his own culture (as we saw in the passage from *De Ira* I above) as well as (b) the risk of an inflexibility inappropriate for moral contexts which is featured so prominently in the *De Beneficiis*. Before going on to consider the 'law of mortality' and how Seneca puts it to work, I want to underline again some general features of Seneca's views on law and nature.

First, the uniform operations of nature and natural processes are frequently and significantly described as being law-like, and even when Seneca considers the possibility (whether counterfactual or not) of something happening which violates this law he stays within the framework of concepts derived from law. For such descriptive laws of nature are only violable by a direct authoritative edict—either another law (what we might think of as a *privilegium*) or a command overriding the law.[22]

Second, 'law of nature' often designates fundamental principles of Stoic ethics, such as the principle that nothing is good except the honourable and nothing bad except the shameful. In this sense there is a 'law of life' similar to the more generally Socratic 'art of life'. These law-like principles are general and the key to their usefulness is the flexibility with which they are applied to the specific cases which form the principal focus of most moral deliberation. Another of these laws is the statement of the basic notions of Stoic axiology, the realization that considerations external to virtue (such as pleasure and wealth) play a subordinate role in the good life—hence the application of the notion of natural law to the idea, shared with Epicurus, that there are natural limits to pleasure. Such laws are both descriptive and prescriptive: they describe what the world is like, just as much as the 'laws' governing the behaviour of the tides do, but they also establish guidelines for human behaviour. Another substantive application of natural law does the same: the basic bond of sociability and kinship among all humans is, in Stoic eyes, a basic biological fact, but the *ius humanum* which rests on it is the requirement that we behave accordingly.

Such features of nature are law-like in several regards: their uniformity of application, their impersonal application, and their authoritative relationship to human beings. The most important and certainly the most common single application of the notion of natural law in Seneca brings the various aspects of the idea together. The 'law of mortality', the inevitable fact of our precarious mortality—something which had been as central to human nature as rationality itself, since the time of Homer—is a natural law. According to this law, we all must die but cannot know when. This is one of those brute facts which apply to all and none can avoid. It is not at all a feature of Stoic physics in particular or any specifically Stoic doctrine. Lucretius and other Epicureans and indeed the entire subphilosophical consolatory tradition rest heavily on this idea.

[22] See above and *De Otio* 5.5.

But for Seneca the idea is expressed as a law of nature in a specifically Stoic way.

For Seneca, this law of precarious human mortality is a basic principle for ethics, comparable to the axiological principles already mentioned and used similarly as a guideline in the practical tasks of moral life: deliberation, deciding, and advising. And although we may suspect that Seneca must have acted in the light of this law of nature when he faced his own suicide, we mostly see him in the role of advising. This arises in an important letter, number 70.

In this letter, the first of book 8 of the collection, Seneca opens with reflections on the swift passage of life. Life, he reminds Lucilius, is not always worth hanging on to, since (following the basic Stoic axiology) it is not a good—that is reserved for living well (70.4). This basic principle is not, in fact, called a 'law' here, as it is elsewhere, but the discussion which follows does provide a clear illustration of how such moral laws of nature are to be followed.

There is one small detail in this section of letter 70 which is particularly important. In 70.9 Seneca is looking at cases where delaying in life is appropriate even when a certain death is imminent. Socrates is his first example:

Socrates could have ended his life by starving himself and could have died by lack of food rather than by poison. Nevertheless he passed thirty days in jail, waiting for death, not in the belief that 'anything could happen and that such a long time gave grounds for many hopes'. Rather, [he stayed] in order to submit to the laws (*ut praeberet se legibus*) and to make available to his friends Socrates in his final days.

The context here is unmistakably the *Crito* and *Phaedo* of Plato. The benevolent desire to make himself available for continuing conversations with his friends is a clear reflection of the opening pages of the *Phaedo*, indeed, of the entire ambience of that dialogue with its moving emphasis on the warm personal and philosophical bonds between Socrates and various members of his school. But the desire to submit to (more literally, 'make himself available to') the laws—or perhaps to the Laws—is more significant for us. For in the *Crito* Socrates engages in direct conversation with the Laws of Athens, which make the case for submission to the law of the city. Socrates is there urged not to escape prison, and it is clear that Seneca has applied this to a rather different form of escape, since it is the prospect of suicide before the execution which he has in view. But in Seneca's application and in Plato's dialogue, the issue is the relationship between Socrates and the laws, and in both contexts Socrates honours his obligation to the laws.

What does this have to do with natural law? Are the laws of the *Crito* not civic laws personified rather than laws founded on Stoic cosmic rationality? They are, but at the same time they stand for something considerably more important than the contingent laws of the city of Athens. For the determinative feature of their exhortation to Socrates is not their ability to compel him (their power in that regard is clear enough) but their appeal to his sense of reasonableness and fairness. In a nutshell, they remind Socrates that basic principles of fairness and rationality govern all of his behaviour. He has entered into a bargain by living in Athens, an agreement to abide by the laws in return for enjoying the benefits of Athenian law and culture. And he is deemed by the Laws to have undertaken this agreement in a willing and informed spirit. Hence if he were to fail to obey the Laws he would be acting in a manner which is either unjust or foolish: unjust if he abandons the agreement to his own benefit and to the detriment of the other party (hence the importance of the claim that flouting the Law counts as destroying it in so far as it is in his power)[23] or foolish if he does not appreciate the nature of the agreement he has undertaken.

Hence when Seneca gives as one of Socrates' motivations for passing the thirty days before execution in prison his desire to *praebere se legibus* he is reminding us of Socrates' commitment to follow wherever the *logos* may lead and to stand by his agreements. I suggest that Seneca sees our relationship to the law of nature, in particular the law of mortality, on this model. Nature can be portrayed as another person (as in the wonderful

---

[23] It is the fact that harm would be done to the Laws which also brings the situation under the injunction against returning harm for harm.

passage from book 3 of Lucretius[24]), one with whom agreements can be made and with whom understandings can be reached. And if that is the case, then our obligation to follow the law of nature (which, we should remember, is intimately dependent on the full apparatus of Stoic cosmological theory) will be grounded in our commitment to rationality and fairness. This moral commitment to a law dependent on the outdated cosmology of ancient Stoicism will not be heteronomous, as critics of law-based theories of morality often fear. If I am right, a good Stoic follows cosmic nature because he is rational enough to understand the agreement he has undertaken and fair-minded enough to respect it. It is a further consideration that he is rational enough to understand that resistance to the law of nature is futile. But this further consideration leaves the misleading impression that in following nature we are yielding to the brute force of the natural world, something which one might well do but would hardly help us to rebut the charge that Stoicism is heteronomous.

But at least with regard to human mortality that is not how Seneca thinks that things work. There are laws of nature which govern our mortality, laws in terms of which we must decide how to handle the particular situations of life. But our acquiescence in those laws is not motivated by a sense of capitulation to the brute force of overmastering fate. We follow nature (or follow the facts, as Lawrence Becker puts it)[25] for the same reasons that Socrates put himself at the disposal of the laws: their claim on us is reasonable and fair. To the extent that the choice to acquiesce is our own and is based on our sense of justice and rationality, there is no threat of heteronomy.

The best illustration of this is, as I hinted earlier, found in the consolations, though I think it is also present elsewhere. In section 17 of the *Consolatio ad Marciam* Seneca portrays the terms of the law of human mortality as being fair and open (*neminem decipio*) so that complaint against it would be

---

[24] *De Rerum Natura* 3.931–65.
[25] In *A New Stoicism* (Princeton, 1998) Becker himself sometimes seems to think that our motivation to capitulate is based upon mere realistic capitulation to the brute force of natural limitations.

unreasonable: *post has leges propositas si liberos tollis, omni deos invidia liberas, qui tibi nihil certi spoponderunt*. He offers a comparison for human life in 18. Marcia is to imagine being born as rather like going to visit a tourist destination (Syracuse, in this case); as you debate whether to go, a well-informed adviser explains both its attractive and its irritating features. Now suppose that the advice is being given to someone about to be born. The adviser begins: 'You are about to enter a city shared by gods and men, all-embracing, bound by definite and eternal laws' (18.2). The laws, then, represent the terms and conditions of human life. They are prior to any particular person, fair, impersonal, and fixed. In being born we choose to be bound by such laws, and to rebel against them at the moment of death is irrational.

Let us look more closely at sections 17 and 18 of the *Consolatio ad Marciam*. First, 17.6–7:

Nature says to us all: 'I deceive no one. If you raise sons, you could have good-looking or ugly ones. Maybe you will have many sons: one of them could just as well save his country as betray it. You have no reason to abandon the hope that they will be so worthy that no one would dare to blame you on their account; still, imagine that they will be so shameful that they will themselves be a curse to you. Nothing stops them from performing your funeral rites and nothing stops you from being eulogized by your own children, but prepare yourself for the task of having to cremate one of them as a young boy, a youth, or an old man—for the age doesn't matter, since any funeral attended by a parent is painful.' If you raise children after these laws have been promulgated, you are freeing the gods from any trace of resentment, for they haven't promised you anything reliable.

It is striking here that the seemingly harsh facts of life, elsewhere called the law of mortality, are presented to us by nature in a speech which is honest and frank. There are facts of nature which we all know—or are deemed to know—and these are public and impersonal, like laws posted on public display. Anything we undertake in light of these laws is done on one's own responsibility. It is either unfair or irrational to complain about the application of laws to which one has willingly bound oneself. The parallel with the *Crito* is close.

But if the fragility of human life is just part of the deal for us, it is one thing to apply it to choices like having children. But what of the very choice to live oneself—for that would be the better parallel to Socrates' choice to live in Athens. He, after all, didn't choose to be born there any more than anyone chooses to be born into the wide world. So one might think that the voluntary nature of the bargain is compromised. It was not in fact compromised for Socrates, because he chose freely to stay in Athens and enjoy the benefits of life there. So too for a Stoic. We choose to stay in life and enjoy its benefits. There is, we might say, a constructive choice to live if we agree to stay in life to enjoy its benefits and if it is the case that *if* we had had the choice to be born or not we would have chosen to do so voluntarily.[26] The need for this choice to be truly voluntary is certainly one of the reasons why Seneca emphasizes so frequently that one can always commit suicide when one doesn't like the bargain of life.[27] In a similar vein, at letter 91.15, Seneca considers our proper reaction to the often unpredictable power of *fortuna*:

None of this is reason for outrage. We have come into a world where life is governed by these laws. If it suits you, obey. If not, leave however you like. Be outraged if any unfair conditions have been set down for you in particular; but if the same necessity binds the mighty and humble, then be reconciled with fate, by which all things are settled.

In Seneca's view, remaining alive is part of the bargain, proof that we adhere to the contract voluntarily.

Seneca, however, does not just assert this; he argues for it, in his own rhetorical way. In sections 18 ff. of the *Consolatio ad Marciam* Seneca considers life as a whole and the terms on which it might be lived:

---

[26] Compare Rawls's use of the fiction of the original position to bring out the underlying nature of our commitment to just social institutions. It is as though we made an agreement based on certain facts. There are analogous features in most uses of social contract theory to justify political institutions. What Seneca is doing here is applying this kind of reasoning to human life as a whole.

[27] See also *Ep.* 70.15: *Bono loco res humanae sunt, quod nemo nisi vitio suo miser est. Placet? Vive. Non placet? Licet eo reverti unde venisti.* No one, then, has any right to complain about the quality of his or her life.

Come then, compare the entry into life as a whole to this image. You were debating whether to visit Syracuse, and I explained to you all its potential pleasures and its potential annoyances. Suppose that I am similarly advising you as you are about to be born. You are about to enter a city shared by gods and men, all-embracing, bound by definite and eternal laws, revolving with the tireless duties of the heavenly bodies. There you will see stars without number shining, you will see everything filled with the light of a single star, the sun which marks with its daily course the intervals of day and night and divides more evenly with its annual course summers and winters. You will see the nightly progress of the moon, borrowing from meetings with her brother a gentle and diminished light, alternately hidden and visible all around the world, changing as it waxes and wanes, constantly unlike its most recent self.

Seneca extends his somewhat florid recital of the wonders of nature in what follows, but then balances it with an honest disclosure of the contrasting drawbacks.

You will see five stars pursuing different paths and moving in opposition to the headlong motion of the cosmos. The fortunes of entire peoples depend on the smallest of their movements and the most important and most trivial events are shaped by whether a favourable or unfavourable star advances. You will marvel at masses of clouds and falling waters and twisted lightning bolts and the fracture of the heavens. When you have had your fill of the spectacle of the heavenly bodies and turn your eyes down to the earth, another category of things awaits you, amazing in its own way: on one hand the broad expanse of fields stretching off without limit, on another the lofty peaks of mountains rising in huge snow-capped ranges; waterfalls and rivers spreading from a single source to east and west and groves nodding with their lofty treetops and so many forests with all their animals and the contrasting harmonies of birds; varied urban locales and tribes remote and difficult of access, some holed up on high mountains and others cut off by rivers and lakes; cultivated fields and wild orchards; and the gentle outflow of streams among the meadows and pleasant bays and shores leading into a harbour; so many islands scattered across the deep, separating the seas from each other by their presence. What of the shining gemstones and gold washed in the sands of rapid streams and fiery torches in the midst of the land and even in the middle of the sea, and the ocean which binds the lands together, dividing the continuity of peoples with its three bights and surging with boundless licence? Here you will see animals far larger than land animals swimming among the troubled waters which billow even without a wind, some heavy and moving themselves with an awkward governance, some rapid and more swift than speedy oars, some ingesting the waves and spouting them forth with great danger to those who sail by; here you will see ships seeking unknown lands. You will see nothing untried by human courage and you will yourself be both spectator and a significant part of the endeavour: you will learn and teach the arts, some of which provide for life, others of which adorn it, others of which govern it.

But there will also be a thousand plagues for body and soul: wars, pillaging, poison, shipwrecks, bad weather, and the bitter longing for one's loved ones—and their deaths, perhaps easy deaths and perhaps bound up with pain and suffering. Think about it and ponder what you want: to get to your goal this is the path you must depart on.

What will the prospective visitor to the shores of human life decide when faced with this depiction of the terms and conditions?

You will answer that you want to live. Of course you will. In fact, in my opinion, you will not go after anything that you would grieve about if part of it were taken away. So, live in accordance with the agreement (*vive ergo ut convenit*). You say, 'nobody asked my opinion'. Well, our parents gave their opinion for us when, after learning the conditions of life, they accepted us into life.

Life, as Seneca portrays it, is so wonderful that anyone would choose to live on the terms offered. It may have been our parents who made the proxy choice for us by deciding to let us live, but (and this is common to many contract models of justice) the contractual obligation is, in fact, our own. If, *per impossible*, we had been able to choose to live on those terms or not at all, anyone would so choose—a not surprising view for a Stoic to hold. So, we are, like Socrates with regard to the laws of Athens, parties to a bargain which it would be as unjust as it would be inconsistent to repudiate. Hence when the law of mortality comes into our deliberations, as it certainly must, we embrace the law not because it is the brute force of nature; we embrace it because we are by nature rational beings, committed by nature to rational consistency and the kind of detached, impartial fairness characteristic of the law. Seneca is not the first philosopher to exploit the appeal of something like contract law in unfolding a model of practical rationality, nor is he the last. But he is without a doubt committed to this conceptual strategy in a manner completely coherent with the rest of what we know about Stoic natural law. To the extent that our implicit choice is a voluntary adherence to a bargain, like that made by Socrates in the *Crito*, the Stoic attitude to the inevitabilities of fate and natural law, deprecated so often for bad faith or heteronomy, proves to be as 'autonomous' as any reasonable critic would want a moral choice to be.

9

Reason, Rationalization, and Happiness in Seneca

In ancient Stoicism of all periods, the cultivation of rationality is taken to be the key to happiness. Following the Socratic ideal, the Stoics focused their efforts on the care of the soul, convinced that this was a necessary condition for human happiness and that perfection in this endeavour was indeed a sufficient condition. They held, further, that the adult human soul was essentially rational: reason permeates the entire soul and there are no distinct anti-rational forces within it which require cultivation or appeasement. It is true that they allowed for a division of the soul into eight 'parts', but seven of these play such a clearly subordinate role that in practice only the 'leading part' of the soul, the *hēgemonikon*, needs to be considered. (The subordinate seven are, of course, the five senses, necessary for supplying information about the world, the reproductive function, necessary for passing on our human nature to our offspring, and the power of utterance, necessary for interaction with other rational and articulate agents.)

Hence the Stoic recipe for happiness is, on the surface, simple—unbelievably simple, in fact. Cultivate reason and you will be happy. The leading part of the soul, which is reason through and through, has four powers or capabilities: presentation, assent, impulse, and reason. Of these, the first is obviously connected with the five sensory parts of the soul, though it also goes beyond them in its function to include a considerable amount of processing, memory, and concept formation. Impulse has a central role to play in the generation of actions, and assent functions in both practical and theoretical ways. Reason, as a distinct capacity, seems to have an important role in the production of articulable experience on the basis of our material interaction with the outside world.[1]

But it is the perfection of the *hēgemonikon* as a whole which constitutes human happiness. Care of the rational soul means the cultivation of our *hēgemonikon*. And the cultivation of our mind—as I will call the *hēgemonikon* from here on in, for the sake of convenience—is itself the work of reason. The mind functions in two modes, as it were, the theoretical and the practical, and both of these are involved in the project of rational self-improvement which leads to happiness. Our rationality is both the agent of this improvement and its object. When one sets out to use the mind to improve the mind, this will inevitably involve a form of bootstrapping, and to this extent the entire Stoic project will be vulnerable to certain pitfalls. In this essay I want to discuss one such pitfall with particular attention to the Roman Stoic Seneca. Seneca is a good choice to focus attention on. For though a 'later' Stoic who wrote in Latin and therefore somewhat disprized in the world of professional ancient philosophers, he has had enormous historical influence. Writing in Latin rather than Greek guaranteed him greater impact in much of the Western tradition, and the simple fact that so many complete works survived gave him an edge over the giants of earlier Stoicism whose treatises had perished prematurely.

That Seneca is committed to these essential Stoic ideas is clear. Consider, for example, letter 76.8–11.

8. Everything depends on its own good. Productivity and the flavour of the wine commend a vine, speed commends a stag; you ask how strong a back draught animals have, for their sole function is to haul a load; in

---

[1] I present and discuss the evidence for this construction of Stoic psychology in chapter 2 of Inwood, *Ethics and Human Action in Early Stoicism* (Oxford, 1985).

a dog the most important thing is keen smell if it is supposed to track beasts, running if it is supposed to catch them, boldness if it is to attack and bite them. In each thing, that for which it is born and by which it is judged ought to be its best. 9. What is best in man? Reason. By this man surpasses the animals and follows the gods. Therefore perfected reason is our proper good and all other traits are shared by man with animals and plants. Man is strong—so are lions. He is beautiful—so are peacocks. He is swift—so are horses. I don't say that he is outdone in all these respects; I am not asking what his greatest feature is, but which one is his very own. He has a body—so do trees. He has impulse and voluntary motion—so do beasts and worms. He has a voice—but how much more ringing is the voice of dogs, how much sharper that of eagles, how much deeper that of bulls, how much sweeter and more flexible that of nightingales. 10. What is proper to man? Reason. This, when upright and complete, has fulfilled the happiness of man. Therefore if each thing, when it has perfected its very own good, is praiseworthy and attains the goal of its own nature, and if reason is man's very own good, then if he has perfected this he is praiseworthy and has reached the goal of his own nature. This perfected reason is called virtue and this same thing is what is noble (*honestum*). 11. Thus the unique good in man is that which uniquely belongs to man. For at this point we are asking not what is good but what is the good of man.

As we learn also in letter 124, Seneca is commited to the notion that there is a distinct good for each natural kind, a 'good' relative to its nature which will fulfill it. But the overall good is human good (so anthropocentric is their theory) and this consists in man's distinctive attribute which he shares only with the gods, reason. Perfect reason, Seneca says, and man is happy.

At this level of generality, then, Stoic theory is simple. For any given animal, if you want to know what its optimal condition is, find its distinctive attribute, perfect it, and you get the *finis* (*telos*) of that species. When the animal in question is man, this *finis* is called happiness. Hence, perfect reason (our distinctive good), and happiness follows with analytic certainty. If that were all there is to it, ancient Stoic ethics could be summarized quickly; the detailed work of describing and prescribing the perfection of reason would be difficult in practice, but conceptually straightforward. But in fact there are some pitfalls, and the one I want to focus on is reflected in the middle term of my title.

Rationalization is a term seldom used except to criticize. It normally designates a process of using reasons to justify some *fait accompli* in a manner which is at worst disingenuous or insincere and at best indifferent to the independent acceptability of the reasons invoked. We think this is a bad thing, for the most part, because we think that justifications should be constrained by a requirement that they be based in truth, understood in realist terms; in fact, if we want a label for a rationalization which asserts its acceptability by these standards, we just call it a justification, and we reserve this term of opprobrium for defective cases.

There is a common criticism of ancient Stoicism, especially later Stoicism, which consists essentially in the charge that they sought happiness through rationalization rather than through more reputable rational means. According to this criticism, they held that the happy life was a life in accordance with nature and sought to bring our minds into that harmony with events in the world by using reason to help us adjust to the world, rather than using it to care for the soul in the true Socratic spirit, by working to improve our rational capacities as such. And in fact the Stoics did hold that the happy life was one lived in accordance with nature, and the most authoritative version of this formula emphasized that both human nature and the overall nature of the cosmos were to be included in this project of harmonization.[2]

The charge of rationalization is made with regard to our need to harmonize ourselves with the nature of the cosmos, with the 'will of Zeus', as it is sometimes put, in order to achieve that 'smooth flow of life' which is identified with happiness. In its clearest form, this accusation claims that we abuse our reason to convince ourselves that we in each case want the occurrence of what in fact happens: when unpleasant things occur which cannot be changed,[3] being mindful of the need to live in

---

[2] DL 7.88–9; Stobaeus, *Ecl.* ii. 75.11–76.15. See *CHHP*, 684–5.

[3] It is natural to focus on our reactions to unpleasant circumstances and other constraints, since there is usually very little difficulty in harmonizing our desires

accordance with nature, we use our rationality to bring about changes in ourself such that we not only accept but even embrace such events and circumstances in nature. We achieve happiness through reason, but through a reason which has been co-opted. In pursuit of happiness, we make our peace with the world at any cost. In personal ethics this strategy manifests itself as a policy of 'making do' substituted for a more honest policy aimed at the improvement of oneself and the world, a policy which pays due heed to our intuitions about the autonomy and rational integrity of moral agents.

I introduce the term autonomy quite deliberately. For many critics of Stoicism have taken the view that a strategy of using reason to adapt one's desires to the world violates human autonomy, that it entails making something outside of human reason our moral benchmark and criterion. In Julia Annas's version of this criticism, this led to the explicit charge that Stoicism (Seneca is one of her examples) entails heteronomy.[4] Whether one's background assumptions are Kantian or eudaimonist, we want *our* reason to be in control, to set the standards. We don't want an ethics based on the assumption that the principal function of our own rationality is to help us come to grips with forces more powerful than ourselves.

In a recent discussion of Frankfurt's notions of autonomy, David Zimmerman trades heavily on this criticism of Stoicism.[5] Though Zimmerman makes no pretence of studying the ancient Stoics, he does use Seneca (a 'later Stoic') as a reference point for some aspects of his critique of Frankfurt, holding that

with events we regard as good and compatible with our plans. There can be exceptions, though. Despite a desire for personal wealth, I may have to work at reconciling myself with the sudden prosperity which comes when a lottery ticket received as a gift pays off handsomely, *if*, that is, I have some antecedent and deeply held disapproval of lotteries.

[4] *The Morality of Happiness*, 160–2, where she points particularly to later Stoicism as being vulnerable to this critique. Since then she has quite reasonably generalized the point, saying (in correspondence) that 'I think it would hold for any attempt to inculcate Stoic ethics on the basis of Stoic metaphysics alone, without reference to the kind of considerations that are relevant to using your reason about your final end'.

[5] 'Making Do: Troubling Stoic Tendencies in an Otherwise Compelling Theory of Autonomy', *Canadian Journal of Philosophy*, 30 (2000), 25–53.

certain aspects of his theory of free will and autonomy are dangerously vulnerable to the kind of criticisms normally thought to apply to Stoics, especially to Seneca. I will say a bit more about Zimmerman's case in a moment, but allow me first to say why this critique seems especially relevant to my present concerns. When considering Seneca's theory of the 'will',[6] I have recently suggested that one of its central features is a concern with second-order intentional states somewhat like those that Frankfurt exploits in his own theory of free will and autonomy. Exercising one's own will (i.e. being free or autonomous) for both Seneca and Frankfurt, I argue, is in large measure a question of having certain beliefs and desires about one's own beliefs and desires—a necessary condition for any project of self-improvement or self-shaping. So when Zimmerman suggests that Frankfurt's theory is vulnerable to some of the same criticisms as later Stoic theories are, and precisely because of defects in the way he formulates the role of higher-order intentional states, he is on to something of genuine importance, not just about Frankfurt, but also about Seneca and the entire project of self-consciously using reason to attain happiness. I would not claim that Frankfurt's and the Stoics' theories stand or fall together, but it is certainly worth considering why they share this apparent vulnerability to the charge that they stoop to rationalization where a more detached rationality might naturally be preferred.

As an example of Seneca's typically Stoic views, Zimmerman cites (courtesy of Bernard Williams) a passage from *De Beneficiis* book 3.[7]

It is a mistake to think that slavery goes all the way down into the man. The better part of him remains outside it. The body belongs to the master and is subject to him, but the soul is autonomous (*sui iuris*), and is so free that it cannot be held by any prison.... It is the body that luck has given over to the master; this he buys and sells; that interior part cannot be handed over as property.

---

[6] 'The Will in Seneca', Ch. 5 above.
[7] *Ben.* 3.20, cited by Williams at *Shame and Necessity* (Berkeley, 1993) 115, by Zimmerman, 'Making Do', 26. I use the translation in Williams.

This doctrine (which some might think was a stirring vindication of the dignity of the human spirit amidst the greatest possible adversity) is alleged to embody 'seriously unacceptable moral implications'. Zimmerman thinks that Seneca's Stoicism drives him to a conception of autonomy which no one could seriously embrace, except by a kind of adjustment of one's attitudes, in bad faith, in the face of uncontrollable adversity. He suggests that the typically ancient body/soul dualism of Seneca maps onto Frankfurt's distinction between first-order and higher-order desires. The key (and dangerous) similarity is expressed thus:

But I do take Frankfurt and Seneca to agree on the following conception of how one can *achieve* autonomy:

> A person who has a rich array of first-order desires which she cares about at time t, but who is subjected at time t + 1 to harsh physical and psychological constraints which prevent her from satisfying them, can nonetheless achieve personal liberation at t + 2 and thereafter in part by somehow altering the content of these first-order desires so that those in the new set are in accord with the constricted options still available to her.[8]

In effect, one can reason one's way to a full acceptance of one's lot in life, no matter how bad it is, and thereby be happy, provided that one's powers of rationality are sufficient to work their magic on one's first-order desires. That we might learn to accept and even to embrace slavery or some other grave misfortune by such use of reason, instead of seeing it for the ultimate indignity incompatible with human happiness—which is what it really is—this, Zimmerman thinks (and many others would agree), is proof that reason has been perverted to an unworthy end, that rationalization has displaced the true cultivation of perfected human reason. He illustrates the challenge to Frankfurt's theory with an imaginary story about a fast-living Russian entrepreneur (Epictetov) who is kidnapped by terrorists and learns to make do by bootstrapping his way into a new character, drawing on the resources of his childhood religious education long since abandoned. Under the constraints of a prison,

[8] Zimmerman, 'Making Do', 27.

Epictetov finds happiness by turning himself into a kind of person he never thought he could be, a devoutly resigned, saintly man able to find peace in the hell of his concentration camp.[9]

Such a use of reason to reshape one's character violates any reasonable conception of autonomy. *We* cannot (and here I agree with Zimmerman) see this as an expression of human freedom or autonomous action because, no matter how much Epictetov identifies with his new self, no matter how much he now wants to want his own suffering, *we* know that he would never have chosen such a life unless circumstances forced him into a situation as unnatural as it is undesirable. Epictetov has used his mental resources to attain happiness, but stands convicted of having rationalized his way to bliss instead of getting there by a straightforward cultivation of reason.

Zimmerman's interest in this scenario is the unacceptable 'Stoic' consequence it poses for Frankfurtian theory, and the main thrust of his discussion is the formulation of revisions to the theory which protect it from such consequences. The *basic* strategy on this point (though it is certainly not the only one needed, in Zimmerman's view)[10] is to build in some historical conditions which make the way we got into the situation which provokes our project of reshaping our selves relevant to the assessment of our freedom and autonomy.[11] For if we require only that our second-order desires cohere with the newly produced first-order desires (or that we fully endorse our new desires), then rational adaptation to dreadful circumstances will turn out to be autonomous happiness, provided that our self-brainwashing is effective enough. To block this, we have to say something like this: one isn't responsible for actions (including those of character reformation) if one undertakes them 'out of motives and/or for reasons the strength and/or importance of which he has knowingly induced in himself at some time

---

[9] Zimmerman, 'Making Do', 35 ff.

[10] I should note here that I am oversimplifying his discussion for my own purposes: ibid. 40 ff.

[11] Ibid. 33.

only in order to make the best of an intrusive history of external implantation' or some other external compulsion.

Zimmerman's interest in the finer details of Frankfurt's theory can be set aside for my purposes. I don't doubt that Frankfurt's theory of freedom, the will, and responsibility leads him down Stoic pathways—about which Zimmerman says 'I hope that Frankfurt would not welcome this Stoic implication of his hierarchical account of the unfreedom of coercion.'[12] And I don't doubt that most of us (even those with Stoic sympathies) find something odd about claiming that 'the slave, the battered housewife and the sweatshop worker...[by] intentionally freeing themselves from the desires they are prevented from satisfying by coercive circumstance...succeed in rendering themselves more autonomous than they would have been if they had done nothing but suffer under the constraints imposed by their tormentors.' But I want to direct attention to the underlying question about Stoicism: does Stoicism, especially in Seneca's version, teach us to rationalize in this way, to reshape our characters and beliefs to help us cope with constraint and coercion? Does it induce us to 'make do' in the face of adversity? Is this the use of reason which they claim makes us happy?

The short answer is, no. Of course, Seneca like other Stoics does believe that the person whose reason has been perfected will be happy regardless of circumstances. And he holds that reason is the only tool which can bring about this improvement in our soul. What we need to see, then, is why this doesn't count as mere rationalization. To put it briefly, it doesn't count as rationalization because a central feature of rationalization does not apply to it, because the counterfactual condition built into our understanding of rationalization (the very one which makes it objectionable) is not satisfied. We are rationalizing when we hold beliefs pertinent to our situation which we would never have held *if not for* the motivation provided by unsatisfactory external circumstances. Suppose, to use Zimmerman's example, we are enslaved. We might well console ourselves with

[12] Ibid. 40.

the reflection that civil freedom is of no moral importance and that therefore our happiness and autonomy are not damaged by it.[13] If this view is one which we are motivated to hold (or to induce in ourselves) *only* because of our circumstances, then obviously we are rationalizing. But if we have reasons to hold this view independently of our own personal and unpleasant circumstances (whether actual or potential—for even an irrational fear of enslavement might induce us to adopt this view as a pre-emptive defence), then it won't count as rationalization if we preserve our happiness by coming to hold this view.

So provided that we are actually motivated by independently good reasons to hold the relevant doctrines, the reform of our desires and values which reason carries out will not be mere rationalization in the face of a hostile or frustrating world (either actual or potential). We may assume that a given agent at least claims he has adequate reasons for adopting those doctrines (for if he admits that he believes that death is nothing to us—for instance, *in order to* quash his fear of death—then he will fail to convince even himself in the efficacious way he needs; successful rationalization normally requires some self-deception). The problem remaining, then, is to decide whether a given agent who uses Stoic doctrine and Stoic arguments to achieve happiness is in fact in good faith when accepting such reasons as adequate. This, it is worth noting, is harder to do when the critic holds to his or her own account that the relevant doctrines are both false and inadequately supported.

I should add here as well that there is one piece of evidence from ancient Stoicism that might well be taken to show that they are prone to subordinate beliefs to desires for moral improvement in precisely this way. Epictetus, at *Diss.* 1.4.27, says 'If one had to be deceived in order to learn that of externals and things outside our power none concern us, I for one would

---

[13] As above, I am allowing happiness and autonomy to blend together here. I am not supposing that there are no relevant differences between them. But like many people I think that there are necessary connections between them. I would claim (in a spirit of eudaimonism) that happiness in any form is incompatible with a radical loss of the relevant form of freedom (which we may call autonomy).

consent to a deception from which I would live with a smooth current of life and without annoyance' (tr. Dobbin). As disturbing as this readiness to embrace morally useful self-deception might be, this is clearly counterfactual. Still, if one wants an explicit example of the kind of bad faith we are facing, this is a useful text since it shows us what such rationalization would look like if flushed out of its alleged hiding places.

Much of the critique of later Stoicism rests, I believe, on this. We simply don't accept that a man like Seneca (or Epictetus or Marcus Aurelius) *really* believed on independent grounds in the doctrines which preserve tranquillity. Hence to show that it is the genuine cultivation of reason which makes us happy, rather than rationalization, we must consider the independent reasons the Stoics had for holding them. I cannot now make the case generally for all Stoics and all relevant doctrines. Seneca alone is my immediate theme and even with him not all relevant doctrines can be scrutinized.

(One particularly important set of doctrines concerns god and the nature of the cosmos. If all that happens is determined by the will of Zeus and Zeus himself is the rational nature which causally determines all events for the best, then to wish for anything that does not occur is not only futile but impious; if our rational nature when perfected is really identical with that of Zeus, as Stoics claim, then to wish for anything which does not occur or to regret anything which does is to repudiate one's own nature as much as it is to reject Zeus.)[14]

---

[14] A defence of the independent tenability of these doctrines, in fact, even dealing with the occurrence of these themes in letter 66, would extend my essay unbearably and entail a consideration of a great deal in earlier Stoicism as well as perhaps of the main themes of Plato's *Timaeus*. As far as Epictetus is concerned, the objectionable passage quoted above needs to be qualified not just by emphasis on the fact that its claims are counterfactual, but also by attention to another crucial passage from the *Dissertationes*, 2.6.9–10. Here, paraphrasing Chrysippus, Epictetus makes it clear that the willing embrace of misfortune depends on our actually knowing the future (which is impossible for human beings) as well as on our conviction that the misfortune which will afflict us is not only inevitable but also a product of fate (i.e. of the divine, rational powers whose nature we share) and so for the ultimate good of the cosmos. I am grateful to Don Morrison for pointing out the relevance of this passage to my argument.

My immediate plan is to undertake a somewhat simpler task. One important Stoic doctrine concerns the difference between what is good (or bad) and what is of a lesser kind of value, and the bearing these have on human happiness; it derives in part from an ultimately Socratic argument, based on the premise that the only genuine good is something which cannot be misused.[15] I will look, then, at just one of his *Epistulae Morales*, number 66,[16] which deals with Stoic value theory and show that Seneca had independent reasons for holding that those things whose loss we quite naturally regret (such as our civil freedom or bodily health) do not contribute to human happiness.

Letter 66 marshals a wide range of arguments on exactly our concerns. Its theme is the value in a human life of virtue in favourable and in unfavourable circumstances, and its arguments (or many of them) are, it seems to me, of independent merit. It requires no bad faith on *our* parts as readers to accept that solely on the basis of such arguments one might very well come to believe that our happiness is not harmed by adverse circumstances. When Seneca uses these arguments to improve his own soul and that of Lucilius, he is reasoning with his readers in his own characteristically rhetorical way; he is not, I maintain, rationalizing.

The letter opens with a personal anecdote. Seneca reports to Lucilius that he has recently visited a former fellow-student of philosophy. Seneca is well on in years, and so is his friend Claranus. Time has apparently treated him kindly in the intellectual department, but has been most unkind in the matter of his physical condition. The discrepancy between his intellectual vigour and physical decrepitude is so great that Seneca even suggests that Claranus has been providentially provided as an exemplar, as a demonstration that intellectual merit is independent of physical condition (just as the political greatness of a man is often independent of his social origins, if that is what *potest ex casa vir magnus exire* in 66.3 means). Seneca's sum-

---

[15] See *CHHP*, ch. 21 sections V, VI and pp. 693–4.

[16] If time permitted, it would be worthwhile to consider the thematically similar letters 71 and 74 (esp. 20 ff.).

mary of what Claranus' case demonstrates already raises our theme: 'the mind is not spoiled by deformity of the body; rather, the body is adorned by mental beauty' (66.1–4). For in the *quaestio* which follows (presented as a summary of the conversation between Seneca and Claranus, 66.4–6) Seneca defends the position that *all* goods are equal, and in particular that despite the varying circumstances[17] in which goods might be found there is equal value in what the Stoics call primary goods[18] (which we would choose for their own sakes) and other, secondary goods (which we would embrace only if necessary, since they are manifested in unfortunate situations, *in materia infelici expressa*).[19] How, he asks, can all goods be equal when one set is such as to be chosen and the other such as to be avoided?

Seneca's answer builds on an explication of what he calls the primary good, which turns out to be virtue.[20] But virtues in Stoicism are defined as ideal dispositions of the human mind (*talis animus virtus est*). In 66.6 the key features of such a mind are given:

Virtue is this kind of mind: a mind which (1) contemplates the truth, (2) is experienced in the matter of what should be pursued and what avoided, (3) assigns values to things in accordance with nature and not on the basis of mere opinion, (4) involves itself in the whole cosmos and devotes contemplative activity to all of its acts, (5) is focused on

---

[17] Note: *triplex eorum condicio* in 66.5.

[18] *Prima bona*, illustrated by three examples drawn not from technical Stoic theory but from 'common sense': joy, peace, the safety of one's fatherland. What the examples indicate is not an unconditional Stoic good, but things which are typically chosen in unconstrained circumstances. It is typical of Seneca to begin with non-technical language which provides an open entry point into the argument for his readers. When, in the next paragraph, he refers to the *primum bonum* (see below) he evidently has a different and more technical sense in mind; the overlapping terminology seems regrettably clumsy.

[19] *Secunda bona*. The examples here are endurance of torture and self-control during serious illness. Seneca also notes a third type (*tertia bona*), illustrated by the right kinds of gait, facial expression, and gesture. These play no role in the discussion which follows.

[20] See n. 18. Good is defined more generally as 'virtue and what participates in virtue'. See *CHHP*, 691 and Stobaeus, *Ecl.* ii.57.21–58.1. At DL 7.94–5 we learn that what participates in virtue and so is good includes virtuous people and virtuous actions.

thought and action in a balanced manner, (6) is great, energetic, unconquered by hardship and pleasures alike and submissive to neither circumstance, (7) rising above everything which happens to befall it, (8) is very beautiful, well-ordered with regard to both charm and strength, (9) is sound and sober, undisturbed and fearless, immune to violent blows, neither elated nor depressed by the events of fortune.

These are the general characteristics of virtue, the primary good, and no one would reasonably deny that such a soul is a good thing. In 66.7 Seneca notes that virtue has a wide range of appearances (*species*), since it manifests itself differently in accordance with the varied circumstances of life and the actions it calls for. But, he claims, these *species* do not affect the basic disposition which constitutes virtue. Virtue itself does not get greater or lesser even though it takes on different qualities as it reflects the condition of the actions it will have to undertake.

This way of understanding the relationship between the basic disposition and its manifestations in action has much to be said for it. On the same model one might plausibly isolate a disposition such as physical strength, which remains the same underlying disposition even though it will appear very different if one is called upon to lift a fifty-pound sack of wheat or a slice of toast; one is not weaker just because one doesn't have to exert one's strength, and similarly one is not less virtuous just because one's resilience is not being severely tested at the moment. Seneca is, of course, taking for granted that we have particular concern for long-term dispositions of the soul.

In 66.8–9 Seneca moves on to other features of virtue. He notes that anything which is 'touched'[21] by virtue takes on some of its admirability. As the limiting case of goodness, virtue cannot actually get bigger or stronger. Since it is 'straight', 'true', and 'balanced', it cannot become more of any of these attributes; these are absolutes, whether applied to virtue or more literally to things like lines, propositions, or bodily conditions. Virtue has been described as something complete (*perfectum*), and completeness is the sort of attribute which a subject

---

[21] That is, which participates in virtue by being produced by it (actions) or characterized by it (virtuous people).

either has or lacks. If a mental disposition is not, then, straight, true, balanced, and complete, it is not virtue. If virtue or any of its key attributes (such as nobility, fittingness, justice, lawfulness) could be increased, then they would not yet be virtue. In 66.10 he adds the claim (so far unsupported but not in itself implausible) that good is a univocal term when applied to virtues: *bonum omne in easdem cadit leges*. The result of this is that personal and public utility converge and that what is worth pursuing (personal utility) is inseparable from what is praiseworthy (public utility). This is an important part of any argument for the unity of virtue, but one that goes back to early Stoicism and its Socratic roots. The conclusion Seneca draws then is complex: virtues are all equal; so are the actions produced by virtue and the agents who possess it (66.10).

In all of this there are a couple of key moves. One is the standard Stoic equation of primary good with virtue. Another is the understanding of virtue as a limiting instance of a range of traits, which makes it invariable in degree. Third, and perhaps more contentious, is the claim that virtue shares its essential attributes with its actions and products, including its invariance in degree. The second of these moves is particularly vital for the success of Seneca's argument, and he moves quickly to reinforce it by invoking the doctrine that 'virtues' are relative to different kinds of beings (plants and animals have each their own forms of excellence) but that human virtue is of superior importance and has a unity and stability which other things lack.[22] *una inducitur humanis virtutibus regula; una enim est ratio recta simplexque* (66.11). The reason given to support this is man's special connection to divinity. As rational beings we share the nature of the gods and the heavenly bodies, and everything divine has an unvarying nature. Hence our reason and virtue are similarly uniform. Since there can be no relevant difference of quality among divine things, our virtues (which are relevantly similar) are also free of variation in degree. If true human good is like this, then its various manifestations cannot vary in degree. 'So joy and a brave and determined endurance of

[22] See *Ep.* 76 above.

torture are equal, since in each there is the same greatness of mind, relaxed and unstrained in the one case aggressive and tense in the other' (66.12). Seneca concludes this argument with an example drawn from military experience and a rousing summary.

As rhetorically complex as this is, the basic argument is clear enough. The primary good is virtue, a limiting case of many desirable traits in the mental dispositions of human beings. The divine nature of human virtue reinforces its claim to be a stable and invariant limiting case, a perfection in its very nature. The invariance of virtue is an essential trait, so other things which take their goodness from virtue (such as agents and actions) are similarly invariant. Hence any manifestation of any virtue is equal to any other, and we should accept that intelligent rejoicing at how well things are going is just as good as a discerning endurance of misfortune and torment. Q.E.D.

Seneca reinforces this basic argument by the device of entertaining hypothetical objections. In 66.14–17 he concedes that virtue in the best case and virtue in the worst case do differ, but not in so far as it is virtue. It is the raw material, the circumstances of its exercise, which is the locus of the difference. And indeed, if virtue as an unvarying and stable disposition is abstracted from its circumstantial manifestations, it is hard to see why *its* qualities should be affected by those circumstances. For in the standard Stoic theory of value, virtue and vice have a different kind of value than that which characterizes virtually everything else, including all external and bodily circumstances. Seneca relies explicitly on the definition of virtue developed earlier, but also on familiar Stoic theory.[23] But the argument does not stop here.

A new supporting consideration is invoked at 66.16-17: if such circumstantial aspects of action could diminish or enhance the underlying disposition itself, then nobility (the key feature of virtue) would lose its unity and therefore perish. Seneca realizes that this bold claim needs some support (*Quare? Dicam*). Nobility must be totally voluntary, never begrudged.

---

[23] See Inwood *Ethics and Human Action*, ch. 6.

If it is tainted by hesitation, fear, or regret, it loses its best feature (which is at the same time a necessary condition for virtue), its own internal harmony of desire and belief (*sibi placere*). Self-doubt and hesitation utterly undermine nobility and so virtue. Conflict among our beliefs and motivations eliminates the harmony and stability which are essential if the mental disposition is to have the traits which make it virtue.

At section 18 Seneca anticipates the objections of an imaginary interlocutor, no doubt a hedonist: 'I know what he might reply to me at this point: you're trying to persuade us of the proposition that it makes no difference whether someone experiences pleasure (*gaudium*) or lies upon the rack and wears out his torturer.' Seneca notes (and passes by) one obvious *ad hominem* rejoinder, that Epicurus, a hedonist, holds that a wise man will feel pleasure while roasting in the bull of Phalaris. Seneca prefers a better line of argument in reply (66.19 ff.).

Standard doctrine distinguishes between what one would select (*electio*) and what one chooses.[24] Nothing in traditional doctrine denies that there are differences of selective value among moral indifferents, so that there can be a huge difference between pleasure and pain. If asked to make a selection, any agent will of course pursue the former and avoid the latter, simply on the grounds that the one accords with our nature as the other violates it. The underlying doctrine here is 'axiological dualism', the Stoic view that there are two incommensurably different kinds of value and that happiness depends on one, not the other. Hence he can say (66.19–20):

19. As long as [pleasure and pain] are assessed in this manner [in terms of selective value], they differ from each other by a big margin; but when it comes to virtue, each instance of virtue is equal, the one accompanied by happy circumstances and the one accompanied by regrettable circumstances. 20. Aggravation and pain and anything else which is dispreferred have no weight; they are overwhelmed by virtue. Just as the brilliance of the sun obscures very small lights, so virtue, by its magnitude, crushes and stifles pains, annoyances, and injustices. And whatever virtue shines on, anything which appears without it is there

[24] Ibid. 201–15.

extinguished. Dispreferred things, when they co-occur with virtue, make no more impact than a rain shower does on the ocean.

This is standard doctrine, and even the examples of the light of the sun and the ocean are familiar[25] if slightly misleading analogues for the incommensurability of virtue. And the standard doctrine is supported by an argument which is quite independent of any consideration of how we handle suffering virtuously, the so-called 'use argument' which can be traced back to the august figure of Socrates himself.[26]

But instead of relying solely on an invocation of the familiar technical doctrine, Seneca offers an argument from the behaviour of good men, which is in effect an appeal to our intuitions (66.21–7). First, he alleges, a good man will not hesitate in his pursuit of the noble. He will not be deterred by the prospect of torture from maintaining his commitment to virtue, which is like his commitment to another good man.[27] Virtue, like a virtuous companion, is a source of genuine benefit and security, so anything virtuous retains its value despite circumstances, just as a friend retains his value despite being a poor and starving exile. To confirm this intuition, Seneca asks us to compare our reaction to two equally good men, one poor in externals and the other rich; no one would have a preference for the virtue of one over the other, so the same judgement will be made about circumstances as about the men: 'virtue is equally praiseworthy in a strong and free body as it is in a sickly and enslaved body' (66.21–2).

This argument forces our attention onto a highly relevant feature of virtue, its univocity and its abstractability from external circumstances. By focusing on persons in contrast to their bodies and money rather than on the abstraction 'virtue' in

---

[25] Cicero, *Fin.* 3.45.

[26] Mentioned by Seneca as familiar at *Ep.* 120.3. See also *CHHP*, ch. 21, sections IV–VI.

[27] Compare Letter 71.17, where Seneca points out that if you deny that all goods are equal you will have to conclude that Socrates and Cato were not happy (since their circumstances were unfortunate, and so less than maximally good, but if less than maximally good, then not happy). That notion, he says, is so bizarre that no one would entertain it.

contrast to broadly defined circumstances of life, Seneca merely grasps the issue by its most persuasive handle. His sustained comparison between our pursuit of things and the bonds of friendship between people (*quod amicitia in hominibus est, hoc in rebus adpetitio*, 66.24) is an effective analogical argument with genuine argumentative bite. It draws on intuitions we all possess about friendship as well as about virtue: we would not treat virtuous friends differently just because of changing external circumstances, so why treat other instances of virtue (such as actions in bad circumstances) any differently just because of different external circumstances? The existence of a personal attachment and love for virtue (which is what a good person has)[28] raises it above variations in circumstance, just as our love for our own children and our sentiments for our native land have similar resiliency. Virtue loves all of her actions with the even-handed love of a parent for her children (66.27).

This analogical argument has persuasive force because there really are important similarities between our attitudes towards our loved ones and towards other things of value. I suggest that this similarity lies in the common ancient view that rational interactions with the world are all structured by value judgements about the things dealt with. Such value can be the object of distinct focus, whether in people or in things, and in both parts of the analogy Seneca detaches for consideration the valued aspect of each, the virtue which underlies the goodness which produces true benefit for the person involved. This abstraction of value from the circumstances is made explicit in the section which follows (66.28–34). After repeating the point that absolute terms (like *aptum* and *planum*, and therefore also *honestum*) cannot vary in degree, he observes in section 30 that those who think that goods of favourable and unfavourable circumstance are unequal must in fact be concentrating on the external circumstances rather than on what is good in each situation (66.30). It is the job of reason, he says, to make such assessments and reason's assessment is guided by the values of

---

[28] In letter 71.5 Seneca refers to 'falling in love with virtue' in connection with the same thesis as is defended here in 66.

reason: that is, its value judgements seek out what is reliable and invariant. Only reason can do the kind of focusing and abstraction which generates such stable value judgements. Reason is able to guide our planning and decision making because it is *inmutabilis et iudicii tenax* (66.32). In this respect it stands in stark contrast to the senses (66.35 ff.) which cannot synthesize over time. The senses cannot deal with the future and so cannot take charge of the *rerum ordo seriesque* and so produce what every eudaimonist theory aims at: *unitas vitae per rectum iturae*. This, Seneca says explicitly, is why it is reason which makes the decisions about what is good and bad.

Seneca has argued, then, that reason rather than our senses is the mental faculty appropriate for making the value judgements which guide long-term eudaimonist planning. Since reason is in charge, it will make its judgements according to its distinctive nature: reason is able to abstract and generalize, to attend selectively to relevant features of a situation, and to plan for the future. In doing so, he holds, reason distinguishes relevantly similar features and values them similarly.

Returning to Zimmerman's critique, I want to make a couple of observations. First, the body/soul dualism which struck him as so rebarbative is clearly visible in Seneca. Letter 66 is, in fact, typical in this regard. Seneca does regard the mind as a kind of 'inner citadel' and frequently treats our own body as an external, no more part of our morally relevant self than our wealth or our civil status. We may now ask why he does so. Zimmerman presumes the common answer, that this is a rationalization designed to help us cope with the unpleasant necessities of life. Others might prefer the suggestion that Seneca has acquired a bad case of sentimental Platonism from excessive brooding on the *Phaedo*—in which Socrates notoriously and light-heartedly distinguishes between his body and his self just on the point of his tragic death. ('How shall we bury you?' asks Crito. 'In any way you like, if you can catch me and I do not escape you', Socrates replies, *Phd.* 115c–d.) But here, in one letter at least, we can see a more philosophically interesting answer. Woven through the admittedly complex rhetoric of the letter—which I have certainly not subjected to the full

Reason, Rationalization, and Happiness 269

analysis which it deserves—we can, I think, discern the following patterns of thought.

Decisions about how to act in life, what attitudes to hold and what actions to undertake, will always be guided by value judgements. Actions based on such judgements will shape our character and determine the moral quality of our life. These value judgements will inevitably be entrusted either to the senses or to the reason, to our body or to the mind. Which is more appropriate? Reason. And why is that? Because reason has certain characteristics and abilities: reason can grasp the future, can generalize, and can distinguish different aspects of complex situations. This gives it the ability to deliberate and select, to be in control of decisions as the senses cannot be. Further, we have a prior commitment to attaining happiness over a whole life (this being the shared goal of all eudaimonist systems), and only reason's capacities enable it to attain the unity and consistency which that long-term goal demands.

That is why we put reason in charge of reshaping our lives. In addition, it is reason which we share with the gods (this is a commonplace of ancient thought, one shared even by the Epicureans), and the gods are (on the basis of separate arguments in natural philosophy) identifiable with the nature that governs the world as a whole. Hence *our* reason tracks nature when it functions well and the *summum bonum* can be described indifferently as the perfection of human reason or as 'comporting oneself in accordance with the will of nature' (66.39).

When reason assesses complex situations which are mixtures of the favourable and the unfavourable—like the case of a good man struggling with horrendous physical frailty—it does so in its own typical way. It abstracts and groups the various characteristics and features of the situation in the manner which is most defensible in argument. Hence Seneca *argues* for the proposition that the virtue displayed in such a situation should be taken together with the virtue displayed in other situations, abstracted from its distinguishable bodily context so that its most important trait, its rational perfection, is the central focus of moral evaluation. It is true that in order to do so he must draw the boundaries of the self in such a way that the body falls outside them, that he is pushed towards a degree of body-soul dualism which can seem not only disingenuous for a Stoic corporealist but can also appear to be more Platonic than Stoic. But if my partial analysis of this letter is on the right track, he does so not because he is rationalizing away the unpleasantness of life in order to attain a superficial and short-sighted form of happiness. Rather, he does so because he genuinely believes that this is where the argument leads, that this is what *ratio recta* tells us is true about human beings and our place in the world. The arguments on which he has relied the most are conceptual (that virtue is a perfection and that perfections as a class cannot vary in degree), endoxic (that our common conception of a good man's behaviour does not allow for fickle situational revision of our decisions and value judgements), and analogical (that there is an important similarity between our attachment to friends and our love of virtue itself, and that our relationship to our actions is relevantly similar to our relationship to the circumstances in which they occur). None of these arguments is deductively compelling, but none falls outside the quality range we are accustomed to in the best ancient philosophers.

This letter, like many others, has an unmistakeable anti-Epicurean theme. We do not, of course, have direct access to any of the arguments on the other side—the objections are all filtered through Seneca's own authorial voice. But that should not obscure the fact that he raises objections to his own positions and then does his best to answer them rationally. We do not have any good reason to think that Seneca does anything other than to follow those arguments as conscientiously as he can, trying like most philosophers in the ancient world, Platonist, Stoic, and even Epicurean, to perfect his reason in order to attain happiness.

10

Getting to Goodness

It is a fundamental tenet of Stoicism that the entire repertoire of human concepts comes directly or indirectly from our sensory experience, interpreted broadly. Here (for convenience) is a familiar set of texts which tells us most of what we know about Stoic theories on the acquisition of concepts.[1]

Diogenes Laertius 7.52–3

52. According to the Stoics, 'sense-perception' refers to [a] the *pneuma* which extends from the leading part [of the soul] to the senses and [b] the 'grasp' which comes through the senses and [c] the equipment of the sense organs (in which some people are impaired). And [d] their activation is also called sense-perception. According to them the grasp occurs [a] through sense-perception (in the case of white objects, black

---

I am particularly indebted to Robert Todd, Margaret Graver, Phillip Mitsis, and Tony Long for helpful criticism on various versions of this essay.

[1] The fundamental piece of modern literature on the topic is M. Pohlenz's account in *Grundfragen der stoischen Philosophie* (Göttingen, 1940), 82–99: 'Die Entstehung der sittlichen Begriffe'; at pp. 99–103 he moves on to the question of our *prolēpsis* of god; still very valuable is F. H. Sandbach, '*Ennoia* and *Prolēpsis*', *CQ* 24 (1930), 44–51; repr. in A. A. Long (ed.), *Problems in Stoicism* (London, 1971), 22–37 (citations are to the reprint). The most penetrating recent work on this topic is Dominic Scott, 'Innatism and the Stoa', *Proceedings of the Cambridge Philological Society*, ser. 3, 30 (1988), 123–53 and *Recollection and Experience: Plato's Theory of Learning and its Successors* (Cambridge, 1995). In this chapter I attempt to demonstrate in some detail the independent contribution Seneca makes to a problem in moral epistemology which stands in need of both philosophical and historical clarification.

objects, rough objects, smooth objects); and [b] through reason (in the case of conclusions drawn through demonstration, for example, that there are gods and that they are provident). For of conceptions, some are conceived on the basis of direct experience, some on the basis of similarity, some on the basis of analogy, <some on the basis of transposition,> some on the basis of composition and some on the basis of opposition. 53. Sensibles are conceived on the basis of direct experience; on the basis of similarity are conceived things [known] from something which is at hand—as Socrates is conceived of on the basis of his statue; on the basis of analogy things are conceived by expansion, for example, Tityos and the Cyclops, and by shrinking, for example, a Pygmy. And the centre of the earth is conceived through analogy with smaller spheres. On the basis of transposition, for example, eyes in the chest. On the basis of composition the Hippocentaur is conceived of; and death on the basis of opposition [to life]. Some things too are conceived of on the basis of transference, for example, the things said (*lekta*) and place. And there is a natural origin too for the conception of something just and good.[2] Also on the basis of privation, for example, someone without a hand. These are their doctrines on presentation, sense-perception, and conception.

Aetius 4.11.1–5

(= *Dox. Gr.*, 400–1) The origin of sense-perception, conceptions, and internal reason.

1. The Stoics say: When a human being is born, the leading part of his soul is like a sheet of paper in good condition for being written on. On this he inscribes each and every one of his conceptions.

2. The first manner of writing on it is through the senses. For when one perceives something, white for example, one retains a memory after it goes away. When there are many memories similar in kind then we say one has experience. For experience is the plurality of presentations similar in kind.

3. Of conceptions, some come into being naturally in the stated ways and without technical elaboration, but others, already, come into being through our teaching and efforts. The latter are called only conceptions, while the former are also called preconceptions (*prolēpseis*).

---

[2] See *De Stoic. Rep.* 1041e = *SVF* iii.69 = LS 60B and commentary p. 375; also Pohlenz, *Grundfragen*, 88 f., Sandbach, '*Ennoia* and *Prolēpsis*', 28, and Cherniss ad loc. (*Moralia*, vol. xiii, pt. 2 (Loeb Classical Library; Cambridge, MA, 1976), 489–1).

4. But reason, according to which we are termed rational, is said to be completely filled out with preconceptions at the age of seven years. And a concept is a phantasm in the intellect of a rational animal. For when a phantasm occurs in a rational soul, then it is called a concept, taking its name from 'mind' (*ennoēma*, from *nous*).

5. Therefore, all the phantasms which strike irrational animals are *only* phantasms and those which occur in us and in the gods are phantasms in general and specifically concepts. (Just as denarii and staters, on their own, are denarii and staters, but when they are given to pay for a ship-passage, then they are called 'ship money' in addition to being denarii [and staters].)

Sextus, *M* 8.56–9 (*SVF* 2.88)

56 ... For every thought comes from sense-perception or not without sense-perception and either from direct experience or not without direct experience. 57. Hence, we shall find that not even the so-called false presentations (for example, those occurring in sleep or madness) are independent of things known to us through sense-perception by direct experience ... 58. And in general one can find nothing in our conceptions which is not known to oneself in direct experience. For it will be grasped either by similarity to what is revealed in direct experience or by expansion or reduction or compounding. 59. So, for example, [it is] by similarity when we conceive of the Socrates we do not see on the basis of a statue of Socrates which we are looking at; by expansion, when on the basis of an ordinary human we conceive of someone who is not like 'a grain-eating man but rather like a wooded peak among high mountains'; by reduction when by reducing the magnitude of an ordinary human we acquire the conception of a Pygmy; by compounding when on the basis of human and horse we conceive of the Hippocentaur, which we have never experienced. So, sensory experience must precede every conception and therefore if sensible things are eliminated then necessarily every thought is eliminated along with it.

Cicero, *De Finibus* 3.33–4

33. 'Good', which has been used so frequently in this discussion, is also explained with a definition. The definitions offered by [the Stoics] do differ from each other, but only very slightly; for all that, they are getting at the same point. I agree with Diogenes who defined good as that which is perfect in its nature. He followed this up by defining the

beneficial (let us use this term for *ōphelēma*) as a motion or condition which is in accord with what is perfect in its nature. And since we acquire conceptions of things if we learn something either by direct experience or by combination or by similarity or by rational inference, the conception of good is created by the last method mentioned. For the mind attains a conception of the good when it ascends by rational inference from those things which according to nature. 34. But the good itself is not perceived to be good or called good because of some addition or increase or comparison with other things, but in virtue of its own special character. For honey, although it is the sweetest thing, is nevertheless perceived to be sweet not because of a comparison with other things, but because of its own distinctive flavour; in the same way the good, which is the subject of our discussion, is indeed most valuable, but that value derives meaning from its distinctive type and not from its magnitude. For value (which is called *axia*) is not counted as either good or bad; consequently, however much you might increase it, it will still remain in the same general category. Therefore, there is one kind of value which applies to virtue, and it derives its meaning from its distinctive type and not from its magnitude.

My concern here is with one particular concept: the good. For it is both unusually important and deeply problematic. Its importance stems from its role in the improvement of a human life. Achieving the human *telos*, becoming happy, is a matter of acquiring the good for oneself. But since human beings are rational animals, we can neither acquire the good nor benefit from it unless we also *understand* it; we must achieve knowledge of the good if we are to be happy, and this knowledge is the acquisition of a certain and unshakeable grasp. This is problematic not just because of the breathtakingly high standard for knowledge set by the Stoics, but because of the peculiar relationship of the good to human experience. For the good is taken to be virtue and what participates in virtue;[3] and virtue is manifested only in wise persons, who are the principal example of things which participate in virtue (the other examples being the actions performed by such people and perhaps some of their character states and relations). And wise persons are, as we

---

[3] Stobaeus, *Ecl.* ii.57; cf. *M* 11.2, which nicely emphasizes the connection of this formulation to the notion of genuine benefit.

know, extremely rare (if not altogether unexampled) on the normal Stoic view of things. If, as we expect and as the practice of Stoic moral pedagogy presupposes, the achievement of virtue, happiness, and the good is in principle open to anyone, how can this be? How can anyone even learn what goodness is (let alone acquire an unshakeable grasp of it) if no one is at all likely to encounter an actual instance of it in their experience?

The text of Cicero cited refers back to an earlier passage on the nature of the good in *De Finibus* 3, sections 20–5. This section tells us a good deal about our development of a notion of the good, and has been much discussed, most recently by Michael Frede in 'On the Stoic Conception of the Good'.[4]

20. Let us move on, then, since we began from these natural principles and what follows should be consistent with them. There follows this primary division: they say that what has value (we are to call it that, I think) is that which is either itself in accordance with nature or productive of it, so that it is worthy of selection because it has a certain 'weight' which is worth valuing (and this [value] they call *axia*); by contrast, what is opposite to the above is disvalued. The starting point being, then, so constituted that what is natural is to be taken for its own sake and what is unnatural is to be rejected, the first appropriate action (for that is what I call *kathēkon*) is that the human being should preserve itself in its natural constitution; and then that it should retain what is according to nature and reject what is contrary to nature. After this [pattern of] selection and rejection is discovered, there then follows appropriate selection, and then constant [appropriate] selection, and finally [selection] which is stable and in agreement with nature; **and here for the first time we begin to have and to understand something which can truly be called good. 21. For a human being's first sense of congeniality is to what is according to nature; but as soon as he gets an understanding, or rather a conception (which they call an *ennoia*) and sees the ordering and, I might say, concord of things which are to be done, he then values that more highly than all those things which he loved in the beginning, and he comes to a conclusion by intelligence and reasoning, with the result that he decides that this is what the highest good for a human being consists in, which is**

---

[4] Chapter 3 of K. Ierodiakonou (ed.), *Topics in Stoic Philosophy* (Oxford, 1999).

to be praised and chosen for its own sake. And since it is placed in what the Stoics call *homologia*, let us call it agreement, if you please. Since, therefore, this constitutes the good, to which all things are to be referred, honourable actions and the honourable itself—which is considered to be the only good—although it arises later [in our lives], nevertheless it is the only thing which is to be chosen in virtue of its own character and value; but none of the primary natural things is to be chosen for its own sake.

22. Since, however, those things which I called appropriate actions proceed from the starting points [established] by nature, it is necessary that they be referred to them; **so it is right to say all appropriate actions are referred to acquisition of the natural principles, not however in the sense that this is the highest good, since honourable action is not among the primarily and naturally congenial things. That, as I said, is posterior and arises later.** But [such action] is natural and encourages us to choose it much more than all the earlier mentioned things. But here one must first remove a misunderstanding, so that no one might think that there are two highest goods. For just as, if it is someone's purpose to direct a spear or arrow at something, we say that his highest goal is to do everything he can in order to direct it at [the target], in the same sense we say that our highest goal is a good. The archer in this comparison is to do all that he can to direct [his arrow at the target]; and yet doing all that he can to attain his purpose would be like the highest goal of the sort which we say is the highest good in life; actually striking [the target], though, is as it were to be selected and not to be chosen.

23. Since all appropriate actions proceed from the natural principles, it is necessary that wisdom itself proceed from them as well. **But just as it often happens that he who is introduced to someone puts a higher value on the person to whom he is introduced than to the person by whom he was introduced, just so it is in no way surprising that we are first introduced to wisdom by the starting points [established] by nature, but that later on wisdom itself becomes dearer to us than the things which brought us to wisdom.** And just as our limbs were given us in such a way that they seem to have been given for the sake of a certain way of life, similarly the impulse in our soul, which is called *hormē* in Greek, seems not to have been given for the sake of any old type of life but

for a certain kind of living; and similarly for reason and perfected reason. 24. Just as an actor or dancer has not been assigned just any [type of] delivery or movement but rather a certain definite [type]; so too life is to be lived in a certain definite manner, not in any old [manner]. And we call that manner 'in agreement' and consonant. And we do not think that wisdom is like navigation or medicine, but rather like the craft of acting or dancing which I just mentioned; thus its goal, i.e. the [proper] execution of the craft, depends on it itself and is not sought outside itself. There is also another point of dissimilarity between wisdom and these crafts, viz. that in them proper actions do not contain all the components [lit. parts] which constitute the art; but things called 'right' or 'rightly done', if I may call them that, though the Greeks call them *katorthōmata* [morally perfect actions], contain all the features of virtue. Only wisdom is totally self-contained, and this is not the case with the other crafts.

25. But it is misguided to compare the highest goal of medicine or navigation with that of wisdom; for wisdom embraces great-heartedness and justice and an ability to judge that everything which happens to a [mere] human being is beneath it—and this does not apply to the rest of the crafts. But no one can possess the very virtues which I just mentioned unless he has firmly decided that there is nothing except what is honourable or shameful which makes a difference or distinguishes one [thing or situation] from another.

In this passage, which I have quoted at some length highlighting what I take to be the particularly important parts, Cicero describes how over the course of our maturation we come ideally to develop a conception of the good. The emphasis throughout is on the fact that this is a posterior development rooted in an initial grasp of what is naturally advantageous in some less final sense. As the end of section 20 indicates, the good comes to be in us (*inesse*) at the same time as we begin to understand it (*intellegi*). This development of our concept of the good requires certain prior developments in us; in addition to the basic idea of advantage or utility, we also have to acquire a notion of the ordering or concord in the actions which are somehow incumbent on us owing to our nature. This is clearly a necessary condition for the evaluative and affective change which follows and for the cognitive development which ensues.

Perhaps Cicero also thinks of it as a sufficient condition (this would be a reasonable inference from 'as soon as' in section 21), but in fact he also describes the cognitive development as an inference based on *cognitio* and *ratio*. At the same time as we transfer our affective allegiance to this new value, we also think our way through to the conclusion that this ordering is the locus of the highest good for humans.

Cicero says very little here about the nature of this reasoning process. But he does make it clear that it cannot be a simple matter of empirical generalization derived from our experiences of natural and appropriate action. As he says, 'honourable action is not among the primarily and naturally congenial things. That, as I said, is posterior and arises later.' The rather mysterious character of this reasoning is not clarified by the highlighted comparison in section 23. Cicero is, however, clear and emphatic on a point also made by Diogenes Laertius (7.53). However it happens, this process of coming to grasp the good is something natural: 'and there is a natural origin too for the conception of something just and good'.

The mystery of this inference is not cleared up by *De Finibus* 3.33. There, after giving a standard list of the means of concept formation, Cicero specifies that the good is grasped by rational inference (*collatio rationis*; compare *cognitione et ratione collegit* at 3.21) and not by the other means. All he says is that the basis for the inference is the primary natural things and that the process is a kind of ascent. The reference to the role of order and harmony among actions directed at those natural things is missing; we have no opportunity to integrate the two passages any more closely than this. Frede's discussion ('On the Stoic Conception') of the passage emphasizes the purported naturalness of the developmental process which the Stoics envisaged and the psychology presupposed by the Stoic theory, and his reflections on Stoic ideas about teleology and value theory are important. But they do not, unfortunately, answer the critical question which emerges from Cicero's text and from other evidence about Stoic theories of the good: if the notion of the good comes to us by a process of reasoning, as a rational inference, how is that process supposed to work?

The best hint we can detect in the Cicero text comes from 3.20–1. Without yet having a concept of the good, people select things and actions quite naturally. And because we are a well-adapted species, we make adaptive or appropriate selections just as naturally. That kind of activity will fall into a pattern, of course, since the environment we deal with is characterized by large-scale regularities and since our nature is stable. From reflection on this regularity we draw some conclusions, and the Stoics would like us to draw the conclusion that regularity and order lie at the core of goodness. Why should we go along with this invitation?

Let us grant the Stoic theorist a small handicap advantage. Let us grant that the regular appropriate selections on which we reflect include not just our own experience but that of others. Let us also focus on cases of natural preferences which border closely on virtue as it is conventionally understood, granting for example that one of the regularly occurring appropriate selections involves actions which benefit another person—care for our own children in accordance with one of the most fundamental traits of our nature. With this sort of action in view, how do we apply what Cicero says in 3.20–1, in the selection highlighted above?

How can any amount of reflection on the selections referred to there induce a rational agent to hold that the orderliness of such behaviour is the locus of our good, rather than the substantive appeals which attracted us naturally to select such actions to start with? Once we have come to appreciate the value of the orderliness and consistency of such actions, they are no longer to be chosen for their own sakes at all.[5] It is perhaps not difficult to imagine that generalization across many such experiences might induce us to hold that it is good

---

[5] The relationship between the value such actions have and the value of the good is a major topic of Frede's discussion. He suggests (91–2) that our remaining concern for such things is now 'completely derivative' and that 'if things which have mere value are not desirable in themselves, then the desire for them in a rational person *can only* [my emphasis] be the desire for them as mere means to the good'. I don't think this is the right account of the relationship between preferred indifferents and the good, but the point is peripheral to my present concerns. See my discussion in *CHHP*, ch. 21, sections IV to VI.

to be consistent in caring for our children, or that it is consistently good to care for our children, or that it is good that everyone should care for their own children; but it is not so easy to see why we should conclude that consistency is what is good and that getting the children fed and clothed is not to be chosen for its own sake.

What Cicero has given us, clearly, is a description of a Stoic theory and not any account of the argument underlying it. We should not, I think, expect to find the argument here, since his concern is clearly to communicate to his readers an *external* picture of the theory and not to present the arguments which would rationally compel acceptance of it (if there were any at his disposal) nor to present the inferential process which, according to the theory, we undergo in order to acquire the notion of the good and so transform our lives into eudaimonistic success stories. Even after looking closely at Cicero's evidence, then, we are back where we started, with an unanswered puzzle. By what rational process do the Stoics think we acquire the notion of the good?

The list of processes by which concepts are formed is short, as we have seen. Direct experience, similarity, analogy, transposition, composition, and opposition are mentioned by Diogenes Laertius. Sextus' list includes direct experience, expansion, reduction, and compounding. According to Aetius, some concepts require the intervention of teaching and effort, while others seem to emerge directly (he says 'naturally') from the accretion of repeated similar experiences. I would suppose that the kind of repeated similar experience envisaged here counts as 'direct experience' in the lists of Sextus and Diogenes and that the similarity mentioned by Diogenes falls under the more reflective and self-conscious processes which Aetius correctly says require teaching and effort. The analogy mentioned by Diogenes includes and may be exhausted by the processes of reducing and expanding in Sextus' list. Cicero's list includes direct experience, combination, and similarity, but adds rational inference seemingly to cover the case of good. The way he describes its operation is not only inadequate to explain what he is driving at (as we have seen), but it also makes clear that, whatever rational inference is, it does not include the use of our reason to project changes of scale or degree onto the concept in question. The dualism in Stoic value theory makes mere extrapolation inadequate to the job of accounting for the notion of the good.[6]

There was, then, a problem for Stoics in accounting for the possibility of our acquisition of the concept of the good.[7] It is clearly meant to be a concept open to us through natural, empirical means. Yet at the same time it seems to transcend the realm of ordinary experience and to embody an ideal of human perfection which we neither experience in our ordinary lives nor attain with any significant frequency. The starting points for coming to understand the good, the experience of what is mundanely useful or advantageous, are accessible enough; but the required development of such 'utility' towards the ideal of perfect moral utility is virtually impossible to account for within the framework of Stoic epistemology. It is one thing to set out a theory which builds on the assumption that we can learn about the good. But it is quite another to have a defensible account of how we are supposed to be able to do so within the context of Stoic epistemology. In our consideration of Seneca's contribution to this problem, we will need to focus on how this gap is to be bridged.

This is the starting point for my consideration of Seneca's discussion of how the notion of the good is acquired, and the realization that there *is* a real problem in this area for Stoics is crucial for my assessment of how his discussion is meant to work. I shall try to support the view that Seneca at least intends to make a serious contribution to the problem and that his discussion in letter 120 is at least coherent and interesting;[8] whether he should be thought to have helped the situation very much is a different question, one to which I will return at

---

[6] But that does not mean that the idea of the good is not sometimes illustrated by examples which involve differences of degree: *Fin.* 3.45.

[7] It is this problem which provoked Bonhöffer (in *Epictet und die Stoa* (Stuttgart, 1890)) to postulate an innate concept of the good (relying on *De Stoic. Rep.* 17). See the discussion of Pohlenz, *Grundfragen*, 82–99.

[8] Contra Pohlenz, see next note.

the end of my essay. But whether or not his contribution is constructive, some features of his approach to the problem are of independent interest; and (more important for my own immediate concerns) the realization that Seneca is working on a legitimate problem in Stoic moral epistemology helps us to see what is going on in one of his more important letters.

Seneca discusses the good many times in his letters. But for our purposes, the best place to pick up the story is in letter 117. Here, Seneca asks whether *sapere* is good. That *sapientia* is good is taken for granted on the basis of Stoic theory, and Seneca reminds his readers that on the official Stoic view *sapere*, 'being wise', cannot be good since it is an incorporeal predicate rather than a body—they hold that the good is a body. Seneca takes this as a prime instance of a subtle metaphysical distinction which serves no philosophical purpose, and argues against the denial that *sapere* is good. In section 6 he describes his own position in tackling this issue:

I do not hold the same view and I think that our school (*nostros*) gets into this position because they are still impeded by their preliminary constraint (*primo vinculo tenentur*) and they are not permitted to change their formula. We are accustomed to give considerable weight to the preconception (*praesumptio*, i.e. *prolēpsis*) of all people and our view is that it is an argument that something is true if all people believe it; for example, we conclude that there are gods for this reason among others, that there is implanted in everyone an opinion about the gods and there is no culture anywhere so far beyond laws and customs that it does not hold that there are *some* gods. When we debate the eternity of souls, it has considerable weight with us that there is a consensus among people who either fear the gods of the underworld or worship them. I use this public mode of persuasion: you won't find anyone who does not think that both wisdom and 'being wise' are good.

One can argue about how much weight the *consensus omnium* argument ought to have, but there is no doubt at all that it has a serious role in Stoic epistemology. The fact that everyone agrees that *p* is a reasonable premiss in an argument for many conclusions, especially in theology; Seneca thinks, with other Stoics, that there are some universal conceptions shared naturally by all humans and that the fact that they are shared is an important (though not necessarily compelling) consideration in favour of the truth of at least some philosophical opinions.[9] In this letter Seneca may or may not succeed in his criticism of Stoic metaphysical distinctions as untrue and unfruitful. But it will help to bear this passage in mind when we turn to the letter which most interests me, 120.[10]

Letter 120 deals explicitly with what he calls a minor *quaestio*, our question of how we come to have the notion of the good and honourable. As a brief summary will show, the discussion falls largely within the ambit of familiar Stoic epistemology, but there is a perhaps puzzling excursus which sketches a picture of the Stoic sage in rather platonic-looking terms, the function of which in the letter is not immediately obvious. Here is the outline of the letter (referring to the normal section numbers in the Oxford Classical Text) which I will follow in discussing the argument of the letter.

1–3 prefatory remarks
4–5 the main argument
6–8 examples
8–11 details of the cognitive processing
12–18 the sage
19–22 conclusion

1–3. These are prefatory remarks. Lucilius' request for an account of how the concept of the *bonum honestumque* comes to us leads to a short discussion of the relationship between good and honourable

---

[9] See the helpful discussion of this general issue in Dirk Obbink, '"What all Men believe must be true": Common Conceptions and *consensio omnium* in Aristotle and Hellenistic Philosophy', *Oxford Studies in Ancient Philosophy*, 10 (1992), 193–231. Useful background is also to be found in Malcolm Schofield, 'Preconception, Argument and God', in M. Schofield, M. Burnyeat, and J. Barnes (eds.), *Doubt and Dogmatism* (Oxford 1980), 283–308.

[10] Pohlenz, *Grundfragen*, 82–99, discusses this problem in general, acknowledging the contribution of Sandbach and making clear why Bonhöffer's views must be wrong (see esp. pp. 88 ff.). At pp. 86–8 he considers letter 120. He fails, in my view, to grasp what Seneca is doing in large measure because he over-assimilates his discussion to the doctrine of the earlier school as known from DL and Cicero, and also through an excessive readiness to conclude that Seneca simply loses track of his main question and veers off onto another theme in mid-letter. I hope to show by my discussion that Seneca's account has more coherence than Pohlenz suspected.

(as I shall translate *honestum*). Stoics hold that they are distinct but not extensionally separable concepts (*divisa* but not *diversa*).[11] He criticizes those who hold the notion of the good as useful in any sense which diverges from the honourable. He does not, of course, deny that the good is useful, but rather is insisting that the appropriately technical sense of usefulness be relied on. If the honourable is that for which one can give an account of why it is the right thing to do, then an overly broad notion of the useful (one which includes wealth, horses, wine, and shoes) must be wrong. The notions of good and honourable are distinct (*duo*) but unified (*ex uno*), in the sense that they are extensionally equivalent. Only the honourable is good (*nihil est bonum nisi quod honestum est*) and the honourable is necessarily good (*quod honestum, est utique bonum*). Seneca moves quickly here in support of this claim, merely alluding to the 'use' argument which goes back to Socrates: wealth, high birth, and physical strength are often misused, so they cannot be good. It is typical of Seneca's rhetoric that he bluntly dismisses the notion of the good used by his opponents as 'base' or 'cheap' (*tanta fit apud illos boni vilitas*) before rolling out his own arguments.

4–5. This section gives the main argument about how we in fact acquire our conception of the good and the honourable. Natural acquisition is ruled out (since nature only gives us the *semina scientiae*). So too is chance (the idea that virtue—anticipated as the proper candidate for the good—could be learned in this way is dismissed as a wholly implausible suggestion).[12] Let me translate the next bit. In what follows, it is worth noticing Seneca's use of past tenses here and throughout the letter. It is taken for granted that we already have the notion of the good;

---

[11] This extensional equivalence is sustainable as long as one uses the strictest notion of good (which relies on a strict Socratic notion of genuine benefit). If a looser notion is used, then the good is a broader concept within which the honourable and the strict good fall. In saying that extensional equivalence is at issue here, I look to the remarks in 3: nothing is good except what is honourable, which both highlights the extensional character of his claim and clearly invokes only the strict notion of good.

[12] Pohlenz, *Grundfragen*, 86, takes this passage to refer simply to grasping a concept *kata periptōsin* (see DL 7.52–3), but this, while possible for *incidisse*, seems implausible in view of *casu*.

the only question is how we came to have it, so that references to a prior process of concept acquisition should not be surprising.

> We believe that it [virtue] has been inferred by the observation and comparison of actions done repeatedly. Our school holds that the honourable and the good are understood by analogy... Let me explain what this analogy is. 5. We had a familiarity with bodily health; from this we also realized that there is a certain health of the mind. We had a familiarity with bodily strength; from this we inferred that there is also mental power. Certain generous deeds, certain kindly deeds, certain brave deeds had amazed us; we began to admire them as though they were perfect. There were hidden in them many failings which were concealed by the appearance (*species*) and splendour of some outstanding deed; these failings we pretended not to notice. Nature orders us to exaggerate what is praiseworthy, and there is no one who hasn't elevated glory beyond the truth. Hence it is from these actions that we have derived the appearance of some great good.

We recognize here the language of the Stoic theory of concept formation. Repeated observation of actions and the critical comparison of them with the aid of analogy fit well within Stoic epistemology. What is less obvious on the surface is the role of a kind of abstraction. Just as bodily strength has helped us to generate the notion of mental strength, so too the common features of various admirable deeds (deeds of generosity, kindness, courage) taken together give us the notion of complete virtue. 'The observation and comparison of actions done repeatedly' is the foundation for our conception of virtue.

But at this point Seneca faces the problem from which I began in this essay, an urgent problem for Stoic theory. There are always, in the world of our experience, failings 'concealed by the appearance and splendour of some outstanding deed'. Since we do not observe sages, the good actions we see done repeatedly must in fact be flawed, undermined by hidden failings. How is this cognitive process supposed to work, and how does this help us get reliably to the notion of goodness? As he notes, we 'pretended not to notice' the failings (*haec dissimulavimus*).

This is hardly the sort of move which inspires confidence in the reliability of our inference. But what Seneca says next is very important. It is Nature herself who predisposes us to amplify the significance of praiseworthy traits.[13] And it is not just a predisposition to do so, it is the 'command' of nature, which I take to mean that Seneca is here treating Nature not just as an explanation for the skewed cognitive behaviour we demonstrate in privileging the praiseworthy over the defective in our understanding of things. It is also the right way for us to behave.[14] That such cognitive bias is in fact universal is supported with an observation: everyone exaggerates *gloria* beyond the truth. Seneca's claim, then, is that this universal tendency to accentuate the praiseworthy is rooted in human nature by Nature and that this cognitive bias towards goodness is vital for our ability to derive, from the defective examples of good behaviour which we actually observe in our experience, a sound notion of virtue, the *ingens bonum*. It is not at all clear that anyone who does not share a Stoic confidence in the providential care of Nature for our species should be reassured about the reliability of this process.

6–8. The two heroes invoked here, Fabricius and Horatius, function as signal *exempla* of striking good deeds drawn from the tradition which any Roman would rely on in developing a conception of virtue. As we would expect, it is their deeds rather than their total characters which we consider. What they have created for us is an image of virtue (*haec et eiusmodi facta imaginem nobis ostendere virtutis*). I suggest, then, that Seneca uses these two examples to put flesh on the bones of his claims in 4–5; and that means that we should not suppose that Fabricius and Horatius are meant to be perfect exemplars. In 4–5 Seneca emphasized the process of developing a conception of virtue; as he said, 'we began to admire them *as though* they were perfect'. No matter how admirable such figures may be in the widely shared tradition, they cannot on their own define virtue. Such men were not sages. They surely had hidden flaws. But

---

[13] Pohlenz, *Grundfragen*, 87, takes this to refer to concept formation by *auxēsis*, as in the case of perceptual concepts in the text of DL above. But the point seems to be quite different.

[14] Letter 121 which follows immediately makes extensive use of providential nature's way of setting us up as persons to explain how humans come to care for virtue as part of their own human identity.

Nature has inclined us to downplay such defects, indeed to deceive ourselves into not attending to them, in order to give us an essential starting point for the notion of what is good and honourable.

It is, I think, important for what follows that Fabricius and Horatius play their role in helping us form a conception of virtue despite two apparent drawbacks. They are, as noted, not themselves virtuous in the full Stoic sense; hence their use in derivation of the concept of virtue is as complicated as it is important. They help to inspire and also to justify the concept of good without themselves being perfect exemplars of it. And more seriously, they are (as we are perhaps more aware of than Seneca himself) mere creatures of tradition. The Horatius we know is not someone whose deeds we observe first hand in the forum. Perhaps unlike some of the anonymous examples adduced in the letter, he is a character we know from literature, tradition, and history. If one were forming the conception of, say, 'horse' one would prefer to analyse one's observations of a number of real horses rather than traditions and second-hand reports about horses, no matter how authoritative. Perhaps here Seneca is relying to some extent on the epistemological value of a widely shared, virtually universal tradition. As we saw in letter 117 (and as is particularly evident in discussions of theological concepts) the Stoics were prepared to give real weight to the fact that certain views are deeply embedded and widely held cultural norms;[15] the fact that Horatius and Fabricius are not subject to our immediate observation is counter-balanced by the universality of his culture's admiration for their deeds.[16]

8–11. In this section Seneca illustrates at greater length some of the cognitive processing involved in extracting from our experience of defectively good deeds a conception of virtue. First,

---

[15] Rather like Cicero; see my 'Rhetorica Disputatio: The Strategy of *De Finibus II*', in Martha Nussbaum (ed.), *The Poetics of Therapy* [*Apeiron*, 23.4 (1990), 143–64].

[16] I do not want to suggest that Seneca himself would relativize the value of their universal acceptance; rather, the fact that he does not seriously consider cultural variance makes it easier for him to regard what seem to us like culturally bound examples as being 'universal'.

Seneca notes the importance of contrary examples.[17] The fact that some vices are superficially similar to virtues has a role to play in helping us to learn goodness in a world which lacks clear examples of virtue. The close similarity (note *confinia, similitudo*) of prodigality to generosity, of negligence to easy-goingness, and of rashness to courage makes our experience potentially deceptive (note *mentitur*). But it is this very deceptiveness which encourages us (rather, drives us, *coegit*) to focus more closely and make the subtle distinctions of kind which are needed. Furthermore, we distinguish one-off deeds from *patterns* of good activity. We distinguish men brave in only one sphere of life from those whose courage covers their entire range of behaviour. Such analysis enables us to abstract the merits of the action from the defects of the agent (*factum laudavimus, contempsimus virum*, sec. 9).

In section 10 Seneca makes a transition which is crucial to his discussion. Having dealt with examples of defective virtue and praiseworthy deeds done by imperfect agents (both named historical figures and presumably contemporary anonymous examples), he introduces as a contrast the agent of maximally consistent good deeds (*alium vidimus*):[18] kind to friends, restrained to his enemies, responsible in his management of public and personal affairs, displaying *patientia* and *prudentia* appropriately when circumstances call for endurance or action, manifesting generosity and gritty determination as needed. But more important for Seneca's argument, this sort of person is *dispositionally* good.

Moreover, he was always the same and consistent with himself in every act; not 'good' by planning but owing to his character he advanced to the point where he not only could act rightly but could not act other than rightly.

---

[17] Again, Pohlenz, *Grundfragen*, 87, identifies this with concept formation *kat' enantiōsin* as in DL's account.

[18] As we will see, the claim that 'we have seen' such a person (*vidimus*) is highly contentious. Without a sage to observe in the flesh, how could we have seen such an agent?

In such an agent, Seneca says (11), we got our understanding of perfected virtue and subsequently analysed it into the four cardinal virtues of the tradition.[19]

At this point Seneca has outlined the raw materials of the problem and can restate it with more point—hence I would myself want to mark a strong break in the middle of 11: *ex quo ergo virtutem intelleximus?* seems to start a new paragraph. The answer is formulated in an interesting way:

> It was shown to us by his orderliness (*ordo*) and fittingness (*decor*) and consistency (*constantia*), the mutual agreement (*concordia*) of all his actions and the greatness which rises above everything. This is the source of our understanding of the happy life which flows smoothly and is completely in its own power.

The central role is played by orderliness, consistency, and an apt fitting together of a maximal set of actions. One observation worth making is that the language used by Seneca here cannot fail to recall what Cicero said at *De Finibus* 3.21.[20] For Cicero it is the *rerum agendarum ordo et concordia*, for Seneca it is the *ordo* of the agent and (among other things) the *omnium inter se actionum concordia* which grounds the understanding (*intellegentiam vel notionem* in Cicero, *intellegere* in Seneca) of virtue and the virtuous life.[21]

If we think of the Cicero text as relevant to Seneca's aim here in letter 120, then it is fair to say that already Seneca has given us more to work with in terms of understanding how Stoics are supposed to get a notion of goodness out of a defective world

---

[19] Interestingly, this not only commits Seneca to the unity of virtues as a bit of Stoic theory, but also to the idea that unified virtue is epistemologically prior. And this is not unreasonable, since for Seneca as for other Stoics maximal consistency is one of the most reliable markers of virtue.

[20] Pohlenz, *Grundfragen*, 87.

[21] I don't doubt that Seneca is intentionally recalling Cicero here. Not only is it intrinsically likely that he should be familiar with and draw on the most authoritative account of Stoic ethics yet produced in Latin; but Cicero has already been invoked in book 20 of the letters. Letter 118 opens the book with an unmistakable allusion to *Ad Atticum* 1. Just as Horace intrudes particularly in this book of letters (*Ep.* 119, 120), so too Cicero (as often, the literary model he aims to outdo). If the pertinence of letter 118's allusion to Cicero is doubted, note the recurrence of the Vatinius example (alongside Cato) at 120.19. I think Seneca often writes with Cicero's philosophical works in mind and sees himself as in some ways his rival.

than Cicero himself did. He has addressed the problem left by conventional Stoic moral epistemology by pointing out some features of our moral life which contribute to our ability to make the qualitative leap to a conception of virtue on the basis of merely partial experience of good action.

12–18. At the beginning of 120.12, though, Seneca again takes stock and makes what should, I think, be recognized as a new start. He asks, *quomodo ergo hoc ipsum nobis apparuit?* and undertakes to explain (*dicam*). It is important to get clear, if we can, about what it is that Seneca undertakes to be explaining at this point. 'So how did this itself appear to us?' one might translate literally. But what is the *hoc ipsum*? It must be one of two things: either the *beata vita* described at the end of 11 in such conventional Stoic terms, or the *bonum et honestum* we have been asking about all along. In favour of the former are proximity and the smooth unfolding of the letter's themes. In favour of the latter is the fact that this one question has been the main theme throughout, recurred to often;[22] if we mark a new paragraph here, it would not be implausible to imagine Seneca jumping back to his main question with this formulation.

Whether Seneca is asking about the origin of our image of the happy life or of our conception of the good is still unclear to me. But this is not an impediment to our grasp of the letter, if only because these two will converge in any case. For here, in 12, we stand at its turning point. Having taken the traditional Stoic problem about how we can derive a concept of good from a world which gives us no sages to observe, and having filled out Cicero's reply, based as it is on comparison and analogical analysis of our experience of the world as it is, Seneca is clearly not done with the issue. The tack which his letter takes at this point is intended, I think, to make a further contribution to the problem, though it is not obvious that other Stoics would be as happy with this contribution as they might be with the earlier one.

---

[22] And, though this is a weak consideration, the occurrence of *apparuit* at the beginning of 13 below.

In 12 Seneca begins a detailed and laudatory description of the wise and happy person he has been discussing. (I think this must be the same character, though *vir ille* does not show this on its own; but combined with the words *perfectus adeptusque virtutem* which echo *perfectam virtutem* of 11 the *ille* must surely be anaphoric.) This man never curses fortune, accepts what happens without sadness, thinks of himself as a sort of soldier-citizen of the universe, taking hardship as part of his duty (12). Such a man necessarily looked (*apparuit*) great to us; and so he has an important epistemological role to play in the world: 'He gave many people an understanding of himself and shone forth just like a light in the darkness and turned everyone's attention onto himself, since he was calm and relaxed, a match for divine and human affairs equally' (13). Here, perhaps, is a further suggestion about how we can come to know the good in a world such as ours. Not only does Nature urge us to exaggerate the good and neglect the bad; Seneca is also suggesting here that our experience of one great man can have such impact that he directly communicates a grasp of what he is and stands for (the *intellectus sui*) to a significant number of people. The fact that such a figure can attract the attention of *everyone* (*advertitque in se omnium animos*) shows how such an idealized character of tradition builds a *consensus omnium* which can then play a critical role in building the concept of the good.

In 14–18 Seneca elaborates the picture of such a sage in terms which cannot fail to evoke a conception of human perfection more platonic than what we normally think of as Stoic. It is, perhaps, worth quoting at length (15–18) to underline this point:

Lucilius my friend, it is the most powerful proof that a mind comes from some loftier place if it judges these things it deals with to be base and narrow, if it is not afraid to take its leave. For it knows where it is going to go and remembers where it came from. Don't we see how many troubles plague us and how badly this body suits us? We complain about headache sometimes, stomach ache other times, and again about chest troubles or a sore throat. Now our muscles trouble us, now our feet, then diarrhoea, then a runny nose. Sometimes our blood is too abundant, sometimes too thin. We are besieged from all sides and then driven out. This is normally the experience only of those living in a foreign environment.

But even though we are stuck with such a crumbling body we nevertheless aim at the eternal and with our ambition we seize the full extent of what the length of a human life can accommodate, not content with money or power in any amount. What could be more outrageous or more stupid than this? Nothing satisfies those who are about to die, indeed who are dying already. Every day we stand closer to the end and each day pushes us towards the place from which we must fall. See what blindness afflicts our minds. What I refer to as future occurs at that very moment and most of it is already in the past. For the time that we have lived is in the same place as it was before we lived. So we are wrong to fear our final day, since each and every day contributes just as much to our death. The step during which we collapse is not the one which makes us tired; it just announces our fatigue. The final day reaches death; each day approaches. Death plucks at us; it does not snatch us. So a great mind, one aware of its better nature, certainly takes care to comport itself honourably and industriously in the post to which it is stationed, but it does not judge that any of its surroundings are its own. A traveller hurrying by, it uses them as though they are on loan.

These are widely shared, even universal experiences. On this account we are all mere sojourners in our bodies, or exiles, deceiving ourselves about our significance in this world. One of the considerations which drives the sage to this detachment from the body is the demand for consistency in act and motivation which has already been urged. The rapid variation of bodily misfortunes is a sign that we are not at home in our bodies; in addition we act with reckless folly in supposing that such a body can sustain long-term plans. The vulnerability of our bodily existence is such that consistent follow-through is only possible if our ambitions for our life can be fulfilled *even if* the body fails us. This drives us to the detachment Seneca recommends, for only by standing back from the body and seeing that every day in it contributes to our eventual death can we plan reliably for the very long term. Thus, the lofty mind remembers his origins and acts in light of them (15); this is how a great mind shows its awareness of its better nature. The imperatives of rational consistency over the long term, when combined with the unreliability of the body as such, clearly motivates the 'platonic' detachment of body and soul exhibited here. And since the experience of bodily vulnerability is universal, so too is our susceptibility to the importance of such an ideal of long-term consistency.

19–22. In 19 Seneca begins his conclusion, and in so doing he focuses on one feature of the sage just imagined, his *constantia*, an idea which remains central right to the end of this letter. In sections 10–11 it was the contrast of the inconsistent with the consistent agent which Seneca made central. In the conclusion he returns to this, emphasizing that it is *aequalitas* and *tenor* which are the mark of genuineness (19) and that *fluctuatio* is the clearest mark of a bad disposition (20). Waverers are excoriated (*alternis Vatinii, alternis Catones sunt*, etc. 19) and a satire of Horace is invoked to give the point literary support.

The inconsistent pattern of activity of most human beings is elaborated further in 21, and in 22 the final argument is marshalled. An agent who cannot sustain a single character is not only not virtuous, but does not even qualify as a single recognizable agent:

This is most powerful proof that a mind is unwise (*imprudens*). It goes around as one person after another and is inconsistent with itself, and I think nothing is more shameful than that. Consider it a great thing to play the role of one person. But except for the sage, no one plays a single role; the rest of us are multiple. At one point we will seem prudent and serious to you, at another financially reckless and frivolous. We change roles frequently and put on a mask opposite to the one we just removed. So demand this of yourself. You undertook to present yourself in a certain way; preserve that self right through to the end. Make it possible that you can be praised, or at least that you can be identified. It could fairly be said of the man you saw yesterday, 'Who is he?' That is how much he has changed.

Without a deep commitment to consistency we cannot live a single life at all, let alone a life which is consistent and therefore happy.

Let's take stock of letter 120 as a whole, then. Seneca seems to me to be aware in a sharply focused way of a serious question in Stoic moral epistemology, how we can obtain an understanding of good in a world without sages. He begins with a sharpening of the notion of 'good' so that it is properly distinguished from the merely useful and then sketches his problem in terms familiar from Stoic epistemology. Our natural proneness to seek out and focus on the praiseworthy is then invoked to explain how it is that our experience of morally imperfect persons can be put to reliable use in unearthing a notion of the good. Further stimulus to analysis is derived from reflection on the close relationship of vices with their corresponding virtues. Most important, though, is the contrast of consistent behaviour with inconsistency; this is the key not just to our understanding of the good by observation but also to our becoming good. But the most original contribution to this Stoic reflection on the epistemology of goodness comes from the 'platonic' excursus on the nature of the sage, which suggests that a ruthlessly clear recognition of the distinction between body and mind is the price one must pay for sustaining the consistency that is the mark of virtue. The platonism of the letter, if that is what it is, appears in the guise of what one must embrace in order really to understand the good.

Referring to this excursus in the middle of the letter as 'platonic' in tone brings us to a question, important but evaded until now. The sage is introduced in section 10. But what is the status, ontologically, of this moral paragon? Is he an existent human being subject to our observation? Or is he an ideal sage, not available for literal observation but somehow available to us for reliable grasping despite his physical unavailability? Or are we meant to recognize in him an invocation of some unique historical figure like Socrates (or Cato?), no longer open to our observation but nevertheless available to us through historical tradition?

Let us look again at the language Seneca uses of this ideal character. Above I argued that he is the person introduced in section 10 (*alium vidimus*), where the use of the perfect tense and the singular pronoun suggested that there is a real person at issue here of the same type as the inconsistent agents invoked earlier; *intelleximus in illo* (11) refers back to this person, as does *vir ille* (12). Yet we can hardly believe that we have in fact seen such a person with any frequency, if ever. Since he echoes Socrates in the *Phaedo* by regarding himself as being on military duty while living in this world (12), by never complaining about his fate and functioning as a beacon of moral exemplarity (13), it is hard not to wonder if Socrates lurks behind the general description of our sage (at 22 this character is formally called a *sapiens*). Yet it seems important to acknowledge as well that Seneca suggests that we do not need some historically unique individual to play this role in the argument, since in 19 he refers back to the portrait thus: *cum **aliquem** huius videremus constantiae*. The hint is that anyone with the appropriate characteristics would do.

My suggestion—and it can be no more than that—is that Seneca actually does intend us to think of the exemplary force of those few 'historical' sages like Socrates (or Cato), characters who have at some point in the past instantiated virtue in a perfected form. Yet he does not want to suggest that anyone outside the historically privileged time in which they lived can derive from them, by the 'normal' empirical processes of concept formation, a veridical concept of virtue. These sages have a vital function in our moral epistemology, but it is one which demands that we acknowledge their special place in our tradition. Socrates (and in this Cato is similar) is cognitively available to Seneca (and to us) as an exemplar because of the rich narrative concerning him and because of his special status in the philosophical tradition. He can be invoked by allusion, and need not be the unique character of this or that Socratic dialogue. He is, through this literary tradition, as available to us as the ordinary characters we actually do experience (either directly or through our tradition, as is the case with Horatius and Fabricius). However, his primary use in our moral epistemology is not as a direct model for imitation or analysis, but as a foil in the analytical process of concept formation. It is the idealized *persona* of a Socrates which we use as a point of reference in assessing our experience of the ordinary world of defective agents. The sage is a whetstone for our analysis of moral experience, not something we are expected to grasp and use directly in a veridical manner. This sort of sage is perhaps as much a part of Nature's plan for us as is the proneness to exaggerate the praiseworthy which she has embedded in our natures.

If one accepts this function for the idealized sage, the process of getting a grasp of the true conception of goodness can proceed by the otherwise empirically based rational process of concept formation that Stoics regularly apply to all concepts. As the early part of the letter shows, there is a great deal in the defective actions of quasi-virtuous agents which is grist for the kind of analogical analysis that underlies any empirical concept formation. But whereas most concepts (even those derived from teaching and reason) can be generated veridically from one's experience, the concept of the good requires something more, it requires an ideally consistent person to contrast to the empirical persons of our experience if our conceptual imagination is to do its job. This demand does make the notion of good unique in epistemological terms. But the process is clearly *supposed* to keep its feet on the ground and is *supposed* to pass for a phenomenon which is not just natural to us as humans but also naturalistic. It is not clear to me whether this demand can be satisfied if the process can depend on the availability of a merely literary ideal which is not subject to direct observation and therefore not in itself veridical about the notion of good. (To be sure, those generations privileged to see a Cato or Socrates directly would have a particular advantage.)

The curious status which Seneca assigns to the notion of good and his oblique suggestions about how we attain it (if I am right about it) make sense in the context of the philosophical tradition within which Seneca was working. The naturalness of the idea of good was a matter of some ambivalence and difficulty in the Stoic tradition long before Seneca (to say nothing of its role in the thought of Plato and Aristotle). Readers of Cicero's *De Finibus* 3 were surely aware of the problem; the doxographical account in Diogenes Laertius ('and there is a natural origin too for the conception of something just and good', 7.53) asserts the naturalness of the concept but fails to resolve it. If Seneca is suggesting in an indirect way that a notion of the ideal sage can play a serious role in our 'natural' derivation of the concept of good, then he is addressing an open and interesting question in his own moral tradition, something worth taking into account no matter how we assess the success of his venture.

I would like to add one further confirmatory reflection. If the idealized sage plays such an indispensable role in our coming to know the good, then of course it follows that the concept of the good is one of those which is known through reason. And Seneca takes up this question too in the same book of letters. The theme of letter 124 is exactly this, whether good is grasped by the senses or by the understanding (124.1), and one or two features of this letter (though merely sketched in passing) will, I hope, complement my discussion of letter 120.

The first five sections of this letter establish its essentially anti-hedonist theme and rely heavily on the familiar argument that hedonists are necessarily lumbered with an implausible moral epistemology which makes brute sensory awareness the ultimate criterion. This theme is not of interest here, except in so far as Seneca uses the associated duality of sense and reason to support his argument that a person's rational nature, in contrast to the body, is his or her true self—thus replacing pleasure with *gaudium* as the affective marker for the happy life (124.21–4, *gaudium* in 24). But it does concern us here to notice the first and only serious objection which Seneca allows his opponent to raise. At 124.6 the objector says:

Just as every science and art ought to arise from and grow out of (*ex quo oriatur et crescat*) something self-evident and grasped by the senses, so the happy life derives its foundation and starting point from what is self-evident and subject to sense-perception. Surely you say that the happy life takes its starting point from what is self-evident.

This argument strikes at the very problem Seneca wrestles with in letter 120, the foundations of our notion of the good. If Stoic epistemology is really empirically based, then it ought to have perceptual observations as its ultimate criterion. And as they are committed to giving an empiricist account of the development of all concepts, they ought also to recognize the empirical foundations of the concept of the good. Yet in this letter Seneca has just maintained that sensory foundations lead inexorably to a hedonistic conception of the good. And the principal argument of this entire letter is devoted to responding to the challenge posed in section 6. Clearly this is a problem which seriously engages Seneca's philosophical interests.

It would tax the reader's patience to look as closely at the range of argument in letter 124 as we have at letter 120, but I want to point quickly to two features. First, it relies on much of the basic Stoic classification of living things: plant-like things, non-rational animals, rational animals before the acquisition of reason, animals with developed reason, animals with perfected reason—a hierarchy of value, a classificatory hierarchy, and also an ontogenetic hierarchy which captures the developmental history of human beings from their plant-like foetal stage to the perfection of their virtue. Thus this letter builds on the developmental discussion of letter 121[23] and we find, I think, good reason for interpreting the book which contains all three of these strikingly technical discussions as a thematically integrated whole. And second, Seneca concludes letter 124 (21-4) with a picture of human nature very like that of letter 120, a picture in which humans are essentially their reason, are fundamentally alien from their body, and thus are properly grouped with gods not animals. The arguments which support this particularly Stoic narrowing of the concept of human nature had long been contentious, of course—they were a principal theme of the dialectic in *De Finibus* 4 and 5. They seldom carry conviction with modern readers and I don't propose to explicate them or defend them here.[24] But once those arguments are made and their conclusion embraced (as Seneca

---

[23] In his discussion (*Grundfragen*, 89–94) Pohlenz takes the theory of *sunaisthēsis* and *oikeiōsis* to be necessary for understanding the Stoic account of how we acquire the concept of the good. But in that discussion he provides no readily understandable account of how the final acquisition of reason might validate our notion of the good, that is, no account of how this natural development might also be sufficient. Pohlenz's compromise between innatist and empirical theories of how we acquire the notion of the good is aimed more at reconciling the testimony of a wide range of sources than it is at sorting out how the theory and argument are supposed to work. See too Sandbach, '*Ennoia* and *Prolēpsis*', 34.

[24] Nevertheless the argument in 16–17 that non-human animals are objectively incomplete because they cannot grasp past and future times as we can has considerable interest.

embraces it), the conclusions he draws are as naturalistic and as conventionally eudaimonistic as one could wish: 'You are a rational animal. So what is the good in you? Perfected reason. Summon this to its final goal (*ad suum finem*), allow this to grow as great as it can.' This is the key to the happy life, and one thing which letter 120 showed was that the kind of intellectual processing required for coming to grasp the concept of goodness (and so to acquire the happy life) is only accessible to creatures like us. Unfortunately it would take a longer and perhaps more difficult argument to show why it is that in this letter Seneca's emphasis on the fact that human reason is distinct from that of animals leads him so quickly to bundle us together with the divine.

* * *

I conclude that Seneca is in his own way contributing to the development of a Stoic position on an important but difficult problem in Stoic moral epistemology. But it would be wrong to conclude without venturing at least a rapid assessment of his success. Let me restate the problem as I see it for the Stoics. The good is a concept indispensable to human happiness, since getting a clear notion of what the good is forms a necessary condition for happiness. Happiness itself will require knowledge (a firm and unshakeable grasp) of it, but it is obviously necessary to get clear about what the good is in the first instance. Stoic accounts of how we acquire any concepts at all emphasize the empirical character of the process, yet empirical means alone do not suffice to yield from our experience the notion of goodness which Stoic theory requires, not even when one allows for the standard processing techniques familiar from our sources. The virtually transcendental notion of goodness on which Stoic theory relies cannot be obtained from mere extrapolation.

If I am right, Seneca thinks that we can explain how reflection on the experience of imperfect but laudable agents can veridically generate a notion of perfect goodness. We do this in part by careful abstraction from their acts, aided by a providentially natural tendency to focus on the good. But more important is the role of an ideal of a perfect agent (even one uninstantiated or attested only in literary tradition) in focusing our attention and helping to distinguish those features which constitute goodness. Seneca, following his predecessors including Cicero, holds that consistency of action and planning across a life has particular weight, and seems undeterred by the realization that such consistency can only be assured by detachment from the body, identification of our self with our mind, and by the privileging of those elements in us which we share with the divine over those which we share with beasts.

If analysis of our experience is carried out in the light of these two ideals, the sage and god, Seneca thinks, we will be able to see in that experience where goodness lies with a certainty otherwise lacking. I suspect that this is true, that our imperfect world will only yield a model of perfection when it is scrutinized against a standard higher and more pure than we can ever meet in our experience. And I am also prepared to concede that this would work, if we indeed have such a model in our consciousness to apply. But at the same time, this wonderful project will certainly fail for us. First, we, unlike Seneca, will insist on subjecting those ideal figures to the same scrutiny. We will ask, or should ask, how we can be sure that so-and-so really was a sage (or, if that's what sagehood is, how we can be sure that it really is such a good thing); we will ask how, if godhead is perfection, we could know it well enough to enable its use as a stimulus for a conceptual breakthrough. If our notion of the good is necessarily no more secure than our conception of the sage and god, then invoking them to ground our notion of good is a strategy that will work only with an audience favourably disposed. Justification is always easier under such circumstances.

But let us concede that we can rely on such ideals; there is another worry. If we actually do have such a model, why should we bother with our experience? Why not invoke this ideal directly and embrace a frankly theocentric conception of the good? Why not simply claim that our grasp of god and wisdom is innate, and is merely awoken by our experience of near-misses like Fabricius? Can fully Platonic recollection be far behind? I fear not. Seneca, in the empiricist spirit of Stoicism, thinks of his godlike ideals as helping us to discern what is perfect amidst a world of imperfect instances. But this is astonishingly close to thinking of the world of imperfect instances as stimulating a recollection of the ideal.

For Plato as for Seneca, there is a yawning gap between our experience of imperfection and our conception of the genuinely good. Seneca, I think, really did make a genuine advance over his Stoic predecessors in how he thought this gap might be bridged. But in so doing he brought Stoic moral epistemology to the threshold of Platonic recollection. Little wonder that, in the next generation, Epictetus seems to have taken the next step and accepted the reality of innate ideas.[25] There is an inevitable dialectic between the limitations of embodied human experience and the human striving to ground our notion of perfection. In the first century AD the Stoics were, without fully realizing it, solving the problems of Stoic moral epistemology by working their way back to the *Meno*.

---

[25] Scott, of 'Innatism and the Stoa', 140, takes his readers from letter 120.4 of Seneca, which looks like a clear expression of an anti-innatist view ('Nature could not have taught us [the concept of the good]; she has given us the seeds of knowledge but has not given us knowledge'), to Epictetus, *Diss.* 2.11.2–3, an apparently clear expression of innatism on the same point ('Who, on the other hand, has not come into being with an inborn concept of good and evil, fine and base...?').

11

Seneca on Freedom and Autonomy

It is hardly a new notion that the idea of 'freedom' was crucially important to Stoic thought. But it is an issue which has been bedevilled by a number of misconceptions and confusions, most significantly the mistaken notion that 'freedom' was an important part of the debate on determinism and responsibility—which is for us most often cast in terms of fate and 'free will' or determinism and human freedom. In the wake of an important recent book, though, *Determinism and Freedom in Stoic Philosophy* by Susanne Bobzien, it is possible to disentangle these issues and to see how novel Epictetus' contribution was. As Bobzien shows in her chapter 7, the concept of freedom and the concept of 'what depends on us' were originally quite distinct in Stoicism and it is only after Epictetus that we find them definitively linked.

This short essay was first published as a contribution to a festschrift for Richard Sorabji, in honour of the path-breaking work he has done on philosophy in the Roman imperial period, with particular emphasis on the interaction of pagan philosophy and non-pagan traditions. In particular, his enthusiastic engagement with Seneca's philosophical achievements has been a major stimulus for a great deal of recent work. In discussing, however superficially, the relationship between Stoic and Platonic strands in Seneca's thought and their relationship to some themes in the historian Josephus, I hope at least to suggest some areas and approaches where further exploration might be fruitful.

In its origins, 'freedom' is a political term, one which philosophers adopted and put to creative use in the psychological and ethical sphere. In place of freedom from enslavement or command by others, it came to represent, in Bobzien's words (339), 'total independence of the person from all passions and from all wrong desires'. In Greek Stoicism before Epictetus, there is no connection between freedom and fate or freedom and responsibility. A wise person is free because nothing inside or outside him tells him what to do, and the 'him' so liberated is the rational aspect of the total person. We are free if *no* tyrant, not even our own passions, can push us around. As in the *Protagoras* of Plato (where 352 b–e wonderfully captures the political origins of this metaphor), our reasoning is not pushed around by our desires and pleasures. So just as in the political sphere a person is paradigmatically free if he is not a slave and a nation is free if it does not pay tribute or take peremptory orders from an imperial power, so too within our own soul. Freedom in Greek philosophical thought, especially in Stoicism, is an internalization of a social and political reality. According to Bobzien—and she is surely right—the idea of freedom in Epictetus is fundamentally the same; his distinctive contribution is to claim that this kind of freedom is dependent on our having a proper understanding of what is truly in our power and handling *that* issue correctly.[1]

In all of this, Bobzien has done the philosophical world a service, in part by clearing away the erroneous conflation of freedom and free will which many—and I include myself in this charge, as does Bobzien—have unthinkingly perpetrated. As far as the Greek tradition is concerned, freedom might fairly be said to have found its proper place in her account.

But the most interesting thing, in my view, about the philosophical scene in the first century AD is that by then it was no longer limited to what was going on in Greek. As I have argued elsewhere,[2] in that century the philosophical scene in Roman cultural circles was becoming interestingly bilingual and Seneca

---

[1] S. Bobzien, *Determinism and Freedom in Stoic Philosophy* (Oxford, 1998), 342–3.
[2] 'Seneca in his Philosophical Milieu', Ch. 1 above.

the Younger—a man who knew a thing or two about freedom and its absence in the political sphere—found himself in the enviable position, for a Roman, of working out his own philosophical insights in a conceptual framework delimited by his own language rather than by Greek. Greek was, of course, still the prestige language of philosophical discourse. But Seneca had philosophical concerns of his own that went beyond merely adapting Greek thought for his Roman audience or working out the implications of Stoicism for the morality of the elite to which he belonged, and he routinely expressed those concerns in his own language—a bold if not always successful move.

Bobzien's account matters for our understanding of Seneca. For her account explains why Seneca does not connect *libertas* with the 'free will' and responsibility problem. That nexus develops later and so when Seneca deals with the issue of moral responsibility the language of freedom is not part of the story. But in addition Seneca's interest in freedom, *libertas*, can offer us something beyond what Bobzien uncovers in her careful analysis of the Greek tradition, and since the philosophical world was increasingly bilingual and bicultural in the first century AD, it may turn out to matter what was happening philosophically to the concept of freedom on the Latin side of things too. So I propose to deal primarily, in this context, with Seneca's notion of *libertas*.

Freedom is such a central idea in Roman political culture that we should not expect Seneca's—or anyone's—philosophical exploitation of it to be a straightforward matter. At least since Wirszubski's *Libertas as a Political Ideal at Rome during the Late Republic and Early Principate*[3] there has been a series of books and articles probing different aspects of the ideology of *libertas* in Roman politics. Most recently this theme has become one important focus of a significant new work, Matthew Roller's *Constructing Autocracy: Aristocrats and Emperors in Julio-Claudian Rome*.[4] Roller shows how intimately connected

---

[3] C. Wirszubski, *Libertas as a Political Ideal at Rome during the Late Republic and Early Principate* (Cambridge, 1950).

[4] M. Roller, *Constructing Autocracy: Aristocrats and Emperors in Julio-Claudian Rome* (Princeton, 2001).

the idea of liberty is with the dominant social paradigm of slavery and argues that in Roman elite culture (for our purposes the only one that matters) it is a largely negative concept, the opposite of being enslaved either literally or (as is more relevant) metaphorically. Seneca features prominently in Roller's discussion, of course, and brings out a great deal of importance about the social and political significance of his reflections on freedom for his fellow aristocrats. But Roller limits himself to this aspect of Seneca's Stoicism, seeing him (as he puts it in another context)[5] 'as a Roman aristocrat in the first instance, who presents Stoic ethics to his social peers (the implied audience) as a way out of certain contemporary ethical binds'. I want to go beyond this undoubtedly important aspect of Seneca's Stoicism and to suggest that his reflections on freedom and autonomy work to push back new frontiers within Stoic philosophy itself as well, since for me (as Roller rightly says) Seneca 'is first and foremost a Stoic philosopher'. Let us see, then, what philosophical novelty Seneca may have brought to the idea of freedom.

There are four philosophically interesting aspects of *libertas* in Seneca which I would like to discuss. The first and most unsettling for us lies in its connection with death. The second deals with a form of freedom that accompanies wisdom: a sage's freedom consists in part in the fact that he is free from harm that others might inflict on him, a freedom which depends on adopting a typically Stoic conception of harm. Third is the connection of freedom with the acceptance of god or fate. And finally, in many contexts Seneca explores the notion that the most important kind of freedom is a mental freedom, freedom from various passions and disorders. In what I think of as the richest and most puzzling application of the idea of freedom Seneca connects this kind of freedom to cosmological insights based on Stoic natural philosophy.

Let's start with death.[6] The idea that Seneca's interest in the moral standing of suicide was unusual within the Stoic school

---

[5] Ibid. 80 n. 27.

[6] Richard Sorabji has hinted at some of what I want to say about the liberating potential of suicide for Seneca in his *Emotion and Peace of Mind: From Stoic Agitation to Christian Temptation* (Oxford, 2000), 214.

was urged with particular force by John Rist; the importance of the idealization of freedom in this connection of thought is the central theme of ch. 13 of his *Stoic Philosophy*.[7] In his view Seneca's attitude to suicide is essentially un-Stoic. 'Fundamentally Seneca's wise man is in love with death' (p. 249). Not only is this a one-sided view, and so properly subjected to a healthy correction by Miriam Griffin in her discussion of the question.[8] But this extreme interpretation means that Rist must allow for occasional 'lapses' by Seneca into a more orthodox Stoic view (e.g. 249–50). Perhaps a less extreme interpretation can be more unified. This is what Griffin offers in her account, but even she misses what I think is the most important aspect of Seneca's approach to death and freedom, the central importance of 'agency'. For it is the possibility of being an agent in the proper sense of the word which is most decisively though paradoxically preserved by a timely or even premature death by one's own hand. In her splendid analysis of the Stoic orthodoxy of Seneca's views (pp. 372–83) this aspect is scarcely mentioned, though she does correctly emphasize that 'freedom' in the sense of free will is not what is at stake in Senecan *libertas* (383–4). For Griffin, the most important feature of Seneca's individual views is his enthusiasm for 'martyrdom' (386).

Here we cannot avoid introducing the highly ambiguous character of Cato the Younger, a man who was in Seneca's eyes a powerful symbol of philosophical progress, in large measure because he took his own life rather than live under political conditions incompatible with his political values. His ambiguity stems from the fact that the republican institutions for which he died were not those which Seneca himself valued most highly. Seneca is himself a ready supporter of the imperial regime (far too ready, some might say), so some might suspect him of confusion or muddle in his keenness to lionize the republican martyr. A look at how Cato's freedom is handled by Seneca will show that this ambiguity has its roots in subtlety rather than confusion.

---

[7] J. Rist, *Stoic Philosophy* (Cambridge, 1969). See especially pp. 247–50, where the liberating potential of suicide is emphasized.

[8] M. Griffin, *Seneca: A Philosopher in Politics* (2nd edn., Oxford, 1992), ch. 11.

Consider first *De Providentia*. In section 2.10 Seneca is arguing that a god who has special affection for men of virtue might welcome the sight of strong men struggling against adversity.

I do not see, I say, what Jupiter could deem more beautiful to contemplate on this earth (if he were to turn his attention this way) than the sight of Cato, after the repeated defeat of his faction, still standing upright amidst the wreckage of the state. He says, 'although everything has fallen into the hands of one man and although the land is guarded by his legions as the oceans are by his fleets, though the gates are occupied by Caesar's troops, nevertheless Cato has an escape route; he will make a road to freedom with one hand. His sword, unstained and innocent even in the civil war, will in the end perform virtuous and noble deeds: it will give to Cato the freedom which it could not give to his fatherland. Brave mind, tackle a task you have planned for so long, tear yourself away from human affairs. Already Petreius and Juba have gone to battle and lie dead, slain each by the other's hand, a brave and remarkable convergence of fate, but not one which befits my greatness. It would be as shameful for Cato to seek death from someone else as it would be for him to seek life.'

Cato is, Seneca adds, an *acerrimus sui vindex* (2.11). Similarly in section 6.7 the emphasis is on being in control, the agent of one's situation not the victim: 'Above all watch out that you not be caught against your will (*invitos*). The way out is open. If you don't want to fight you can flee.... Just watch for it and you will see how short and easy is the road which leads to freedom.' Dying, he says, is shorter and easier than being born, which is itself a sign of god's providence. 'Let every time and every place teach you how easy it is to reject nature and to shove its gifts back in her face; amidst the altars and the sacred rituals of those who give sacrifice, while you pray for life, practice for death' (6.7–8).

What, then, is so admirable about the pursuit of death? First and foremost that it is a mark of agency even amidst misfortune. In circumstances where it is most difficult to act, to be in control, there too we can have freedom of action. And if the only expression of that freedom is death, that is no cause for concern (death is, for any Stoic, a mere indifferent). What

Jupiter admires and what he recognizes as worthy of the greatness he himself possesses is the independence and self-determination of the agent. That is freedom, and this is the sort of narrative Seneca has in mind in the climax of the great letter 95 on the topic of moral instruction, when he says (95.72) that 'it will be beneficial not only to say what good men are generally like and to sketch the form and outline of their characters, but to tell stories about and to set out in detail what they were like—for example, Cato's famous, final, and most courageous wound through which freedom released his soul'.

This same general point is made with macabre force as well in *De Ira*, in a passage famous because of its gruesome colourfulness. In 3.14–15 Seneca dwells on a tale drawn from Herodotus. Here is the story in the fine translation by the late John Procopé:

14. (1) King Cambyses was too fond of wine. Prexaspes, one of his dearest friends, advised him to drink less, declaring drunkenness in a king with the eyes and ears of all upon him to be a disgrace. The king answered: 'to show you that I never lose control of myself, I will now prove to you that the wine leaves my eyes and hands in full working order.' (2) He went on to drink more generously than usual, out of larger cups. Heavily drunk, he ordered his critic's son to go beyond the threshold and stand there with his left hand over his head. Then he drew his bow and shot the boy through the heart—that, he had said, was his aim. He had the breast cut open. He showed the arrow stuck directly in the heart. He looked at the father, asking whether his hand had been sure enough. 'Not even Apollo', the father replied, 'could have aimed better.'

(3) Confound the man, a slave in mind if not in station! There he was, praising something which it was too much even to have witnessed, finding occasion for flattery in the dissection of his son's breast and the palpitation of the heart in the wound. He should have disputed the question of glory with him and called for the shot to be repeated, that it might please the king to show a yet surer hand in aiming at the father. (4) O bloodthirsty king! He deserved to have everyone's bow turned on him. And yet, execrable as he is to us for ending the banquet with punishment and slaughter, to praise the shot was still more criminal than to make it. But how *should* a father have behaved as he stood over

his son's body, witness and cause of his killing? We shall see. The point now at issue is clear, that anger can be suppressed. (5) Not cursing the king, he uttered not a word even of grief, though he felt his heart transfixed no less than his son's. You can say that he was right to choke back his words; expressions of anger would have denied him the role of a father. (6) You can even think that he behaved more wisely in that misfortune than he had when he gave advice on moderation in wine-bibbing to a man who was better employed drinking wine than blood—when his hands were on the wine cup, at least that meant peace. He joined the ranks of those whose catastrophes have shown what it costs the friends of kings to give good advice. 15. (1) I have no doubt that Harpagus offered some such advice to *his* Persian king. It annoyed him into serving up the man's children at a feast and repeatedly asking him if he liked the seasoning. Then, seeing him with a stomach full of woe for himself, he ordered their heads to be brought in and asked him what he thought of the bounty. Words did not fail the poor man, his lips were not sealed. 'Dinner with a king', said he, 'is always delicious.' What did he achieve by this flattery? He was spared the leftovers. I am not saying that a father should not condemn anything that the king does, I am not saying that he should not try to punish such monstrous ferocity as it deserves; I am just proving, for the moment, that even anger generated by enormous affliction can be concealed and compelled to use words that express the opposite.

(3) It is necessary to bridle your indignation in this way, especially if your lot is to have this sort of life and be invited to the royal table. That is how you eat there, how you drink there, the sort of answer that you make there—you just have to smile as your family dies.

The key part of this text for us is what follows (15.3 continues):

But is the life worth that much? We shall see. That is a different question. We have no consolation to offer for a prison so gloomy. We are not going to advise men to endure the butcher's commands. We shall simply show that in any slavery the way lies open to freedom. One's affliction is mental, the misery one's own fault, if one can put an end to it, together with oneself. (4) I shall say both to the man with the luck to have a king who shoots arrows at the heart of his friends and to him whose master gorges the father with the entrails of his son: 'Why the groans, madman? Why wait for an enemy to avenge you through the downfall of your nation, or for some mighty monarch to swoop down from afar? Wheresoever you cast your eyes, there lies an end to affliction. Look at that precipice—down it runs the way to freedom. Look at the sea there, the river, the well—at its bottom lies freedom. Look at that tree, short and shrivelled and barren—there on it hangs freedom. Look at your throat, your windpipe, your heart—all are ways of escape from slavery. But perhaps the ways out which I have shown are too toilsome for you, too demanding on spirit and strength. Are you asking for the road to freedom? Take any vein you like in your body!'

I have quoted this passage at length not only as an example of Seneca's macabre power as a writer, but because its conclusion, with its hyperbolic enthusiasm for different ways of killing oneself, is a passage often cited to confirm Seneca's morbid and unorthodox devotion to death. But settling for that reaction to the passage passes over how Seneca's argument is meant to work. What matters most here is not the awfulness of the circumstances from which we escape (though they are certainly maximally awful), and not the emphasis on how easy it is to kill oneself. What matters is the advice he gives to men in the grip of tyrannical circumstance: 'We shall simply show that in any slavery the way lies open to freedom.' It is the *possibility* of freedom, the *availability* of a way out that Seneca stresses.[9] His concern is primarily with people who suffer unbearably, forget that they have an alternative, and then complain about the cruelty of fate. In Seneca's view those complaints are unwarranted: no slavery is so great that free action cannot be exercised and if we choose not to die then we cannot reasonably complain about our lot.[10] It is worth remembering that in this long narrative of suffering and human misery, Seneca defers deciding on what would be the right thing for the victim to do and focuses solely on the possibilities open to him (14.4): 'But how *should* a father have behaved as he stood over his son's body, witness and cause of his killing? We shall see.' And in

---

[9] His exaggerated emphasis on the ready availability of the ways to die might be compared to the way we use counterfactual situations in our own moral argument. Imagine the victim with a suicide pill which works instantly and painlessly and can be carried on one's person legally at all times. Or better: imagine the agent augmented with a thought-activated death implant.

[10] For another aspect of this idea in Seneca, see 'Natural Law in Seneca', Ch. 8 above.

15.3: 'But is the life worth that much? We shall see. That is a different question.'

The significance of this line of thought is made clearer in the *Consolatio ad Marciam* (20.3): 'slavery is not an annoyance when, if you get tired of your master, you can cross to freedom with a single step. Life, I deem you dear thanks to death.' This adds a valuable corrective. The availability of death is a source of freedom, provides room for proper agency and creates room for *deciding* on how one ought to act even when we seem to be most constrained by external factors, because it guarantees the perpetual possibility of action. Of course we may live under a master (who does not?). But even such slavery is a pleasure just in so far as we can walk away from it when *we* get tired of it. Choice is at the heart of agency, and *libertas* here comes down to a typically Senecan concern for agency.[11]

The same theme runs through the letters as well, a source so rich that the quickest survey will have to suffice.

In letter 12.10 for example, in the midst of the Epicurean *envoi*, Seneca emphasizes that the ready abundance of paths to freedom should make us grateful to god for setting things up in such a way that 'no one can be *held* in this life: it is always possible to trample constraints under foot.' A similar Epicurean context frames 22.5–6, which expresses an anxiety about the possibility that one's ability to choose death (the *libertas recedendi*) might be taken away by circumstances—that is the proper basis for choosing suicide in many circumstances.[12]

---

[11] Hence, though it should scarcely need to be said, 'freedom' for Seneca does not involve any incompatibility with earlier Stoic conceptions of determinism and responsibility (or with those of Epictetus). 'Agency'—which is our term, of course—is as compatible with Chrysippan determinism as is the preservation of 'what is up to us'. Seneca's *libertas* does not, then, represent a move towards a dual potestative theory; it is a feature of moral choice within the compatibilist framework characteristic of the entire Stoic school. Suicide is the focus of 'freedom' *not* because the choice which leads to it is metaphysically different from other decisions we make, but because the focus of the choice being made is a central value (life itself) which truly puts to the test our entire moral character. The choice to give up your life is the ultimate declaration of one's conviction that it is an indifferent rather than a good, that it does not contribute to human happiness.

[12] At *Ep.* 104.21 Seneca says that Socrates can teach us how to die when it is necessary and Zeno before it is necessary.

In 26.10, again in the Epicurean context of the conclusion to a letter, the connection between death and agency is again reinforced.

'Practise death'—the adviser who says this is telling you to practise freedom. He who learns to die unlearns slavery. Death is above every form of power, or at least beyond its reach. What are the jail-cell, imprisonment, and shackles to him?

He has an open door. Only one chain holds us in bondage, the love of life—which though it should not be rejected utterly ought nevertheless to be reduced, so that if circumstances ever do demand it nothing will hold us back or prevent us from being ready to do immediately what needs to be done on any given occasion.

In 66.13 the suicide to which Scipio drove the Numantians under siege is recognized as being as virtuous as Scipio himself. Someone who knows that he can die is not fully besieged and can 'die in the embrace of freedom'. The connection of free agency with death and the availability of suicide is fully articulated at 70.14–16, where Seneca openly rebuts those philosophers who hold that suicide is immoral. Letter 77 too is rich with examples of death as freedom, where the point of each example is that the suicide is thereby preserving his own agency: he *acts* rather than suffers. As in letter 70, it is held to be a good thing about our circumstances on earth that *tam prope libertas est* (70.15). The freedom which comes from taking action in one's own death is the opposite of sloth and inertia (*Ep.* 70. 16) and its result is happiness (*nemo nisi vitio suo miser est*), the kind of satisfaction produced by acting on one's own inclinations (*placet? vive; non placet? licet eo reverti unde venisti* (70.15)) rather than allowing oneself to be passively influenced by circumstances and the choices of others. Agency in contrast to passivity is the benefit of maintaining a loose grip on life.

Another perspective on freedom in Seneca concerns the peculiarly clear understanding that the sage has of the Socratic meaning of harm and benefit. In *De Constantia Sapientis* section 9.2–5 Seneca concedes that there is a very large number of dangers and threats, but nevertheless maintains the Stoic paradox that the sage cannot suffer harm:

The sage escapes these dangers, since he knows not how to live for hope or for fear. Add to this the fact that no one takes an injury unmoved, but is upset when he senses it; but there is no upset in a man who is free of mistakes, controls himself, and possesses a deep and calm tranquillity. For if injury touches a man he is both moved and driven on. But the wise man lacks anger, which is aroused by the appearance of injury and he could not lack anger unless he also lacked injustice—which he knows cannot happen to him. This is the source of his dignity and his light-heartedness; this is why he is elevated with a constant joy. So far is he from being pained by offences inflicted by circumstances and men that the injury itself is of use to him, for he tries his strength with it and tests his virtue. So, I beg you, let us be reverent towards this proposition and listen with fairmindedness while the wise man is exempted from injury. It is not that your own impertinence is in any way reduced, nor is the violence of your greedy desires or your blind recklessness and pride. This freedom is won for the wise man without any impairment to *your* vices! I am not arguing that you cannot inflict injury, but that he casts aside all injuries and protects himself with endurance and strong-mindedness. In the same way at the sacred games many have won victory by wearing out the blows of their attackers by resolute endurance; think of the sage as being of this sort, one of those who has achieved by long and consistent training the strength to endure and wear down all hostile attacks.

Later in the book, at 19.2, Seneca distinguishes this sort of freedom, which has its roots in the proper understanding of values which enables him to rise above assaults and injuries, from the freedom which consists in simply not putting up with affronts directed at us and asserting our rights with angry indignation. This more conventional kind of 'freedom' is, he maintains, *intemperans libertas*.

The treatise *De Vita Beata* relies on a similar understanding of *libertas* in several places. For example, in 3.4 the constant tranquillity which comes from rising above irritations and grievances is deemed a form of *libertas*. Fear and pleasure are the emotions which underlie the opposite state, a form of *feritas*, beastliness, which corresponds to the *intemperantia* of *De Constantia* 19. A similar path to peace of mind is advocated in *De Vita Beata* 4.5, where the freedom which constitutes this eudaimonic state is attributed to 'rising above fortune'. In section 9 this *libertas* is linked once again to the intrinsically valuable (note *pretium sui*) state of happiness: the *summum bonum* is 'the strength of a mind which cannot be broken, foresight, loftiness, health, freedom, harmony, and dignity'.

In this context we can better assess one of those Senecan maxims which so often is cited to show how foreign from our notion of moral strength his Stoicism is. At the end of *De Beata Vita* 15 he sums up: 'we are born into a monarchy; freedom is to obey god'. If our freedom consists in submission to a higher power, no matter how special it might be from the normative perspective, we will quite rightly find this an unappealing notion of freedom. We are, perhaps, liberated from one form of slavery just to take on a greater and more limiting servitude. But as the passages we have been looking at show, and as the very context of chapter 15 confirms, even in a passage which *sounds* so theological, the real key to our *eudaimonia* is a clear understanding of human values and *not* simply submission to higher power.

In brief, Seneca is here arguing that the ideal life cannot be one which combines virtue and pleasure, on the grounds that 'any part of what is honourable must be itself honourable and the highest good will not have its own integrity if within itself it finds anything which is unlike its better aspect' (15.1). Even the joy we take in being virtuous or acting virtuously is not an unconditional good, despite the goodness of what occasions it. It is a good, but one which follows from the highest good and not one of its components. This much is familiar Stoic doctrine (15.2). Seneca then explains in his own way (15.3):

But he who forges an alliance, even an unequal one, between pleasure and virtue, undermines whatever strength the one has through the vulnerability of the other good; he sends beneath the yoke that freedom which is unconquered only if it knows that nothing is more valuable than itself. For it begins to need fortune, and that is the greatest form of servitude; then comes a worried life, suspicious, fearful, trembling before chance, hanging on brief moments of time.

Inclusion of pleasure in one's goal makes its foundation unstable. If you care in that way about pleasure you are bound to work with one eye on the vulnerabilities which come from having a body. This impairs our ability to obey god just as it would impair our ability to act patriotically. That is why it is essential to exclude physically dependent states like pleasure from our ultimate motivation, the good. Doing so means that we can take proper account of a law of nature (*lex naturae*, 15.5) which holds that a good soldier is bound to be wounded or even die. The point is that concern for pleasure would impede the performance of military duty; since one is bound to be in physical danger one can only maintain consistency if one brackets out one's concern for pleasure. Heeding the ancient precept 'follow god' is part of a package of values which ensures the integrity and internal consistency of our life—surely a necessary condition for freedom from fear and confusion. And in the case of a soldier, it also leads to the preservation of our *patria*, the state whose freedom is the necessary condition of our own.

Obeying god, then, is a matter of adopting the values which make our mission in the cosmic state (a kingdom) possible; without those values we will fail to do what we must, due to fear and pleasure, and we will fail to maintain the consistency which the happy life requires. Our freedom comes from obedience to god because obedience to god requires commitment to the same values that guarantee our liberation from distress (15.7), not because we are to find our freedom in simple subordination to some higher power. (In this context I have to pass over the interesting issues of fate and human choice which may also be at play in this complex text.)

For similar reasons the freedom of the wise man which is contrasted to the 'half-freedom' of Cicero (who is represented as whining weakly about his political misfortunes)[13] in *De*

---

[13] To a great extent Seneca's emphasis on the ready availability of death supports a general condemnation of complaint about one's fate on the grounds that there are always alternatives. For example, in *Ep.* 117.21 Seneca says that philosophy should teach us how to handle misfortune: 'Teach me how to sustain grief without groaning myself, good fortune without groaning from others, how not to wait around for the final and inevitable moment, but to take refuge there myself when the time seems right.' Immediately after this (117.22–4) he criticizes people who merely wish for death amidst misfortune—how hypocritical or muddled it is to wish for death in a kind of despair over one's situation when one can either just kill oneself or endure; as

Brevitatae Vitae 5 can properly be described thus: the wise man is characterized by 'a freedom which is intact and solid, he is unbound and autonomous (*sui iuris*) and loftier than the others. What [not who] could be above the man who is above fortune?' If Stoic freedom were just a matter of following god or fate, then the autonomy here described would make no sense and there would be an answer to the question: god would be higher than the wise man. But of course he is not. It is for this reason too that in letter 8.7–8 Seneca claims that freedom is a result of service to philosophy and not of service to god or fate.

Human freedom, then, comes not from mere political freedom; nor does it come merely from aligning oneself with the overwhelming power of god and fate. It comes from a philosophical and moral breakthrough in one's life, a realization that things of the highest value to non-philosophers are in the end indifferent to human happiness. In letter 22.11 he says that the appropriate dedication to freedom will eliminate *perpetua sollicitudo*, the mental anguish which comes from muddling up one's values and moral commitments. Clear thinking about such things will itself be a liberation. In letter 75.18 Seneca concludes similarly: we can emerge from the 'sewer' of life to something lofty and noble; what awaits us there is *tranquillitas animi et expulsis erroribus absoluta libertas*—mental peace and the unconditional freedom which comes from driving out the mistakes we too often make in thinking about our lives. Then he asks: 'what is this freedom? to fear neither men nor gods; to desire neither shameful things nor excesses; to have within oneself the greatest power; it is a good beyond price to be one's own'. The same sort of freedom is invoked at letter 80.4–5 and even more bluntly in letter 123: 'a great part of freedom lies in having hungers which know their place and can endure affronts' (123.3).

The connections between this freedom, the desires and fears which are its enemies and so the source of slavery, and philo-

---

he says, 'let me die' 'are the words of a weak mind, angling for pity'. Knowing that death is readily available forces us to take a genuine responsibility for our reactions to events and so we can 'sustain grief without groaning'.

sophy itself are complex. In letter 37.4 Seneca reflects on simple stupidity. It is

a low, base, dirty and slavish thing, subordinate to all kinds of very cruel passions. These masters are very severe, sometimes giving orders by turns, sometimes in concert with each other. Wisdom eliminates them from you and wisdom is the one true freedom. One road leads to freedom, and it is a straight one. You will not go astray; just walk with a steady pace. If you want to subordinate everything to you, subordinate yourself to reason; you will rule many people if reason rules you. From reason you will learn what to undertake and how to do so; you won't just blunder into things. You won't be able to show me anyone who knows how he has come to want what he wants. He has got there not by deliberation but driven by blind impulse. Fortune comes upon us as often as we come upon fortune. It is shameful not to proceed but rather to be swept along then suddenly, in the midst of a vortex of circumstance to be stunned and ask, 'How did I get here?'

As Seneca says in letter 51.9, it is when you *understand* fortune that she ceases to have power over you;[14] that is why freedom comes with philosophy.

The kind of philosophy which brings us freedom is a solid knowledge of the real values of things which affect our concrete human lives and which if misunderstood, misevaluated, or muddled will enslave us to our passions. In letter 104 this kind of knowledge is contrasted with geographical and ethnographic knowledge which does not make us better people (15 ff.). The travels which bring us this sort of knowledge are mere wanderings until we learn 'what is worth fleeing, what is worth pursuing, what is necessary and what superfluous, what is just and what is unjust, what is honourable and what is dishonourable'.

The relationship of this sort of freedom to more lofty forms of philosophical knowledge is set out at some length in a crucially important passage of letter 65, which is one of the more technical letters in the collection. Its topic is the different conceptions of causation of the various philosophical schools. As is his custom, Seneca digresses at one point to justify this kind of technical

[14] Compare Bobzien, *Determinism*, 342, on Epictetus.

exploration, ever eager to avoid the appearance of moral irrelevance.

16. I am not wasting time even now, as you think. For if all those issues are not chopped up and dispersed into this kind of pointless sophistication, they elevate and relieve the mind, which, being burdened by its great load, desires to be set free and to return to the things it used to be part of. For this body is a burden and a penalty for the mind. It is burdened by its weight and is in chains unless philosophy comes to it and urges it to take its ease before the sight of nature and directs it away from what is earthly and towards the divine. This is its freedom, this is its free range. From time to time it slips away from the prison in which it is held and is refreshed by the sight of the heavens.

17. Artisans who work on some quite detailed job which wearies their eyes with concentration if they rely on bad and uncertain lighting, these artisans make an appearance in public and treat their eyes to the light in some region devoted to the public leisure—just so the mind, enclosed in this sad and gloomy dwelling, seeks open space and takes its ease in the contemplation of nature.

18. To be sure, he who is wise and pursues wisdom sticks to his body, but with the best part of himself he is elsewhere and focuses his thoughts on higher matters. Like a soldier under oath he thinks that this life is a tour of duty; and he has been shaped in such a way that he neither loves nor hates life and he puts up with mortal matters though he knows that higher things remain.

19. Do you ban me from an investigation of nature, drag me away from the whole and confine me to a part? Shall I not investigate the principles of all things? Who gave them form? Who made distinctions among things which were melded into one and enmeshed in passive matter? Shall I not enquire who is the artisan of this cosmos? How so great a mass was reduced to lawlike structure? Who gathered the scattered bits, who separated what was combined and brought shape to things lying in unsightly neglect? Where did this great light come from? Is it fire or something brighter than fire?

20. Shall I not ask these questions? Shall I remain ignorant of my origins? Am I to see these things just once or am I to be born many times? Where am I to go from here? What residence awaits the soul when it is freed from the laws of human servitude? You forbid me to meddle with the heavens, i.e. you order me to live with bowed head.

21. I am greater than that and born for greater things than to be a slave to my body, which I think of as no different than a chain fastened about my freedom. So it is this that I offer to fortune, so that she will stop right there; I permit no wound to get through the body to *me*. This is the only part of me which can suffer injustice. A free mind lives in this vulnerable dwelling.

22. That flesh will never drive me to fear, never to pretence unworthy of a good man; I shall never lie to show 'respect' for this paltry body. When the time seems right, I shall dissolve my partnership with it. Even now, however, while he clings to it, we will not be partners on equal terms. The mind will reserve all rights to itself. To despise one's body is a reliable freedom.

Here there is something new, and something worth exploring at some length on another occasion.[15] For here there is another notion, one clearly drawn ultimately from the *Phaedo* of Plato. Our freedom here is not merely a matter of knowing the real value of things like money, pleasure, pain, and life itself. It comes from identifying one's mind with the universe, not with one's body. The fact that human origins lie in the heavens and that one's mind will return to its origins when the body falls away—this is the source of dignity. To deny us the opportunity to study cosmology is to make us live with bowed heads. Doing philosophy involves understanding the emotions, human values, pleasure and pain. It involves the optimally rational planning of one's life in a sense which is clearly eudaimonistic and naturalistic. But here in letter 65 we learn that part of our freedom lies also in identifying our selves with our minds rather than our bodies and in thinking about the cosmos rather than about our own immediate world. So if there were to be a place where Seneca's otherworldliness cut into his naturalism, this would be it.[16] But even here, as I think a careful reading of the letter and this passage in particular shows, Seneca has kept the focus on freedom in this life and not on the divine understood in such a way that our human autonomy was somehow

---

[15] But see also G. Maurach, *Seneca: Leben und Werk* (2nd edn., Darmstadt, 1996), 169–71.

[16] See Rist, *Stoic Philosophy*, 247–50.

compromised by our attitude to it. We are free owing to our detachment from the body in our thoughts and we are free because our nature is like that of the divine. For Stoics, after all, the cosmos as a whole is not opposed to nature but is nature itself. The cosmic perspective is naturalistic.

Before I conclude, I want to point briefly to the presence of the same theme in a rather unlikely place. The Jewish historian Josephus (like other Greek-speaking intellectuals who affiliated themselves closely with Romans) was part of the Latin-speaking world as well as the Greek, and in his *Jewish War* he found occasion to deal with some themes similar to those I have been discussing in Seneca. It is difficult to say if there can be any relevance of Seneca's ideas to those of Josephus, but there are certainly some intriguing parallels between what Seneca believes about the relationship between freedom and death and the magnificent speech of Eleazar in the final hours of Masada.[17] Just as Seneca seems often to anticipate Epictetus' views in this area, perhaps we can see something similar with respect to Josephus.

The similarity becomes apparent in Josephus' account of the motivations and ideological rhetoric of the leaders of the final suicidal siege at Masada, especially Eleazar.[18] That Eleazar and his followers took the desire for *eleutheria* as their central goal is clear from *Jewish War* 2.443, where their longing for freedom is extended to cover their reasons for taking a particular position in the brutal struggles within the Jewish community (cf. 7.254–8). But it is most striking in the great speech of Eleazar at the climax of book 7 (323–36, 341–88). Especially in the second half of this speech, described by Josephus as a second effort to stiffen the spines of those wavering in their determination to accept the suicide pact, Eleazar connects freedom, self-inflicted death, autonomy of choice, and human dignity with a cosmic

---

[17] For some background see D. Ladouceur, 'Masada: A Consideration of the Literary Evidence', *GRBS* 21 (1980), 245–60, and 'Joseph and Masada', in L. Feldman and G. Hata (eds.), *Josephus, Judaism and Christianity* (Detroit, 1987), 95–113. I am grateful to Tim Barnes for the references.

[18] It would be worth recalling Seneca's comments on the suicides at the siege of Numantia (*Ep.* 66.13 and above).

perspective; and he does so in a way which recalls Seneca's configuration of this theme. A full discussion of this point is not possible here; but a reading of the second half of the speech will, I think, be impressive, especially if careful attention is given to 7.344: 'it is death which gives freedom to our souls and sets them free to escape to their pure and proper place, where they will be untouched (*apatheis*) by all misfortune.' Though the philosophers he invokes to support his point are Indian and the doctrine owes much to Platonism, the thought and language are also Stoic.

It does not, of course, follow that Josephus was in any measure directly influenced by Seneca. There are more than enough common influences to make that the most economical hypothesis. And there is certainly nothing as distinctively Stoic in Eleazar's speech as what there is in Seneca. So perhaps the appearance of common ground comes only from their shared openness to Platonic influences. I suspect, though, that there is more to it than that. The Greco-Roman intellectual world of the first century AD provided Josephus with a language, a set of terms, which owed a good deal to Stoicism as well as to other schools, but also with an intellectual framework to work in, a framework which had absorbed the perspectives of both Stoicism and Platonism. Any writer struggling with the themes of freedom, autonomy, and the threats to them—as both Seneca and Josephus did in their own ways—will quite naturally have been led to similar solutions. That a highly constrained world can provide room for autonomy only as long as the 'door is open', as Seneca might say, is not surprising. That it can be difficult to keep the door open and to find the resolution to go through it is, in part, the lesson we learn from Josephus' narrative of the death of the rebels at Masada.

12

Seneca and Self-assertion

> It is pleasant to be with oneself as long as possible when one has made oneself worth spending time with. (*Ep.* 58.32)

This essay is, in a sense, the continuation of a line of thought about moral psychology in Seneca first broached in Chapter 5. Between the composition of the two a little over seven years passed. The occasion of the first essay was a conference paper and the earliest version of it was entitled 'The Will and the Self in Seneca'. But the longer I worked on that paper and the more critical feedback I received, the more self-less it became, until in the end it was entitled simply 'The Will in Seneca'.

I am grateful to the organizers of the conference on 'Seneca and the Self' at the University of Chicago, 4–6 April 2003, for the invitation to speak and to all those present, especially David Wray and Jonathan Beere, for their helpful critical comments. I am also deeply grateful to Graham Burchell for allowing me to see his translation of Foucault's *L'Herméneutique du sujet* in advance of publication. I want also to thank the members of the New York Colloquium in Ancient Philosophy (which allowed me to try out my discussion of Foucault's treatment of the *Alcibiades* at its meeting of 21 February 2004), and especially to John Partridge, Iakovos Vasiliou, and Katja Vogt. Further refinement to some of the ideas in this essay emerged from the opportunity to present it at the *Seminaire de philosophie hellénistique et romaine* sponsored by l'Université de Paris XII (29 May 2004); I am very grateful indeed to my host, Alain Gigandet, for his generous assistance, both intellectual and practical. Gretchen Reydams-Schils and David Konstan also offered stimulating challenges and constructive advice on the final version. For particular comments on this essay and for constant philosophical inspiration over the last twenty-four years I am grateful to Tony Long.

This autobiographical reflection is not mere self-indulgence. The Senecan self disappeared from that early paper for definite reasons and as a result of philosophical preferences and methodological predilections which haven't gone away. The preferences are for ontological minimalism in interpreting Stoic philosophy of mind (and much else)—not postulating any entities beyond those strictly necessary to account for the phenomena under consideration—and the predilections are for relying on close scrutiny when advancing views about what ancient thinkers thought. Those commitments led not only to the effacement of the self in that earlier paper but also to the minimization of the will itself. In fact, the 'self' survived only indirectly, since in the end I argued that the appearance that there is a robust conception of 'will' in Seneca arises primarily because of his interest in the reflexive nature of moral self-improvement. What struck me most, then and now, is how often Seneca talks about giving commands or orders to oneself. I argued that this way of writing about command creates the *illusion* of a will; it is an illusion because, as I see it, there is no distinctive ontology behind the idea of the will in Seneca, nothing about the mind of the agent which goes beyond the moral psychology worked out by his predecessors earlier in the history of the Stoic school. The claims made for the will in chapter 5 are made for the self here. The result of this renewed investigation, I hope, is a reassertion of the essential Stoic conservatism of Seneca's theory of mind that nevertheless recognizes his importance for the later development of ideas about the will and the self.

In keeping with my minimalist principles, I begin by asking what is meant by talking about Seneca and the self. As I do so, I am keenly aware of the pioneering stand taken by Tony Long in his 'Representation and the Self in Stoicism'. He explained there what he meant by a 'philosophy of the self'.[1] Such a philosophy is concerned with 'the conceptualisation and history of the individual or person' and 'its special concern is "representation"', by which he means:

---

[1] A. A. Long, *Stoic Studies* (Cambridge, 1996), 265.

the way in which individual human beings perceive themselves, or what it is for them to have a first-person outlook on the world or first-person experience. The self in this sense is something essentially individual—a uniquely positioned viewer and interlocutor, a being that has interior access of a kind that is not available to anyone else.

Long's sense of the project is that it involves what seems in hindsight to be a Foucauldian aim of tracing an historical and culturally variable account of the 'ways in which we Westerners view ourselves, what we take ourselves, in first-person reflection, to be' (p. 266). In this discussion he focuses on what he takes the distinctive contribution of Epictetus to have been (with a constructive sidelong glance at Hierocles and some serious framing by way of contrast with Aristotle). But he does not tackle Seneca here. Still, his argument that Epictetus made a very important contribution to the broad evolution of a Western sense of who we are and how we view ourselves is powerful, and it has helped us to understand why Epictetus has at many times been central to European moral reflection. But despite the use of the term 'being' in the quotation above, even Long's sensitive analysis seems to reveal very little that is new in the ontology of the human mind which Epictetus uses.[2] If a 'self' is some isolatable part or aspect of us, it will have to be

---

[2] *Per litteras* Long clarifies that 'Epictetus' use of [the self] hardly registers a novel ontology of the mind. But what he does with the language of "I" etc. may still be novel in interesting philosophical ways, especially if... "*the* self" is a function of language, unlike the parts/dispositions of the soul/mind'. This seems to me to be exactly right. At the end of this essay I return to the issue of how a certain way of writing/speaking about the moral engagement of a person with the world might generate a sense that there is a distinct entity, the self, without, nevertheless, committing oneself to a Foucauldian claim that the self is a distinct 'being'. It might seem controversial to claim that Foucault commits himself to any ontological claims at all—indeed it is hard to see whether or not he does so in *The Care of the Self*. But it is clear that (whatever hesitation he might have and whatever inconsistencies there may be across his later works) he does make a significant ontological claim, at least in the foundational argument of the *L'Herméneutique de sujet* which I discuss below. Long's own commitment to ontological claims is similarly ambiguous. He has accepted the minimalist claims made here, but when he writes about representation in relations to the self, it is only natural to ask, 'representation of *what*?' If there is not something distinct to represent, why invoke it at all? My aim in this essay is at least to remove this ambiguity from the discussion of Seneca.

seen as something familiar from earlier philosophy. My present question is whether this is also true for Seneca.

To facilitate this I want to look very briefly at the portrayal of Seneca, and especially the *Epistulae Morales*, given by Paul Veyne. In his 1993 book, now translated as *Seneca: The Life of a Stoic*,[3] he is insistent about Seneca's merits as a philosopher (p. ix):

> Despite his clarity [sic], Seneca still must be taken seriously as a philosopher. The time is past when he was regarded as a belletrist lightly brushed with philosophy, studied only by specialists in Latin literature. His clarity reveals a firm conceptual foundation, that of Greek Stoicism in its authentic form: Seneca practiced neither a debased nor a vulgarized philosophy aimed at the supposed 'practical spirit' of the Romans.

Veyne goes on to justify his plan to ground his treatment of Seneca primarily in the *Epistulae*.

> Their exposition of Stoicism starts from the self, the *I* of the neophyte Lucilius, to whom they offer a knowingly graduated course in Stoicism and a series of exercises in self-persuasion. They start from the interest the *I* has in becoming a Stoic, and create the perception that the *I* is all-powerful, that only it matters, and that it can be sufficient unto itself. In order for unhappiness and death not to matter, it is enough to consider them as nothing; if the world is hostile, it is enough to ignore it; the *I* can do this, and the only thing that matters to it will remain, itself. This is so attractive that one wishes to believe it, and it is the reason the *Letters* are captivating reading from their opening pages.

> There is, then, a contemporary application of Stoicism, precisely that suggested by the *Letters*, directed as they are to the person of a disciple: an egocentric Stoicism. It is no coincidence that the revival of Seneca began, in France at least, in the early 1980's, in a certain publishing circle connected with Michel Foucault, living under the threat of AIDS. In the face of death, the *I*, with its capacity for denial, is the only weapon remaining to us.

---

[3] P. Veyne, *Seneca: The Life of a Stoic*, tr. D. Sullivan (New York, 2003).

This homage to Foucault's centralization of the idea of the self in Seneca's work (seen perhaps most clearly in part two of *The Care of the Self*) raises more questions than can be dealt with here.[4] It is surprising, perhaps, that Veyne does relatively little with the notion of 'self' in the rest of his intriguing and at times brilliant exposition of 'Greek Stoicism' and Seneca's presentation of it in the *Epistulae*. The reason for this is given immediately (p. x):

> Stoicism has thus become, *for our use* [my emphasis], a philosophy of the active turning in on itself of the *I*, and of a determined denial of a menacing or absurd world. It was nothing of the kind in its own day, but the *Letters* permit us to view it as such.... The role of this reinterpretation of Stoicism in Michel Foucault's interior life as he was writing his last book... is well known.

Veyne thus values at the same time both the historically authentic account of Stoicism which Chrysippus might recognize as his own and the projective exploitation of it by Foucault which he, Veyne, regards as particularly meaningful in our own philosophical world. As Veyne says (pp. x–xi):

> The paradox is that a point of detail within Stoic doctrine, the autonomy of the *I* and the possibility of a transformative work of the self on the self, has become a means of survival for us despite the disappearance of everything whose existence Stoicism affirmed: nature, god, the unity of the self. For us, Stoicism is an 'immune system' in the biological sense of the word: the individual can rely on the self for support in defense against a world (contrary to that seen by Stoic optimism) not made for him.

For Veyne it is important that Seneca's 'self' corresponds quite closely to something central to Greek Stoicism. Otherwise the self-saturated Seneca constructed by Foucault will turn out to be even more of a projection of his post-modern agenda than

---

[4] It gives us enough to discuss that I am choosing not to pursue some possibly rewarding lines of thought stimulated by Christopher Gill's wide-ranging book *Personality in Greek Epic, Tragedy, and Philosophy: The Self in Dialogue* (Oxford, 1996). Gill takes a much broader cultural perspective on these themes than I can accommodate here; his approach to the contributions respectively of philosophical and literary works to conceptual history is quite different from my own.

he claims it to be. If Foucault's Senecan 'self' is not traditionally Stoic or (worse yet) if it is not even truly Senecan, then the relationship between Foucault's argument and the ancient world risks losing its claim to be an interpretation or a reinterpretation of something rooted in the ancient world he so dearly loved and from which he drew so much inspiration.

Hence it becomes quite important to settle what is meant by talking about the self in Seneca. The first obstacle to overcome, in my view, is that we (or at least I) often don't think hard enough about what we mean by 'self' on its own—as opposed to the representation of self or how we view ourselves—in our own reflections. Since reading Charles Taylor's *Sources of the Self* [5] I have tended to think of this primarily as a notion defined by a modern philosophical agenda, and I think that Long is quite right to have cited Taylor's work at the outset of his own essay. But it is one thing to look back from our own philosophical concerns and quite another to scrutinize the work of a long-dead philosophical predecessor as closely as one can, just to see what he or she may have been up to. Hence, in order to provide a more rigorous context for the evaluation of what Seneca has done, I propose to turn instead to Seneca's ancient philosophical predecessors to get some sense of the philosophically significant notions of a self in his background—or at the very least, to help me to figure out what ancient language about the self might look like.

There are many places to look, not surprisingly in a culture which accepted the Delphic maxim 'Know yourself' as being of central interest in many ways. But two undeniably interesting texts come readily to mind. Heraclitus famously but obscurely said that he had gone in search of himself (*edizēsamēn emeōuton*, B101 DK) and Aristotle claimed that a friend is 'another self' (*allos autos, EN* 1166ª32). In each of these cases we might wonder how much of a 'self' is being invoked. When Heraclitus searches for himself, he uses a simple reflexive pronoun to indicate the object of his search. Charles Kahn once proposed a very robust reading of this short fragment. The only way it

---

[5] C. Taylor, *Sources of the Self* (Cambridge, 1989).

makes sense to search for oneself, as opposed to someone else, is 'if my self is somehow absent, hidden or difficult to find'.[6] He detects here something 'distinctly modern' and a clear anticipation of 'the modern or Christian idea that a person may be alienated from his own (true) self'. He might have added that on some interpretations such a notion might be as Platonic as it is modern or Christian. Now, this is an ambitious claim, though Robinson's rejection of it is too deflationary;[7] the ancient interpretation that this fragment refers only to Heraclitus' autodidactic pretensions seems inadequate. Even so, it would surely be sufficient, in explaining the apparently deliberate paradox of this fragment, to suggest that a person might be hard to figure out—as it might well be, even if it were not divided or alienated.

Kahn's interpretation moves too rapidly from the fact that seeking can be reflexively directed to an assumed explanation of that fact, and this move has significant implications for the ontology of the mind. But is the move quite so obvious? Can I not somehow need to investigate myself without having a concept of a normative self that is distinct from the enquiring human being or a quasi-Platonic division within one human being? Why should enquiry into myself divide me or alienate me any more than feeding myself, scratching myself, or loving myself does?

If there *is* something interesting and new about the self in Heraclitus, the language used to express it seems to be no grander and no more distinctive than the first-person reflexive pronoun. And perhaps it is the use of the first person rather than the use of the reflexive that seems to make the difference here. For Kahn gives us no reason to think that the consequences he detects would follow from a use of the reflexive pronoun in the second or third person—what would we, in fact, conclude from a claim by Heraclitus that 'you went in search of yourself' or that 'Pythagoras went in search of himself'? The mere use of a reflexive pronoun cannot commit us to accepting that Heracli-

---

[6] C. H. Kahn, *The Art and Thought of Heraclitus* (Cambridge, 1979), 116.

[7] T. M. Robinson (ed., tr., and comm.), *Heraclitus: Fragments* (*Phoenix*, Supp. 22; Toronto, 1991), 147.

tus introduced a novel conception of the self, even if it is the object of a rich and interesting cognitive verb. I don't mean to deny that Heraclitus had something new and important (both epistemologically and morally) to say about the nature of a person; his enigmatic remarks about *psuchē* in B 45 (DK) suggest as much. But the claim of interesting novelty about the self rests precisely on the assumption that there is an important new idea *beyond* the identification of self with soul which Heraclitus may have pioneered and was apparently taken for granted by the time of Plato's *Apology*.

Unlike Heraclitus B 101 (DK), Aristotle's famous phrase 'another self' is not expressed with a mere reflexive pronoun, but with an intensive pronoun. But when Aristotle says, parenthetically, that a friend is an *allos autos* he is in fact summarizing the general point being made throughout *EN* 9.4, which is that the relationship one has with a friend is derived (conceptually, at least) from the relationship one has with oneself. I love myself—and I love my friend. I like spending time with myself—and with my friend. I want the genuine good for myself—and for my friend. This basically reflexive meaning of 'self' is then nominalized with the phrase *allos autos* (which eventually gives us the familiar locution *alter ego* as well). It is this nominalization of the intensive pronoun which seems, perhaps, to generate a noun 'the self' and to create a category of 'the self' as some kind of distinct aspect or part of the person.[8]

That, at any rate, is one story about the self in the *Nicomachean Ethics*. But I think that the phrase *allos autos* does no such

[8] I take this opportunity to note the importance to the issue of our having, in English, the noun 'self' to focus on when we discuss these issues. The penultimate version of this essay was translated into French for presentation at a seminar in Paris, and in doing so Alain Gigandet had to render the manifold occurrences of the noun 'self' back into the nominalized pronouns used to discuss this question in French. This, of course, casts the question in just the same form that Foucault used—a form which can make the ontological presuppositions much more difficult to determine. The use of the noun 'self' in English also masks the role of the first person (with its accompanying epistemological privilege) in contrast to the third person. From this I derive two things: a suspicion that English-language writers dealing with Foucault's theory may well be overstating its ontological implications; and a determination to exercise an unusual level of care in determining what ontological commitments Foucault is in fact taking on in his theory.

thing, and I would be prepared to bet that any open-minded reader of *EN* 9 would come to a similar conclusion. It may be terribly important that Aristotle thinks of friendship on the model of the relationship which one ideally has with oneself; but this doesn't generate anything new in the ontology of the human being, nor should it lead us to suspect it. For Aristotle the person is no more and no less than what the *De Anima* and (for example) *EN* 1.13 say it is.

Plato, of course, like Aristotle has a conception of the human being which involves internal divisions in the soul. There are rational and irrational aspects of people which can be and often are in conflict of some sort. So it is no surprise that (like Aristotle) Plato thinks that one is identifiable with one's better part, with one's reason. In this tradition, the true self is really only one's reason, though there is a difference between how the various parts of the person are thought to become unified when (if ever) the person becomes ideally developed or perfectly rational. Either the non-rational parts of the person become utterly well behaved and optimally compliant or they become somehow assimilated to the perfected rational part, which is then thought of as an ontological unity. The 'self' or 'true self' in this tradition is one's reason and is distinguishable from the whole person; it is one's true or rational self which is 'in charge of' the moral improvement of the entire person.

When asking whether a writer makes a contribution to the tradition of thinking and writing about the self as such, it makes a difference whether he or she works with a conception of the 'self' that has identifiable ontological implications or whether that thinker just uses reflexive pronouns in the course of his or her intellectual work. If I *am* a self or *have* a self in the more robust sense, then there may well be (perhaps should be) things that are true of that self which wouldn't be true of Brad Inwood, and vice versa. I might (to pick up one of Kahn's suggestions) fall short of my true self (which is eloquent and philosophically ingenious while the dull old Inwood writing this chapter is merely clear and deflationary). Or (thinking of Kahn's suggestion of a divided Heraclitean self or of a Platonically divided self) I might want to deliver a pep talk to my self in the fear that otherwise I'd never get my book written—since my real self is slothful and despondent while there is something in me that aims to do better. And if I really wanted to improve my lot in life I would go beyond the pep talk and make a serious attempt to *train* my recalcitrant self into better habits. That would be a genuine care of my self—or should I write, of myself?

But even this way of thinking and acting would not, I think, involve any sense of the self beyond what we find in Heraclitus, Plato, Aristotle, or Chrysippus (whose notion of 'self' is surely to be identified with the *hēgemonikon*, the unitary rational soul).[9] I would like to suggest that despite Foucault's claims even Seneca's conception of the self doesn't involve anything more substantial or robust in the way of mental ontology. That is to say, it seems to me that Veyne is right to hold that the fundamentals of Seneca's philosophical outlook (at least in this regard) are all well within the notions of self to be found in the earlier traditions of ancient psychology.

But with respect to Foucault, I must concede that it is often difficult to tell when (and whether) he thinks that Seneca is contributing something novel to our conceptions of the self and when he is merely drawing our attention to facets of the ancient conception of the self which seem interestingly or even surprisingly different from those we think we know in our own practice or from the notions we have formed about the Christian tradition. In *The Care of the Self* the emphasis seems to me to be very heavily on retrospective historical explorations emphasizing the kind of differences between ancient and modern (or medieval) ideas which, frankly, do not surprise professional historians of ancient thought. But the story told in *L'Herméneutique du sujet*[10] is more detailed. It not only includes a richer account of the supposed historical background to developments that occur in the early imperial period and a more insistent emphasis on the way a wide network of allegedly quite systematic ascetic training practices in the pagan world anticipates and

---

[9] Recall his argument for locating it in the heart: it is where the chin points when we say the word *egō* (Galen, *PHP* 2.2.10; cf. *SVF* ii.911, LS 34J).

[10] Collège de France lectures from 1982, published as *L'Herméneutique du sujet* (Paris, 2001).

shapes the *askēsis* normally associated with monastic Christianity.[11] But it also makes clear, in a crucial early lecture, that Foucault did rest much of his theory on a claim of ontological novelty in the ancient theory of the 'self'.[12] For it seems to have mattered greatly to Foucault that he be able to claim that such a self-shaping *askēsis* had roots and a conceptual structure independent of Christian doctrine—indeed, that it was pre-Platonic. Many parts of this story (especially the now sadly outdated account of early Pythagoreanism in the 13 January lecture) are disappointing as cultural history; but even if one grants for the sake of argument a fair bit of Foucault's account of early Greek

---

[11] Compare also ch. 2 of *The Technologies of the Self*.

[12] In discussion with colleagues more familiar with Foucault than I, in particular Thomas Bénatouïl, I have learned that it remains controversial to claim that Foucault's '*soi*' commits him to a novel mental ontology. While recognizing that even in the *L'Herméneutique* Foucault is often less than clear about ontology (which he officially misprizes, at any rate, by comparison with epistemology), I do think that the texts of Foucault discussed below show clearly that at least in the *L'Herméneutique* he is committed to a new mental ontology—which one might well expect from the identification of the self with the 'subject' as well. Bénatouïl has emphasized in conversation that one indication that Foucault may not be committed to ontological novelty is his failure to nominalize the pronoun *soi*—he writes of *le souci de soi* and not of *le souci du soi*. This subtlety is masked in the usual English translation, unfortunately. But even on this criterion Foucault emerges as being at least intermittently committed to regarding the *soi* as something distinct from the rational soul. Foucault himself uses *le soi* from time to time in the *L'Herméneutique* (for example p. 241) and treats it as a distinct goal for a moral agent to attain on p. 255 (*parvenir à soi*). Further, some of the more knowledgeable and sympathetic interpreters who have contributed to the collection *Foucault et la philosophie antique* (ed. Frédéric Gros et Carlos Lévy (Paris 2003)) slip effortlessly into the substantivized expression of the Foucauldian theory. Bénatouïl himself cites these very texts of Foucault on pp. 36 and 42 of his contribution and uses the locution in his own voice on p. 40 (*la découverte de formes spécifiques du soi*); Laurent Jaffro refers to a *technologie du soi* on p. 71 and to the *conception stoïcienne du soi* on p. 54; surely his reference to the *soi stoïcien* on p. 69, even without the definite article, also suggests ontological commitments. Though the simple form *soi* vastly predominates over the clearly nominalized *le soi* in Foucault's text, the safest conclusion seems to be that Foucault does make significant ontological claims for the self in the *L'Herméneutique* (though it *may* be inconsistent of him to do so) and that the ontological claim is not merely an unfortunate effect of the English expression 'the self'. Still, if determined and sympathetic Foucauldians dismiss the ontological claims as merely loose talk and deny that Foucault ever made new ontological commitments, his influence on interpreters of Seneca has had an unfortunate influence which I hope here to undo.

practices of self-shaping, he nevertheless still fails to establish that the Senecan self is interestingly novel.

The question about the ontology of the self which is central to my present concerns seems an obvious one to raise, and indeed it was raised in a pointed way by Foucault himself in this course of lectures—dispelling for once the pervasive ambiguities found in other texts. Towards the end of the second lecture on 6 January (p. 39) Foucault says that when the Platonic *Alcibiades* makes 'care of oneself' a central theme for the last portion of the dialogue, a theme uniting personal and political issues in an intimate way, the question of what this 'self' is must arise: 'quel est donc ce soi dont il faut se soucier quand on dit qu'il faut se soucier de soi?' Foucault's view of what is going on at 129b is interesting. He claims that Socrates' question boils down *not* to the mere enquiry 'What is a human being?'—a query that would be in line with the ontologically minimalist view of 'self' that I am defending—but to the richer question 'What is the subject?' That is, 'What is the *auto*?' Or, as he puts it in the next lecture (13 January, first lecture, p. 52), it is not a matter of knowing what you are in the sense of knowing your own capabilities, spirit and mind, whether you are mortal or not; rather 'c'est en quelque sorte une question méthodologique et formelle mais, je crois, tout à fait capitale dans tout ce mouvement... [Quel est] ce rapport, qu'est-ce qui est désigné par ce pronom réfléchi **heauton**, qu'est-ce que c'est que cet élément qui est le même du côté du sujet et du côté de l'objet?' Foucault acknowledges the obvious similarity of this text in the *Alcibiades* to many others in which the 'self' just is the soul or the rational soul; but he insists here (p. 53) that the meaning of self as soul here is quite different from what it is elsewhere in Plato.[13] Foucault's analysis of the way the idea of 'using' is

---

[13] In *Technologies of the Self*, 25, Foucault contrasts care of the self as 'care of the activity' and as 'care of the soul-as-substance' and refers to caring for 'this principle of activity'—which suggests an ontological difference just in so far as substances and activities are normally and properly thought of as ontologically different. Yet, perhaps confusingly, on the same page Foucault emphasizes that this care of the self as a principle of activity depends on knowing 'of what the soul consists' and also that 'to take care of oneself *consists of* knowing oneself' (25–6). Even allowing for the

used in the decisive argument at 129e–130c leads him to hold (pp. 54–7) that there is a significant difference between soul as a substance and soul as a subject and to assert that it is the latter idea which is in play in the *Alcibiades* and in the tradition of self-care (Platonic, Pythagorean, and especially Stoic) which derives from precisely this text. But whether the soul using body is different from, e.g., the soul as it is portrayed in the *Phaedo* is not definitively settled here, since Foucault relies crucially on his interpretation of 129b to give 'using' this surprising level of importance in the argument that concludes at 130c.[14]

If Foucault were right about the *Alcibiades* here and if he is right about the cultural centrality of this text in shaping the later tradition (which is a quite separate issue), then much of what he claims about the revolutionary developments of the early imperial period (including Seneca, of course) would have considerable force. But I want to argue that this is not what is going on in this section of the *Alcibiades*. If I am right about Foucault being wrong, then the case for ontological minimalism is considerably strengthened, since (as we can now see since the publication of *L'Herméneutique*) it is on his interpretation of this Platonic text that Foucault rests virtually his entire case for claiming that there is an ontologically interesting novelty to consider. We should recall too that the main claim he wishes to make about the distinctiveness of the imperial tradition of the care of the self is the uncoupling of the 'practice' as sketched in the Platonic *Alcibiades* from the political function it plays in the fourth century BC. I think there is another argument (distinct from the question of the nature of the reflexive relationship) to be made that this uncoupling of self-cultivation is much less

full complexity and subtlety of Foucault's views, we are nevertheless left with the sense that the self Foucault detects in the *Alcibiades* is ontologically novel when compared with the soul as represented in other Platonic dialogues.

[14] It is disappointing that Foucault fails to note the role of *archein* (see 130a3) in the argument. In order to focus on the idea of soul using body that interests him (it is in fact relatively rare in this sense in Plato), he ignores the more familiar (indeed unremarkable) idea of soul ruling over body. Yet it is precisely this idea of ruling which actually clinches the argument by elimination at 129e–130c. A frank acknowledgement of how the argument works would, again, weaken his claim that Plato is here employing a unique conception of soul as self.

important than Foucault claims—indeed, Veyne seems to make part of that case in his discussion of Seneca—but that would be the subject of a more extensive project in cultural history. For present purposes I think we need only see that the 'self' which is being cultivated involves no new commitments in philosophical anthropology or mental ontology.

That this is the case in the *Alcibiades* seems clear. The key moment in the discussion, as Foucault himself recognizes, comes at 129b, where in pursuit of the question 'What are we, ourselves?' Socrates claims that the key to learning who we ourselves are might well be found in finding what the 'itself' itself is (*auto to auto*).[15] Foucault is adamant that the answer to this question is not to be found in a declaration of what a human being is, that the relation of reflexivity involved in taking care of oneself is itself an independent object of enquiry, the 'subject' or the 'self' in a robust sense (p. 52, e.g.). Very little argument is offered in support of this, and I think most readers would find Denyer's explanation adequately convincing.[16] Denyer notes that the use of *auto* to single out the feature common to all cases of a given type is common in Plato, often though not always being a designation for a Form. As he says on p. 212 of his edition:

---

[15] There are uncertainties about the text here, but Foucault accepts the reading *auto to auto* which Nicholas Denyer (*Plato: Alcibiades* (Cambridge, 2001)) also prefers (and rightly so, in my view). However, Foucault interprets this reading differently than Denyer (whom I follow). Effectively, Foucault would translate *auto to auto*, the object of inquiry, as 'the same [element] itself' i.e. the element which is itself both the subject and the object of the verb—and it is the fact that subject and object are the same that makes the clause reflexive. Denyer's translation and the explanation of it are far more natural interpretations of the Greek phrase in context; Hutchinson ('Alcibiades', in J. Cooper and D. Hutchinson (eds.), *Plato: Complete Works* (Indianapolis, 1997)) translates it much as Denyer does: 'how can we find out what "itself" is, in itself?'; and the recent French translation by Chantal Marboeuf and J.-F. Pradeau (*Platon: Alcibiade* (Paris, 1999)) confirms Hutchinson's good judgement on this point (see p. 166 and Pradeau's n. 121, citing previous scholarship on this difficult text). Foucault's interpretation seems to me to require a number of presuppositions about what is going on in the argument which are not borne out by a closer consideration of the context.

[16] Denyer, *Alcibiades*, ad loc.

Thus 'to discover the itself itself' would be to find a formula which spells out the common feature of those cases in which the expression *autos* can rightly be applied. This formula would explain the common feature that entitles us to speak of e.g. the *Oresteia* itself (as opposed to e.g. its various productions and performances), of Athens itself (as opposed to e.g. her various territories and inhabitants), and in particular of Alcibiades himself (as opposed to e.g. his various possessions and organs).

And indeed in the pages which follow Socrates and Alcibiades come to the conclusion that a human being is the soul as opposed to the body which it uses as an organ or the possessions he or she might have—this has been a key part of the lesson to be learned by the young Alcibiades throughout the dialogue. He has to learn that taking care of himself is not a matter of taking care of his property or his body but rather a matter of seeing to the cultivation of his soul.[17] Care of the self in this dialogue seems to be a matter of doing what Socrates recommended at *Apology* 29d–e, taking care of one's soul so that it might be as good (i.e. virtuous) as possible.

It is true that at 130c–d Socrates comments that perhaps there is a more exact (*akribes*) answer to be given. 'However, instead of the itself <itself>, we have in fact been investigating what each himself is.' This is Denyer's translation of his own conjecture and in the commentary (p. 217) he both defends the translation (with or without the supplement the meaning is essentially the same) and notes that the lack of exactness is fully in line with the task Socrates set for them at 129b, which

[17] There is another difficult textual issue at 128e10, where the direct tradition unanimously gives *auton*, the indirect tradition suggests perhaps *autōn*, and Denyer prints the conjecture *anthrōpon*. Hutchinson translates this important sentence 'Well then, could we ever know what skill makes us better if we didn't know what we were?' The word 'us' renders *autōn*—a paraphrase glossing over a manifestly corrupt text. For *auton* seems quite impossible here. It cannot be the intensifying pronoun, standing not only without an adjacent noun to modify but without one obviously to be supplied from the immediate context. Nor can it be the personal pronoun 'him'—that would lack a plausible antecedent in the context. The sense required is obvious: Hutchinson correctly glosses the crux with 'us' and Denyer has proposed a conjecture which expresses the same interpretation and seems to me to be palaeographically quite plausible. Retaining *auton*, however, would not support Foucault's interpretation of the argument.

was to develop an understanding of what it means quite generally to say what a thing itself is. Here they have only shown what a human being itself is—far too narrow an answer. Yet what is missing here is not an answer to the sort of deep formal and methodological question that Foucault supposes Socrates is seeking. It is that most familiar of Socratic desiderata, a fully general account of what the phenomenon under consideration *itself* really is. We have a partial answer, one good example of what a thing 'itself' is. If we can find a few more cases like this (which Socrates doesn't bother to do here since, as he notes at 130d, this answer is probably good enough for present purposes), then we can generalize to an account of the itself itself. But what is left out doesn't seem at all to point to the kind of 'rapport...désigné par ce pronom réfléchi...cet élément qui est le même du côté du sujet et du côté de l'objet' that Foucault intuits (*L'herméneutique*, 52).

To be sure, when Socrates settles for a provisional half answer he often leaves us with a suspicion that *something* larger might be afoot (as with the adumbration offered of the Form of the Good in the *Republic*). And perhaps something larger is in the offing here too. But if so, there is no reason to think it would be the structural reality of a reflexive relationship; more likely it would be something like an essence, what it *really* is to be the thing in question. The discussion with Alcibiades shows that what it *really* is to be a person is to be a soul using a body (rather than a body + soul compound or a mere body). Perhaps a similar analysis of other examples of '*X* itself' would lead eventually to the notion of *to ti ēn einai*. Perhaps not. But even if it did lead to that ultimate conclusion when developed, it would not on that account be proper to invoke that later and fuller development as an account of what is going on in the text of the dialogue before us (indeed, Socrates says that we don't need to). After all, the provisional short-cut account of the Form of the Good, just in the form we meet it in the *Republic*, became the foundation of much later Platonic metaphysics and despite that later development most scholars would not want to claim that those later Platonic developments are the actual sense of the text in the *Republic*.

It is reasonably clear, then, despite the difficulties inherent in the *Alcibiades*, that Foucault's urge to reify reflexivity here, and so to produce a subject-self, goes far beyond what the text (or a relatively conservative reading of it) requires. His own interpretation of the text is perhaps not quite impossible, but it must, I think, be recognized as extravagant and unmotivated. On the more conservative interpretation (that is, the interpretation less dependent on presuppositions about the nature of the self to be found in it), Socrates is asking what *auto to auto* (the intensifier 'itself' taken in isolation) is and *not* what *auto to heauton* is (the reflexive pronoun used of humans taken by itself)—which is perhaps what Foucault was assuming at one point in his lecture (e.g. on p. 52). If, in fact, the essential structure of a reflexive relationship were the focus of discussion, Plato would have had a way to make that clear.

A final consideration against Foucault's reading of the *Alcibiades* is even simpler. Socrates and Alcibiades consider a number of examples of the relationship of using and caring for things, as at 128 where caring for a thing itself and caring for the possessions of a thing are contrasted (feet and shoes are one example). At 131 the discussion shifts to knowing and loving rather than using or caring for. In the entire discussion there is no hint of any deep or interesting complexity in the contrast between the thing itself and its appurtenances. In the entire discussion there is no hint that it makes the slightest difference to the nature of the action whether the object of caring for, using, or knowing is reflexive or not—indeed, the force of the argument from parallelism *relies on* there being no interesting difference between what it means to care for a reflexive and for a non-reflexive object.

We need go no further with the *Alcibiades*. I think that we must reject Foucault's claim that the 'self' which the *Alcibiades* argues we should care for introduces to the ancient tradition some interesting novelty, either epistemological or ontological, either methodological or formal. And since his claims seem to rest in large measure on the view that this dialogue (whatever its date and authorship) is what brings about the new and robust sense of 'care of the self' which then gets de-politicized and further internalized in the imperial period, this dialogue on its own gives us no reason to expect that there will be any deep, novel, and interesting sense of the self in Seneca.

Perhaps, though, we should consider the possibility that the ontological novelty can be detected in the later period—something which might be thought to give greater credibility to his reading of the Platonic text (though that kind of historically backwards reading would be pretty bad method, in my view). After all, Foucault does put considerable emphasis on the fact that the novel ideas he constructs and explores are characteristic of the first two centuries AD (e.g. *Care of the Self*, 39). Recalling that Seneca is almost the earliest author he discusses from that period, we should consider whether Seneca's texts give us warrant for the claims he makes. Even while outlining the pre-imperial origins of the 'care of the self', Foucault points to the 'fullness assumed, in Seneca, by the theme of application of oneself to oneself' and claims that Seneca 'commands a whole vocabulary for designating the different forms that ought to be taken by the care of the self and the haste which one seeks to reunite with oneself': *se formare, sibi vindicare, se facere, se ad studia revocare, sibi applicare, suum fieri, in se recedere, ad se recurrere, secum morari, ad se properare* (*Care*, 46). He detects the same basic interests in Epictetus (whose 'self' is no doubt the *prohairesis*) and Marcus Aurelius; and so the general impression is left that here at least Foucault is maintaining that something significant and new is to be found in Seneca and the other imperial Stoics. And when one considers these claims against the background of *L'herméneutique*, it at least appears that Foucault is making ontological claims for the self.

But as I argued in 'The Will in Seneca', such language does not establish that there is anything new with regard to the ontology of the self or the moral psychology. If there is in fact less novelty in the earlier tradition than Foucault thought, and if we give due credit to the continuity with earlier Socratic and Pythagorean conceptions of self-evaluation and self-shaping, then it is reasonable to conclude that there is in this later period nothing *fundamentally* new in the idea of moral education that couldn't be found, for instance, widely spread in the Hellenistic period. But before we conclude that there is *nothing at all* that is new about the self in Seneca and that Foucault has done no more than to project his own anxieties into his history, we ought to take account of the general though often unfocused perception which so many readers of Seneca have had—that he *does* emphasize or valorize the self in a distinctive way.

There are several grounds for this impression. One is quite simple. Seneca quite often chooses to distinguish his own position on a philosophical issue from that of the leading members of the school in previous generations. He is capable of taking an independent stand on points of substance and routinely uses his own philosophical judgement—and he tells us that he is doing so. Hence in the *Quaestiones Naturales* (7.22) he announces his independence of mind in almost defiant terms: *ego nostris non assentior*. And in letter 113.23 he indulges in explicit self-justification: 'You shouldn't think that I am the first of our school to speak independently of established doctrine and to form my own opinion,' pointing out that even Chrysippus and Cleanthes disagreed with each other on points of metaphysical psychology.[18] As an independent-minded Roman writing against the background of Greek authority, Seneca has, I suggest, a need to assert his own point of view that goes beyond the usual demands of philosophical controversy. This was made clear at the beginning of the letter (*Ep.* 113.1): 'but I proclaim that I am myself of another opinion [than my predecessors]. I think that there are some topics which are appropriate to those who wear Greek-style shoes and cloaks.' The self assertion which has sometimes been taken as evidence for Seneca's eclecticism is, perhaps, better regarded as a sign that Roman writers, self-conscious about their relative lack of cultural capital, had to blow their own horns rather more than their counterparts writing in Greek did. And there is nothing like a touch of condescending xenophobia about the Greeks to help a Roman to do so.

This is not to say that Seneca's independence is not genuine—he is not straining to demonstrate a freedom of thought

---

[18] Think too of his strident declaration of intellectual independence at *De Vita Beata* 3.2.

which he does not really have. The same might also be said of Cicero's stance as an Academic. Cicero often asserts his freedom as a philosopher to give his assent to whatever view strikes *him* as most credible. Many readers find this overly emphatic. In a sense, *of course* everyone takes the view that seems most credible to oneself, and Academics are not particularly special in this regard. (But the more self-conscious one is about epistemological worries, I think, the more likely one is to advert explicitly to this fact.) Cicero puts his own independence of judgement on public display as forcefully and as repeatedly as he does because of a certain level of cultural anxiety. A Roman, writing about philosophy *as a Roman*—that is, in Latin—asserts himself with a kind of defiant pride. If Seneca is doing this too, as I think he is, then here is one small part of the impression that the 'self' is playing a new and larger role in his thought.

There is another feature of Seneca's philosophical writing which contributes to the apparent novelty of his focus on the self. Consider the role of *exempla* in philosophical exposition and argument. Chrysippus draws on Medea's behaviour in his account of the passions; Seneca retails anecdotes about Cato the Younger, Horatius Cocles, and others; Cicero runs the gamut of *exempla* and in the *De Officiis* puts Regulus to particularly good use. Nothing novel or exciting here—but we might ask whether Seneca has a particular taste for *self*-exemplification, for citing his own experience alongside that of others. Catharine Edwards has made some stimulating suggestions and there is probably more work to be done along this line.[19] But it is helpful to keep this in mind when assessing, for example, the striking passage about self-examination that Foucault has frequently exploited, *De Ira* 3.36.[20]

---

[19] Catharine Edwards, 'Self-scrutiny and Self-transformation in Seneca's Letters', *Greece and Rome*, 44 (1997), 23.

[20] *Care of the Self*, 60–2; *Fearless Speech*, 147–50. See also *L'Herméneutique*, 24 March second lecture, p. 461 and n. 17. Foucault quite rightly emphasizes (*Fearless Speech*, 148) that the language here is not exclusively judicial and forensic, that administrative review of different sorts is also invoked by Seneca's metaphors here. See my 'Moral Judgement in Seneca', Ch. 7 above. Nevertheless, for Foucault's purposes and mine the difference between formal judicial power and other forms of authoritative review matter less than Seneca's readiness to adapt the language of an

All our senses, in fact, must be trained to endure. They are naturally capable of endurance, once the mind stops corrupting them. It [the mind] should be summoned each day to give an account of itself. Sextius used to do this. At the day's end, when he had retired for the night, he would interrogate his mind: 'What ailment of yours have you cured today? What failing have you resisted? Where can you show improvement?' Your anger will cease or moderate itself, if it knows that each day it must come before a judge. Could anything be finer than this habit of sifting through the whole day? Think of the sleep that follows the self-examination! How calm, deep and unimpeded it must be, when the mind has been praised or admonished and—its own sentinel and censor—has taken stock secretly of its own habits. (tr. Procopé)

Here Seneca is giving general advice about mental training as a part of character formation. And he begins by citing, as an example of how this can be done, the experience of Sextius, who had been one of his teachers. What Sextius used to do, it seems to me, was reflexive self-criticism: though it is the *animus* that is being interrogated by the speaker, Sextius, there is no sense of a divided or detached self in this practice any more than there is in Heraclitus' search for himself or in a Platonic concern about self-control (*sōphrosunē*)—and perhaps not even that much. The example of Sextius is useful for moral education, of course, but that is not what particularly interests Foucault and others so much. What grips readers is the personal example which follows.

I make use of this opportunity, daily pleading my case at my own court. When the light has been taken away and my wife has fallen silent, aware as she is of my habit, I examine my entire day, going through what I have done and said. I conceal nothing from myself, I pass nothing by. I have nothing to fear from my errors when I can say: 'See that you do not do this any more. For the moment, I excuse you. In that dispute you spoke too pugnaciously. Don't have anything in future to do with ignorant people—those who have never learned don't want to learn! You were franker than you should have been in admonishing that person. You did not help him—you just annoyed him. In

---

asymmetrical and interpersonal power structure to the internal workings of the human mind.

future, don't just consider the truth of what you are saying, but whether the person to whom you are saying it can endure the truth. While good men are glad to be admonished, the worse a man is, the more keenly he resents any guidance.'

This *prosopopoiia* of self-admonition continues for another full page, but its general character is clear already.

What are we to make of such a passage? Foucault uses it as evidence for a practice of spiritual self-examination going back to Pythagorean practice.[21] Foucault points to Porphyry's *Life of Pythagoras* 40 (and to Diogenes Laertius 8.22)[22] to establish its Pythagorean credentials, but as Burkert says[23] this and the other sources in fact contain recommendations for memory training rather than spiritual exercises as a means to character improvement or transformation—a point also made by Cooper and Procopé in their notes to the Seneca text;[24] this is also the point of Cicero's *De Senectute* 38 (cited as a parallel). In fact, there really isn't any evidence that I can find for a Pythagorean practice of daily spiritual review (as opposed to memory training). It is Sextius himself, in fact, whose personal habit Seneca cites, and he should get the credit for such a spiritual practice—if there is any credit to be given for what strikes me as a sensible but scarcely brilliant way of improving one's self-knowledge.[25]

And yet this passage impresses everyone. There are two reasons for this. One is the groundless assumption (constructed,

[21] *Care*, 60–1; *L'Herméneutique*, 13 Jan., first lecture p. 48 and nn.; *Fearless Speech*, 146: it is a 'daily requirement', a 'custom', or a 'habit'. It is worth noting that the use of Porphyry as evidence for pre-Platonic Pythagorean practice is controversial.

[22] *Care*, 245 at n. 58, correcting the apparent editorial error.

[23] W. Burkert, *Lore and Science in Ancient Pythagoreanism*, tr. E. Minar (Cambridge, MA, 1972), 213 and n. 19.

[24] Cooper and Procopé, *Seneca*, 110. There is no merit in their attempt to invoke *Ep*. 28.10 as a parallel for the general spiritual practice—Seneca is here merely urging self-inquisition on a forensic model (which seems to be the real point of the parallel). *Ep*. 28 is citing Epicurus on the need for knowledge of one's own faults (an obvious and familiar point about the utility of self-knowledge) if moral improvement is to occur. Daily spiritual practice is not mentioned. Horace *Serm*. 1.4.133-9 is perhaps closer to that model, but still seems to be far short of what Foucault has in mind.

[25] See also Foucault's remarks in *L'Herméneutique*, 457–67, the final lecture of the course (esp. 461 ff.)

as far as I can tell, by Foucault who misread the parallel Pythagorean evidence about memory training) that it represents a quasi-institutional practice—if this were true it would be a crucial fact about institutions of moral training in the ancient world otherwise unknown outside the early Church. The other is the stunning vividness of Seneca's self-exemplification. When he goes beyond saying 'Here's a neat thing that Sextius did to help out with his character improvement' to reinforce the point with the example of his own experience, we *are* impressed. But why? All Seneca is really saying is, 'I've tried it too—and it works.' But since he purports to be speaking from his own experience he can dramatize the example in a most compelling way, a way that would be scarcely possible if he made such claims about the effectiveness of the technique on the basis only of someone else's experience. But before we get swept away by the mere fact of convincing self-exemplification, it won't hurt to recall that Seneca is just as capable of making other people's experience, historical *exempla* of various sorts, equally vivid. When Horatius postures heroically in letter 120, when Cato faces his final decision on several occasions, and so forth, it is always with comparably vivid realism. This is what brilliant writers can do with their *exempla*. What is striking here is that Seneca uses his own experience as evidence to reinforce the experience of Sextius. This enhances the impact—perhaps it actually does improve the argument since the evidence might be thought to be more reliable in so far as it relies on first-person experience. But I don't think it gives us anything new about the self or about the 'practices' which govern it in Seneca's world.

I think that one could say pretty much the same thing for other striking passages where the shift to writing about himself heightens the effect. Consider letter 58, sections 34–6.

34. But if the body is useless for its duties, why wouldn't it be appropriate to escort the failing mind out the door? And perhaps it is to be done a little before it ought to be, to avoid the situation where you are unable to do it when it ought to be done. And since there is a greater danger in living badly than there is in dying swiftly, he is a fool who doesn't buy out the risk of a great misfortune by paying a small price in time. Few

make it to their deaths intact if old age is greatly prolonged; many have a passive life, lying there unable to make use of themselves. In the end, there is no crueller loss in life than the loss of the right to end it.

35. Don't listen to me reluctantly, as though this maxim already applies to you, and do evaluate what I am saying. I will not abandon my old age if it leaves me all of myself, but that means all of the better part. But if it starts to weaken my intelligence, to dislodge its parts, if what it leaves me is not *a life* but just being alive, then I shall jump clear of a decayed and collapsing building.

36. I shall not flee disease by means of death, as long as it is curable and does not impede the mind. I will not do violence to myself because of pain. Such a death is a defeat. But if I see that I have to suffer pain ceaselessly, I will make my exit, not because of pain but because it will be an obstacle for me with regard to the whole point of living. He who dies because of pain is weak and cowardly, but he who lives for pain is a fool.

The point being made about the relationship between the soul and the body in section 34 is clear enough. And in terms of what the self actually is, nothing Seneca says in this whole passage goes beyond the kind of body–soul dualism crystallized in Plato's *Phaedo* and adopted so readily (and yet compatibly with traditional Stoicism) by Seneca. But the personal element of urgency which enters in 35–6 is overpowering and effective. It makes us see so much more vividly what is involved in the decision by one's mind to let the body go. The intrusion of Seneca himself into the argument makes a difference without, I think, changing anything about the self.

It is Seneca's decision as a writer to make this insertion that should draw our attention. It is both a deliberate and controlled act by an immensely artful writer *and* a natural and unproblematic feature of the genre of letter writing. What could be more natural than that I talk about myself when I write a letter to a friend? What could be more natural than that I should reveal a personal insight or vulnerability? Or than that I should wield a pointed *tu quoque* argument with someone whom I *know* shares my basic values and inclinations? Having decided to write philosophical letters, Seneca can and indeed should intrude himself into the argument often and effectively.

And yet, even though Seneca's own personal experience plays such a role in his writing (not just in the letters, but most naturally there), even though there is so much that is confessional and even though he relies on self-exemplification to a degree that makes his more analytically inclined readers worry about the generalizability of his conclusions, despite all of this Seneca is not an autobiographical writer. Although we learn about various incidents in his early life and about his family, we cannot (as Catharine Edwards,[26] among others, has noted) construct even a merely intellectual biography for Seneca from his own works. There is no connected autobiographical narrative to be constructed even by an historian as skilled as Miriam Griffin.[27] Still, the autobiographical element which is present primes at least some of us[28] to think of Augustine, whose *Confessions* really do create a connected and philosophically urgent autobiographical narrative, one in which the fate of the 'self' is a large part of its point. Despite the use Seneca makes of autobiographical elements (and again, there is less of it in Seneca than there is in Cicero), there is nothing like the 'self' of Augustine. However, we might suspect that Seneca inspired Augustine; or perhaps that our reading of Augustine primes us to look for something similar in Seneca.

The importance of literary factors for generating this sense of self in Seneca's corpus can be illustrated from the letters as well. It is now widely accepted, as it was not when Foucault wrote *Le Souci de soi* in apparent ignorance of Miriam Griffin's work and in predictable reliance upon Pierre Grimal's study,[29] that the correspondence of Seneca with Lucilius is to a great extent fictitious. Like the dialogues of Plato, Seneca's letters are a literary representation of a philosophical exchange which is to some extent imaginary. We cannot, of course, be sure that Lucilius and Seneca didn't have a real-life philosophical relationship any more than we can know that what Alcibiades says in his wonderful biographical tribute to Socrates near the end of

---

[26] 'Self-scrutiny', 23–4. [27] Griffin, *Seneca*.
[28] Including Edwards, 'Self-scrutiny', 25, 28. See also Foucault, *Technologies*, 27.
[29] P. Grimal, *Sénèque, ou la conscience de l'empire* (Paris, 1979).

the *Symposium* isn't true. But once we accept that the letters are a literary artefact, the possibility of an underlying biographical reality isn't really quite as interesting any more. This might also be said of other prose works of Seneca, which are dedicated to real people about whom we often know a good deal. How relevant the particular interests and biographical facts of such dedicatees actually were is usually hard to determine—with the possible exception of the *De Clementia* addressed to Nero.[30]

Lucilius and Seneca are characters in the letters. We have an epistolary exchange—but only one side of it—as the author's preferred literary form. Fictitious epistolography is a widespread ancient genre and in the long run I think it would be a mistake to make a serious evaluation of the letters without taking any knowable generic constraints into account. But for present purposes a somewhat simpler point might suffice. If a literary correspondence like this is going to be a success, and especially if it is going to be a success in the wake of Cicero's correspondence (which has the advantage of being genuine and sometimes even two-sided), then it needs to have verisimilitude. It has to sound and feel like a real correspondence. And that pretty much requires a powerful, even over-powering first-person voice. With the possible exception of the literary diary, it is hard to think of any form whose success depends more on the realistic presence of the first-person voice. And so, in letter after letter of the work which for most people defines *who* Seneca is and what he stands for as a writer, we get this 'self'. In his letters, but elsewhere as well, of course, Seneca as a writer creates a powerful sense of dialogical reality. That is to say, like Plato in the more vivid Socratic dialogues, Seneca creates in the minds of his readers an illusion of reality by generating strongly defined *personae* in conversation with each other.[31]

---

[30] Again, I should note that I have been greatly enlightened by Catharine Edwards's thoughts along the same lines in her 1997 discussion of these matters.

[31] It is worth recalling that Demetrius (*On Style*, 223–4) follows Artemon in holding that letters and dialogues are intimately related: Artemon held that 'the letter is, as it were, one half of the dialogue'. This is nowhere truer than in the case of Seneca's letters. We learn a great deal about Lucilius just by reading what his epistolary partner has to say. And in the real world of professional biographers the availability of one half of a correspondence is a find of the highest importance.

I have a last suggestion about the appearance of the self which Seneca generates so convincingly but so unstably. Its origin too is in a text of Foucault's which it might well be worth getting behind. I now have in mind not *The Care of the Self* but rather *Fearless Speech*; not all of it, of course, but only the stretch in which he deals so suggestively with the 'dialogue' *De Tranquillitate Animi* (150 ff.). For Foucault, this text 'exhibits a model or pattern for a type of self-examination'. *De Tranquillitate* is a curious text, but an important one for understanding Seneca's method of philosophical writing and Foucault is right to devote serious attention to it. But its effectiveness in evoking a sense that there is a distinctively Senecan kind of 'self' also turns on matters of form. But that form is baffling. Let me share my puzzlement.

First, if we approach the text from Foucault's reading we learn that 'the text is supposed to be a letter written to Serenus incorporating the latter's request for moral advice'.[32] Since the work is preserved among the *dialogi* this will surprise the pedestrian reader, as it certainly surprised me.[33] Foucault can, while in hot pursuit of a fruitful idea, make the occasional exegetical mistake, but this seems a stunning error. Less so, perhaps, when one considers what the scrupulous Maurach has to say in *Seneca: Leben und Werk* (123–4), that 'Seneca stellt einen Brief des Adressaten Serenus voran und antwortet dann auf dessen Frage. Man kann diese Form als Vorform der späteren 'Epistulae Morales' betrachten...jedenfalls wird auf diese Weise das Epistular-Dialogische an Senecas Traktaten hier so deutlich betont wie sonst nirgends.'

The idea that the form is in effect epistolary is explicable when one considers how close the epistolary in Seneca is to the dialogical—which is just what Maurach has seen so clearly.

---

[32] *Fearless Speech*, 151. At p. 86 of the *L'Herméneutique* Foucault is somewhat more circumspect about the nature of the text here, but his commitment to its fundamentally epistolary nature is still evident.

[33] As to the meaning of the term *dialogus* I incline to Griffin's view (*Seneca*, 412–15) that it refers to *sermocinatio* as a technique within a work and that it may originally have been used for 'all the prose works aside from the letters and speeches', even those not now labelled *dialogi* on the basis of the MS tradition.

What makes Foucault's mistake so piquant, though, is that since Haase's edition it has been generally accepted that we should *supply in the text* indications of speakers at the beginning of chapter 1 (Serenus) and chapter 2 (Seneca).[34] That is to say, this is the one 'dialogue' we have which is formally dialogical. If the tone and authorial stance of Seneca seem particularly epistolary in this dialogue, this confirms the fundamentally dialogical character of the letters: it is just nice to 'hear' (as it were) the other side of the dialogue for once, and however briefly.

Now the actual content of the *De Tranquillitate* is certainly about the care of the self—the 'self' of the dialogue partner, in this case. Since Serenus is seeking a 'cure' from Seneca, he must of course give a true and honest account of his symptoms and of his state of moral progress. The self-conscious candour he displays in 1.5 when he discusses his *summus amor parsimoniae*—remember, he takes the trouble to say that this is not *in ambitionem...compositum*—can be compared with much in Seneca's letters (e.g. *Ep.* 87.5: *Parum adhuc profeci: nondum audeo frugalitatem palam ferre; etiamnunc curo opiniones uiatorum*). The confessional and self-asserting qualities of the dialogue are very much the same as those in the letters—and for a very good reason. Not only is the subject matter often the same (as it is in this case), that is, the improvement of one's soul construed on the medical model so convincingly explored for the entire Hellenistic period by Martha Nussbaum. But the literary strategy and constraints are also relevantly similar. The drama of moral improvement is enhanced by the dramatic illusion of real people talking to one another.[35] As in Plato, so in Seneca: verisimilitude works.

But perhaps one might say at this point that I have succeeded only in showing how right Foucault was, that the intensely personal element in the care of the soul is precisely what we mean by saying that Seneca breaks new ground in establishing a

[34] Reynold's apparatus reflects this. K. Abel (*Bauformen in Senecas Dialogen* (Heidelberg, 1967)) agrees that there is only a short lacuna to be filled at the head of the work.

[35] See Griffin, *Seneca*, 353-4, for the fictitious character of the 'dialogue' in *Tranq.*

concept of self. In a way that is true—after all, I set out to try to identify what it was that creates the sense we all share that something 'self'-ish is afoot in Seneca and am only denying that there is any interesting or innovative ontology behind it. And perhaps that denial is of little interest except to those who are narrowly preoccupied with the ontology of the mind.

But *De Tranquillitate* is not that simple a text. After its overtly dialogical and personal opening (Serenus really does bare his soul), Seneca's advice actually turns out to be surprisingly generic in its content. In his reply to Serenus' *cri de cœur*, after quite brief attention to his interlocutor's particular case, Seneca proposes: 'let us investigate in a general manner [or: on a universal scale] (*in universum*) how tranquillity may be achieved; you will take as much as you want from the *publicum remedium*. Meanwhile vice as a whole has to be dragged out on display (*in medium*) and from this each person will recognize the part that is his or her own' (*Tranq.* 2.4–5).

To be sure, this generic approach is said to be for Serenus' personal benefit; but it is not personal advice. His 'self' is not scrutinized particularly closely. Indeed, the advice within the main body of the dialogue about attaining tranquillity is often about the self and one's management of it, but often it is not. In fact, the overall picture is one of pragmatism and of continuity with the moral precept tradition of the early school. Hence the usefulness of several passages in the reconstruction of general Stoic views.[36] Comparison can be made here and there to the general precepts of letter 94 and in several places we see the importance of not turning inward too much.

Consider, for example, what Seneca says about the Stoic Athenodorus. In 3.1 his advice to turn one's energies *outward* to public affairs—that is, to turn away from too much preoccupation with oneself—is supported by Seneca, even though in his speech Serenus has made it clear that he does lots of that kind of thing, too much perhaps. When Athenodorus balances this with a need to turn inward and 'go private' when times become

---

[36] For example, the texts on *reservatio* (*hupexairesis*) in sections 13–14. See Inwood *Ethics and Human Action*, 119 ff.

difficult, Seneca makes it clear that Athenodorus does so too easily (4.1) for his own taste: 'My dearest Serenus, Athenodorus seems to have given in too much to circumstances and to have retreated too quickly. I would not deny that one must sometimes yield, but the retreat should be gradual, with one's standards and military honour safe.' The picture here, as elsewhere in Seneca, is that a fine balance must always be struck, that the inner life and the outer life must be regulated according to one's circumstances, but that the agent must be always in control of how this is done. This is perfectly general advice, not tailored to any particular individual, really, and its pertinence to Serenus is that acting in the light of such advice will enable him (as it would anyone else) able to exert this kind of control.

One could go through this entire treatise with an eye on this issue: how much of the advice is personal and directed at an interesting individual as such and how much is generic advice offered so that we might all learn to choose the relevant items from the menu. I don't have time to do that here. But I think it would be noted how much emphasis there is on a fine balance in moral hygiene between the reflective and the outgoing, between the inward and outward-looking. Indeed, towards the end of the treatise Seneca makes the need for balance explicit (17.3):

One must also retreat into oneself a good deal. For dealing with people unlike us upsets our careful composure, renews the passions and aggravates all the weakness in the soul which has not been thoroughly healed. Still, one must also blend and alternate the two, solitude and busy-ness. The one makes us long for other men, the other for ourselves. Each is the cure for the other.

Overall, self-reflexive activity and advice are not privileged in *De Tranquillitate*. The advice on externals is just as frequent and just as important. The inner citadel is explicitly said to be not enough for human happiness.

Let me conclude. I've tried to sort out what it might and might not mean to talk about a new or distinctive sense of the self in Seneca's philosophical works. I've pushed for a strong negative answer on the question of whether there are any new ontological commitments in the philosophy of mind. If there are any such commitments they don't seem to centre around the notion of the self. As Veyne says, Seneca's core philosophical commitments are conservative. Similarly, I don't think that there are interesting new conceptual breakthroughs in the area of moral education or moral improvement. This was a common theme from the fourth century BC onwards and I don't think we have adequate grounds for following Foucault in detecting dramatically new techniques of self-shaping in Seneca—I certainly think we need to be very cautious about regarding them as quasi-institutionalized practices new to the environment of the early empire.

But there does seem to be something new and interesting in Seneca's talk about 'self' and display of his authorial 'self', and I have argued that the sense that all perceptive readers get about this 'self' is not illusory. I have suggested that this sense has its roots in several features of Seneca's literary stance and authorial practice (his self-assertion as an independent thinker, his readiness to use himself as an *exemplum* or as particularly persuasive evidence, his peculiarly dialogical technique in the letters and in at least some of the dialogues). This sense of 'self' that we get, then, is in one way a mere artefact of literary technique. What is not yet clear to me—and perhaps it will remain unclear—is when we may reasonably regard such literary artefacts as philosophical innovations. This depends, no doubt, on the conception of the philosophical which one brings to the study of an ancient author; but it may also depend on what the subsequent tradition has done with such literary artefacts. Suppose, just for the sake of argument, that Seneca's self assertion (which falls so far short of autobiography that one cannot really write a coherent narrative of Seneca's life based on all the confessional bits he has chosen to give us) helped to inspire a writer like Augustine, whose *Confessions* have seemed to many to introduce a new form of 'self' to our philosophical tradition. If Augustine really did so and if Seneca's more narrowly literary 'self' was part of the provocation, what does that say about the boundaries between literary and philosophical facts in the study of the ancient world?

BIBLIOGRAPHY

ABEL, K., *Bauformen in Senecas Dialogen* (Heidelberg, 1967).

ALBERTI, A., 'Il volontario e la scelta in Aspasio', in A. Alberti and R. W. Sharples (eds.), *Aspasius: The Earliest Extant Commentary on Aristotle's Ethics* (*Peripatoi*, Band 17; Berlin and New York, 1999), 107-41.

ALGRA, K. *et al.* (eds.), *Cambridge History of Hellenistic Philosophy* (Cambridge, 1999).

ANAGNOSTOPOULOS, G., *Aristotle on the Goals and Exactness of Ethics* (Berkeley, 1994).

ANNAS, J., 'Cicero on Stoic Moral Philosophy and Private Property', in M. Griffin and J. Barnes (eds.), *Philosophia Togata* (Oxford, 1989), 151-73.

——. *The Morality of Happiness* (Oxford, 1993).

ANSCOMBE, G. E. M., *Intention* (2nd edn., Ithaca, 1963).

AUSLAND, H. W., 'On the Moral Origin of the Pyrrhonian Philosophy', *Elenchos*, 10 (1989), 359-434.

AXELSON, B., *Senecastudien: Kritische Bemerkungen zu Senecas Naturales Quaestiones* (Lund, 1933).

BARNES, J., 'Bits and Pieces', in J. Barnes and M. Mignucci (eds.), *Matter and Metaphysics* (Naples, 1988), 223-94.

——. *Logic and the Imperial Stoa* (Leiden, 1997).

BECKER, L., *A New Stoicism* (Princeton, 1998).

BELLINCIONI, M., '*Clementia Liberum Arbitrium Habet*', *Paideia*, 39 (1984), 173-83; repr. in M. Bellincioni, *Studi Senecani e Altri Scritti* (Brescia, 1986), 113-25.

——. *Potere ed etica in Seneca: clementia e voluntas amica* (Brescia, 1984).

BILLERBECK, M., *Der Kyniker Demetrius* (Leiden, 1979).

BOBZIEN, S., *Determinism and Freedom in Stoic Philosophy* (Oxford, 1998).

——. 'The Inadvertent Conception and Late Birth of the Free-Will Problem', *Phronesis*, 43 (1998), 133-75.

BONHÖFFER, A. F., *Epictet und die Stoa* (Stuttgart, 1890).

BRATMAN, M., *Intention, Plans, and Practical Reason* (Cambridge, MA, 1987).
——. *Faces of Intention: Selected Essays on Intention and Agency* (Cambridge, 1999).
BROK, M. F. A. (ed. and tr.), *L. Annaeus Seneca: Naturwissenschaftliche Untersuchungen* (Darmstadt, 1995).
BRUNSCHWIG, J., 'On the Book-title by Chrysippus: "On the fact that the ancients admitted dialectic along with demonstration"', in H. Blumenthal and H. Robinson (eds.), *Aristotle and the Later Tradition* (*Oxford Studies in Ancient Philosophy*, Supp. vol.; Oxford, 1991).
BURKERT, W., *Lore and Science in Ancient Pythagoreanism*, tr. E. Minar (Cambridge, MA, 1972).
CHAUMARTIN, F.-R., *Le De Beneficiis de Sénèque: sa signification philosophique, politique et sociale* (Paris, 1985).
CHERNISS, H. (ed. and tr.), *Plutarch: Moralia*, vol. xiii, pt. 2 (Loeb Classical Library; Cambridge, MA, 1976).
CODOÑER, C. 'La physique de Sénèque: Ordonnance et structure des "Naturales Quaestiones"', *ANRW* II.36.3 (1989), 1779–1822.
COOPER, J. M. and PROCOPÉ, J. F. (eds. and trs.), *Seneca: Moral and Political Essays* (Cambridge, 1995).
CORCORAN, T. H. (ed. and tr.), *Seneca: Naturales Quaestiones*, 2 vols. (Loeb Classical Library; Cambridge, MA, 1971).
COULOUBARITSIS, L., 'La psychologie chez Chrysippe', in H. Flashar and O. Gigon (eds.), *Aspects de la philosophie hellénistique* (Entretiens sur l'antiquité classique, t. 32; Geneva, 1986).
DAVIDSON, D., *Essays on Actions and Events* (Oxford, 1980).
DEFILIPPO, J. and MITSIS, P., 'Socrates and Stoic Natural Law', in P. Vander Waerdt (ed.), *The Socratic Movement* (Ithaca, NY, 1994), 252–71.
DE LACY, P. H. (ed.), *Galen: De Placitis Hippocratis et Platonis*, 3 vols. (*Corpus Medicorum Graecorum* V, 4, 1, 2; Berlin, 1978–84).
DENYER, N., *Plato: Alcibiades* (Cambridge, 2001).
DIELS, H., *Doxographi Graeci* (Berlin, 1879; repr. 1965).
DIELS, H. AND KRANZ, W., *Die Fragmente der Vorsokratiker* (Berlin, 1952).
DIHLE, A., *The Theory of the Will in Classical Antiquity* (Berkeley, 1982).
DOBBIN, R. F. (tr. and comm.), *Epictetus: Discourses. Book I* (Oxford, 1998).
DODDS, E. R. (ed.), *Plato: Gorgias* (Oxford, 1966).

DONINI, P.-L., *Le scuole, l'anima, l'impero: la filosofia antica da Antioco a Plotino* (Turin, 1982).
——. 'The History of the Concept of Eclecticism', in J. M. Dillon and A. A. Long (eds.), *The Question of 'Eclecticism': Studies in Later Greek Philosophy* (Berkeley, 1988), 15–33.
DONINI, P. and GIANCOTTI, G.-F., *Modelli filosofici e letterari* (Bologna, 1979).
DÜLL, R., 'Seneca Iurisconsultus', *ANRW* II.15 (1976), 365–80.
EDELSTEIN, L. AND KIDD, I. G. (eds. and trs.), *Posidonius*, 3 vols. (Cambridge, 1972–99).
EDWARDS, C., 'Self-scrutiny and Self-transformation in Seneca's Letters', *Greece and Rome*, 44 (1997), 23–38.
FILLION-LAHILLE, J., *Le De ira de Sénèque et la philosophie stoïcienne des passions* (Paris, 1984).
FINNIS, J., *Natural Law and Natural Rights* (Oxford, 1980).
FOUCAULT, M., *The Care of the Self*, tr. R. Hurley (New York, 1986).
——. *Technologies of the Self*, ed. L. Martin, H. Gutman, and P. Hutton (Amherst, MA, 1988).
——. *Fearless Speech*, ed. J. Pearson (Los Angeles, 2001).
——. *L'Herméneutique du sujet* (Paris, 2001).
FRANKFURT, H., 'Alternate Possibilities and Moral Responsibility', *JPh* 66 (1969), 829–39; repr. in id., *The Importance of What We Care About* (Cambridge, 1988), ch. 1.
——. 'Freedom of the Will and the Concept of a Person', *JPh* 68 (1971), 5–20; repr. in id., *The Importance of What We Care About* (Cambridge, 1988), ch. 2.
FREDE, M., 'The Stoic Doctrine of the Affections of the Soul', in M. Schofield and G. Striker (eds.), *The Norms of Nature* (Cambridge and Paris, 1986).
——. 'On the Stoic Conception of the Good', in K. Ierodiakonou (ed.), *Topics in Stoic Philosophy* (Oxford, 1999), 71–94.
GARNSEY, P. and SALLER, R. P., *The Roman Empire: Economy, Society and Culture* (Berkeley, 1987).
GERCKE, A., *Seneca-Studien* (*Jahrbücher für classische Philologie*, Supp. 22; Leipzig, 1895).
——. *Senecae Naturalium Quaestionum Libri VIII* (Bibliotheca Teubneriana; Leipzig, 1907).
GIGON, O., 'Senecas *Naturales Quaestiones*', in P. Grimal (ed.), *Sénèque et la prose latine* (Entretiens sur l'antiquité classique, t. 36; Geneva, 1991), 313–39.

GILL, C., 'Personhood and Personality: The Four-*personae* Theory in Cicero, *De Officiis* I', *Oxford Studies in Ancient Philosophy*, 6 (1988), 169–99.

——. *Personality in Greek Epic, Tragedy, and Philosophy: The Self in Dialogue* (Oxford, 1996).

GLUCKER, J., *Antiochus and the Late Academy* (Göttingen, 1978).

GRAVER, M., 'Therapeutic Reading and Seneca's Moral Epistles' (Diss. Brown University, 1996).

GRIFFIN, M., 'Philosophy for Statesmen: Cicero and Seneca', in H. W. Schmidt and P. Wülfing (eds.), *Antikes Denken—Moderne Schule (Gymnasium*, Beiheft 9; Heidelberg, 1988), 133–50.

——. *Seneca: A Philosopher in Politics* (2nd edn., Oxford, 1992).

——. 'Seneca and Pliny', in C. J. Rowe and M. Schofield (eds.), *The Cambridge History of Greek and Roman Political Thought* (Cambridge, 2000), 532–58.

GRIFFIN, M. and ATKINS, E. M. (eds. and trs.), *Cicero: On Duties* (Cambridge, 1991).

GRIMAL, P., 'L'Épicurisme romain', in *Actes du VIIIe Congrès de l'Association G. Budé*, (Paris, 1969), 139–68.

——. 'Nature et limite de l'éclectisme philosophique chez Sénèque', *Les Études Classiques*, 38 (1970), 3–17

——. *Sénèque, ou la conscience de l'empire* (Paris, 1979).

——. *La Langue latine, langue de la philosophie: actes du colloque organisé par l'École Française de Rome* (Rome, 1992).

GROS, F. and LÉVY, C. (eds.), *Foucault et la philosophie antique* (Paris, 2003).

GROSS, N., *Senecas Naturales Quaestiones: Komposition, Naturphilosophische Aussagen und ihre Quellen (Palingenesia* 27; Stuttgart, 1989).

HAASE, F., *Seneca: Opera quae supersunt* (Bibliotheca Teubneriana; Leipzig, 1852).

HADOT, I., *Seneca und die griechisch-römische Tradition der Seelenleitung* (Berlin, 1969).

HINE, H. M. (ed.), *L. Annaeus Seneca: Naturalium Quaestionum Libros* (Bibliotheca Teubneriana; Stuttgart and Leipzig, 1996).

HOLLER, E., *Seneca und die Seelenteilungslehre und Affektpsychologie der Mittelstoa* (Kallmünz, 1934).

HUTCHINSON, D. (tr.), 'Alcibiades', in J. Cooper and D. Hutchinson (eds.), *Plato: Complete Works* (Indianapolis, 1997).

INWOOD, B., 'A Note on Desire in Stoic Theory', *Dialogue*, 21 (1982), 329–31.

——. *Ethics and Human Action in Early Stoicism* (Oxford, 1985).
——. 'Goal and Target in Stoicism', *Journal of Philosophy*, 83 (1986), 547–56.
——. 'Commentary on Striker', *Proceedings of the Boston Area Colloquium in Ancient Philosophy*, 2 (1987), 95–101.
——. 'Rhetorica Disputatio: The Strategy of *De Finibus* II', in Martha Nussbaum (ed.), *The Poetics of Therapy* [*Apeiron*, 23.4 (1990)], 143–64.
——. 'Review of T. Rosenmeyer, *Senecan Drama and Stoic Cosmology*', *Classical Philology*, 86 (1991), 248–52.
——. 'Why do Fools fall in Love?', in R. Sorabji (ed.), *Aristotle and After* (Bulletin of the Institute of Classical Studies, Supp. 68; London, 1997), 55–69.
——. 'Stoic Ethics I', in Keimpe Algra *et al.* (eds.), *Cambridge History of Hellenistic Philosophy* (Cambridge, 1999)
——. 'Review of J. Zetzel, *Cicero: On the Commonwealth and On the Laws*', *BMRC*, 2000.
IOPPOLO, A. M., *Aristone di Chio e lo stoicismo antico* (Naples, 1980).
——. 'Il monismo psicologico degli Stoici antichi', *Elenchos*, 8 (1987), 449–66.
IRWIN, T. H., 'Who discovered the Will?', in J. Tomberlin (ed.), *Ethics* (Philosophical Perspectives, vol. 6; Atascadero, CA, 1992), 453–73.
KAHN, C. H., *The Art and Thought of Heraclitus* (Cambridge, 1979).
——. 'Arius as a Doxographer', in W. W. Fortenbaugh (ed.), *On Stoic and Peripatetic Ethics: The Work of Arius Didymus* (New Brunswick, NJ, 1983), 3–13.
——. 'Discovering the Will', in J. M. Dillon and A. A. Long (eds.), *The Question of 'Eclecticism': Studies in Later Greek Philosophy* (Berkeley, 1988), 234–59.
KENNETT, J. and SMITH, M., 'Frog and Toad Lose Control', *Analysis*, 56 (1996), 63–73.
KENNY, A., *Action, Emotion, and Will* (London, 1963).
——. *Will, Freedom, and Power* (Oxford, 1975).
——. *Aristotle's Theory of the Will* (New Haven, 1979).
KIDD, I., 'Moral Actions and Rules in Stoicism', in J. M. Rist (ed.), *The Stoics* (Berkeley, 1978), 247–58.
LADOUCEUR, D., 'Masada: A Consideration of the Literary Evidence', *GRBS* 21 (1980), 245–60.
——. 'Joseph and Masada', in L. Feldman and G. Hata (eds.), *Josephus, Judaism and Christianity* (Detroit, 1987), 95–113.

LAKOFF, G. AND JOHNSON, M., *Metaphors We Live By* (Chicago, 1980).
LAPIDGE, M., 'Stoic Cosmology and Roman Literature, First to Third Centuries A. D.', *ANRW* II.36.3 (1989), 1379–1429.
LÉVY, C., *Cicero Academicus* (Rome, 1992).
——. 'De Chrysippe à Posidonius: variations Stoïciennes sur le thème de la divination', in J.-G. Heintz (ed.), *Oracles et prophéties dans l'Antiquité* (Strasbourg, 1997), 321–43.
LONG, A. A., *Stoic Studies* (Cambridge, 1996).
LONG, A. A. and SEDLEY, D., *The Hellenistic Philosophers*, 2 vols. (Cambridge, 1987).
LUTZ, C., 'Musonius Rufus: "The Roman Socrates"', *YCS* 10 (1947), 3–147.
LYNCH, J., *Aristotle's School: A Study of a Greek Educational Institution* (Berkeley, 1972).
MARBOEUF, C. and PRADEAU, J.-F. (trs.), *Platon: Alcibiade* (Paris, 1999).
MAURACH, G., 'Zur Eigenart und Herkunft von Senecas Methode in den *Naturales Quaestiones*', *Hermes*, 93 (1965), 357–69; repr. in G. Maurach (ed.), *Seneca als Philosoph* (Wege der Forschung, Band 414; Darmstadt, 1975), 305–22.
——. (ed.), *Seneca als Philosoph* (Wege der Forschung, Band 414; Darmstadt, 1975).
——. *Geschichte der römischen Philosophie: eine Einführung* (Darmstadt, 1989).
——. *Seneca: Leben und Werk* (Darmstadt, 1991; 2nd edn., 1996).
MELE, A., *Springs of Action* (Oxford, 1992).
MITSIS, P., 'Moral Rules and the Aims of Stoic Ethics', *Journal of Philosophy*, 83 (1986), 556–7.
——. 'Natural Law and Natural Right in Post-Aristotelian Philosophy: The Stoics and their Critics', *ANRW* II.36.7 (1994), 4812–50.
——. 'Seneca on Reason, Rules and Moral Development', in J. Brunschwig and M. Nussbaum (eds.), *Passions and Perceptions* (Cambridge, 1993), 285–312.
MUTSCHMANN, H. (ed.), *Divisiones quae vulgo dicuntur Aristoteleae* (Leipzig, 1906).
NUSSBAUM, M., 'The Discernment of Perception: An Aristotelian Conception of Private and Public Rationality', *Proceedings of the Boston Area Colloquium in Ancient Philosophy*, 1 (1985), 151–201.
——. *The Fragility of Goodness* (Cambridge, 1986).

OBBINK, D., '"What all men believe must be true": Common Conceptions and *consensio omnium* in Aristotle and Hellenistic Philosophy', *Oxford Studies in Ancient Philosophy*, 10 (1992), 193–231.

OLTRAMARE, P. J., *Sénèque: Questions Naturelles* (l'Association Guillaume Budé; Paris, 1961).

PLEZIA, M. (ed.), *Aristotelis Epistularum Fragmenta cum Testamento* (Warsaw, 1961).

——. (ed.). *Aristoteles: Privatorum Scriptorum Fragmenta* (Bibliotheca Teubneriana; Leipzig, 1977).

POHLENZ, M., *Grundfragen der stoischen Philosophie* (Göttingen, 1940).

——. 'Philosophie und Erlebnis in Senecas Dialogen', *NAWG*, phil.-hist. Kl. 1.4.3 (1941), 55–118; repr. in id., *Kleine Schriften*, 2 vols. (Hildesheim, 1965), 384–447.

——. *Die Stoa*, 2 vols. (4th edn., Göttingen, 1970).

RAWLS, J., 'Two Concepts of Rules', *Philosophical Review*, 64 (1955), 3–32.

REHM, A., 'Anlage und Buchfolge von Senecas *Naturales Quaestiones*', *Philologus*, 66 (1907), 374–95.

REYNOLDS, L. D. (ed.), *Seneca: Ad Lucilium epistulae morales*, 2 vols. (OCT; Oxford, 1965).

RIST, J., *Stoic Philosophy* (Cambridge, 1969).

——. (ed.), *The Stoics* (Berkeley, 1978).

——. 'Are You a Stoic? The Case of Marcus Aurelius', in B. F. Meyer and E. P. Sanders (eds.), *Self-Definition in the Greco-Roman World*, vol. 3 of *Jewish and Christian Self-definition* (Philadelphia, 1982).

——. 'Seneca and Stoic Orthodoxy', *ANRW* 36.3 (1989), 1993–2012.

——. *Augustine* (Cambridge 1994).

ROBINSON, T. M. (ed., tr., and comm.), *Heraclitus: Fragments* (*Phoenix*, Supp. 22; Toronto, 1991).

ROLKE, K.-H., *Die bildhaften Vergleiche in den Fragmenten der Stoiker von Zenon bis Panaitios* (Hildesheim, 1975).

ROLLER, M., *Constructing Autocracy: Aristocrats and Emperors in Julio-Claudian Rome* (Princeton, 2001).

SALLER, R. P., *Personal Patronage under the Early Roman Empire* (Cambridge, 1982).

SANDBACH, F. H., '*Ennoia* and *Prolēpsis*', *CQ* 24 (1930), 44–51; repr. in A. A. Long (ed.), *Problems in Stoicism* (London, 1971), 22–37.

SCHAUER, F., *Playing by the Rules: A Philosophical Examination of Rule-Based Decision-Making in Law and in Life* (Oxford, 1991).

SCHMEKEL, A., *Die Philosophie der mittleren Stoa* (Berlin, 1892).

SCHOFIELD, M., 'Preconception, Argument and God', in M. Schofield, M. Burnyeat, and J. Barnes (eds.), *Doubt and Dogmatism* (Oxford 1980), 283–308.

——. *The Stoic Idea of the City* (Cambridge, 1991).

SCOTT, D., 'Innatism and the Stoa', *Proceedings of the Cambridge Philological Society*, ser. 3, 30 (1988), 123–53.

——. *Recollection and Experience: Plato's Theory of Learning and its Successors* (Cambridge, 1995).

SEDLEY, D., 'Chrysippus on Psychophysical Causality', in J. Brunschwig and M. Nussbaum (eds.), *Passions & Perceptions* (Cambridge, 1993), 313–31.

SMYTH, H. W., *Greek Grammar* (Cambridge, MA, 1956).

SORABJI, R., *Necessity, Cause and Blame* (London, 1980).

——. *Emotion and Peace of Mind: From Stoic Agitation to Christian Temptation* (Oxford, 2000).

STAHL, G., *Aufbau, Darstellungsform und philosophischer Gehalt der Naturales Quaestiones des L. Annaeus Seneca* (Diss. Kiel, 1960).

——. 'Die *Naturales Quaestiones* Senecas: Ein Beitrag zum Spiritualisierungsprozeß der römischen Stoa', *Hermes*, 92 (1964) 425–54; repr. in G. Maurach (ed.), *Seneca als Philosoph* (Wege der Forschung, Band 414; Darmstadt, 1975), 264–304.

STEWART, Z., 'Sejanus, Gaetulicus, and Seneca', *AJP* 74 (1953), 70–85.

STRIKER, G., 'Antipater, or the Art of Living', in M. Schofield and G. Striker (eds.), *The Norms of Nature* (Cambridge and Paris, 1986), 185–204; repr. in G. Striker, *Essays on Hellenistic Epistemology and Ethics* (Cambridge, 1996), 298–315.

——. 'Origins of the Concept of Natural Law', *Proceedings of the Boston Area Colloquium in Ancient Philosophy*, 2 (1987), 79–94; repr. in G. Striker, *Essays on Hellenistic Epistemology and Ethics* (Cambridge, 1996), 209–20.

——. 'Following Nature: A Study in Stoic Ethics', *OSAP* 9 (1991), 1–73; repr. in G. Striker, *Essays on Hellenistic Epistemology and Ethics* (Cambridge, 1996), 221–80.

STROHM, H., 'Beiträge zum Verständnis der *Naturales Quaestiones* Senecas', in *Latinität und alte Kirche* (Festschrift Hanslik) (*Wiener Studien*, Beiheft 8; Vienna, Cologne, and Graz, 1977), 309–25.

STROUX, L., 'Vergleich und Metapher in der Lehre des Zenon von Kition' (Diss. Heidelberg, 1966).
TAYLOR, C., *Sources of the Self* (Cambridge, 1989).
TICE, D. M. and BAUMEISTER R. F., 'Controlling Anger: Self-induced Emotional Change', in D. M. Wegner and J. W. Pennebaker (eds.), *Handbook of Mental Control* (Englewood Cliffs, NJ, 1993), 393–409.
TIELEMAN, T., *Galen and Chrysippus on the Soul* (Leiden, 1996).
TODD, R. B., 'The Stoics and their Cosmology in the First and Second Centuries A.D.', *ANRW* II.36.3 (1989), 1365–78.
TURRINI, G., 'Il frammento 34 di Senofane e la tradizione dossografica', *Prometheus*, 8 (1982), 117–35.
VANDER WAERDT, P., 'Philosophical Influence on Roman Jurisprudence? The Case of Stoicism and Natural Law', *ANRW* II.36.7 (1994), 4851–4900.
——. 'Zeno's *Republic* and the Origins of Natural Law', in P. Vander Waerdt (ed.), *The Socratic Movement* (Ithaca, NY, 1994), 272–308.
——. (ed.), *The Socratic Movement* (Ithaca, NY, 1994).
VEYNE, P., *Bread and Circuses*, tr. B. Pearce (London, 1990).
——. *Seneca: The Life of a Stoic*, tr. D. Sullivan (New York, 2003).
VOELKE, A.-J., *L'Idée de volonté dans le stoïcisme* (Paris, 1973).
VON ARNIM, J., *Stoicorum Veterum Fragmenta*, 3 vols. (Leipzig, 1903–24).
WACHSMUTH, C., *Ioannis Stobaei Anthologium*, 5 vols. (Berlin, 1884–1912).
WAIBLINGER, F.-P., *Senecas Naturales Quaestiones: griechische Wissenschaft und römische Form* (Zetemata Monographien, Heft 70; Munich, 1977).
WALLACE-HADRILL, A. (ed.), *Patronage in Ancient Society* (London, 1989).
WATSON, G., 'The Natural Law in Stoicism', in A. A. Long (ed.), *Problems in Stoicism* (London, 1971).
WEGNER, D. M. and PENNEBAKER, J. W. (eds.), *Handbook of Mental Control* (Englewood Cliffs, NJ, 1993).
WHITE, N. P., 'Two Notes on Stoic Terminology', *AJP* 99 (1978), 111–19.
WIGGINS, D., 'Deliberation and Practical Reason', in A. O. Rorty (ed.), *Essays on Aristotle's Ethics* (Berkeley, 1980), 221–40.
WILLIAMS, B., *Shame and Necessity* (Berkeley, 1993).
WIRSZUBSKI, C., *Libertas as a Political Ideal at Rome during the Late Republic and Early Principate* (Cambridge, 1950).

ZELLER, E., *Die Philosophie der Griechen* (5th edn., Leipzig, 1923).
ZILLMAN, D., 'Mental Control of Angry Aggression', in D. M. Wegner and J. W. Pennebaker (eds.), *Handbook of Mental Control* (Engelwood Cliffs, NJ, 1993).
ZIMMERMAN, D., 'Making Do: Troubling Stoic Tendencies in an Otherwise Compelling Theory of Autonomy', *Canadian Journal of Philosophy*, 30 (2000), 25–53.

INDEX OF SUBJECTS

Academic, the Academy 16–17, 42, 67, 124, 165, 224, 341
added opinion (*to prosepidoxazomenon*) 45–6
agency 306–7, 310–12
agreement, *see* contract
air 182–3, 193–5
ambiguity 20, 84, 89
analogy 168–9, 171, 173, 175–6, 182–3, 285
Anaxagoras 176
anger Ch. 2 *passim*, 69, 144–5, 153–5, 208–10, 217–18, 226, 308–11, 313
    see also passion
animals, *see* beasts
Antiochus of Ascalon 224
Antipater 115, 126–8
apatheia 20, 235–6, 239, 321
    see also passions
Apollonius of Mynda 186
appropriate, see *kathēkonta*
Aquinas 135
Aratus 225
Arcesilaus 44, 68
Ariston of Chios 102, 105–7, 111, 114–17, 127, 130
Aristotle and Aristotelianism 16–17, 26, 42, 44, 50–1, 58, 65–7, 71, 73–4, 79, 81–2, 92–3, 96, 99, 105, 112, 119, 124, 134–5, 137, 142, 146, 148, 151, 154–5, 163–5, 181–2, 189, 202, 227–8, 296, 324, 327, 329–31, 347
Asclepiodotus 183, 195

askēsis 331–2
assent 22, 46, 52, 55–6, 59, 60–3, 143, 219, 249–50
Attalus 14, 15, 36–7, 198–9
Augustine 134–5, 137, 346, 352
Aulus Caecina 198
autonomy 101, 110, 140, 230, 248, 252–6, 258, Ch. 11 *passim*, 326
axiology (good, bad, and indifferent) 39, 74–8, 80–4, 101–3, 108–9, 111–12, 120, 123, 128–30, 202, 228–9, 236, 239–41, 258, 260–70, 274–9, 281, 284, 298, 307, 311–17, 319

beasts, irrational animals 4, 47, 148, 250–1, 273, 298, 300
beneficia, *see* favours
bilingualism and translation 11–13, 18–22, 303–4, 320–1, 341
biography of Seneca Ch. 1 *passim*, 346–7, 352

Callisthenes 183
Cambyses 308–11
cannibalism 101–3
casuistry 76–8, 92, 128
Cato the Younger 235–6, 266, 289, 293–6, 306–8, 341, 344
causes 166, Ch. 6 *passim*
    multiple causation 183
celestial phenomena 185–90, 232–1, 246–7, 318
Chaldaeans 196

Index of Subjects

children 244, 247, 267, 279–80, 308–11
Chrysippus 12–13, 18, 22–31, 33–4, 43–5, 47, 49, 51, 56–7, 60, 63–4, 67–8, 73–4, 86, 92, 97–8, 101, 103, 107, 111, 114, 117, 119, 120, 135, 137, 142, 154, 158–9, 162, 165, 179, 225–6, 229, 259, 326, 331, 340–1
Cicero 7–8, 11, 13, 16–20, 28–9, 43, 55, 102, 104, 110–11, 114–15, 120–1, 123–5, 127–9, 131, 158–9, 165, 181, 203, 224–5, 230, 266, 273–80, 283, 287, 289–90, 296, 300, 315, 341, 343, 346–7
circumstances 109–11, 260–1, 264, 266–7, 270, 312–13
Cleanthes 24, 31, 43–4, 67, 71, 73, 83, 94, 114–17, 119, 127, 130, 157–9, 225, 340
clemency, *see* forgiveness
comets 185–90, 192–3, 232
common sense 74–6, 89–90
concepts and concept acquisition Ch. 10 *passim*
confatalia 197–8, 234
conflagration 172
consensus omnium 282–3, 287, 292
consistency 149–50, 217–18, 220–3, 248, 264–70, 276–80, 288–90, 292–4, 300, 314–16
consolation 179–80, 184–5, 197, 199–200, 237–8, 240, 309
contract 237–9, 242–5, 247–8
Cornutus 12–13
cosmos, cosmology 39, 68, 92, 122–3, 157–9, 163, 165, 168, 173, 177, 181–2, 186, 191–2, 194–5, 200, 231–6, 239, 244–7, 252–3, 261–2, 259, 269, 305, 315, 317–20
craft, *see* skill
cycles 168–9, 175

Danube 175
death 226, 229, 235–48, 258, 292–3, Ch. 11 *passim*
deception 258–9
decision 150, 173, 219–22, 228, 247
decreta, see *praecepta*
definition 38, 101, 103, 150, 177, 220, 227, 264, 273
deliberation 38, 44, 99–100, 106, 111, 115, 118, 202, 226, 228, 240–1, 247, 317,
Demetrius the Cynic 12, 16, 116, 120
Democritus 177, 183, 190
determinism 302, 304, 311
divination 176–7, 195–9
dialectic 15, 168, 172
dialogi 348–9
Diogenes of Babylon 115, 126–8, 273
disposition 262–4
divine, the, gods, the etc. 4, 39, 68, 152, Ch. 6 *passim*, 299–300, 272, 298, 314–16, 326
  divine and human nature ch. 6 passim, 231–6, 244–6, 251, 263, 269, 319–20
doxography 26, 31, 33, 35, 41–2, 53, 101–2, 296
dualism Ch. 2 *passim*, 33–5, 40–1, 59–60, 87–8, 100, 194, 250, 255, 265, 268–70, 281, 291–3, 298–9, 314–15, 317–20, 334–7, 344–5

earthquakes 163, 178–85
eclecticism 21, 23–4, 27–8, 32, 42, 50, 63–4, 165, 340
empirical method 168–9, 181–2, 185–90
Epictetus 12–13, 15, 21, 25, 63, 68, 104, 120, 130–2, 137, 220, 258–9, 301–3, 311, 317, 320, 324, 339

Index of Subjects

Epicurus and Epicureanism 16, 40, 67, 71, 80, 106, 123, 163–5, 169, 180, 183, 229–30, 234, 236–7, 240, 265, 269–70, 311–12, 343
epistemic limitations 76–9, 80, 110, 113, 117–18, Ch. 6 *passim* (esp. 187–90, 196, 200), 222–3, 211–18, 232, 235, 240, 281, 285, 294–6, 299–301
epistemology 3, 4, Ch. 6 *passim*
epistolarity 345–9
equity and fairness 206–7, 209–18
essence 337
ethics and the social/political 71–3, 79–81, 85–93
Etruscans 177, 195–9
Eudorus 17, 71–2
examples 341–5
experience 159, 170, 179, 181, 184

faculty psychology 133, 139, 142, 155
fairness 237–40, 242–5, 248
fate 158, 171, 178–9, 195, 197–8, 200, 233–5, 305, 316
favours Ch. 3 *passim*, 141–2,
fear 179–81, 184–5, 199–200
fire 182–3, 195
  atmospheric fire 190–3
first-person Ch. 12 *passim*
flatulence 177
flood 170–3, 177
forgiveness (clemency, leniency, mercy, pardon, pity) 69, 78–9, 153, 205–7, 213–15, 218, 234
formula 111, 120–5, 128, 177, 207–8, 210, 212–15, 218
Foucault, Michel 324–7, 329, 331–41, 343–4, 346, 348–50, 352
Frankfurt, Harry 134, 143, 148, 151, 253–7
'free will' 151, 254, 302–4, 306

freedom 141, 151, 233, 254–8, Ch. 11 *passim*
friendship 80, 92–3, 106, 140, 241, 266–7, 270, 329
function 250–1

Galen 28–30, 51, 64
geography 163
goal (*telos, finis*) 40, 114, 117, 119–20, 127–9, 159, 167, 181, 247, 251, 269, 274, 276–7, 290, 299, 314, 320
gods, *see* divine
good 250–1, 261–8, Ch. 10 *passim*
  see also axiology
good deeds, *see* favours
good faith 112, 258–60
gratitude 233–4
  see also favours
greed 228, 236, 313

hail 175–7
halo 192–3
happiness Ch. 9 *passim*
health 102, 147, 260–1, 285, 314
hedonism 265, 297–8
Heraclitus 199, 327–9, 330–1, 342
heteronomy 243, 248, 252–3, 314–16
hierarchy of nature 39–40
Hierocles 223, 324
historians 166, 174–6, 184, 186
honourable, *honestum* 9, 80–1, 84, 112, 115, 123–4, 206, 211, 227–8, 236, 240, 251, 267, 276–8, 283–7, 290, 292, 314, 317
human nature 125, 127, 333–7
  see also divine

ideal, idealism 72, 92–3, 95, 97, 101, 110, 123, 126, 129, 204, 214, 218, 221, 249, 261, 281, 291, 293–7, 299–301, 314, 330

Index of Subjects

impulse (*hormē*) Ch. 2 *passim*, 97,
    139, 147, 222, 249–51, 276
incest 101, 103
indifferent, *see* axiology
ingratitude 211–13
    see also favours
intention 73, 77–8, 80–5, 87, 89, 91,
    93, 153, 167, 205, 254
intuition 99, 106, 118, 202, 266–7

Josephus 320–1
joy (*gaudium, chara*) 85
Julius Caesar 11, 85, 153, 230
Jupiter, *see* Zeus
justification 252, 300
judgement 29, 42–3, 52–3, 57, 60–3,
    78–80, 99, 103, 108, 113, 118,
    141, 145, 150–6, 165, Ch.7
    passim, 225, 266–70, 340–1

kathēkonta (appropriate action) 62,
    70–1, 93, 101–6, 108, 111–12,
    114, 116–17, 119, 122, 124–5,
    128–30, 227, 241, 275–6,
    278–9, 288, 344
katorthōmata (right action) 71, 74,
    81, 101–5, 119, 129–30, 277

law Ch. 4 *passim*, 136, 152–3,
    226–7, 241–2
    see also natural law
lekta 44–6, 54, 57, 62, 272
leniency, *see* forgiveness
lightning and thunder 194–9
limits 229, 236, 240
logic 162
Lucretius 11, 164, 184, 240, 243

Marcus Aurelius 11, 25, 68, 259, 339
Mark Twain 54
martyrdom 306, 320–1
Masada 320–1
mental ontology 134, 323–5, 330–5,
    339, 350–2

mercy, *see* forgiveness
metaphor 31–8, 50–1, 89–90, 92,
    126, 147, 153, 160, 176, 201–4,
    207, 217, 219, 222–3, 226, 237,
    239, 303, 305, 341
meteorology Ch. 6 *passim*
military duty 238, 291, 295, 315, 318
mind 191–2, 221–2, 249–50, 260–2,
    300, 322–3
mirrors 193
moral development 99–100
moral progress (*prokopē,
    profectus*) 75, 90, 100, 110, 116,
    119, 124, 138–40, 149, 162,
    166–7, 228, 250–2, 349, 352
moral psychology 3, 5, Ch. 2 *passim*,
    322–3
moral reasoning, moral choice Ch. 4
    passim
moral theory, ethics 4, 5, 14, 15, 16
mortality 123, Ch. 8 *passim*, Ch. 11
    passim
Musonius Rufus 12, 14–16, 104

nature Ch. 6 *passim*, 251–3, 259, 269,
    275–6, 285–6, 291, 318, 326
    see also cosmos, cosmology
natural law 96, 105, 107–8, 123,
    159, 169, 172–4, 179, 184–5,
    Ch. 8 *passim*, 315
natural processes 231–6, 239
Natural Questions, order of
    books 161–2
Nero 12, 69, 72, 205, 208, 223, 230,
    347
Nile 174–5

oikeiōsis 68, 122, 125, 275–9
officia 210–12, 228
    see also duty. *kathēkonta*
openness 243–4
optics 193
order and harmony 275–6, 288–90
    see also consistency

Index of Subjects

Panaetius 37, 42, 68, 73, 100, 114–15, 123, 129–31, 189
Papirius Fabianus 9–11, 14–15, 171
paradoxes Ch. 3 *passim*, 19, 101, 113, 152, 261, 267, 312–14
pardon, *see* forgiveness
passions Ch. 2 *passim*, 148, 154–5, 235, 317
   see also anger
patronage 69
Peripatetic, *see* Aristotle and Aristotelian
persona, role 122, 129–31, 207, 212, 218–19, 224, 293–5, 309, 347
personal identity 52
philosophy, parts of 162–3, 191–9
physics 14–16, 68, 122, 191–4
   physics and ethics 236–7
   physics and theology 162–3
   see also cosmos, cosmology; theology
pity, *see* forgiveness
Plato and Platonism 16–17, 26, 29–35, 38–42, 44, 50, 63–4, 67, 80, 97, 136–7, 155, 165–6, 184, 194, 201–2, 212, 224–7, 241–2, 259, 268, 270, 283, 291, 293–4, 296, 300–1, 302–3, 319, 321, 328–39, 343, 345–7, 349
pleasure 40, 85, 93, 123, 146, 211, 220, 228–9, 236, 240, 246, 262, 265, 297, 303, 311, 313–15, 319
pornography 193
portents 192
Posidonius 27–30, 33, 38, 41–2, 53, 55, 63–4, 68, 114, 163–4, 175–6, 183, 195, 199
pneuma 45, 182–3, 271
practical syllogism 99, 202
praecepta and *decreta* 108–11, 116–26, 149–50, 167, 227–8, 230, 234, 350–1

prayer 157–9, 167
preconception (*prolēpsis*) 272–3, 282
preferred/dispreferred indifferents 81, 89–90, 102–3, 111, 265–6, 279
   see also axiology
prescription, prohibition Ch. 4 *passim*
presentation (*phantasia*) 46, 48–9, 52–3, 56–7, 222, 249, 272–3
Presocratics 163, 195
prohairesis 21, 93, 132–3, 137, 220–2
propatheiai 41–63
proposition 45–6, 262
psychological inertia 47, 50, 56, 60, 64
punishment 61, 154, 206–10
Pyrrho and Pyrrhonism 16, 102
Pythagoreanism 15, 332, 334, 339, 343–4

Quellenforschung 27–30, 38, 42, 53, 64, 69–71, 163–4

rain 233
rainbow 193
rationalization Ch. 9 *passim*
Rawls, John 109, 245
reason, rationality 43–63, 139–40, 191–2, 231, 233, 235, 240, Ch. 9 *passim*, 330
reason and the senses 180–4, 189, 194, 268–70, Ch. 10 *passim* (esp. 297–9)
recollection 300–1
reflexivity 143–52, 155–6, 334–8
regula 111, 119–21, 123, 128, 210, 221–2, 263
   see also standard
representation 323–4, 327
responsibility 56, 147, 151, 234, 244, 257, 302–4, 311, 316
rigidity 217–18, 220–3, 239

Index of Subjects

rule of thumb 109–11, 113, 131
rules Ch. 4 *passim*
   rule-case deduction 96, 98–9, 110, 128, 202

sage and non-sage 3, 4, 74–85, 90–1, 97, 100–1, 107, 109–11, 113, 115, 124, 141–2, 152, 206–9, 214–18, 221–3, 228, 234, 274–5, 285–7, 291–7, 300, 306, 312–14
Schauer, Frederick 109–11, 124, 126
schools of philosophy, Seneca's attitude 3–4, Ch. 1 *passim*, 23–4
second-order 84, 139, 143, 145, 148–52, 154–5, 254, 256, Ch. 9 *passim*
selection (vs. choice) 100, 129–30, 265–6, 269, 275–6, 279
self 52, 143–56, Ch. 12 *passim*
   self-awareness 207–11, 218–19
   self, care of 326, 331–4, 336, 338–9, 343, 349–50
   self-command 145–8
   self-examination 341–3
sense-perception 194, 271–4, 280, 297–8
Sextius and the Sextians 9–12, 15–16, 35–7, 210–11, 342–4
skill (*ars, technē*) 86–8, 92, 121, 227, 240, 277
slavery 141, 233, 254–5, 257–8, 303, 305, 310–11, 314, 316, 318–19
snow 177
social bonds, society 65–9, 122, 125–7, 230–1, 239
Socrates 97, 102, 104, 154, 202, 225–6, 235, 240–5, 247–9, 252, 260, 263, 266, 268, 272–3, 284, 294–6, 311–12, 333, 335–9, 346–7
Sotion 10, 15

soul 249–50, 329–30
soul, care of 249–52, 254, 259, Ch. 12 *passim*
standard (*kanōn, regula*) 87–8, 119, 120, 221–2, 229
Stoicism, Seneca's attitude to 3–5, 23–30, Ch. 2 *passim*, 68–70, 97, 135–7, 163–4, 176–7, 183–4, 187, 200, 305–6, 310, 325–7, 340–1, 350
straight (*rectus*) 37, 77, 85, 149, 157, 220–1, 262–3, 268, 270, 317
stupidity 36–7, 317
subterranean water and wind 169, 178, 182–3
suicide 113, 147, 241–2, 245, Ch. 11 *passim*
superstition 176–7, 180–2, 185, 196–9
Syracuse 244–7

Tacitus 160
Taylor, Charles 327
technicality 81, 83–5
telos, see goal
Thales 182
theodicy 198
   see also fate
theology 191–2, 282–3, 287
tranquillity 144, 236, 259, 313–14, 316, 350
tradition 287, 294–7, 299–301
tragedies by Seneca 5–6
trial, internal 219
tyranny 153, 230, 303, 308–11
type/token 98, 102–5, 108, 111, 122

unfamiliar events 180, 185, 232
'use' argument 266, 284
   see also Socrates; axiology

value, *see* axiology
virtue 36–7, 51, 55, 66–9, 71–3, 76, 80, 82, 84–5, 89, 92–3, 95,

Index of Subjects

102–4, 107, 116–17, 120, 122, 125, 128–30, 149, 167, 184, 217, 220–3, 236, 240, 251, 260–70, Ch. 10 *passim* (esp. 274–5, 277, 279, 284–90, 294–5, 298), 307, 313–14
voluntarism 135–6, 139, 141

wealth 11, 65, 91, 102, 115, 123, 125, 173, 214, 228–9, 240, 253, 268, 284
will and the voluntary 21–2, 49, 53–6, 58–60, 63, 79–81, 83–5, 90, 93, 117, 153, 245, 247–8, 252, 254, 257, Ch.5 *passim*, 233–4, 307, 322–3
wind 177–8
wise person, wisdom, *see* sage

Xenophanes 189–90

Zeno of Citium 24–5, 30–1, 43–4, 54, 68, 72, 97, 101, 103–5, 114, 117, 136, 158, 208, 311
Zeus/Jupiter 157–8, 198, 212, 223, 225, 252, 259, 307–8
zodiac 187

INDEX LOCORUM

SENECA THE YOUNGER

Epistulae Morales

1.10	215	48.2–3	230–1
4.10	123, 229	48.9	237
5.7	71	49.2	152
6.7	71	51.9	317
8.7–8	316	52.1	150
9.2	20	52.14	146
9.6	71	57.3–6	43, 45, 54
11	144	58	17, 40, 163
11.5–7	60	58.32	322
12.10	311	58.34–6	344–5
13.7	120	59.6–9	35–6
14.18	71	61.1	149
16	144	63.15	238
18.3	147	65	17, 34, 40, 163
20.4–6	149–50	65.1	147
22.1–2	119	65.15–22	191
22.5–6	311	65.16–22	317–20
22.7–8	106	65.19	232
22.11	316	65.20–2	228–9
25.4	123, 229	66	259–70
26.3	146–7	66.13	312, 320
26.10	312	66.32	147, 220–1
27.2	149	67.2	152
27.9	123, 229	70	241–3
28.10	219, 343	70.4–11	228
30.11	238–9	70.11	113
34.2–3	137–8, 144	70.14–15	229
37.4	317	70.14–16	312
37.4–5	37–8, 137, 139–40	70.21	141
37.5	150	70.25	146
45.3–4	219	71	115, 260
45.9	123, 229	71.1	106, 119
		71.2	120

Index Locorum

71.2–3	152	94.7	238
71.5	267	94.36	77
71.16	235	94.37–9	227
71.17	266	95.2	149
71.17–20	221	95.8	141
71.27–29	41	95.9	124
71.29	45, 60	95.18	146
71.29–33	221–2	95.43–4	228
71.36	137–9, 150	95.49	152
72.8	36–7	95.51–3	230
74	260	95.54	228
75.18	316	95.57	228
76	263	95.58	150
76.8–11	250–1	95.62	221
76.22	236	95.72	308
76.23–4	235–6	98.4	144
76.34	144	99.15–21	145–6
77	312	101.5	235
77.6	141	101.7–8	235
77.12	238	103.3	122
78.2	146–7	104.3	146
80	144	104.21	311
80.4	137, 140–1	106.10	147
80.4–5	316	107.6	147
81	75–81, 90, 112, 215–16, 218	107.6–12	235
		107.10–11	158
81.3	159	108	14–15
81.13	137, 141–2	108.6	229
81.31	212	108.21	220
83	144	109.14 ff.	115
84.11	112	109.16	150
85.29	147	113	43–4, 51, 55, 60–1, 143
87.1	152		
87.5	349	113.1	322
89	17	113.23	322
90.4	123	116.1	146
90.19	147	116.4–5	100
90.27	144	116.5–6	37
90.34	191, 229	116.8	152
91.15–16	144, 238, 245	117.6	282–3
92	38–41	117.19	191, 232
92.9	147	117.21–4	315–16
92.26	147	117.23	146
94 and 95	107–9, 112, 115–23, 127, 130	118	289
		119	289

119.15	228	\multicolumn{2}{l	}{*De Beneficiis* (151, 158–9, 205)}
120	281, 283–98, 344	1.3–4	68
120.3	266	1.3.4	92
121	286	1.4	167
123.3	316	1.4.1	92
123.16	238	1.4.2	66
124	251, 297–9	1.10.5	220
124.14	120	1.15.2	66
		2.14.1	219
\multicolumn{2}{|l|}{*Natural Questions* (Ch. 6 passim)}	2.17.3–4	92
NQ 1	190–3	2.18.1	104
1 Pref.	34	2.18.4	228
1 Pref. 3	233	2.18.7–8	151–2
NQ 2	193–9	2.26.2	211
2.35.35–8	234–5	2.31–5	75–6, 85–91
2.38.3	141	3	227
2.48	14	3.6	223
2.50	14	3.6–8	213–15
2.59.3	145	3.7.5	211
NQ 3	166–74	3.7.5–8	213–14
3 Pref. 16	123, 228	3.7.7	77
3.12	149	3.12.2–3	212
3.15.3	123, 232	3.14	112
3.16.4	123, 232	3.18.2	230
3.29.3	232	3.20	254–5
3.29.7	232	3.21.2	122
NQ 4–5	174–8	3.21.3	141
4b.5.1	216–17	3.30.1	141
NQ 6	178–85	3.31.3	104
6.1.12	232	3.36	167
6.2.1	145	4.9–11	112–13
6.32.12	123, 238	4.11.5	211–12, 221
NQ 7	185–90	4.12.1	120
7.12.4	232	4.17	68
7.22	340	4.17.3	123, 230
7.25.3	232	4.28.3	233
7.28.2	232	4.33.1	77
		4.39	68
\multicolumn{2}{|l|}{*De Clementia* (73, 69, 66, 205, 347)}	4.41.2	66
		5.2	167
1.5–6	205–6	5.4.1	141
1.19.2	123	5.7.5	146–7
2.2.2	152, 219	5.12.7	141
2.7	206–8	5.12–17	75, 81–5

5.14.2	141		2.1.1–2	160
5.20.7	147		2.1.4	141, 145–6
5.25.5–6	117–18		2.2.1	141, 154
6.3.1	229		2.3.5	154
6.4.2	104		2.4.2	154, 220–1
6.6.1–2	212		2.12.3–4	146–8
6.21–2	152		2.14	155
6.23.1–2	233–4		2.17	155
7.1.3–7	116, 120		2.19–21	145
7.1–2	123		2.22–4	153
7.2.2	227–8		2.26.4–5	150–1
7.8.3	237		2.27.2	231
7.12.6	237		2.28	210
7.18.8–9	230		2.28.2	227
			2.28.4	238

De Providentia

1.2	231–2		2.30	153
2.10–11	307		2.32	147
3.1	237		2.33–6	155
5.6–7	233		2.35	141
6.7–8	307		2.35.2	147
			3.10	64
			3.13.7	146

De Constantia Sapientis

9.2–5	312–13		3.14–15	155, 308–11
19	313		3.23.4	147
			3.26.3	210
			3.29.2	218

De Ira (69, 66, 205)

bk. 1	47–51		3.34.2	150
1.7.4	153		3.36	210–11, 219, 341–3
1.8	64			
1.8.1	141			

Consolatio ad Marciam

1.9.2	147		2.3.2	141
1.14.2–3	209		8.3	144–5
1.14–19	209–10		10	237
1.15.3	153		17–18	243–8
1.16.5–6	226, 235		20.3	311
1.16.6–7	208			
1.16.7	43, 54, 56, 57, 145		*de Vita Beata*	
1.17.1	153		1.4–5	220
1.17.7	210		3–4	313
1.18.3–6	217–18, 222		3.3	237
bk. 2	143		5.3	152
2.1–4	17, 22, 27–30, 41–6, 51–63, 219		6.2	152, 220
			9	313–14
2.1.1	152, 154		9.2–3	220

9.3	152	*de Brevitate Vitae*	
15	238, 314–15	1.18–9	230
15.5	123	5	315–16
		10	144
de Otio		15.5	228
1.2–3	219		
3.1	24–5	*Consolatio ad Polybium*	
5.5	232–3, 240	10–14	237–8
de Tranquillitate animi (348–51)		*Consolatio ad Helviam Matrem*	
2.3	20	6.8	123, 237
2.8	32–3, 147	13.2	123, 237
6	144	18.9	147
17	144		

OTHER AUTHORS

Aëtius 4.11.1–5		ii.89.4 ff.	33–35
	272–3, 280	ii.96.20–2	103
		ii.102.8–9	101
Aristotle		ii.104.6–9	75
EN		ii.108.28	101
1.13	330	fr. 29 = SVF ii.528	158
bks 8–9	92–3		
9.4	329	Chrysippus	
1110^{a}17–18	151	SVF ii.527	68
1155^a	66	SVF ii.763	165
1163^{a}9–23	92	SVF ii.885	165
1166^{a}32	327, 329–30	SVF ii.911	331
EE		SVF iii.276–7	165
1225^{b}8	151	SVF iii.314	97, 107, 120, 229
1226^{b}30–2	151		
De Anima	330	SVF iii.462	31, 47, 55–6
		SVF iii.510	119
ps.-Aristotle			
Letter 3	65–6	Cicero	
		De Natura Deorum	
Arius Didymus		bk. 2	159
(in Stobaeus *Eclogae*)		2.37	181
ii.57–8	101–2, 261, 274	2.154	68
ii.70.11	105	*De Fato* 40	43, 55, 61
ii.75–6	252	*de Finibus*	
ii.76	159, 170	bk. 3	296

Index Locorum

3.20–5	275–80, 289, 296	7.94–5	261
		7.107	103
3.32	104	7.108–9	104–5
3.33–4	273–4, 280	7.121	101, 103, 111
3.33	278	7.125	101
3.45	266, 281	7.127	45
bks 4–5	298	7.151–5	159
De Re Publica	224	8.22	343
De Legibus	224		
1.18	225	Epictetus	
1.53–6	225	*Enchiridion*	
ad Atticum 1	289	30	104
de Officiis		*Diss.*	
bks 1–2	125–6	1.4.27	258–9
1.7	114	1.17.16	13
1.9	114–15	1.26.5–7	104
1.107	129	2.6.9–10	259
bk 3	123–9	2.10.7	104
3.20–2	230	2.10	130
3.89	70–1	2.11.2–3	301
3.90	104	2.14.9–13	120
De Senectute		3.2.4	71
Tusculan Disputations		3.3.5–10	104
3.74–9	179	4.12	130

Cleanthes *Hymn to Zeus*	157–9, 225	Galen *PHP*	
Demetrius *On Style*		2.2.10	331
223–4	347	4.2.30	47
Democritus		4.2.28–38	51
B117	190	4.5.12	51

Diogenes Laërtius		Gellius	
7.40–1	158	*Noctes Atticae*	
7.41	71	14.1.11–12	187
7.46	165	19.1	44, 45
7.52–3	271–2, 280, 283–4, 286, 288, 296	Heraclitus	
		B45 DK	329
7.84	71, 116	B101 DK	327–9
7.85–6	220		
7.87	159, 170	Hierocles	
7.88	107	(at Stobaeus *Ecl.* i. 63.6) 223
7.88–9	252		
7.94	102, 105	Horace *Sermones* 1.4.133–9 343

Josephus
Jewish Wars
2.443   320
7.323–88   320–1
7.254–8   320

Lucretius
DRN
3.931–65   243

Plato
Apology
29de   336
Crito   241–8
Phaedo   241, 319
Phaedo
115c–d   268
Alcibiades
129–131   333–9
Meno   301
Gorgias   212
Gorgias
483e3   224
Protagoras
352b–e   303
Republic 504b 337
Timaeus   259
Theaetetus 201 201

Pliny *NH*
2.200   180

Plutarch
Adv. Col. 26   43, 55
Comm.Not. 21   74–5
Sto. Rep. 12   74
Sto. Rep. 1035a   158, 162
Sto. Rep; 1041e   272

ps.-Plutarch
Lib.Aegr. 6   29

Porphyry *De Vita*
     Pythagorica 40   343
Seneca the Elder *Contr.* 2.
     Pref.3–4   9–10
Suas. 2.12   14

Sextus
M 8.56–9   273, 280
M 11.2   274
M 11.64–7   102, 111

Xenophanes
B18 DK   189